Sustainable Development Law in the UK

Sustainable development is now widely accepted as a political objective in the UK and elsewhere but to what extent has the UK's rhetoric on sustainable development become a reality? The aim of this book is to critically examine the UK's approach to promoting and delivering sustainable development. It begins by providing a detailed account of UK law on sustainable development by reviewing the various policy, institutional and legal mechanisms used by the UK since the 1980s and by devolved administrations since devolution took effect in 1999. Progress has been slow, too slow and, according to the scientists, time is running out. To deal with this lack of progress, the book advocates increasing the status of ecological sustainability and sustainable development through the introduction of a wide range of legal mechanisms which would compel the change needed. The book calls for ecological sustainability, or respecting the Earth's environmental limits, to be afforded the status of legal principle and argues that with ecological sustainability at its normative core, sustainable development could provide an effective framework for decision making and governance. It argues that to support this approach and ensure consistency, the time has come for sustainable development to receive explicit legal backing. Over and above its symbolic and educational value, legislation can impose mandatory rules on policymakers and decision makers, often with meaningful consequences both inside and outside the courtroom. To this end, the book contributes to the theory on sustainable development governance by suggesting three possible legislative approaches for such intervention. The volume concludes that while a lack of leadership on sustainable development may hinder the introduction of these innovations, once introduced, these innovations would equally provide much needed support for effective leadership towards a sustainable future.

Andrea Ross is a Reader in the School of Law at the University of Dundee and has taught and researched in the areas of public and environmental law for over 18 years. Before becoming an academic she qualified as a Barrister and Solicitor in Ontario, Canada.

Sustainable Development Law in the UK

From rhetoric to reality?

Andrea Ross

publishing for a sustainable future

First published 2012
by Earthscan
2 Park Square, Milton Park, Abingdon, Oxon OX14 4RN

Simultaneously published in the USA and Canada
by Earthscan
711 Third Avenue, New York, NY 10017

*Earthscan is an imprint of the Taylor & Francis Group,
an informa business*

British Library Cataloguing in Publication Data
A catalogue record for this book is available from the British Library

Library of Congress Cataloging in Publication Data
Sustainable development law in the UK: from rhetoric to reality /
Andrea Ross.
    p. cm.
    Includes bibliographical references and index.
    1. Environmental law–Great Britain. 2. Sustainable development–Law
and legislation–Great Britain. I. Title.
    KD3372.R67 2012
    344.4104'6–dc23

2011024264

ISBN: 978-1-84971-287-3 (hbk)
ISBN: 978-1-84971-288-0 (pbk)
ISBN: 978-0-20315-008-5 (ebk)

Typeset in Galliard
by Graphicraft Limited, Hong Kong

Printed and bound in Great Britain by the MPG Books Group

To my parents, Donna and Alan

Contents

Acknowledgements

Many people have helped me make this book a reality and I owe them all considerable gratitude. In many respects this book is a culmination of a large part of my research from the past 13 years and draws on articles that I have previously published. I am grateful to colleagues, reviewers and editors who gave me advice and feedback on all those pieces.

Importantly, the book would never have happened without the support of a British Academy Research Development Award that funded the research into the relationship between sustainable development strategies, indicators and legal duties. It also afforded me the benefit of three marvellous research assistants. Hilary Grimes helped me through the jungle of sustainable development indicators, while both Emma Blundell and Tomilola Akanle kept me straight on the referencing and style required by Earthscan, as well as checking it all made sense. I am also very grateful to the School of Law at the University of Dundee for providing me with the luxury of a semester's sabbatical from teaching to really progress the book.

I am very grateful to Jeremy Rowan Robinson and Robin Churchill who provided valuable advice on the content and structure of the book and to Earthscan for taking on the project and being so enthusiastic about it. The four anonymous reviewers of the proposal deserve many thanks for their positive reviews and constructive comments. I have also received very valuable feedback on earlier drafts of various chapters from other colleagues, including: Elizabeth Kirk, Greg Lloyd, Karen Morrow, Aylwin Pillai, Colin Reid and Sharon Turner.

So much of this book builds on the previous work of other writers in several disciplines who have contributed to the literature on delivering sustainable development. The efforts of the Sustainable Development Commission must be specifically noted. The outcome of the project would have been much poorer without access to its guidance, advice, reviews and reports for every part of the UK. Its loss is a significant blow to the delivery of sustainable development in the UK.

Finally, none of this would have been possible without the support, encouragement and, in the end, patience of my family, Ian, Stuart, Iain and Katrina.

I have endeavoured to ensure the book is up-to-date to May 2011. Despite all this support and my own best efforts, given the nature of the topic and the amount of material in the book, it would not surprise me at all if there are failings in the final product, and I take full responsibility for them.

Andrea Ross
University of Dundee
May 2011

Table of cases

Table of legislation

International

Instruments

European Union

Secondary Legislation

Northern Ireland

Primary Legislation

Wales

Measures

Secondary Legislation

Other national legislation

Abu Dhabi

Canada

Federal

Poland

South Africa

United States of America

Abbreviations

Table of Abbreviations

ADPH Association of Directors of Public Health
AMSDE Annual Meeting of Sustainable Development Experts
BGPSD British Government Panel on Sustainable Development
BRE Better Regulation Executive
CBD Convention on Biological Diversity
CESP Centre of Expertise in Sustainable Procurement
CET central England temperature
CEU Council of the European Union
CIESIN Center of International Earth Science Information Network
CMPS Centre for Management and Policy Studies
CoSLA Convention of Scottish Local Authorities
CSCSS Cabinet Sub-Committee on Sustainable Scotland
CSD Commission on Sustainable Development
DCMS Department for Culture, Media and Sport
DCSF Department for Children, Schools and Families
DECC Department of Energy and Climate Change
DEFRA Department for Environment, Food and Rural Affairs
DESA Department of Economic and Social Affairs
DETR Department of Environment, Transport and the Regions
DOE Department of Environment
DPSIR driver (or driving force), pressure, state, impact and response
EA Environment Agency
EAC Environmental Audit Committee
EAP environmental action plan
EC European Community
ECOSOC Economic and Social Council
ECT environmental and clean technologies
EEAC European Environment and Sustainable Development Advisory Councils
EEC European Economic Community
EHS environmentally harmful subsidies
EIA environmental impact assessment
EMAS Eco-Management and Audit Scheme
EPI environmental performance index
EPI environmental policy integration

ERD Environment and Rural Development Committee (Scottish Parliament)
ESDN European Sustainable Development Network
EU European Union
GDP gross domestic product
GHG green house gas
GMC Green Ministers Committee
GNI gross national income
GPI genuine progress indicator
GVA gross value added
HC House of Commons
HEFCE Higher Education Funding Council for England
HIE Highlands and Islands Enterprise
IA impact assessment
IHPC In House Policy Consultancy
IISD International Institute for Sustainable Development
IPA integrated policy appraisal
IPCC Intergovernmental Panel on Climate Change
ISEW index of sustainable economic welfare
IUCN Union for the Conservation of Nature
JPOI Johannesburg Plan of Implementation
MoD Ministry of Defence
MPs members of Parliament
NAO National Audit Office
NAW (the Assembly) National Assembly for Wales
NDPB Non-Departmental Public Bodies
NGO non-governmental organization
NHS National Health Service
NIAO Northern Ireland Audit Office
NICS Ireland Civil Service
NIE Northern Ireland Executive
NSDS national sustainable development strategy
NSMC North-South Ministerial Committee
ODPM Office of the Deputy Prime Minister
OECD Organisation for Economic Co-operation and Development
OFMDFM Office of the First Minister and Deputy First Minister
(Northern Ireland)
OGC Office of Government Commerce
PIU Performance and Innovation Unit
PSA public service agreement
RAE Rural Affairs and the Environment Committee (Scottish Parliament)
RCEP Royal Commission on Environmental Pollution
RDA Regional Development Agency
SA sustainability appraisal
SCBD Secretariat of the Convention on Biological Diversity
SCP sustainable consumption and production

SD sustainable development
SDAPs Sustainable Development Action Plans
SDC Sustainable Development Commission
SDCS Sustainable Development Commission in Scotland
SDCW Sustainable Development Commission Wales
SDI sustainable development indicators
SDiG Sustainable Development in Government
SD SIT Sustainable Development Specific Impact Test
SDPB Sustainable Development Programme Board
SDS sustainable development strategy
SDU Sustainable Development Unit
SEA strategic environmental assessment
SEC European Sustainable Development Strategy
SEDD Scottish Executive Development Department
SEPA Scottish Environment Protection Agency
SMART specific, measureable, accountable, realistic and time related
SNH Scottish Natural Heritage
SNP Scottish National Party
SOGE Sustainable Operations on the Government Estate
SPP Scottish Planning Policy
TICC Transport, Infrastructure and Climate Change Committee
(Scottish Parliament)
UK United Kingdom
UN United Nations
UNCED United Nations Conference on Environment and Development
UNDESA United Nations Department of Economic and Social Affairs
UNDP United Nations Development Programme
UNECE United Nations Economic Commission for Europe
UNEP United Nations Environment Programme
UNESCO United Nations Educational, Scientific and Cultural Organization
UNFCCC United Nations Framework Convention on Climate Change
UNGA United Nations General Assembly
VAT value added tax
WAG Welsh Assembly Government
WCED World Commission on Environment and Development
WCS World Conservation Strategy
WIT Welsh Integration Tool
WSSD World Summit on Sustainable Development
WWF World Wildlife Fund

Part I
Turning rhetoric into reality

1 Introduction

One of the biggest challenges facing any author writing on sustainable development is its opaque meaning. This author is no exception. The concept of sustainable development originates from attempts to reconcile the environmental protection and human development agendas. More specifically, sustainable development was devised to be a means of addressing mounting concerns about the incompatibility of maintaining a healthy environment with promoting economic growth as the main driver for development, while at the same time addressing the widening gap between the quality of life in developed countries and developing countries (Grainger, 2004: 3). As such, the solution proposed, sustainable development, is an explicit recognition that human society is intrinsically linked to wider ecological processes and the Earth's natural resources (French, 2005: 10). To be truly sustainable, decisions need to consider long-term consequences of human activity on the planet as a whole and on its inhabitants. In many cases, this is very difficult when short-term pressures (such as poverty, unemployment, the prospect of re-election, etc.) are so powerful. Moreover, tensions and differences surround the relative importance of various factors to sustainable development and the priority which ought to be afforded to each. These factors include the pursuit of economic growth, the role of technology, the limits of the Earth's ecosystems, and levels of distributional justice within the current generation and between generations.

By design then, sustainable development evolved into a multifaceted concept to permit and encourage concurrent dialogues on environmental protection, social and economic development, human rights, governance, justice and other issues amongst states, individuals and organizations with very different views, priorities and agendas. The result is a concept that is very hard to pin down. Some commentators argue that sustainable development legitimizes 'business as usual' patterns of economic growth or, at the other extreme, requires a fundamental reworking of the global socioeconomic order. Still others in the deep ecology movement have argued that sustainable development is a contradiction in terms, in that growth and environmental protection are enemies (Alder and Wilkinson, 1999: 141).

This book critically examines the UK's approach to implementing sustainable development. Specifically it has four main aims. First, it provides, for the first time, a detailed account of UK law on sustainable development. Next, it provides a critical review of the various policy, institutional and legal mechanisms used by the UK since the 1980s and by the devolved administrations post-devolution, to implement sustainable development. Third, it shows that a new legal status for ecological sustainability and sustainable development is needed to ensure the effective implementation of sustainable development in the UK, and explains how this new legal status is consistent with the UK's institutional and legal culture. Finally, it shows how this could be made operational through the introduction of a wide range of legal actions for compelling the change needed.

The analysis reveals that while much of the institutional and policy architecture for delivering sustainable development is in place in the UK, sustainable development continues to be only incorporated into policy and decision making when governments see obvious short-term gains; important principles, priorities and good practice are often ignored altogether. Indeed, the policy and institutional mechanisms developed to implement sustainable development objectives are developed, used and repealed on an ad hoc basis. It is argued that this is due to three key factors. First, there is a lack of leadership for sustainable development in the UK. Second, the UK's approach to sustainable development has varied over time and between jurisdictions and sectors so that no consistent understanding of sustainable development with clear priorities and a framework for decision making exists in the UK. Finally, there are misunderstandings as to the role and importance of sustainable development in decision making, especially in relation to related objectives such as economic growth and tackling climate change.

Following on from these conclusions, the book argues that ecological sustainability or respecting the Earth's environmental limits should be afforded the status of legal principle and that, with ecological sustainability at its normative core, sustainable development could provide an effective framework for decision making and governance. It then argues that to support this approach and ensure consistency, the time has come for sustainable development to receive legal backing. Over and above its symbolic and educational value, legislation will impose mandatory rules on policy and decision makers, often with meaningful consequences both inside and outside the courtroom. Three possible legislative approaches for such intervention are then offered. The volume concludes that a lack of sustainable development leadership may hinder these innovations, but conversely if they are introduced, they will promote and support effective leadership.

While the international law on sustainable development is well covered (French, 2005; Rieu-Clarke, 2005) and while some analysis has been made of the contribution of law in implementing sustainable development in the USA and New Zealand (Dernbach, 2009; Miller, 2011), research on a national level is rare and it has not previously been done for the UK. Also, while some of the policy and institutional mechanisms have been covered by other disciplines such as geography and political science, no book has been published from a legal perspective (Purvis and Grainger, 2004; Jordan and Lenschow, 2008). Excellent information does exist in non-governmental organization, government agency and special reports, but these have not been tied together to demonstrate the evolution of the implementation process.

This book addresses this gap in the market. It aims to provide an authoritative account of the UK and devolved governments' approaches to the implementation of sustainable development from a legal perspective. Following a detailed analysis of the legal, institutional and policy mechanisms used in the UK since the late 1980s and those of the devolved administrations since 1999, it aims to critically assess how each of the mechanisms – and consequently the administrations – has performed. In doing so, it shows how the UK's institutions and legal culture have influenced the choices made, the effectiveness of those choices and how these need to be kept in mind when suggesting new approaches. The book uses its analysis of the UK approach from a legal perspective to propose several possible ways that the law can be used to move the UK closer to the reality of sustainable development.

Some important explanations as to the coverage and structure of the book are worth noting at the outset. First, this book refers to sustainable development law in its broadest sense, with one important exception. As used here, the term encompasses the legal and moral norms that underpin sustainable development, such as ecological sustainability, justice including environmental justice and the other 'environmental principles'. It also covers the institutional and administrative framework used to support sustainable development as a framework for governance. This includes overarching statutory or policy duties and objectives, leadership, cabinet committees and parliamentary committees, as well as strategy, budgeting and review processes. Finally, sustainable development law also covers the operational toolkit of measures designed to implement sustainable development, on the ground and day to day, through various forms of spending reviews, targets, assessments, consultation requirements and indicators. The extent to which these processes are, or ought to be, mandatory is also explored. The key omission from the definition of sustainable development law used in this book is any specific examination of the role of the private law in promoting or hindering sustainable development, as this would be the subject of a whole other book. As such, the book does not cover the contributions of contract and commercial law, property law, tort or delict in the promotion of sustainable development. That said, in places reference is made to some of the norms behind private law rules to explain why public law mechanisms may be needed to actually promote change (Chapter 12).

Second, the focus of this book is on the law and governance of the UK. This includes the laws, policies, institutions and decisions made at the devolved levels in Scotland, Wales and Northern Ireland in the context of implementing sustainable development. To provide a full, accurate and up-to-date account of the full range of institutional, policy and legal measures and decisions used in each of the administrations would be impossible. Instead, the volume tracks the development, evolution and success of key institutional, policy and legal measures to implement sustainable development over the years. It also identifies specific examples of particularly innovative good practices, as well as examples of movement backwards.

Third, while the UK approach has undoubtedly been influenced by both bottom-up and top-down drivers, the focus of the book is on the law and policy that applies to the UK and the devolved administrations in the UK. It does not expressly deal with local government however innovations at local and private level will be referred to sporadically, especially in relation to good practice and coordination. Furthermore, as much of the law and policy in the UK has its origins in international conventions (such as the United Framework Convention on Climate Change) or EU directives (such as the Water Framework Directive), where the particular development at international or EU level has had an impact on the UK's approach to sustainable development or is a potential source of how to do things a bit differently, reference will be made to this development. The book does not set out to detail the implementation of sustainable development in the EU. However, EU law is a huge influence on UK law, especially in areas such as environmental protection, agriculture, fisheries, food and trade. All of this will significantly impact on the UK's capacity to implement sustainable development, and the EU's vision of sustainable development will therefore, by necessity, influence that of the UK. The reverse is also true and the UK has often influenced the approach used in the EU. For example, given the impact of EU strategies and action plans on what occurs in the UK, Chapter 4, which examines the understanding of sustainable development, includes an analysis of the EU sustainable development strategies. In the context of operational tools such as strategic environmental assessment, the EU origins are also documented. Where the book explores the value of 'legislating' more generally on sustainable development, the various references to sustainable development and the other environmental principles in the Lisbon Treaty are examined, both in relation to their direct impact on UK sustainable development law and as an alternative way of doing things. In relation to the enforcement and accountability of sustainable development measures, the decisions and potential of the EU and UK courts are also examined.

The fourth point relates to terminology. It is essential that sustainable development is distinguished from climate change, environmental protection, economic development and environmental justice and social justice. The objectives of each quite often overlap, but not always. The best decision in relation to reducing greenhouse gas emissions may or may not be the best for the environment overall, it may or may not be distributed fairly among all people and generations, and it may or may not be economically sustainable (Eriksen and Brown, 2011: ch. 2). This author firmly believes that each of these areas needs their own separate 'champions' and the task of sustainable development as used in this volume is to bring all these objectives to the table, to come up with the most 'sustainable' outcome (Ross, 2009).

For this reason, despite its undisputed importance in relation to delivering sustainable development and its significant influence on more recent interpretations of sustainable development, there is no separate chapter on addressing climate change (Eriksen and Brown, 2011). For similar reasons, the book does not specifically cover particular sectors such as trade, agriculture or transport – there are several very good books that deal with the sustainability of these individual activities (Pretty, 2007; Schiller *et al.*, 2010; Eriksen and Brown, 2011). Importantly, then, the law, policy and institutions aimed at addressing climate change, just like those used for education, employment, trade and environmental protection, all figure as part of this author's broad definition of 'sustainable development law'. The key is that like justice, equality or transparency and openness, sustainable development law permeates all other forms of law to alter the way each is interpreted and delivered.

The book is divided into three parts: Part I Turning rhetoric into reality; Part II The reality of sustainable development in the UK; and Part III A new reality – the way forward. Part I begins by tracing the emergence of sustainable development as a policy objective throughout the world and in the UK. It then examines the research to date on implementing sustainable development and the necessary criteria needed to make this occur. It notes wide agreement in the factors needed for success and, building on the work of the Organisation for Economic Co-operation and Development (OECD) and others, uses four criteria to critically review progress made by the UK and devolved administrations in implementing sustainable development.

These four criteria (common understanding; leadership; stakeholder involvement and knowledge management; and integrative mechanisms) form the backbone of Part II. They are used to analyze the UK's journey towards sustainable development over time and to analyze the various techniques, principles, mechanisms and institutions that both the central and devolved governments in the UK have relied upon to push the sustainable development agenda forward. Those factors that have inhibited progress in any of these areas are also described in the analysis. More specifically, Part II critically reviews the strategies, leadership, stakeholder and knowledge management opportunities used by the UK administrations to implement sustainable development. It then examines the value of various mechanisms in the integration of sustainable development into the heart of government decision making, including institutional changes such as the merging of departmental functions and policy tools like strategic environmental assessment, to implement sustainable development. Part II then explores the use of sustainable development in statutes as a procedural obligation, objective or substantive duty, and the reaction of the UK courts to sustainable development as both a policy and legal obligation. The need to monitor and review the effectiveness of these tools is then considered, focusing on the role of indicators, reporting obligations and scrutiny committees in the UK's implementation of sustainable development. The conclusion from Part II is that while the UK approach to implementing sustainable development has ensured that much of the architecture is in place for moving towards a sustainable UK, it lacks three essential features. These are: strong leadership to drive sustainability forward, a consistent vision of sustainable development that prohibits unsustainable decisions, and mechanisms which support and protect initiatives against political whim and short-termism.

Building on this analysis, Part III considers alternative ways forward. It begins by noting that the UK's approach to date has not worked due to an inconsistent understanding of sustainable development based on weak sustainability. It contends that ecological sustainability or respecting the Earth's environmental limits should be afforded the status of legal principle, and argues that with ecological sustainability as its normative core, sustainable development could provide an effective framework for decision making and governance. It notes, however, that while there is evidence of this type of thinking and practice across the UK, there has not been the necessary groundswell of public and institutional support needed to make it the cultural norm both inside and outside government. Law is a valuable tool for social engineering, and the penultimate chapter makes the case that the time has come for sustainable development to receive legal backing. Three possible legislative approaches for such legal intervention are then offered. The volume concludes that a lack of sustainable development leadership may hinder these innovations but that, if they are introduced, they will promote and support effective leadership.

By examining sustainable development from a legal perspective and the options that the law offers in relation to its understanding and implementation, the hope is to generate more discussion both inside and outside the legal community. This book is littered with examples of good and evolving practice based on the expertise of a wide range of scientists, social scientists, professionals, public servants, voluntary and community groups, businesses and individuals. Unfortunately, the hurdles these initiatives face are often significant and result in good practice being frustratingly ignored, abandoned or repealed. It is hoped that the analysis and arguments set out in this book will inspire calls to protect and support this good practice by all those interested in the capacity of countries to deliver their commitments to sustainable development.

References

Alder, J. and Wilkinson, D. (1999) *Environmental Law and Ethics*, London: Macmillan.

Dernbach, J.C. (ed.) (2009) *Agenda for a Sustainable America*, Washington, DC: Environmental Law Institute.

Eriksen, S. and Brown, K. (eds) (2011) *Sustainable Adaptation to Climate Change Prioritising Social Equity and Environmental Integrity*, London: Earthscan.

French, D. (2005) *International Law and Policy of Sustainable Development*, Manchester: Manchester University Press.

Grainger, A. (2004) 'Introduction', in M. Purvis and A. Grainger (eds) *Exploring Sustainable Development: Geographical Perspectives*, London: Earthscan.

Jordan, A. and Lenschow, A. (eds) (2008) *Innovation in Environmental Policy: Integrating the Environment for Sustainability*, Cheltenham: Edward Elgar.

Miller, C. (2011) *Implementing Sustainability: The New Zealand Experience*, London: Routledge.

Pretty, J. (ed.) (2007) *Sustainable Agriculture and Food*, London: Earthscan.

Purvis, M. and Grainger, A. (eds) (2004) *Exploring Sustainable Development: Geographical Perspectives*, London: Earthscan.

Rieu-Clarke, A. (2005) *International Law and Sustainable Development: Lessons from the Law of International Watercourses*, London: IWA Publishing.

Ross, A. (2009) 'Modern interpretations of sustainable development', *Journal of Law and Society*, 36(1): 32–54.

Schiller, P.L., Brunn, E.C. and Kenworthy, J.R. (2010) *An Introduction to Sustainable Transportation Policy, Planning and Implementation*, London: Earthscan.

2 The emergence of 'sustainable development' and 'sustainable development law' in the UK

This chapter explores the emergence of sustainable development as a policy objective in the UK. It provides a broad overview of the background and evolution of sustainable development in order to fully understand the reasons behind its popularity and the consequences this has had for its implementation. It does this by chronicling the evolution of the concept over time through various historic 'events' and exploring the tensions inherent in sustainable development as a policy objective. More specifically, it shows how a growing awareness of, and concern over, increasing levels of human consumption, environmental degradation, poverty, human suffering and global insecurity led to significant international developments, such as the publication and discussion of *Our Common Future* (the Brundtland Report) in 1987 (WCED, 1987), and the Rio and Johannesburg summits.

Moreover, as the UK is a member of the EU, its law and policy is significantly influenced by developments and approaches taken at EU level. As such, it is essential to examine the impact of EU events on UK law and policy, particularly amendments to the EU treaties. Finally, this chapter explores the substantial constitutional, administrative and political changes that have occurred in the UK itself over the past 40 years and the impact these have had on how the UK implements sustainable development, as well as on the interpretation of, and commitment to, the concept in various parts of the country.

While this chapter is structured hierarchically, examining the evolution of sustainable development first internationally, then nationally and then locally, it is imperative to remember that the evolution has not been purely top-down. Indeed, many of the developments at the international level are the result of bottom-up pressures from grassroots organizations, and local and national governments. Moreover, as the remainder of the book is dedicated to the implementation of sustainable development in the UK and as a consequence, the EU, this chapter, to a very large extent, focuses on international developments.

At this stage, the emphasis is on how the concept of sustainable development has managed to achieve its current status as a key policy objective for governments, international institutions, businesses and voluntary organizations throughout the world, and more specifically, within the national, devolved and local governments of the UK. Chapter 4 explores in detail whether the various publications, conferences and events which have sought to promote and affirm sustainable development internationally and nationally have been instrumental in clarifying its meaning, or have simply contributed to greater confusion and ambiguity.

The emergence of sustainable development in international law

As significant literature already exists on the history of sustainable development in international law and policy (Boyle and Freestone, 1999; French, 2005; Sands, 2003) it is not considered necessary to repeat such an endeavour here. However, it is important to emphasize and analyze the impact of certain key international events and, in particular, the UK's reaction to them. Sustainable development largely evolved out of the need to address significant global and local issues at the same time. These issues can loosely be grouped into three challenges: those relating to development, particularly in poorer countries; those relating to environmental protection; and those relating to global and national security.

As Kirby (1995) notes, although since the Second World War, continuous attempts have been made through aid programmes to accomplish development in poorer countries, relatively little has been achieved. Consistently since that time, one-fifth of the human race faces or has faced serious famine and disease. For instance, increased emphasis on the production of agricultural commodities for export has reduced the scope for production for local consumption, which disproportionately affects the poor (Kirby, 1995: 2–3). In many developing countries, merchants and large landowners have gained power and capital and this has contributed to an increase in the relative poverty of the poor. Pastoral grazing lands have been bought up by urban elites for more mechanized commercial farming with lower labour needs. Commercial logging, large-scale cattle ranching and the expansion of export crops such as coffee, bananas and cotton, have replaced forests, leading to the breakdown of traditional resource management systems and the marginalization and exclusion of the poor. The situation mostly affects indigenous people, women and children (Kirby, 1995: 3).

The next challenge was that of environmental protection. The initial photos of the Earth taken from space, in which it appears as a small bright blue marble of life in an endless universe, are often credited for the increased support for the environmental protection movement. As Grainger (2004: 3) summarizes: 'Mounting and widespread disquiet about the environmental impacts of unfettered human population growth and industrialisation sparked off an "environmental revolution during the 1960s"'. This led to studies arguing for a steady-state economy where people and goods stayed stable and the use of resources was restrained (Meadows *et al.*, 1972: 23–4; Daly, 1973). These studies were challenged with arguments against the doomsday predictions, relying on the Earth's immensity, human ingenuity and technological advances to support the continued pursuit of economic growth (Maddox, 1972: 21–2; Simon, 1981). Despite its critics, however, the environmental movement gathered momentum, and these emergent concerns led to environmental protection being accepted as a minor but significant goal by governments of the leading developed countries. The first major UN conference on international environmental issues, held in Stockholm in 1972, marks a turning point in the development of international environmental politics.

Even by today's standards the Stockholm Declaration is a significant development in environmental law and for sustainable development more generally.[1] In the preamble (paragraph 2), states recognize that:

> The protection and improvement of the human environment is a major issue which affects the well-being of peoples and economic development throughout the world; it is the urgent desire of the peoples of the whole world and the duty of all Governments.[2]

The Stockholm Declaration also led to initiatives at national and regional levels. For example, the European Community published its first Environmental Action Plan (EC, 1973) in the following year.

However, governments still tended to regard a healthy environment as a luxury and something separate from economic activity. Moreover, developing countries took the view that, as it had been the industrialization and development of the North that had created the environmental crisis in the first place, it was the North's problem and the South should not be penalized with restrictions on its development as a result (Grainger, 2004: 3). These attitudes did not begin to change until the 1980s, when there was a realization that the environmental impacts of economic activity could rebound on the whole of humanity, through global concerns such as acid rain, overfishing, desertification, stratospheric ozone depletion and global climate change (Grainger, 2004: 3).

Finally, now, just as in almost every time in history, the Earth continues to be besieged by conflict. Even the end of the Cold War has failed to lead to peace and cooperation. Constant competition between old and emerging powers ensures the continuation of conflict. Most of these conflicts take place in developing countries, thus making survival in these countries even more difficult. Where developed governments are involved, retaliation can be even more destructive. The conflicts take different forms: proxy wars; colonial and post-colonial wars; resource wars; ethnic wars; and terrorist attacks. All devastate vast areas (Kirby, 1995: 6). Such wars include the deliberate killing of civilians, sabotage, the planting of mines, and the destruction of cities, towns, villages, irrigation systems and power installations. Wellbeing is impossible when individuals and communities are facing these threats. As such, individual and communal security, the development of appropriate and accepted mechanisms for dispute resolution, and the promotion of peace and reconciliation are all vital to human and ecosystem wellbeing.

The sustainable development solution

The development, environmental and global security crises interconnect and reinforce one another, thus compounding the impact of each. Sustainable development approaches, as an alternative way forward and as a means of addressing these crises simultaneously, can be traced back to as early as 1972 in the Stockholm Declaration itself.[3] For example, Principle 13 calls on states to 'adopt an integrated and coordinated approach to their development planning so as to ensure that development is compatible with the need to protect and improve environment'.[4] Meanwhile, Principle 9 provides that:

> Environmental deficiencies generated by the conditions of underdevelopment and natural disasters pose grave problems and can best be remedied by accelerated development through the transfer of substantial quantities of financial and technological assistance as a supplement to the domestic effort of the developing countries and such timely assistance as may be required.[5]

Although they do not use the terminology, clearly these principles promote the ethos of sustainable development.

It was not until the early 1980s that conservationists realized that to achieve their goals of conservation, they would have to recognize that others, particularly developing countries, held legitimate goals of development. This vision was promoted in new integrated conservation and development projects, such as the UN Educational, Scientific and Cultural Organization (UNESCO) Man and the Biosphere Programme which combines the establishment of protected areas with initiatives to improve the lives of local people (UNESCO, n.d.).

The term sustainable development first appears officially in the 1980 World Conservation Strategy (WCS). Paragraph 3.2 provides that 'for development to be sustainable it must take account of social and ecological factors, as well as economic ones; of the living and non-living resource base; and of the long-term as well as the short-term advantages and disadvantages of alternative actions' (International Union for Conservation of Nature and Natural Resources, 1980). Sustainable development was thus recommended, especially to developing countries, as a development path that would not produce the same environmental degradation that had occurred in industrialized countries. However, no guidance was offered as to how it would operate or be achieved in practice (Adams, 2001).

The WCS did, however, produce a reaction, and 50 national conservation strategies were adopted (mainly in developed countries) including one in the UK (Johnson, 1983). Nevertheless, Beder (2006: 18) observes that neither the WCS nor its national equivalents had much impact on the wider public or national policies.

The need to reconcile the two agendas remained, and in 1985, the UN General Assembly established the World Commission on Environment and Development (WCED), chaired by Dr Gro Harlem Brundtland, the then Prime Minister of Norway, with membership from 21 diverse developing and developed nations. The WCED focused on two sets of concerns: global environmental degradation; and the discrepancies of social and economic development between the North and the South (WCED, 1987: xi).

The solution proposed in the report of the WCED, *Our Common Future* (the Brundtland Report), was, as in the WCS seven years earlier, to aim for sustainable development. The catastrophe of environment and development could be averted through sustainable development within a framework of equity. Unlike the WCS, the Brundtland Report did define sustainable development – as 'development that meets the needs of the present without compromising the ability of future generations to meet their own needs' (WCED, 1987: 43). Importantly, the full definition, as set out in the report, is not restricted to balancing economic goals against the need to protect the environment and also encompasses broader social ideals like reducing poverty and improving education and health. The Brundtland definition continues:

> It contains two key concepts: the concept of 'needs', in particular the essential needs of the world's poor, to which overriding priority should be given; and the idea of limitations imposed by the state of technology and social organizations on the environment's ability to meet and present future needs.
>
> (WCED, 1987: 43)

Bosselmann (2008: 29) summarizes that 'essentially the Brundtland report is a plea for comprehensive distributive justice between (a) rich and poor, (b) people living today and in the future, and (c) humans and nature'. French (2005: 16) observes that the WCED vision of sustainable development is ultimately premised on two key ideas: the satisfaction of basic needs and that there was essentially only human, not ecological, limitations on the environment's ability to meet these needs. The WCED shifts the focus away from environmental protection in its own right, to it being a means to achieve economic and social development. The result is that sustainable development, as set out in the Brundtland Report, has been subject to criticism from both environmental and economic standpoints (French, 2005: 16).

By October 1987, the goal of sustainable development had been accepted by the governments of 100 nations and approved by the UN General Assembly (UNGA, 1987). However, this overwhelming acceptance is not that remarkable. While the Brundtland definition brings together different and conflicting interests, it is vague and imprecise. By bringing together the disparate agendas and states with disparate interests, the Brundtland approach to sustainable development opened up discourse. However, the cost of this conglomeration is that the conflicts are now internalized into the concept of itself. French (2005: 10–34) neatly categorizes the tensions inherent in sustainable development into those relating to the environment, economy, equity and empowerment. These are discussed in detail in Chapter 4, but it is worth noting here that any interpretation of sustainable development, even within the confines of the Brundtland definition, still requires priorities to be set among: operating within the Earth's limits; equity within the present generation; equity among species; intergenerational equity; the benefits and costs of economic development; wellbeing; and national security.

Therefore, while the Brundtland Report did secure wide public support for sustainable development and establish it as a key objective on the international political agenda, it did so by failing to set clear priorities. The result is that the Brundtland definition can be used to legitimize often conflicting solutions. As Grainger notes it suffers from two crucial flaws. It did not say how continued economic growth could in practice be balanced against the need to conserve resources and natural environments. This arguably put human needs above those of the environment. Second, it was sufficiently ambiguous to enable each of the main interest groups to interpret sustainable development in ways that reflected their own agenda. So governments and campaigners in developed countries believed sustainable development would mean better environmental protection while those in developing countries believed it would bring them more development. (Grainger, 2004: 7)

However, unlike many other reports, the Brundtland Report could not be ignored. As a WCED report, the Brundtland Commission had reported directly to the UN General Assembly and the General Assembly asked for a report on progress after five years. The ambiguous compromise contained in the Brundtland Report effectively allowed the simultaneous existence of multiple interpretations of sustainable development and, as a result, established sufficient common ground between developed and developing countries. The perceived common ground allowed the five-year reporting obligation to swell into an inter-governmental response to the Brundtland Report, produced at what was the largest ever meeting of heads of state. The UN Conference on Environment and Development (UNCED) was held in Rio de Janeiro in 1992. As Kirby (1995: 10) notes, the agenda was dominated by the North and its environmental ideals, which played out primarily by marking the international community's commitment to global environmental matters by opening for signature the UN Framework Convention on Climate Change (UNFCCC) and the Convention on Biological Diversity,[6] both of which had largely been agreed prior to the conference itself.

Grainger (2004: 7) believes that the UNCED made two special contributions to the evolution of sustainable development. First, it succeeded in translating the ideal proposed in the Brundtland Report into a universal ideal for all countries, both developing and developed. What this meant in practice for developed countries, however, was that the goal of increasing environmental protection was rebranded as sustainable development. That said, the conference also provided a political endorsement of sustainable development as an international objective through three non-binding texts: the Rio Declaration on Environment and Development (the Rio Declaration) (UNGA, 1992a), the Non-Legally Binding Authoritative Statement of Principles for a Global Consensus on the Management, Conservation and Sustainable Development of all Types of Forests (the Forest Principles) (UNGA, 1992b) and

Agenda 21, a 470-page plan of action or blueprint for sustainable development (UNGA, 1992c).

The Rio Declaration's 27 principles for the achievement of sustainable development now appear uncontroversial, but at the time they were hotly debated, especially in relation to how much they stress development objectives (Kirby, 1995: 12). Indeed, the first principle is that 'human beings are at the centre of concerns for sustainable development. They are entitled to a healthy and productive life' (UNGA, 1992a). Similarly, Grainger (2004: 7) notes that consensus on *Agenda 21* was only reached by clever and ambiguous language which was wide enough to encompass both interpretations of sustainable development without attempting to resolve contradictions between them. As key issues such as population control have been omitted altogether, *Agenda 21* needs to be seen as more of a political document than a technical manual (Grainger, 2004: 7–8).

Another major achievement at Rio was the emergence of a new collective assertiveness by developing countries (Grainger, 2004: 7). This had a significant influence on the wording of the agreements reached at UNCED, particularly the Biodiversity Convention (UN, 1992), the Rio Declaration and *Agenda 21*. Despite the domination of the agenda by the North, the actual texts of the documents are not distinctly environmental, with many environmental provisions being noticeably ambiguous, and are thus compatible with the conflicting ideals of sustainable development held by developed and developing countries.

A further key contribution was the establishment of a process that has sought to maintain political momentum in sustainable development. *Agenda 21* recommended that the UN establish an international Commission on Sustainable Development (CSD) (UNGA, 1992c). The CSD is to ensure effective follow-up to the Conference, enhance international cooperation, rationalize intergovernmental decision-making capacity for the integration of environment and development issues, and examine the progress of the implementation of *Agenda 21* at the national, regional and international levels (UNGA, 1992c: para. 2). The CSD has produced several reports on best practice in relation to indicators, strategies and frameworks (see Chapters 3 and 9).

Since UNCED, there has been increased momentum generated for improving the links between environmental protection and economic development, both internationally and at national and local levels. National and local *Agenda 21* action plans have been devised and implemented in many countries. Governments are committed to reporting their progress to the CSD and to testing CSD initiatives. The UK is actively involved in the CSD's development and testing of indicators for sustainable development (Chapter 9).

In 1997, a special session of the UN General Assembly, known as 'Rio+5', was held in New York to review progress in the five years since UNCED, as well as progress in the implementation of *Agenda 21*. In the Programme of Action for the Further Implementation of *Agenda 21* adopted at the session, the following warning was issued: 'We acknowledge that a number of positive results have been achieved, but we are deeply concerned that overall trends with respect to sustainable development are worse today than they were in 1992' (UNGA, 1997: para. 4).

It was not until the late 1990s that developed countries started to take any serious notice of the social factors behind sustainable development as iterated in the full text of the Brundtland Report. This shift was first apparent at the 1995 World Summit for Social Development in Copenhagen, where the international community noted that the interrelated nature of sustainable development provides the 'framework for our efforts to achieve a higher quality of life for all people' (UN, 1995: para. 6).

A second, much more significant period of review and assessment occurred at the World Summit on Sustainable Development in Johannesburg in 2002. Following the terrorist attacks in 2001, there was a heightened emphasis on global security. The short political declaration known as the Johannesburg Declaration on Sustainable Development states that: 'the deep fault line that divides human society between the rich and the poor and the ever-increasing gap between developed and developing worlds pose a major threat to global prosperity, security and stability' (UN, 2002a: para. 12).

The results from this meeting were limited. Besides the Johannesburg Declaration on Sustainable Development, the main output is a voluntary and vaguely worded 67 page *Plan of Implementation of the World Summit on Sustainable Development* (UN, 2002b). The Plan did, however, progress the understanding of sustainable development. It notes the need for:

> integration of the three components of sustainable development – economic development, social development and environmental protection – as interdependent and mutually reinforcing pillars. Poverty eradication, changing unsustainable patterns of production and consumption and protecting and managing the natural resource base of economic and social development are overarching objectives of, and essential requirements for, sustainable development.
>
> (UN, 2002b: para. 2)

Disagreements arose over setting targets and timetables for the achievement of certain minimum goals in the *Plan of Implementation*. In the end, the parties did manage to agree on commitments to halve, by 2015, the proportion of the world's population that does not have access to basic sanitation, and to establish a representative network of marine protected areas by 2012. As Grainger (2004: 8) notes, developed countries were just as reluctant to give new financial and other commitments to promote development in developing counties as they had been in the past, while the refusal of the US government to participate in many of the initiatives prevented further progress on the environmental issues. French (2005: 20) is of the opinion that even a cursory reading of the *Plan of Implementation* shows that there is little likelihood of full implementation of *Agenda 21*.

Several events have taken place subsequently which have once again brought environmental and ecological devastation – and the social effects of such devastation – to the forefront of the international political agenda. Some of these events are natural disasters, including the tsunami in South Asia in 2004, Hurricane Katrina in the southern US states in 2005, earthquakes in Haiti and Chile in 2010, and the eruption of an Icelandic volcano in that same year. These disasters were made worse by human activity such as building in risk areas and inappropriate engineering works. This was again apparent following the 2011 triple disaster in Japan whereby an earthquake and tsunami led to a significant nuclear crisis. Other events, such as forest fires and oil spills, are more directly the consequence of human activity, often linked to unsustainable consumption levels and poor governance. The bi-annual *Living Planet* reports, which provide science-based analysis of the health of the planet (World Wildlife Fund *et al.*, 2008), *The Economics of Climate Change: The Stern Review* (Stern, 2007) and the UNFCCC secretariat's annual greenhouse gas (GHG) inventories and reports summarizing the status and trends of GHG emissions (UNFCCC, 2010), have all reiterated the need for more ambitious action.

The legal and political responses to these events and studies have been mixed, especially during times of economic or political crisis. For example, the Kyoto Protocol to the UNFCCC sets binding targets for 37 industrialized countries and the European community for reducing greenhouse gas (GHG) emissions, thus committing industrialized countries to stabilize GHG emissions.[8] These amount to an average of 5 per cent against 1990 levels over the five-year period 2008–2012. Despite an urgent need to replace the targets and timetables set out in the Kyoto Protocol to the UNFCCC, it was announced very early on at the Conference of the Parties in Copenhagen in December 2009 that that there would be no legally binding agreement at the meeting. Instead, after intense wrangling, delegates passed a motion simply taking note of the deal reached during the Conference by several heads of state, rather than formally adopt it. The deal reached contained: a recognition that global temperature rises should be limited to less than 2°C; a promise to provide $30 billion (£18.5) of new and additional financial resources to developing nations between 2010 and 2012; and a goal to provide $100 billion a year by 2020 to help poor countries cope with the impacts of climate change (UN, 2009: paras. 1, 8). These can hardly be said to be any evidence of urgency.

Positive political developments also exist, such as the steady uptake in endorsements for the 'Earth Charter'. Bosselmann (2008: 37) notes that after Johannesburg, just as after Rio, there was a sense of unfinished business. The idea of a new charter that would set forth fundamental principles for sustainable development was discussed in the Brundtland Report and later at the UN 1992 Earth Summit in Rio (The Earth Charter Initiative, 2000). In 1994, Maurice Strong, the Secretary General of the Earth Summit and chairman of the Earth Council, and Mikhail Gorbachev, president of Green Cross International, launched the Earth Charter Initiative with support from the Dutch government. Essentially, the Earth Charter is a declaration of fundamental principles for building a just, sustainable, and peaceful global society for the 21st century (The Earth Charter Initiative, 2000). The Charter is the result of a long period of wide civic engagement and consultation. Its final text was approved by consensus at a meeting at the UNESCO Headquarters in Paris in March 2000. Subsequently, the Charter has been formally endorsed by thousands of organizations representing millions of people, including the UNESCO Conference of Member States, the International Union for the Conservation of Nature, national government ministries, national and international associations of universities, and hundreds of cities and towns in dozens of countries. It has also been endorsed by tens of thousands of individuals, and publicly supported by numerous heads of state.[7]

All of these events at the international level have influenced activity in the EU and in the UK. The relationship, however, is reciprocal. The EU is one of the few jurisdictions to have incorporated sustainable development into its governing treaties. The EU and the UK have also been leaders in the development and testing of indicators for sustainable development. The UK was one of the first countries to respond to the Brundtland Report and one of the first to produce a strategy for sustainable development. Moreover, the grassroots activities at EU and UK levels have been innovative and influential at international level. As the remainder of the book is dedicated to the approaches, mechanisms and institutions for sustainable development in the UK, and to a lesser extent in the EU, what follows is a very brief account of the origins and development of sustainable development in the EU and the UK.

Sustainable development in the European Union

The European Economic Community was originally established in 1957 to deal with the devastation inflicted by the Second World War and to create an economic community mainly through the development of a 'common market'. As a result, the original European Community treaties were silent on sustainable development and, indeed, on the environment.

The European Community (EC or Community) became explicitly engaged with environmental regulation in 1972 when it published its first Environmental Action Plan (EC, 1973). The EU's competence in relation to environmental protection was subsequently extended under the Single European Act in 1986, which added the title of Environment into the European Community treaty, and in the Maastricht Treaty in 1992, which added the precautionary principle to the environment title.[9]

Strategic thinking on sustainable development first appears in the European Community's Fifth Environmental Action Programme entitled *Towards Sustainability*, published in 1993 (EC, 1993). The Fifth Action Programme differed from its predecessors in that it was not only an environmental action programme, but also an implicit sustainable development strategy: 'Behind the strategy set out in this programme is the ultimate aim of transforming the patterns of growth in the Community in such a way as to reach a sustainable development path' (EC, 1993: 55). The document is chiefly dedicated to environmental policy, and the reference to sustainable development is only in the context of integrating environmental concerns into economic and social decision making:

The implementation of such a strategy of sustainable development will require a considerable change in almost all major policy areas in which the Community is involved. It requires that environmental protection requirements be integrated into the definition and implementation of other Community policies not just for the sake of the environment, but also for the sake of the continued efficiency of the other policy areas themselves.

(EC, 1993: 55)

In relation to the treaty itself, promoting sustainable development became an objective of the EC under the Amsterdam Treaty in 1997 which also required environmental protection to be integrated across other policies.[10] The current Article 3 of the consolidated version of the Treaty on the European Union provides that the EU 'shall . . . work for the sustainable development of Europe' and Article 11 of the consolidated version of the Treaty on the Functioning of the European Union provides that environmental protection requirements must be integrated into the definition and implementation of the Union's policies and activities, in particular with a view to promoting sustainable development.[11] As a result, sustainable development, as set out in the Treaty, is the overarching long-term goal of the EU. Importantly, however, none of the provisions establishes sustainable development as a 'legal principle' and there is general consensus that unlike the other environmental principles of integration – polluter pays, prevention and precaution – sustainable development has not achieved the status of an enforceable legal principle in EU law (Macrory, 2004; De Sadeleer, 2005: 311).

These treaty provisions have been used to drive the sustainable development agenda forward, not only at EU level but also in the UK and other EU Member States. Indeed, the biggest influence the EU has on the UK's approach to sustainable development is through its legislation, which is binding on the UK, being a member of the EU. In recent years, the EU has mainstreamed the objective of sustainable development into a broad range of its laws. For example, Article 1 of the Strategic Environmental Assessment Directive provides that:

The objective of this Directive is to provide for a high level of protection of the environment and to contribute to the integration of environmental considerations into the preparation and adoption of plans and programmes with a view to promoting sustainable development, by ensuring that, in accordance with this Directive, an environmental assessment is carried out of certain plans and programmes which are likely to have significant effects on the environment.[12]

The Helsinki European Council in December 1999 requested that action should begin on preparing an EU strategy for sustainable development (European Parliament, 1999: para. 50). In 2001, the European Commission presented its communication, *A Sustainable Europe for a Better World*, as the proposal for 'a

European Union Strategy for Sustainable Development' in Gothenburg (European Commission, 2001). Since some Member States objected to parts of the proposal, the Council members 'welcomed' the draft but did not approve it as official EU strategy. Instead, they included 14 modestly ambitious paragraphs on sustainable development in Europe in the 'Presidency Conclusions' (European Commission, 2001). The key components of this 2001 EU quasi-strategy were:

- The global dimension
- Targeting environmental priorities for sustainability
- Combating climate change
- Ensuring sustainable transport
- Addressing threats to public health
- Managing natural resources more responsibly
- Integrating environment into Community policies.

In March 2000, the European heads of state launched the so-called 'Lisbon Process' at the Lisbon European Council. A key objective of this process was for the EU to become 'the most competitive and dynamic knowledge-based economy in the world, capable of sustaining growth with more and better jobs and greater social cohesion' by 2010 (European Parliament, 2000: para. 5). Since various actors repeatedly criticized the Lisbon Process for its focus on growth and employment and its weak linkage to the EU sustainable development strategy, the European heads of state complemented it with an environmental dimension at the Gothenburg European Council, and reaffirmed that the Lisbon Process should be seen in the wider context of sustainable development.

A lengthy review of the EU sustainable development strategy began in early 2004 and it was not until June 2006 that the European Council adopted 'a single, coherent strategy on how the EU will more effectively live up to its long-standing commitment to meet the challenges of sustainable development' (European Council, 2006: para. 4). The renewed strategy's overall aim is:

> to identify and develop actions to enable the EU to achieve continuous improvement of quality of life both for current and for future generations, through the creation of sustainable communities able to manage and use resources efficiently and to tap the ecological and social innovation potential of the economy, ensuring prosperity, environmental protection and social cohesion.
>
> (European Council, 2006: para. 5)

Importantly, given the intergovernmental nature of the EU, the implementation of the objectives and targets formulated in the EU sustainable development strategy requires efforts from the European level as well as from the EU Member States. Therefore, one of the guiding principles of the EU sustainable development strategy is to establish coherence between policymaking on the various political levels for the implementation of the strategy (European Council, 2006: 5). As such, Member States are requested to include the objectives of the EU sustainable development strategy in their national efforts for sustainable development, in order to 'ensure consistency, coherence and supportiveness' (European Council, 2006: para. 40). This concerns all Member States and their national sustainable development strategies (NSDSs), but is particularly important in countries that develop their first or renew their NSDSs.

It is noticeable that there is no mention of environmental limits in the EU strategy's discussion of environmental protection. In the description of economic prosperity, there is a reference to 'eco-efficient economy which provides high living standards' (European Council, 2006: 4). It remains unclear how an eco-efficient economy corresponds to a sustainable one.

The EU also has key institutions involved in the implementation and promotion of sustainable development. Eurostat collates and analyzes the data on sustainable development and has contributed to research into indicators (Eurostat, 2009). The European Sustainable Development Network also contributes widely to development of best practice through its quarterly reports and conferences. Its members include NSDS coordinators, national coordinators of EU environmental integration and sustainable development policies, experts from the European Commission, representatives from various national councils for sustainable development and national members of the Sustainable Development Working Group of the European Environment and Sustainable Development Advisory Councils (ESDN, 2008).

The EU has also developed mechanisms for promoting sustainable development, such as impact assessments and indicators, as well as clear guidance for integrating environmental protection concerns into EU and Member State policies and decisions – known as the 'Cardiff Process' (European Commission, 1998). The details of these tools are set out in the relevant chapters of this book.

Sustainable development in the UK

Rhetoric on sustainable development appears as early as 1983 in the UK's response to the World Conservation Strategy jointly produced by various non-governmental organisations, including the World Wildlife Fund (WWF), and key government agencies, including the Nature Conservancy Council, the Countryside Commission and the Countryside Commission for Scotland. The response is progressive even by modern standards and provides that:

> Building upon and extending the objectives of the World Conservation Strategy to meet UK conditions requires action in three broad areas: (a) integrating conservation of both living and non-living resources with development; (b) developing a sustainable society in which both physical and psychological needs are fully met; (c) developing a stable and sustainable economy through the practices of resource conservation in all spheres of activity.
>
> (Johnson, 1983: 15)

Moreover, the UK was one of the first countries to respond to the Brundtland Report. Its response: *A Perspective by the United Kingdom on the Report of the World Commission on Environment and Development* ((DOE), 1988) went as far as using the same chapters and headings as in the original report. The response states: 'there can be no quarrel with the [Brundtland principles] as a general definition. The key point is how to translate it into practice, how to measure it, and how to assess progress towards its achievement'.

In 1989, the Government produced a progress report on implementing sustainable development. This report, *Sustaining Our Common Future*, was a first attempt to set out policy aims and measures for the UK specifically directed towards achieving sustainable development (DOE, 1989). The ideas in this report were taken up in 1990 in the UK's first comprehensive environment strategy: *This Common Inheritance: Britain's Environmental Strategy*, where the Government claimed that 'There is, therefore, no contradiction in arguing for both economic growth and for environmental good sense. The challenge is to integrate the two' ((DOE), 1990: para. 1.5). 'Sustainable development' is used cautiously in the document, appearing in Chapter 4, and interpreted as simply balancing economic prosperity against environmental concerns: 'The Government therefore supports the principle of sustainable development . . . To achieve sustainable development requires the full integration of environmental considerations into economic policy decisions' (DOE, 1990: para. 4.5). Any reference to social considerations is made only in relation to how the standard of living in developing countries will improve with both increased economic growth and a clean environment (DOE, 1990: para. 4.6).

Predictably, the UK's first sustainable development strategy, produced in 1994, *Sustainable Development: The UK Strategy* (the 1994 strategy), reflects a bilateral approach:

> Most societies aspire to achieve economic development to secure rising standards of living both for themselves and for future generations. They also seek to protect and enhance their environment now and for their children. Reconciling these two aspirations is at the heart of sustainable development.
>
> (UK Government, 1994: para. 3.1)

The strategy mentions social or development issues only as a by-product of sustainable development or where they are linked to the notion of stewardship or shared responsibility, such as increased public access to information and public participation (UK Government, 1994: 207–12).

At the same time as Rio+5, the political climate in the UK was shifting. In May 1997, the Labour Party came to power with a manifesto that included radical constitutional reforms, including devolution for Scotland, Wales and Northern Ireland, giving further effect to the rights and freedom set out in the European Convention on Human Rights, reforms to both houses of Parliament, and a strong commitment to dealing with what was then referred to as 'wicked issues' such as social exclusion (Labour Party, 1997).

Many of these promises were delivered, and 1998 saw the passage of four very significant constitutional reforms in the form of the Scotland Act 1998, the Government of Wales Act 1998, the Northern Ireland Act 1998 and the Human Rights Act 1998.[13] The 1998 devolution settlements for Scotland, Wales and Northern Ireland produced asymmetrical arrangements among the jurisdictions, as distinct and varied degrees of administrative and legislative duties were devolved (Himsworth, 2007: 32). Devolution has not had popular support in England, and all primary and secondary legislation for England (including that relating to the environment) continues to be enacted by the UK institutions (Hazell, 2001: 266–7). In Wales, the Government of Wales Act 1998 established the National Assembly for Wales ('the Assembly') and devolved certain administrative powers to it, along with the power to pass secondary legislation in specific areas, including the environment.[14] These powers have been extended by the Government of Wales Act 2006 to enable the Assembly to, among other things, make primary laws for Wales, in the form of Assembly Measures, in areas where it has legislative competence.[15] Importantly, the Government of Wales Act 2006 separates the executive, the Welsh Assembly Government (WAG), from the Assembly itself as the legislature.[16]

Scotland has more legislative power. Pursuant to the Scotland Act 1998, the Scottish Parliament is competent to deal with all matters in Scotland other than those expressly reserved for the UK Parliament at Westminster.[17] Specifically, international relations, energy, and aspects of road, rail and marine transport are all reserved. Matters not reserved to Westminster, and thus devolved to the Scottish Parliament, include health, education, policing, criminal justice, environmental protection, agriculture and local government. The Scottish Parliament can legislate on these matters and the Scottish ministers have the power to exercise certain functions within devolved competence.[18]

Under the Northern Ireland Act 1998, the Northern Ireland Assembly is competent to deal with all those matters that are not excepted or reserved to the UK Parliament. Excepted matters are similar to reserved matters in Scotland, and are those that are expressly reserved for the UK Parliament. Reserved matters are those that may be transferred to the Northern Ireland institutions at a later date and include policing and criminal justice. Transferred matters within the competence of the Northern Ireland Assembly include environment, local government and health. The 1998 devolution settlement in Northern Ireland was suspended from 2002 to 2007,[19] and this, combined with the fact that there was a need to clear a substantial backlog of non-implemented EC environmental measures, has meant progress towards sustainable development in Northern Ireland has lagged behind the rest of the UK (Turner 2006a: 55; 2006b: 245).

Other restrictions on the powers of all the devolved administrations include, unsurprisingly, that their lawmaking powers are confined to their respective territorial limits,[20] and importantly, that they cannot make any law which is incompatible with EU law or with rights under the European Convention on Human Rights.[21]

The devolution Acts also expressly provide that they do not affect the power of the UK to make laws for Scotland, Wales and Northern Ireland and, as such, the devolved legislatures and administrations do not enjoy exclusive legislative competence.[22] This distinguishes the settlements from federal systems (Wade and Forsyth, 2004: 131). By convention, the UK Parliament does not enact primary legislation relating to devolved matters in Scotland without the consent of the Scottish Parliament (Page and Batey, 2002: 501).

Interestingly, the UK Parliament imposed a statutory obligation on the Welsh Assembly under the Government of Wales Act 1998 to prepare a scheme for sustainable development.[23] This option was not considered appropriate for the Scottish or Northern Irish institutions, both of which were given competence to enact primary legislation and could therefore arguably impose such an obligation on themselves, if they so desired.

However, more generally, the UK Government contended that:

> Bringing government closer to the people through devolution is itself a policy for sustainable development . . . The new devolved administrations in Scotland, Wales and Northern Ireland have the opportunity to deliver policies for sustainable development which reflect their institutions, their landscape, their culture and their way of life.
>
> (DEFRA, 1999: para. 2.4)

The UK Labour Government's commitment to social issues is evident in its UK strategy for sustainable development produced in 1999, and aptly named *A Better Quality of Life A Strategy for Sustainable Development for the United Kingdom* (the 1999 strategy) (DEFRA, 1999). In it, the Government followed the prevalent approach taken by many countries and the European Community at the time, and adopted a three-pronged approach to sustainable development, whereby economic, social and environmental objectives are achieved at the same time, and the longer-term implications of decisions are considered (DEFRA, 1999: para. 1.9).[24] The approach still advocates the pursuit of high economic growth even for a developed country like the UK, but does contain a greater commitment to intra-generational equity issues both inside and outside the UK.

Accompanying the strategy were numerous innovative tools aimed at improving the delivery of the sustainable development aims set out in the strategy. These tools included a new set of headline indicators designed to be more user-friendly, the establishment of a new Green ministers cabinet sub-committee to monitor the performance within government, and the establishment of the Sustainable Development Commission (SDC) and the House of Commons Environmental Audit Committee to monitor, review and advise the Government on its progress in relation to sustainable development (Chapters 5 and 7).

By 2004, it had become evident to policymakers in the UK that the ecological changes being experienced were, or would soon be, creating unacceptable consequences, and that the weak version of sustainability popular among governments and business was not working. As Bosselmann (2008: 52) observes, the attempt to roll three types of sustainability (ecological, economic and social) into one overarching concept of sustainability left it pointing in multiple directions without any central meaning.

The SDC and academics around the world were calling for sustainable development to be 'the central organising principle of government' (SDC, 2009: 2; Dernbach, 2009: 27–39; Bosselmann, 2008: 175–208). These concerns did have an impact on the next UK strategy, as did devolution. The old 1999 strategy did not reflect the new political reality of a devolved UK with divided competences, and it was not clear which policies, actions and targets applied to all or only part of the UK.

One future – different paths: The UK's shared framework for sustainable development, jointly published in 2005 by all the administrations in the UK, sets out a new approach to sustainable development based on five principles: living within environmental limits, ensuring a healthy and just society, achieving a sustainable economy, promoting good governance, and using sound science responsibly (HM Government *et al.*, 2005: 8; Scottish Executive, 2005; Northern Ireland Office, 2006).[25] The reference to high economic growth is gone and this, combined with an explicit acknowledgement of the Earth's environmental limits, demonstrates a deeper commitment to ecological or strong sustainability. Moreover, the Framework sets out: a shared understanding of sustainable development; a common purpose outlining what the UK is trying to achieve; the guiding principles needed to achieve it; sustainable development priorities for UK action at home and internationally; and indicators to monitor the key issues on a UK basis. At the same time, the UK administration produced a UK strategy for sustainable development entitled *The UK Strategy for Sustainable Development: Securing the Future* (the 2005 strategy), which deals with reserved (or UK-wide) issues and those issues which only pertain to (mainly) England following devolution (DEFRA, 2005).

Following the General Election in 2010, the UK Government was formed by a coalition between the Conservative Party, led by David Cameron, and the Liberal Democrat Party, led by Nick Clegg. The coalition immediately had to deal with a nation in crisis due to mounting public debt, to which a major contributor was the previous government's bailout of the UK financial sector. The initial response was to produce an emergency Budget which sets out a five-year plan to rebuild the British economy, based on the Government's values of responsibility, freedom and fairness (HM Treasury, 2010). It shows how the new Government will carry out Britain's unavoidable deficit reduction plan in a way that strengthens and unites the country. This new model of economic growth is built on saving, investment and enterprise, instead of debt. The aim is to transform the UK economy and pave the way for sustainable, private sector-led growth, balanced across regions and industries. The Budget sets out action in three areas to rebalance the economy and provide the conditions for sustainable growth: deficit reduction, enterprise and fairness (HM Treasury, 2010).

The UK coalition Government aims to become the 'greenest government ever' (Randerson, 2010). While the idea of changing the culture of consumption to one of investment is clearly in line with sustainable development thinking, some of the cuts in public expenditure and services to date appear to be inconsistent with this message. In particular, the decision to cease funding the SDC for a saving of £3–4 million per year appears perverse. The significant contributions of this Commission in the UK's journey towards a sustainable economy are littered throughout this volume and its loss is a significant blow to the move from rhetoric to reality.

Sustainable development in the devolved administrations

Following devolution, the Welsh Assembly immediately set about producing its statutorily required scheme for sustainable development, which was published in November 2000 (NAW, 2000). As for the other two devolved administrations, it was not until after the publication of the *UK's shared framework for sustainable development* in 2005 that the Scottish Executive and the Northern Ireland Executive published their first strategies for sustainable development (Scottish Executive, 2005; Northern Ireland Office, 2006), by which time, Wales was already working on its second scheme. These post-2005 strategies largely use the Framework as a template and then added detail in relation to their own priorities and competences (Scottish Executive, 2005; Northern Ireland Office, 2006).[26] Although these are dealt with in detail in Chapter 4, at this stage, it is useful to observe how over time these strategies have been replaced and are now beginning to deviate more significantly from the Framework.

After the Scottish National Party's success in the Scottish Parliamentary election in May 2007, it replaced the previous government's sustainable development strategy with *The Government's Economic Strategy* and national performance indicators and with one single objective of 'increasing sustainable economic growth' (Scottish Government, 2007: vii). This is clearly inconsistent with the UK vision as set out in its strategy: 'We want to achieve a strong, healthy and just society living within environmental limits' (DEFRA, 2005). The relationship between sustainable economic growth and sustainable development remains unclear, despite the following explanation of the meaning of sustainable economic growth provided by the Scottish Government: 'building a dynamic and growing economy that will provide prosperity and opportunities for all, while respecting the limits of our environment in order to ensure that future generations can enjoy a better quality of life too' (Scottish Government, 2007: vii).[27] The Scottish commitment to growth appears to be a higher priority than living within environmental limits.

The latest sustainable development strategy in Northern Ireland, like its predecessor, while staying true to the principles in the Framework, adds 'promoting opportunity and innovation' to the UK Framework's principles for sustainable development (Northern Ireland Executive, 2010). It also seems to sidestep any strong prioritisation of living within the Earth's limits.

In contrast, the Welsh Assembly Government has recently replaced its strategy with one which explicitly states that: 'Within the lifetime of a generation we want to see Wales using only its fair share of the earth's resources' (WAG, 2009: 11).

Of course, there is much more to implementation than the production of a strategy. Devolved administrations have also introduced diverse and innovative mechanisms for delivering sustainable development. Indeed, in many respects, they have acted as laboratories for more innovative advancements. Porritt (2009) hypothesizes that sustainable development may be an easier concept to operationalize at the sub-national level. In his review of the standing of sustainable development in government in the UK, he notes that the new devolved system has opened up political space for innovation in Scotland and Wales, and that there has been a potentially helpful break with 'path dependence'.

For example, while the UK Government did not impose a duty in relation to sustainable development on the Northern Ireland or Scotland institutions as it did for Wales under the Government of Wales Act 1998, the Northern Ireland Assembly has imposed a statutory duty to promote sustainable development under the Northern Ireland (Miscellaneous Provisions) Act 2006 s. 25,[28] which requires departments and district councils to exercise their functions in the manner they consider best calculated to promote the achievement of sustainable development (Northern Ireland Executive, 2010: 9). Moreover, uniquely for the UK, the responsibility for the production of Northern Ireland's strategy is set within the Office of the First Minister and Deputy First Minister, which at least provides an opportunity for imposing strong leadership from the top level of government.

In Wales, the coordination of sustainable development is led by a crosscutting cabinet committee and, unlike the tradition in the UK Government (also known as Whitehall), the minutes of all its meetings are published. The Scottish Government has chosen to extend the coverage of strategic environmental assessment beyond the scope of the original EU directive to include strategies. It also extended the remit of the Sustainable Development Commission in Scotland to include a full annual review of the Scottish Government's progress towards sustainable development using not only progress against set indicators and strategic objectives, but also auditing policymaking more generally (see Chapter 7 for details).

Sustainable development at grassroots level in the UK

It would be very misleading to say that the sustainable development movement in the UK has been entirely led from the top down. Often, the UK has taken a lead in international discussions, which is usually because of innovative activity already happening in local councils, public bodies, private companies, communities and voluntary organizations within the UK itself. There are numerous examples of UK local authorities, companies and voluntary organizations providing leadership on sustainable development. For instance, Leicester became Britain's first 'Environment City' in 1990. In 1992, it was one of 12 world cities invited to attend the Earth Summit in Rio de Janeiro (Leicester City Council, n.d.). Similarly, the private and voluntary sectors have been active on sustainable development issues for some time. The very first Body Shop store opened on 26 March 1976 in Brighton. Its business – which is based around five core values: support community fair trade, defend human rights, against animal testing, activate self-esteem, and protect our planet – now boasts more than 2500 stores in over 60 countries worldwide (The Body Shop, 2010).

Conclusion

The rhetoric on sustainable development is widespread. However, while its popularity and resilience can largely be attributed to its malleability, behind the broad agreement lies a plethora of inherent conflicts (Alder and Wilkinson, 1999: 141). When differing values combine with the different definitions, sustainable development can be construed as legitimizing 'business as usual' patterns of economic growth or, at the other extreme, requiring a fundamental reworking of the global socioeconomic order. Some in the deep ecology movement have argued that 'Sustainable development is a contradiction in terms, in that growth and environmental protection are enemies' (Alder and Wilkinson, 1999: 141). In sharp contrast, others have described sustainable development as 'the only meaningful cure to the problems that face the world' (Salmon, 2003: 13).

The challenge of not just talking about sustainable development, but actually delivering, has attracted attention at all levels of government right from the start. As early as 1997, the former UK Deputy Prime Minister, John Prescott, observed that 'all of Government [needed] to take the environment and sustainable development seriously, to think through the environmental consequences of policies right from the start, not as a kind of add-on to the main decisions after they have been taken' (EAC, 1998). Indeed, governments at all levels have had to develop an understanding of sustainable development and consider how it should be integrated into everyday decisions and actions in their respective regions, countries and municipalities. As noted by Porritt (2009), and discussed at length in Part II of this volume, much of the architecture needed to secure sustainable development in the UK is in place. However, like many other countries, these mechanisms exist without a clear mandate or understanding of their duties in relation to sustainable development, its relevance to their work or the contribution they could make.

On a positive note, the rhetoric has created a research culture, much of which has been devoted to the delivery of sustainable development. The next chapter reviews this research to uncover remarkably consistent and established criteria for implementation. These criteria are then used as the framework for Part II, which reviews the approaches taken by the UK and devolved administrations to move towards sustainability. It also asks the question why the UK still remains a long way off true sustainability.

Notes

1 The Declaration of the United Nations Conference on the Human Environment (the Stockholm Declaration), 11 *International Legal Materials* (ILM) 1461 (1972).

2 11 ILM 1461 (1972).
3 11 ILM 1461 (1972).
4 11 ILM 1461 (1972).
5 11 ILM 1461 (1972).
6 31 ILM 848 (1992); 31 ILM 818 (1992).
7 For example, see the Government of Mexico (The Earth Charter Initiative, 2007).
8 37 ILM 22 (1998).
9 The Treaty on European Union OJ (1992) C 191.
10 The Treaty of Amsterdam OJ (1997), C 340.
11 Consolidated versions of the Treaty on European Union and the Treaty on the Functioning of the European Union OJ (2008), C 115.
12 Directive 2001/42/EC on the assessment of certain plans and programmes on the environment OJ (2001), L 197/30.
13 The Scotland Act 1998 ch. 46; the Government of Wales Act 1998 ch. 32; the Northern Ireland Act 1998 ch. 47; the Human Rights Act 1998 ch. 42.
14 The Government of Wales Act 1998 s. 1(1); Schedule 2.
15 The Government of Wales Act 2006 ch. 32. Legislative competence is granted either directly through an Act of Parliament or using a Legislative Competence Order.
16 The Government of Wales Act 2006 s. 103: the Welsh Assembly may obtain further powers to pass primary legislation in the future following a referendum.
17 The Scotland Act 1998 Schedule 5.
18 The Scotland Act 1998 s. 53. Under s. 63, the UK Government may additionally transfer functions (including the power to make subordinate legislation) to the Scottish ministers in relation to reserved matters. This is known as 'executive devolution'.
19 See the Northern Ireland Act 1998. The Northern Ireland (St Andrews Agreement) Act 2006 ch. 53 provided for a Transitional Assembly to prepare for the restoration of devolved government. Restoration took place on 8 May 2007.
20 The Scotland Act 1998 s. 29(2)(a); the Government of Wales Act 1998 s. 58(a); the Northern Ireland Act 1998 s. 6(2)(a).
21 The Scotland Act 1998 s. 29(2)(d); the Government of Wales Act 2006 s. 80(8); the Northern Ireland Act 1998 s. 24(1).
22 The Scotland Act 1998 s. 28(7); the Government of Wales Act 2006 s. 107(5).
23 The Government of Wales Act 1998 s. 121. For a discussion on the inclusion of the duty in relation to Wales, see Jenkins, 2002: 578.
24 See European Parliament and European Council (2002) *The Sixth Community Environmental Action* Programme, (OJ) L 242/I, and European Commission, 2001. For a criticism of this approach, see Helm, 2000: 12.
25 Note that Northern Ireland's Sustainable Development Strategy was produced while devolution was still suspended. The Office of the First Minister and Deputy First Minister has produced a plan of implementation for the strategy.
26 Note that Wales has a statutory duty to produce a sustainable development scheme: the Government of Wales Act 2006 s. 79 (previously the 1998 Act s. 121).
27 The Scottish strategy *Choosing our Future* (Scottish Executive, 2005) is now largely a historic document. The new policy is mostly contained in *The Government's Economic Strategy* (Scottish Government, 2007). Also see *Scottish Planning Policy: Proposed Policy Changes Consultation* (Scottish Government, 2009).
28 The Northern Ireland (Miscellaneous Provisions) Act 2006 ch. 33.

References

Adams, W.M. (2001) *Green Development: Environment and Sustainability in the Third World*, 2nd edition, London: Routledge.

Alder, J. and Wilkinson, D. (1999) *Environmental Law and Ethics*, London: Macmillan.

Beder, S. (2006) *Environmental Principles and Policies: An Interdisciplinary Introduction*, London: Earthscan.

The Body Shop (2010) http://www.thebodyshop.co.uk/, accessed 10 October 2010.

Bosselmann, K. (2008) *The Principle of Sustainability: Transforming Law and Governance*, Aldershot: Ashgate.

Bowers, J. (1997) *Sustainability and Environmental Economics: An Alternative Text*, Harlow: Longman.

Boyle, A. and Freestone, D. (1999) *International Law and Sustainable Development: Past Achievements and Future Challenges*, Oxford: Oxford University Press.

Brandt Commission (1980) *North–South: A Programme for Survival*, London: Pan.

Brown, O. (2005) *The Environment and our Security: How our Understanding of the Links has Changed*, Winnipeg: International Institute for Sustainable Development.

Daly, H.E. (1973) *Towards a Steady-State Economy*, San Francisco: W.H. Freeman.

Department for Transport, Scottish Executive, Welsh Assembly Government (2009) *Transport Statistics for Great Britain 2009*, 35th edition, London: Department for Transport.

Department of the Environment (DOE) (1988) *A Perspective by the United Kingdom on the Report of the World Commission on Environment and Development*, London: DOE.

DOE (1989) *Sustaining our Common Future*, London: Department of the Environment.

DOE (1990) *This Common Inheritance: Britain's Environmental Strategy*, London: HMSO.

Department of Environment, Food and Rural Affairs (DEFRA) (1999) *A Better Quality of Life: A Strategy for Sustainable Development for the United Kingdom*, London: DEFRA.

DEFRA (2005) *The UK Strategy for Sustainable Development: Securing the Future*, London: DEFRA.

Dernbach, J. (2009) *Agenda for a Sustainable America*, Washington, DC: Environmental Law Institute.

De Sadeleer, N. (2005) *Environmental Principles: From Political Slogans to Legal Rules*, Oxford: Oxford University Press.

The Earth Charter Initiative (2000) *The Earth Charter*, http://www.earthinaction.org/invent/images/uploads/echarter_english.pdf, accessed 12 August 2010.

The Earth Charter Initiative (2007) 'A wonderful week for the Earth Charter: Mexico reaffirms its support and commitment', http://www.earthcharterinaction.org/content/articles/122/1/A-Wonderful-week-for-the-Earth-Charter.html, accessed 12 August 2010.

Environmental Audit Committee (EAC) (1998) The Greening Government Initiative; Second Report of Session 1997–98, HC 517-II, Q2 (answer given in evidence 28 January 1998).

European Commission (EC) (1973) *Programme of Action of the European Communities on the Environment* (Annex to 'Declaration of 22 November 1973 on the Programme of Action of the European Communities on the Environment'), (OJ) C11 2, 20.12.1973.

European Commission (1993) *Towards Sustainability: A European Community Programme of Policy and Action in Relation to the Environment and Sustainable Development*, Luxembourg COM(92)23, vol. 2.

European Commission (1998) Communication from the Commission to the European Council of 27 May 1998 on a partnership for integration: A strategy for integrating the environment into EU policies (Cardiff) COM(1998)333.

European Commission (2001) *A Sustainable Europe for a Better World: A European Union Strategy for Sustainable Development*, Brussels: European Commission.

European Council (2006) *Review of the EU Sustainable Development Strategy: Renewed Strategy*, Brussels: European Council.

European Parliament (1999) *Helsinki European Council: Presidency Conclusions*, Luxembourg: European Parliament.

European Parliament (2000) *Lisbon European Council: Presidency Conclusions*, Luxembourg: European Parliament.

European Sustainable Development Network (ESDN) (2008) *ESDN Joint Understanding* (updated and adopted by the ESDN Steering Group on 12 September 2008), Salzburg: ESDN.

Eurostat (2009) *Sustainable development in the European Union: 2009 monitoring report of the EU sustainable development strategy*, Luxembourg: Office for Official Publications of the European Communities.

French, D. (2005) *International Law and Policy of Sustainable Development*, Manchester: Manchester University Press.

Grainger, A. (2004) 'Introduction', in M. Purvis and A. Grainger (eds) *Exploring Sustainable Development: Geographical Perspectives*, London: Earthscan.

Hazell, R. (2001) 'Conclusion', in A. Trench (ed.) *The State of the Nations 2001: the Second Year of Devolution in the UK*, Thorverton: Imprint Academic.

Helm, D. (2000) 'Objectives, instruments and institutions', in D. Helm (ed.) *Environmental Policy Objectives, Instruments and Implementation*, Oxford: Oxford University Press.

HM Government, Scottish Executive, Welsh Assembly Government, Northern Ireland Office (2005) *One future – different paths: The UK's shared framework for sustainable development*, London: DEFRA.

HM Treasury (2010) *Budget 2010*, HC 61, London: HM Treasury.

Himsworth, C.M.G. (2007) 'Devolution and its jurisdictional asymmetries', *Modern Law Review*, 70(1): 31–58.

International Union for Conservation of Nature and Natural Resources (ed.) (1980) *World Conservation Strategy: Living Resource Conservation for Sustainable Development*, Gland: IUCN.

Jenkins, V. (2002) 'Placing sustainable development at the heart of government in the UK: The role of law in the evolution of sustainable development as the central organising principle of government', *Legal Studies*, 22(4): 578–601.

Johnson, B. (1983) *The Conservation and Development Programme for the UK: A response to the World Conservation Strategy: An Overview: Resourceful Britain*, London: Kogan Page.

Kirby, J. (1995) 'Introduction', in J. Kirby, P. O'Keefe and L. Timberlake (eds) *The Earthscan Reader in Sustainable Development*, London: Earthscan.

Labour Party (1997) *New Labour: Because Britain Deserves Better*, London: Labour Party.

Leicester City Council (n.d.) From Environment City to Sustainable City http://www.leicester.gov.uk/your-council-services/ep/the-environment/environmental-policies-action/environment-city/, accessed 26 July 2011.

Macrory, R. (ed.) (2004) *Principles of European Environmental Law*, Groningen: Europa Law Publishing.

Maddox, J. (1972) *The Doomsday Syndrome*, London: Macmillan.

Meadows, D.H., Meadows, D.C., Randers, J. and Behrens, W.W. (1972) *The Limits to Growth: A Report for the Club of Rome's Project on the Predicament of Mankind*, London: Pan.

National Assembly for Wales (2000) *Starting to Live Differently: The Sustainable Development Scheme of the National Assembly for Wales*, Cardiff: National Assembly for Wales.

Northern Ireland Executive (2010) *Everyone's Involved: Sustainable Development Strategy*, Belfast: Northern Ireland Executive.

Northern Ireland Office (2006) *Sustainable Development Strategy for Northern Ireland: First Steps towards Sustainability*, Belfast: Northern Ireland Office.

Office of the First Minister and Deputy First Minister (2006) *Plan of Implementation*, Belfast: OFMDFM.

Page, A. and Batey, A. (2002) 'Scotland's other Parliament: Westminster legislation about devolved matters in Scotland since devolution', *Public Law*, Autumn: 501–23.

Pearce, D. (1993) *Blueprint 3: Measuring Sustainable Development*, London: Earthscan.

Porritt, J. (2009) 'The standing of sustainable development in government', http://www.jonathonporritt.com/pages/2009/11/the_standing_of_sustainable_de.html, accessed 12 April 2010.

Randerson, J. (2010) 'Cameron: I want the Coalition to be the "greenest government ever"', *Guardian*, 14 May.

Ross, A. (2010) 'Sustainable development indicators and a putative argument for law: A case study of the UK', in D. French (ed.) *Global Justice and Sustainable Development*, Leiden: Martinus Nijhoff.

Salmon, P. (2003) 'Sustainable development in New Zealand', *RMB*, 5: 13.

Sands, P. (2003) *Principles of International Law*, 2nd edition, Cambridge: Cambridge University Press.

Scottish Executive (2005) *Choosing our Future: Scotland's Sustainable Development Strategy*, Edinburgh: Scottish Executive.

Scottish Government (2007) *The Government's Economic Strategy*, Edinburgh: Scottish Government.

Scottish Government (2009) *Scottish Planning Policy: Proposed Policy Changes Consultation*, Edinburgh: Scottish Government.

Simon, J.L. (1981) *The Ultimate Resource*, Oxford: Martin Robertson.

Stern, N. (2007) *The Economics of Climate Change: The Stern Review*, Cambridge: Cambridge University Press.

Sustainable Development Commission (SDC) (2004) *Shows Promise. But Must Try Harder: An Assessment by the Sustainable Development Commission of the Government's Reported Progress on Sustainable Development over the Past Five Years*, London: SDC.

SDC (2009) *Where Are We Now: A Review of Progress on Sustainable Development*, London: SDC.

Turner, S. (2006a) 'Transforming environmental governance in Northern Ireland: Part one: The process of policy renewal', *Journal of Environmental Law*, 18(1): 55–87.

Turner, S. (2006b) 'Transforming environmental governance in Northern Ireland: Part two: The case of environmental regulation', *Journal of Environmental Law*, 18(2): 245–75.

UK Government (1994) *Sustainable Development: The UK Strategy*, London: HMSO Cm 6467.

UN (1995) *Report of the World Summit for Social Development*, A/CONF.166/9, New York: UN.

UN (2002a) *Johannesburg Declaration on Sustainable Development*, A/CONF.199/L.6/Rev.2, New York: UN.

UN (2002b) *Plan of Implementation of the World Summit on Sustainable Development*, A/CONF.199/20/Res.2, New York: UN.

UN (2009) *Copenhagen Accord*, FCCC/CP/2009/L.7, New York: UN.

UN Educational, Scientific and Cultural Organization (UNESCO) (n.d.) *Man and the Biosphere Programme*, http://portal.unesco.org/science/en/ev.php-URL_ID=6784& URL_DO=DO_TOPIC&URL_SECTION=201.html, accessed 16 August 2010.

UN Framework Convention on Climate Change (UNFCCC) (2010) *Synthesis and Assessment Report on the Greenhouse Gas Inventories*, FCCC/WEB/SAI/2010, New York: UN.

UN General Assembly (UNGA) (1987) *Report of the World Commission on Environment and Development*, A/RES/42/187, New York: UN.

UNGA (1992a) *The Rio Declaration on Environment and Development*, 31 ILM 874.

UNGA (1992b) *The Forest Principles*, A/CONF.151/26 Vol. 3, New York: UN.

UNGA (1992c) *Agenda 21*, A/CONF.151/26 Vol. 1, New York: UN.

UNGA (1997) *Programme for the Further Implementation of Agenda 21*, A/RES/S-19/2, New York: UN.

UNGA (2000) *United Nations Millennium Declaration*, A/Res/55/2, New York: UN.

Wade, H.W.R. and Forsyth, C.F. (2004) *Administrative Law*, 9th edition, Oxford: Oxford University Press.

Welsh Assembly Government (WAG) (2009) *One Wales: One Planet: The Sustainable Development Scheme of the Welsh Assembly Government*, Cardiff: WAG.

World Commission on Environment and Development (WCED) (1987) *Our Common Future*, Oxford: Oxford University Press.

World Wildlife Fund (WWF), Zoological Society of London and Global Footprint Network (2008) *Living Planet Report 2008*, Gland: WWF.

3 Criteria for effective implementation of sustainable development

This chapter explores the difficulties of moving from the rhetoric of sustainable development to its implementation, and the cultural change required within governments for them to become truly sustainable. It canvasses the research into effective implementation of sustainable development, including the criteria used by the UN Commission for Sustainable Development, the Organisation for Economic Co-operation and Development (OECD), the UK's Sustainable Development Commission (SDC) and what are known as the Bellagio Principles, published by the International Institute for Sustainable Development (IISD). It then explains how this book develops the OECD's criteria for implementation for its analysis of the UK approach to sustainable development, drawing on the other studies throughout. The chapter ends with an explanation of how the same criteria are used to provide the broad structure of Part II of this volume. Hence, Chapter 4 examines a common understanding and strategies. The need for clear commitment and leadership is addressed in Chapter 5. The benefits and tools used for stakeholder involvement and efficient knowledge management are explored in Chapter 6, while the various institutional, policy and legal mechanisms which are or have been used to further sustainable development in the UK are reviewed in Chapters 7–10.

Popularity of sustainable development as a policy goal

Following the publication of *Our Common Future* (the Brundtland Report) (WCED, 1987), as observed by Tarlock (2001: 38), 'sustainable development was quickly adopted throughout much of the world as the standard against which public policy should be judged'. There are many reasons for this. First, it is both politically and culturally very difficult to not advocate cleaning the environment, alleviating poverty and improving the wellbeing of humans and the environment, now and in the future. Secondly, the exact meaning of sustainable development remains unclear and the concept is capable of multiple meanings. For instance, in 1996, Fowke and Prasad (1996: 61) identified at least 80 different, often competing or contradictory, definitions of sustainable development. As discussed in detail in the previous and subsequent chapters, the most common definition, the Brundtland definition: 'development that meets the needs of the present without compromising the ability of future generations to meet their own needs' (WCED, 1987), can be construed to support very different political, economic, ecological and social agendas. Groups with very disparate interests can interpret it in ways that reflect their own beliefs and norms. In this way, the Brundtland definition acts as a catalyst for discussion, as it brings together different and conflicting interests. One obvious divide is between developed countries which have used sustainable development to pursue their own environmental protection agendas and developing countries which continue to focus their attention on economic development (Grainger, 2004: 7). Other variations also exist within the Brundtland formula. The differences largely concern the emphasis placed on each of the three components of sustainable development: economy, environment and society. Disparities also exist about the nature of human needs now and in the future and about technology's role in meeting those needs.

The challenge of not just talking about sustainable development but actually delivering has been a concern for all levels of government since its inception. Indeed, governments at all levels have had to develop an understanding of sustainable development and consider how it should be integrated into everyday decisions and actions in their respective regions, countries and municipalities.

At the international level, the Rio Declaration lists a set of principles and objectives which should underpin sustainable development, such as integrating environmental factors into decision making and the need for environmental assessment (UNGA, 1992a). The Declaration is essentially a high-level aspirational declaration. *Agenda 21* (UNGA, 1992b) provides a more detailed account of what is needed. However, it is a very long document and is still aspirational. It provides no guidance as to how to actually go about delivering on these promises (Grainger, 2004: 7–8). In September 2000, 147 heads of states and Governments signed the 'Millennium Declaration' and reaffirmed their support for the principles of sustainable development, including those set out in *Agenda 21* (UNGA, 2000). They also agreed the 'Millennium Development Goals', which include the goal to 'integrate the principles of sustainable development into country policies and programmes and reverse the loss of environmental resources' and importantly, to set specific targets with timetables for each of the goals (UNGA, 2000). That said, targets and timetables alone do not actually promise implementation, and as of 2010, achievement of the goals still remained some way off (UNGA, 2010: 52–64).

Ten years on from Rio, in 2002, the focus of the whole Johannesburg Summit was on the delivery of the promises made in the Rio Declaration and *Agenda 21*. In the *Plan of Implementation*, parties committed themselves to:

> undertaking concrete actions and measures at all levels and to enhancing international cooperation, taking into account the Rio principles, including, inter alia, the principle of common but differentiated responsibilities as set out in principle 7 of the Rio Declaration on Environment and Development. These efforts also promote the integration of the three components of

sustainable development – economic development, social development and environmental protection – as interdependent and mutually reinforcing pillars.

(UN, 2002: para. 2)

Unfortunately, progress towards sustainability has been slow. J. MacNeill (Secretary General of the World Commission on Environment and Development and chief architect and lead author of the Brundtland Report) sees progress towards sustainable development as follows:

> Looking back I think we did get off to a fairly good start in 1987. At the time of our launch in London, I never expected . . . that within a year and extending through Rio, many governments . . . would respond officially to our recommendations and commit themselves to many things including various measures to institutionalize sustainable development . . . But in my view, few governments went far enough and even fewer sustained their efforts.

(MacNeill, 2007: 20)

The research into delivering sustainable development

The research into sustainable development broadly agrees that two significant changes are required for effective implementation. The first change is largely institutional and requires the full integration of environmental protection concerns, and more broadly, sustainable development, into all forms of policy and decision making. The true success of this first change is dependent on the second significant change, which is a cultural acceptance and understanding that prioritizes operating within the Earth's limits and thinking about the long-term effects of policy and decisions. The first change is known as the integration principle, and has procedural and institutional consequences. The OECD has observed that the traditional government procedures for addressing cross-sectoral and intergenerational issues often display a deficit of coherence: constitutional, legal and political obstacles to policy coordination exist partly to maintain a clear distribution of responsibilities and specialization of tasks among sectors and across levels of government (OECD, 2002: 2).

Initially, the integration principle focused on integrating environmental concerns into decision making. This concern has received wide acceptance, and action has been taken to address 'silo' government at all levels. For example, the Treaty on the Functioning of the European Union Article 11 provides that 'Environmental protection requirements must be integrated into the definition and implementation of the Union policies and activities, in particular with a view to promoting sustainable development'.[1] The EU has acted on this commitment by introducing measures such as strategic environmental assessment of plans and programmes by public bodies.[2]

More recently, the integration principle has broadened to include all aspects of sustainable development including concerns about the Earth's limits, and intragenerational and intergenerational equity. The OECD (2002: 2) has stated that in order for public management systems to respond to the challenges presented by sustainable development, specific initiatives are needed by government to better integrate economic, environmental and social goals within the mandate of each existing institution. A lack of effective coordination between sectors and across the various levels of government is therefore one of the major challenges. Similarly, coherence is still lacking between the key choices made by the public sector and those made by the private sector (OECD, 2002: 3).

Thus, integration can help governments make strides towards sustainable societies, but integration alone is not enough to deliver sustainable development. The second change returns to the fact that the implementation process also requires a clear understanding of what sustainable development means in practice and the priorities that ought to prevail when there is conflict. There needs to be a clear vision of what is to be achieved and how it is to be achieved. As such, the definitional issues and cultural change that underpin this clarity of vision and priority cannot be divorced from the implementation process. Indeed, while many states, sub-national and municipal governments, and the private sector have made good progress in creating opportunities and tools for the integration of environmental concerns into decision making, these have had only limited success due to a persistent resistance to set priorities and understand limits. It is only in recent years following *The Economics of Climate Change: The Stern Review* (Stern, 2007), various reports on climate change (World Wildlife Fund *et al.*, 2008) and the ever-worsening state of the Earth's resources that sustain life (SCBD, 2010) that attention has been redirected back towards the interpretation of sustainable development and its actual role in any given society or organization.

The commitments made in Rio, Johannesburg and elsewhere, nationally and internationally, have led to a significant body of research into the actual delivery of sustainable development. While there are many other excellent studies (Dernbach, 2002–2003; Bell and Morse, 2008; WWF *et al.*, 2008; European Council, 2006; Environmental Audit Committee, 2009; Russell and Thomson, 2008),[3] the author has chosen to focus on the work of the key international players in relation to sustainable development guidance and advice, and their UK counterpart. Thus, the contributions of the UN Commission on Sustainable Development (CSD), the OECD, the Bellagio Principles and the UK's own SDC are explored.

The Commission on Sustainable Development

The CSD was established by the UN General Assembly in December 1992 to ensure effective follow-up of the UN Conference on Environment and Development, also known as the 'Earth Summit'. The CSD is a functional commission of the UN Economic and Social Council (ECOSOC), with the ECOSOC's 'Division for Sustainable Development' as its substantive secretariat. The CSD is responsible for reviewing progress of the implementation of *Agenda 21* and the

Rio Declaration on Environment and Development, as well as providing policy guidance to follow up the Johannesburg *Plan of Implementation* at the local, national, regional and international levels.

The CSD has noted that an essential aspect of implementation is the development of the national sustainable development strategy (NSDS) (Division for Sustainable Development, UNDESA, 2002). In research published in 2002, into the development and use of NSDSs, the CSD found that the experience of the previous ten years, as well as current practices, suggest that 'sound and effective national sustainable development strategies have certain elements in common or defining features'. These underlying elements are:

- Country ownership and strong political commitment
- Integrated economic, social and environmental objectives across sectors, territories and generations
- Broad participation and effective partnerships
- Development of capacity and enabling environment
- Focus on outcomes and means of implementation.
                (Division for Sustainable Development, UNDESA, 2002: para. 7)

Moreover, the CSD states that effective implementation of the NSDS requires the follow-up, monitoring and evaluation of what is happening, in order to gain an understanding of 'what works and what does not' (Division for Sustainable Development, UNDESA, 2002: paras. 10, 13).

The CSD contends that the NSDS process needs to be an adaptive process which requires the establishment of mechanisms, policies and legal and institutional frameworks for coordinating and integrating economic, social and environmental aspects. It states that, 'Key measures that need to be taken in this context are: developing a sustainable development strategy culture; institutionalization of the strategy process; putting in place appropriate legal and enforcement mechanisms; and mobilizing, engaging and strengthening national capacity for continuous strategy development process' (Division for Sustainable Development, UNDESA, 2002: para. 15).

Finally, research from the CSD notes that every country needs to determine for itself how best to approach the preparation and implementation of its NSDS, depending upon the prevailing political, historical, cultural and ecological circum stances (Division for Sustainable Development, UNDESA, 2002: para. 4). Thus, there is no 'one size fits all' solution or approach.

The Organisation for Economic Co-operation and Development

The OECD was established in 1961 by Convention.[4] Its original membership of 20 developed countries has expanded to 31, and several other countries have received invitations to join. The OECD brings together the governments of countries committed to democracy and the market economy from around the world to: support sustainable economic growth; boost employment; raise living standards; maintain financial stability; assist other countries' economic development; and contribute to growth in world trade (OECD, n.d.). It does so by encouraging the comparison of policy experiences, seeking answers to common problems, identifying good practice and coordinating domestic and international policies (OECD, n.d.).

Concern about sustainability underlies all of the OECD's work. Its Annual Meeting of Sustainable Development Experts (AMSDE) tracks progress in mainstreaming sustainable development perspectives in OECD country reviews, analyzes, statistics and policy discussions. A summary of the findings is set out each year in an Annual Report (e.g. OECD, 2008).

The AMSDE also oversees specific projects relating to sustainable development. These include identifying approaches for measuring sustainable development and conducting sustainability assessments. The AMSDE highlights good governance practices for institutionalizing sustainable development and for national sustainable development strategies. The OECD works closely with the CSD and other bodies, such as UNESCO (OECD, n.d.).

From its regular reviews, the OECD has collected data on best practice from both developed and developing countries. It used this information in 2002 to develop a checklist to assist the improvement of policy coherence and integration for sustainable development, which was discussed and amended by experts from government, academia and non-governmental organizations who participated in a seminar on improving governance for sustainable development, held in Paris from 22–23 November 2001 (OECD, 2002). The checklist is based on the concept that: 'Good governance and sound public management are preconditions for the implementation of sustainable development policies' (OECD, 2002: 2). Thus, an important issue for the OECD is how to advance the integration agenda. In furtherance of this objective, the OECD, in its checklist, sets out five criteria for the effective implementation of sustainable development: a common understanding of sustainable development; clear commitment and leadership; specific institutional mechanisms to steer integration (including enforcement and monitoring); effective stakeholder involvement; and efficient knowledge management (OECD, 2002: 6).

The Bellagio Principles

The IISD is a Canadian-based, policy research institute that has a long history of conducting cutting-edge research into sustainable development and, through a dynamic portfolio of programmes and projects, has partnered with over 200 organizations worldwide (IISD, 2010). In November 1996, the IISD brought together an international group of measurement practitioners and researchers from five continents in Bellagio, Italy, to review progress towards sustainable development to date, and to synthesize insights from practical ongoing efforts. The result of this meeting was the unanimously accepted 'Bellagio Principles' which are designed to serve as guidelines for the implementation and assessment of the whole sustainable development process (Hardi and Zdan, 1997: 1–7).

The principles are intended for use in determining starting points, specifying content, suggesting scope and offering advice about how to do things right. They provide guidance in starting and improving sustainable development assessment activities, not only to national governments and international institutions, but also to community groups, non-government organizations and corporations (Hardi and Zdan, 1997: 1, 22).

Principle 1 requires a clear vision of sustainable development and goals that define that vision. Principle 2 requires a holistic approach that considers the wellbeing of social, ecological and economic sub-systems, and their state, as well as the direction, rate of change and both positive and negative consequences of human activity. Principle 3 sets out certain substantive elements which are considered essential, including: equity and disparity within the current population and between present and future generations; the ecological conditions on which life depends; and economic development and other non-market activities that contribute to human/social wellbeing. Principle 4 deals with scope and the need for a time horizon long enough to capture both human and ecosystem timescales. It should define the space of study large enough to include not only local but also long-distance impacts on people and ecosystems as well as building on historic and current conditions to anticipate future condition. Principle 5 emphasizes the need for a practical focus that sets out an explicit set of categories or an organizing framework that links vision and goals to indicators and assessment criteria. Principle 6 requires openness, whereby the methods and data that are used are accessible to all, and all judgements, assumptions and uncertainties in data and interpretations are explicit. Principle 7 focuses on effective and appropriate communication. Principle 8 requires the broad participation of key grassroots, professional, technical and social groups, including youth, women and indigenous people (to ensure recognition of diverse and changing values), as well as of decision makers. Principle 9 requires ongoing assessment that has a capacity for repeated measurement to determine trends, and which is iterative, adaptive and responsive to change and uncertainty. Principle 10 requires institutional capacity and, in particular, a clear assignation of responsibility and ongoing support in the decision-making process (Hardi and Zdan, 1997: 2–4).

Essentially, the principles deal with four aspects of assessing progress towards sustainable development. The first principle introduces the need to establish a vision of sustainable development and clear goals that provide a practical definition of that vision for the decision maker. Principles 2–5 deal with the substantive content of any assessment and the need to merge a sense of the overall system with a practical focus on current priority issues. Principles 6–8 deal with the process of assessment and Principles 9 and 10 are concerned with the need to establish a continuing capacity for assessment (Hardi and Zdan, 1997: 1).

The key difference between the principles and criteria from other studies is that they do advocate certain moral, ethical and political norms consistent with stronger versions of sustainable development. In this way, they are less appealing to some states. However, by not simply offering procedural suggestions and by recognizing the need for a real culture change within governments that considers the limits of the Earth and the needs of future generations, they provide more realistic guidance as to what is actually needed to deliver sustainable states.

The UK Sustainable Development Commission

Founded in October 2000, the SDC was the UK Government's independent adviser on sustainable development, reporting to the Prime Minister, the First Ministers of Scotland and Wales, and the First Minister and Deputy First Minister of Northern Ireland. The SDC's role was threefold:

- Advisory: providing informed, evidence-based advice to the government on sustainability
- Capability building: developing the attitudes, skills and knowledge in the government to deliver on sustainable development
- Scrutiny: holding the government to account on progress towards sustainable development and on its operational commitments.

In July 2010, the Government decided to withdraw its funding for the SDC from the next financial year, and it ceased operating on 31 March 2011 (SDC, 2011: chs 8, 10, 11). It was a valuable resource in the UK and, in particular, its insights into the criteria needed to fully implement sustainable development are very useful here.

The SDC maintained that to be meaningful, sustainable development needs to operate at three different levels. First, in terms of helping people understand the 'big picture' or what is actually at stake (SDC, 2004; Porritt, 2009: 10), the SDC long advocated that sustainable development needs to become the central organizing principle of government, instead of being seen as an 'environmental' policy objective (SDC, 2004). The SDC's second requirement is that sustainable development needs to operate in terms of providing a comprehensive framework within which to integrate potentially conflicting priorities (Porritt, 2009: 10).[5] Finally, the SDC maintained that sustainable development must also provide an operational toolkit – in terms of policymaking, performance appraisal, strategy, management systems, procurement, and so on (Porritt, 2009: 8).

Analysis

The contributions set out in the research described above are broadly consistent, and together show that there are now accepted criteria that are considered essential to the implementation of sustainable development.

It was noted earlier that the implementation of sustainable development requires an institutional change which ensures that environmental protection and sustainable development issues are integrated into all policy and decision making, accompanied by a cultural change that indoctrinates a clear and consistent understanding of sustainable development. The CSD surmises that both integration and development of a clear understanding or meaning can only be made operational by establishing, on a continuous basis, four critical processes: political, participatory, technical and resource mobilization processes. The political process involves ensuring the existence of a strong political commitment from the top leadership and the local authorities of a country (Division for Sustainable Development, UNDESA, 2002). The technical process of an NCDS formulation involves various activities: undertaking assessment of the economic, social and environmental situation, identifying problems, setting clear priorities, establishing goals and objectives, developing the investment programme, and monitoring and evaluation. The participatory process entails the full involvement of relevant groups (both government and non-governmental) in appropriate tasks, including strategy design, exchanging information, decision making, implementation, and so on. The resource mobilization process involves ensuring the availability of adequate finance for implementation. It is important to ensure the availability of adequate domestic resources for all projects, as well as the full engagement of the private sector in the strategy development process. Given the strong global interdependence, mechanisms need to be developed for involving the international community in the strategy process, while the individual country remains in full ownership of the process (Division for Sustainable Development, UNDESA, 2002, paras. 7–12). Thus, the criteria are closely interlinked.

Moreover, these criteria are consistent with much of the literature on good governance more generally. The OECD has stated that: 'good governance and sound public management are preconditions for the implementation of sustainable development policies' (OECD, 2002: 2). Similarly, Dernbach (2002–2003: 104–5) has observed that 'much of what is required for national governance for sustainable development is also required for good governance in general. The components of good governance include effective governmental institutions and national laws, a favorable investment climate, informed and science-based decision making, and access to justice'.

The above studies all start from this same general principle and then set out detailed criteria in slightly different ways. While consistent, they offer different perspectives and focus on different characteristics. The OECD and the CSD largely restrict themselves to the procedural and institutional requirements for effective implementation. In contrast, the Bellagio Principles and, to a lesser extent, the SDC include more substantive elements.

Several common threads run through the studies and reports listed above, which can be used to successfully move towards a sustainable society. Part II of this book is broadly structured around the OECD criteria, drawing, where appropriate, from the other studies set out in this chapter and elsewhere. In summary, to effectively deliver sustainable development a nation state must develop the following:

- A common understanding
- Clear commitment and leadership
- Stakeholder involvement and efficient knowledge management
- Appropriate integrative mechanisms (including enforcement tools).

A common understanding

The OECD provides that effective implementation requires a common understanding of sustainable development. Arguably, producing guidelines on the process for developing a common understanding is easier and less politically sensitive than providing guidance on the actual substantive content of what that understanding should be. Yet, it is also likely true that the failure to articulate this substantive content is a reason for the failure of these criteria to actually assist countries to progress. To quote the SDC: 'to be meaningful, people need to understand the "big picture" or what is actually at stake' (SDC, 2004; Porritt, 2009: 10).

Like the other contributions, the Bellagio Principles provide that an assessment of progress toward sustainable development should be guided by a clear vision of sustainable development and goals that define that vision (Hardi and Zdan, 1997: 2). However, the Bellagio Principles go further than some of the other studies in that they offer advice on the substantive content of that vision. They require a holistic look at the whole system and its parts, as well as a consideration of the wellbeing of social, ecological and economic sub-systems, and of both positive and negative consequences of human activity (Hardi and Zdan, 1997: 2). They also set out certain essential elements for the assessment of progress, including equity and disparity within the current population and between present and future generations, dealing with such concerns as: resource use, over-consumption and poverty; the ecological conditions on which life depends; and economic development and other non-market activities that contribute to human/social wellbeing (Hardi and Zdan, 1997: 2).

Clear commitment and leadership

Strong leadership at all levels of governance is a key factor for actually achieving a sustainable society (OECD, 2002: 7–8). Leadership, however, is a double-edged sword. When it is present, policies flourish, and when it disappears, policies like sustainable development flounder (Kavanagh and Richards, 2001: 17). As such, while there is no way to ensure leadership, it is possible to use law, policy and other mechanisms to provide suitable and lasting protection against a lack of leadership in the short term by protecting certain values and imposing certain substantive and procedural obligations. These can also have significant symbolic and, as a result, educational value. Indeed, related to leadership is responsibility, and the Bellagio Principles, instead of focusing on leadership, emphasize responsibility as crucial to success, specifically by clearly assigning responsibility and providing ongoing support in the decision-making process (Hardi and Zdan, 1997: 4).

Stakeholder involvement and efficient knowledge management

The OECD, CSD and SDC all emphasize the importance of effective stakeholder involvement and efficient knowledge management (OECD, 2002: 6; Division for Sustainable Development, UNDESA, 2002; SDC, 2004). Oliver (2003: 34–5) notes that 'participation, in the sense of consultation and being listened to on the part of those affected by possible policy changes, may result in better-prepared and thought out proposals being implemented'. More specifically, public participation and stakeholder involvement are crucial for sustainable development for three reasons. First, participating in decisions about one's future is a good in itself. Participation allows people to feel in control of their lives and this has been found to be an essential component of human wellbeing (Thirion, 2008). Second, by combining different knowledge, public involvement may lead to better problem solving in decision making. Third, involving affected parties means they are more likely to understand the reasoning behind certain decisions and thus, increase acceptability of decisions and in turn increase the likelihood of them being implemented (Oliver, 2003: 34–5).

Once again, the Bellagio Principles are more explicit as to what is required. They require that the assessment of progress towards sustainable development should ensure that the methods and data used are accessible to all and make explicit all judgements, assumptions and uncertainties in data and interpretations (Hardi and Zdan, 1997: 3). Moreover, the assessment should be designed to address the needs of the audience and sets of users, and should also obtain broad representation of key grassroots, professional, technical and social groups, including youth, women and indigenous people, to ensure recognition of diverse and changing values (Hardi and Zdan, 1997: 3). The Bellagio Principles also require the provision of institutional capacity for data collection, maintenance and documentation (Hardi and Zdan, 1997: 4).

The difficulty lies in trying to make the very complicated, complex and unpredictable nature of sustainable development accessible to stakeholders with different backgrounds and objectives, and herein lies the role of effective knowledge management. The OECD checklist describes the link between stakeholder participation and effective knowledge management:

> Scientific knowledge should be the basis for raising awareness in different constituencies and increasing the visibility of the sustainable development concept within and outside government (including in the media). However, since conclusive scientific evidence will not be available for many of the decisions to be made, it is crucial to ensure that sufficient debate occurs to confront values, perceptions and views, in order to take decisions that are more universally acceptable.
>
> (OECD, 2002: 3)

This means governments need to accompany their opportunities for stakeholder involvement with improved scientific data, arbitration processes for managing conflicting knowledge, opportunities for free debate, scenarios to show alternatives and mechanisms for accurately disseminating information to a wider audience.

Appropriate mechanisms for integration

Integration remains crucial to the genuine implementation of sustainable development. Initially, the focus was on integrating environmental concerns into the day-to-day activities of government, and this remains vitally important, especially if we are to operate within the carrying capacity of the Earth's ecosystems. Equally important is the requirement that sustainable development more broadly be integrated into the activities of governance and, specifically, its long-term and intergenerational aspects. Having a vision and framework for sustainable development well set out in a strategy is essential, but it is not enough. There needs to be specific tools aimed at delivering specific objectives. As described by the SDC, sustainable development must also provide an operational toolkit – in terms of policymaking, performance appraisal, strategy, management systems, procurement, and so on (Porritt, 2009: 28). The OECD (2002: 6) similarly expects states to develop specific institutional mechanisms to steer integration. The CSD suggests that these mechanisms should be focused on outcomes (Division for Sustainable Development, UNDESA, 2002). Arguably, these political, administrative and legal mechanisms should also reflect the sustainable development vision and contain decision making within the accepted sustainable development framework.

Meadowcroft identifies four key types of integration mechanisms (Meadowcroft, 2007: 158–9). First, he notes the importance of integration with financial routines. Money is a key resource for government, an important mechanism of internal control and a tool for influencing societal behaviour. Second, he emphasizes the importance of sectoral integration, observing that integration cannot rest solely on the search for the 'win-win alternatives' but also requires trade-offs based on a clear set of priorities. Third, the need to be able to measure and monitor progress is vital and, finally, there needs to be co-ordination with sub-national governments. Central initiatives can only be effective when combined with action at other administrative scales (Meadowcroft, 2007: 159).

The Bellagio Principles take a slightly different approach. Instead of simply focusing on the institutional requirements, they actually make some substantive comment as to what effective tools should do. They note that the assessment should have an adequate scope which adopts a time horizon long enough to capture both human and ecosystem timescales and define the space of study large enough to include not only local, but also long-distance impacts on people and ecosystems (Hardi and Zdan, 1997: 2). They also advocate a practical focus which sets out an explicit set of categories or an organizing framework. This framework links the stated vision and goals to indicators and assessment criteria which then use a limited number of key issues for analysis, and standardized measurement wherever possible, to permit comparisons (Hardi and Zdan, 1997: 3).

All of the contributions include monitoring and review mechanisms as essential to effective progress. Moreover, all emphasize that the results of reviews need to be fed back into the system, which should then evolve to take into account these findings. The Bellagio Principles, for example, state that assessment should be ongoing, be iterative, adaptive and responsive to change and uncertainty, and should also promote development of collective learning and feedback to decision making (Hardi and Zdan, 1997: 4).

Structure of the book

These four criteria (common understanding, leadership, stakeholder involvement and knowledge management, and integrative mechanisms) form the backbone of Part II of this book, 'The reality of sustainable development in the UK'. They are used to analyze the UK's journey towards sustainable development over time and to analyze the various techniques, principles, mechanisms and institutions that both the central and devolved governments in the UK have relied on to push the sustainable development agenda forward. Those factors that have inhibited progress in any of these areas are also described in the analysis. More specifically, Part II consists of seven chapters. Chapter 4 deals with the first criterion – a common understanding – and focuses predominantly on the strategies for sustainable development produced by the UK and devolved administrations to drive their agendas forward. Studies have shown that leadership can be the biggest asset or hindrance to the delivery of sustainable development. Chapter 5 discusses the importance of leadership and commitment by leaders to the sustainable development agenda. It highlights certain mechanisms used by the UK and devolved administrations to promote and support leadership as well as instances where leadership has been lacking or counterproductive. Chapter 6 explores the important governance issues surrounding sustainable development, examining in detail the tools used to promote both stakeholder involvement and efficient knowledge management. The remaining chapters in Part II form a critique of the UK's 'operational toolkit' or the actual integrative mechanisms used to deliver sustainable development in the UK and in the devolved administrations. More specifically, while it is impossible to explore them all, Chapter 7 explores the development and success of various institutional and policy measures used by the UK administrations over the years to implement sustainable development. Chapter 8 explores the UK's use of legislation to further sustainable development. Chapter 9 examines the development, use and review of the sustainability indicators in the implementation process and, finally, Chapter 10 considers the range of tools used in the UK to monitor progress and hold relevant actors to account for their progress or lack of progress.

Conclusion

The research on the criteria needed to effectively deliver sustainable development is broadly consistent and there now exist proven and effective criteria for achieving sustainable development.[6] Moreover, there is evidence in the UK of good practice and innovation for each of the criteria. Indeed, in many respects 'the UK has the architecture in place to actually start delivering sustainable development' (Porritt, 2009: 56). However, as will be discussed, good architecture does not guarantee consistent implementation, nor does it necessarily, at present, stand the test of time. Over time, while some good tools have been reviewed and improved to become excellent tools, other excellent mechanisms have fallen victim to political whim or disfavour. The result is a frustratingly slow progression in which, at present, there is little sign of improvement.

Notes

1 Consolidated versions of the Treaty on European Union and the Treaty on the Functioning of the European Union (OJ) (2008), C 115.
2 Directive 2001/42/EC on the assessment of certain plans and programmes on the environment (OJ) (2001), L 197/30.
3 The European Sustainable Development Network (ESDN) facilitates the exchange of good practices and experiences with Member States. Information on NSDS is available on the ESDN website, see ESDN, n.d. National SDS coordinators provide a link between the EU SDS and NSDS.
4 The Convention on the Organisation for Economic Cooperation and Development, Paris, 14 December 1960, http://www.oecd.org/document/7/0,3343,en_2649_201 185_1915847_1_1_1_1,00.html, accessed 19 August 2010.
5 Note that many different frameworks have been adopted and are being tested. See UN, 2006: 5.
6 Proven in that all the contributions rely on both positive and negative experiences in a variety of countries and contexts.

References

Alder, J. and Wilkinson, D. (1999) *Environmental Law and Ethics*, London: Macmillan.

Bell, S. and Morse, S. (2008) *Sustainability Indicators: Measuring the Immeasurable?*, 2nd edition, London: Earthscan.

Dernbach, J. (2002–2003) 'Targets, timetables and effective implementing mechanisms: Necessary building blocks for sustainable development', *William & Mary Environmental Law and Policy Review*, 27: 79–136.

Division for Sustainable Development, UNDESA (2002) 'Guidance in preparing national sustainable development strategy: Managing sustainable development in the new millennium', Background Paper No. 13, DESA/DSD/PC2/BP13, Rome: Department of Economic and Social Affairs.

Environmental Audit Committee (2009) *Greening Government: Sixth Report of Session 2008–2009*, HC 503, London: House of Commons.

European Council (2006) *Review of the EU Sustainable Development Strategy: Renewed Strategy*, Brussels: European Council.

European Sustainable Development Network (n.d.) 'Country profiles', http://www.sd-network.eu/?k=country%20profiles, accessed 11 May 2011.

Fowke, R. and Prasad, D. (1996) 'Sustainable development, cities and local government', *Australian Planner*, 33(2): 61–6.

Grainger, A. (2004) 'Introduction', in M. Purvis and A. Grainger (eds) *Exploring Sustainable Development: Geographical Perspectives*, London: Earthscan.

Hardi, P. and Zdan, T. (eds) (1997) *Assessing Sustainable Development: Principles in Practice*, Winnipeg: International Institute for Sustainable Development.

International Institute for Sustainable Development (IISD) (2010) *About IISD*, http://www.iisd.org/about/, accessed 21 August 2010.

Kavanagh, D. and Richards, D. (2001) 'Departmentalism and joined-up government: Back to the future?', *Parliamentary Affairs*, 54: 1–18.

MacNeill, J. (2007) 'Leadership for sustainable development', in OECD, *Institutionalizing Sustainable Development*, Paris: OECD.

Meadowcroft, J. (2007) 'National sustainable development strategies: Features, challenges and reflexivity', *European Environment*, 17(3): 152–63.

Oliver, D. (2003) *Constitutional Reform in the UK*, Oxford: Oxford University Press.

Organisation for Economic Co-operation and Development (OECD) (2002) *Improving Policy Coherence and Integration for Sustainable Development: A Checklist*, Paris: OECD.

OECD (2008) *Annual Report on Sustainable Development Work in the OECD*, Paris: OECD.

OECD (n.d.) 'About OECD', http://www.oecd.org/pages/0,3417,en_36734052_367 34103_1_1_1_1_1,00.html, accessed 17 August 2010.

Porritt, J. (2009) 'The standing of sustainable development in government', http://www.jonathonporritt.com/pages/2009/11/the_standing_of_sustainable_de.html, accessed 12 April 2010.

Russell, S.L. and Thomson, I. (2008) 'Accounting for a sustainable Scotland', *Public Money and Management*, 28(6): 367–75.

Secretariat of the Convention on Biological Diversity (SCBD) (2010) *Global Biodiversity Outlook (GBO-3)*, Montreal: Convention on Biological Diversity.

Stern, N. (2007) *The Economics of Climate Change: The Stern Review*, Cambridge: Cambridge University Press.

Sustainable Development Commission (SDC) (2004) *Shows Promise. But Must Try Harder: An Assessment by the Sustainable Development Commission of the Government's Reported Progress on Sustainable Development over the Past Five Years*, London: SDC.

SDC (2011) *Governing for the Future: The Opportunities for Mainstreaming Sustainable Development*, London: SDC.

Tarlock, D. (2001) 'Ideas without institutions. The paradox of sustainable development', *Indiana Journal of Global Legal Studies*, 9: 35–49.

Thirion, S. (2008) 'Involving citizens in defining and measuring well-being and progress', Part II, in *Well-being for All: Concepts and Tools for Social Cohesion* (Trends in Social Cohesion 20), Strasbourg: Council of Europe Publishing.

United Nations (UN) (2002) *Plan of Implementation of the World Summit on Sustainable Development*, A/CONF.199/20/Res.2, New York: UN.

UN (2006) *Global Trends and Status of Indicators of Sustainable Development: Background Paper No.2 DESA/DSD/2006/2*, New York: UN Department of Economic and Social Affairs.

UN Framework Convention on Climate Change (2010) *Synthesis and Assessment Report on the Greenhouse Gas Inventories*, FCCC/WEB/SAI/2010, New York: UN.

UN General Assembly (UNGA) (1992a) *The Rio Declaration on Environment and Development*, 31 ILM 874.

UNGA (1992b) *Agenda 21*, A/CONF.151/26 Vol. 1, New York: UN.

UNGA (2000) *United Nations Millennium Declaration*, A/RES/55/2, New York: UN.

UNGA (2010) *The Millennium Development Goals Report 2010*, New York: UN.

World Commission on Environment and Development (WCED) (1987) *Our Common Future*, Oxford: Oxford University Press.

World Wildlife Fund (WWF), Zoological Society of London and Global Footprint Network (2008) *Living Planet Report 2008*, Gland: WWF.

Part II
The reality of sustainable development in the UK

4 A common understanding – strategies

This chapter examines the first of the Organisation for Economic Co-operation and Development (OECD) criteria – a common understanding – in the context of the UK. It highlights the need for a clear vision of sustainable development that is specific to each particular country, its geography, culture and history. The vision needs to be well understood by leaders and well communicated to stakeholders and the wider public. The chapter explores the evolution of the UK's interpretation of sustainable development. The most common tool for disseminating this vision is the national sustainable development strategy (NSDS). The UK was one of the first countries in the world to produce a sustainable development strategy and this chapter examines the development, content and contribution of the each of the UK's strategies, as well as those introduced by the devolved administrations. Finally, it examines the role of the strategy in relation to other implementation mechanisms, including action plans, training and indicators.

Different visions and definitions of sustainable development

The first of the Bellagio Principles is that the assessment of progress towards sustainable development should be guided by a clear vision of sustainable development and goals that define that vision (Hardi and Zdan, 1997: 1–7). Moreover, if the wider community, and not just the government, is expected to contribute to progressing towards the goal, everyone needs to agree, understand and accept not only the goal, but also the actions required to move forward.

Without a clear vision of sustainable development, it is difficult for anyone inside or outside government to understand clearly what sustainable development means to a nation, region, locality or other organization. Ideally, this vision should be strategic, as without a strategy, all efforts in training, implementation, reporting or monitoring are potentially piecemeal, haphazard, inconsistent and counterproductive (Ross, 2006). The Commission on Sustainable Development (CSD) notes that the 'particular label applied to a national sustainable development strategy is not important, as long as the underlying principles characterizing a national sustainable development strategy are adhered to and that economic, social and environmental objectives are balanced and integrated' (Division for Sustainable Development, UNDESA, 2002: para. 4).

While there is general agreement in the academic community that sustainable development is a good thing, there remains no consensus on the exact meaning of the term. Thus, it is essential for any given state or organization that its strategy sets out its vision clearly and consistently. The clarity and communication of a country's vision is dealt with later in this chapter. First, it is important to explore the boundaries of what is generally considered the appropriate content of sustainable development. One test for appropriateness would be to examine whether the vision falls within the boundaries of the widely accepted 'Brundtland definition' of sustainable development: 'Development that meets the needs of the present without compromising the ability of future generations to meet their own needs' (WCED, 1987: 43). This definition sets wide parameters for countries, regions, organizations and individuals to operate, and allows each to set out its own detailed interpretation of sustainable development based on its particular circumstances. As a result, although the Brundtland definition encourages discourse by bringing together different and conflicting interests, it does suffer from being vague and imprecise. Indeed, most countries, the UK included, do tend to operate within the boundaries of the Brundtland definition of sustainable development. However, very different interpretations with significantly differing priorities and consequences can all be held as consistent with the definition. This section explores these differences in some detail, focusing on the tensions inherent in the definition itself.

French (2005: 10–34) observes three main tensions inherent within the Brundtland definition: tensions as to the environment, tensions in relation to the role of economic growth and tensions in relation to equity and governance. These are worth exploring in detail to determine the scope of potential variance permitted under the Brundtland definition.

In relation to the environment, the question is to what extent should we preserve and conserve those environmental assets that are critical to our well-being and survival as critical natural capital? Tensions exist in relation to the use of these resources, operating within the Earth's limits and the extent to which natural capital can be replaced or offset by human or manmade capital (Pearce, 1993: 15–16; Bowers, 1997: 194). The so-called 'weaker' versions of sustainable development still advocate high economic growth and are based on the premise that technology and international trade will ensure there are always enough resources to meet cultural or human carrying capacity.[1] Indeed, most of the solutions promoted, sought and developed under this technological approach have focused on improving the environmental credentials of the products supplied, with little attention being paid to the demand side of the equation. The result is that while fewer resources are required per unit of energy, transport, food, and so on, more units are being consumed. For example, although modern cars are much less polluting than those in the 1950s, the number of cars on British roads increased from just under 2 million in 1950 to 26.5 million in 2006 (Department for Transport *et al.*, 2009: chs 3, 9).

The next set of tensions revolves around the role of the economy and the market, and the need for economic growth in sustainable development (French,

2005: 26). As Grainger (2004: 12–13) explains, economic growth refers to an increase in an economy's output of goods and services and the overall amount of income that it generates. Measured by gross domestic product (GDP), which prioritizes consumption to generate income, economic growth encourages consumption and production. Improvements in the wellbeing of society as a whole, as reflected in an expanded set of opportunities for the present generation, is broader and referred to as economic development. This concept, however, takes no account of the environmental impacts of the activities needed to generate the income upon which it depends. As noted by Grainger (2004: 13), the theoretical concept of sustainable development differs from economic development as it goes beyond the latter's focus on economic and social dimensions and the notion of intra-generational equity to also consider an environmental dimension as well as an intergenerational equity element.

This leads nicely on to the third set of tensions identified by French (2005: 28), which concerns equity, including tension between the environment and humans, intra-generational equity among states and within states, and intergenerational equity between the present and future generations. While useful in generating a case for long-term planning, intergenerational equity poses many practical and theoretical questions. For example, as there is an infinite number of future people, what weighting should we give their interests and what will be those interests? It is possible that by looking out for future generations, we neglect the present generation and, in particular, the world's poor.

French's final tension inherent in sustainable development involves empowerment (French, 2005: 30–3). To what extent should people be empowered to make their own decisions? Chapter 6 deals explicitly with the mechanisms for stakeholder and public involvement. For these tools to be meaningfully used, however, a culture change which not only accepts, but promotes, empowerment needs to be incorporated into a state or other organization's vision of sustainable development because it recognizes the benefits such empowerment brings.

At the core of empowerment lies a belief that individuals and individual communities are entitled to participate in the decision-making processes that affect their development and environment. There are three elements to this contribution. First, studies in human happiness and wellbeing have found that the key component to human wellbeing is having control over one's own destiny (Thirlon, 2008). Second, the process of seeking stakeholder contribution improves not only the acceptability and usefulness and in turn the legitimacy of the decision, but also the actual quality of the decision (Ross, 2010b: 391). Third, it is easier for stakeholders to implement decisions when they understand their role and the purpose of their actions. In line with this thinking, *Agenda 21* mandates the development and improvement of mechanisms to facilitate the involvement of concerned individuals, groups and organizations in decision-making at all levels (UNGA, 1992b: para. 8.3(c)).

As discussed in detail in Chapter 6, while good practice in relation to governance issues such as transparency, public participation in decision making and access to justice is being developed, the use of such mechanisms is ad hoc and often only when there is a perceived advantage, largely because they are seen as costly, time-consuming and administratively difficult especially at the international level.

Some in the deep ecology movement have argued that 'sustainable development is a contradiction in terms, in that growth and environmental protection are enemies' (Alder and Wilkinson, 1999: 141; Dobson, 1995: ch. 3). In sharp contrast, others have described sustainable development as 'the only meaningful cure to the problems that face the world' (Salmon, 2003: 13). The difficulty is that as it currently stands, more precision is needed. While the Brundtland definition does provide some parameters for judging the acceptability or appropriateness of any definition of sustainability, it gives governments too much flexibility. More recently, many would argue that the Brundtland parameters are insufficiently ambitious. New scientific, including economic, evidence shows that we are not getting the balance right and we are not doing enough to ensure the long-term sustainability of human life on this planet (Stern, 2007).

The meaning of sustainable development in the UK, over time and between levels of government

These definitional conflicts do not only exist outside state boundaries. Indeed, official state interpretations of sustainable development can vary over time as well as between sectors and levels of governance. Within the UK, the definition used by the UK Government has remained far from static. In 1994, sustainable development was described as a trade-off between the environment and economic development (DEFRA, 1994: 7). In *A Better Quality of Life: A Strategy for Sustainable Development* (the 1999 strategy), the Labour Government expanded the definition to include social concerns while still pursuing high economic growth as an objective (DEFRA, 1999).[2] It promoted a view of sustainable development which ensured:

> a better quality of life for everyone, now and for generations to come . . . It means meeting four objectives at the same time, in the UK and the world as a whole: social progress which recognises the needs of everyone; effective protection of the environment; prudent use of natural resources; and maintenance of high and stable levels of economic growth and employment.
>
> (DEFRA, 1999: paras. 1.1–1.2)

Not everyone was convinced this could happen. Helm (2000: 12) observes that 'the 1999 White Paper thus completed the transition of sustainable development from a primarily environmental concept capable of assessment, to a wish list of things that government would like to achieve'.

By 2005, while still not expressly reflecting strong sustainability, the definition of sustainable development in the UK had evolved into a complex concept which involved five guiding principles: living within environmental limits, a just society, a sustainable economy, good governance and sound science (HM Government *et al.*, 2005: 8). *The UK Strategy for Sustainable Development: Securing the Future* (the UK Shared Framework) (DEFRA, 2005) provides further elaboration by separating the principles into two groups, with the first two principles covering the overarching ambitions of the Strategy:

- Living within environmental limits
- Ensuring a strong, healthy, just and equal society.

The three remaining principles describe the necessary conditions for the achievement of sustainable development:

- Achieving a sustainable economy
- Promoting good governance
- Using sound science responsibility.

This approach addresses the significant concerns surrounding environmental limits, the reduction of poverty, and justice concerns. It recognizes the perils of uncontrolled economic growth, sets priority areas and offers certain principles to govern decision making. Thus, over time there has been an evolution of the definition at the UK level.

Despite the UK Framework being heralded as a shared template, over time, the trend in the devolved administrations has been to move away from the approach set out in the Framework, in accordance with their own political priorities. In the case of Wales, there has been a move towards stronger sustainability, while in Scotland, Northern Ireland, and, worryingly, post-2010 in the UK Government the trend has been to return to the pursuit of high economic growth (Porritt, 2011).

The definition in the latest strategy to come out of Wales, entitled *One Wales: One Planet: The Sustainable Development Scheme of the Welsh Assembly Government* (*One Wales: One Planet*) (WAG, 2009), goes much further than the Framework, stating that:

> sustainable development means enhancing the economic, social and environmental wellbeing of people and communities, achieving a better quality of life for our own and future generations: In ways which promote social justice and equality of opportunity; and in ways which enhance the natural and cultural environment and respect its limits – using only our fair share of the earth's resources and sustaining our cultural legacy. Sustainable development is the process by which we reach the goal of sustainability.
>
> (WAG, 2009: 8)

This is by far the strongest interpretation of sustainable development to come out of the UK.

This can be contrasted with the position in Scotland. Since the May 2007 election, the term 'sustainable development' has rarely been used, as the new

Scottish Government has adopted a single purpose: 'To focus government and public services on creating a more successful country, with opportunities for all of Scotland to flourish, through increasing sustainable economic growth' (Scottish Government, 2007a; 2010). This purpose is supported by *The Government's Economic Strategy* (the *Economic Strategy*), which is the guiding strategy of the administration (Scottish Government, 2007a). The Government has stated that it intends to mainstream sustainable development across Government through its commitment to 'sustainable economic growth'. At least theoretically, this significantly alters the emphasis placed on growth compared to what is agreed in the *Shared Framework*, where the objectives include living within the Earth's environmental limits, and ensuring a strong, healthy and just society, and where sustainable economic growth is one of the means of meeting those objectives. Effectively, the Scottish Government has chosen to make one of the enablers in the Framework – sustainable economic growth – its primary aim. That said, based on many of the actions of the Scottish Government, the Sustainable Development Commission in Scotland (SDCS) has concluded that 'taken as a whole, the Purpose, with its emphasis on *"opportunities for all of Scotland to flourish"* requires Government to address wider sustainable development issues' (SDCS, 2009: 6).

The latest sustainable development strategy for Northern Ireland, published in May 2010, is entitled *Everyone's Involved* (Northern Ireland Executive, 2010). The new strategy, like its predecessor produced under direct rule, refers to the UK Framework but it does not share the same substantive vision. Instead of two outcomes and three enablers, there are two ambitions and four necessary conditions. At first sight, the Northern Ireland strategy reflects very similar ideals to the UK Framework. However, it has retained a focus on protecting economic growth and goes to some lengths to emphasize this objective:

> Sustainable development aims to bring viability, stability and opportunity to all of our social, economic and environmental activities and programmes. It does not aim to stop us from growing our economy. It does not seek to obstruct our attempts to improve our society and communities. It does not prevent us from using and capitalising on our natural resources. Rather its goal is to put in place economic, social and environmental measures to ensure that we can continue to do all of these things effectively in the years to come.
>
> (Northern Ireland Executive, 2010: 1)

Thus, despite efforts in 2005 using the Framework, there currently is no consistent UK-wide vision of sustainable development. Moreover, while the documentation, at least from Wales and from the UK before the 2010 election, is consistent, the latest strategies for Scotland and Northern Ireland contain significant ambiguities and inconsistencies. Moreover, the use of the term by the UK coalition Government shows significant regression. The 2011 budget provides that 'to make the UK the best place in Europe to start, finance and grow a business the

Government will introduce a powerful new presumption in favour of sustainable development, so that the default is "yes"' (HM Treasury, 2011: 3). Thus, pursuant to the first of the OECD criteria, a common understanding, the UK administrations are not off to a good start.

Strategies

The vision needs to drive forward the approach taken by a country. *Agenda 21* explicitly promotes national sustainable development strategies (NSDSs) as mechanisms for translating a country's goals and aspirations of sustainable development into concrete policies and actions (UNGA, 1992b). Like many other countries, the various UK administrations have opted to use their NSDSs as the framework or template for their implementation of sustainable development. Approaches which use the national strategy combined with themes around economy, environment and society tend to be well regarded in the literature as 'whole systems approaches' which capture multiple aspects of a system (Hardi and Zdan, 1997: 13). Swanson *et al.* (2004: 41) describe the sustainable development strategy as 'a navigational tool for identifying priority sustainability issues, prioritizing objectives, and co-ordinating the development and use of a mix of policy initiatives to meet national goals'.

Certainly, any common understanding or vision in the strategy needs to reflect the circumstances of its particular area and constituents, whether it be a nation, region, city or business. The CSD emphasizes that:

> Every country needs to determine, for itself, how best to approach the preparation and implementation of its national sustainable development strategy depending upon the prevailing political, historical cultural, ecological circumstances. A 'blueprint' approach for national sustainable development strategies is neither possible nor desirable.
>
> (Division for Sustainable Development, UNDESA, 2002: para. 4)

Furthermore, various studies have concluded that while the robust nature of a strategy's content is essential, so is the process by which it is produced and reviewed. Streurer and Martinuzzi (2005: 455–72) observe that it is the process, rather than the discrete policy outcomes, that is significant. Dernbach notes that this involves:

> the development of an overall sustainability vision and objectives based on an iterative and open process; identification of the institutions and policies that will be used to achieve those objectives; adoption and implementation of the needed laws and policies; and a monitoring, learning and adaptation process that informs and perhaps changes objectives, policies, and implementation.
>
> (Dernbach, 2008: 103)

The CSD also notes that:

> [the] development of the strategy would empower countries to address inter-related social and economic problems by helping them to build capacities, develop procedures and legislative frameworks; allocate limited resources rationally and present timetables for actions. Countries can benefit a lot from formulating strategies both directly (as a result of making development more sustainable) and indirectly (from the process itself).
>
> (Division for Sustainable Development, UNDESA, 2002, Executive Summary)

As highlighted above, the strategic process ideally should include several procedural mechanisms. First, a strategy needs to be subject to a wide consultation process seeking out the views and priorities of experts, regulators, businesses, the voluntary sector, different groups such as children and minority groups, and the wider public. Second, the CSD and others recommend providing clarity through the use of principles, priorities and targets. Finally, the strategic process needs to be subject to both internal and external independent reviewers that are then fed back into the development process. Progress towards the objectives and targets needs to be reported and monitored, and those responsible called to account. This process then leads on to inform the production of the next strategy.

The UK has consistently used its strategy to underpin and set out its sustainable development programme. However, to date, the UK has employed this strategic process without any legislative guidance or direction. In the UK, the goals, priorities and policy tools associated with sustainable development have evolved over time along with the UK's interpretation of the term 'sustainable development' itself. The remainder of this chapter is dedicated to an analysis of the sustainable development strategies in the EU, the UK and the devolved governments. The analysis will include a brief history and then examine the processes in particular which surround the current strategy. Where possible, the strategy's relationship with other strategic agendas will also be considered. So far, there have been three UK-wide strategies and one *Shared Framework for Sustainable Development*. A new strategy from the UK coalition Government had not been produced by September 2011 and is well overdue. The Welsh administration has produced three schemes for sustainable development. There have been two Scottish strategies and two in Northern Ireland. Moreover, as a member of the EU, the UK is influenced and often bound by EU policy and decisions on sustainable development. Thus, it is wise to begin with the EU's strategic approach.

The European Union strategies for sustainable development

Since the 1992 Rio Earth Summit, the EU has played a leading role in supporting sustainable development as a policy objective. Strategic thinking on sustainable development first appears in the European Community's Fifth Environmental Action Programme, *Towards Sustainability*, published in 1993 (European Commission, 1993). The Fifth Action Programme differed from its predecessors in that it was not only an environmental action programme, but also an implicit sustainable development strategy: 'Behind the strategy set out in this programme is the ultimate aim of transforming the patterns of growth in the Community in such a way as to reach a sustainable development path' (European Commission, 1993: 55). The document, however, is chiefly dedicated to environmental policy and the reference to sustainable development is only in the context of integrating environmental concerns into economic and social decision making (European Commission, 1993: 55). The 1998 Cardiff European Council reaffirmed the commitment to integrate environmental concerns into other EU policies and developed a process for so doing ('the Cardiff Process').

It was not until the 2001 Gothenburg European Council that the European Commission presented its communication, *A Sustainable Europe for a Better World*, as the proposal for 'a European Union Strategy for Sustainable Development' (European Commission, 2001). It was a delayed response to the request of the Helsinki European Council in December 1999 (European Parliament, 1999: para. 50).

The key components of the 2001 Gothenburg Strategy (European Commission, 2001) were:

- The global dimension
- Targeting environmental priorities for sustainability
- Combating climate change
- Ensuring sustainable transport
- Addressing threats to public health
- Managing natural resources more responsibly
- Integrating environment into Community policies.

During 2004 and 2005, the Gothenburg Strategy was reviewed in preparation for the adoption of a renewed strategy in 2006, which reaffirmed the overall aim of achieving a continuous improvement in the quality of life, both for current and for future generations (European Council, 2006). The renewed EU SDS sets out a single, coherent strategy on how the EU will more effectively deliver its longstanding commitment to meet the challenges of sustainable development. The structure of the Strategy, however, is far from simple. Its main body is built around seven key challenges, with corresponding operational objectives and targets, as well as associated actions and measures. In addition, a number of key objectives and policy guiding principles serve as a basis for the Strategy (Eurostat, 2009: 29).

The overall aim of the renewed EU SDS is to:

identify and develop actions to enable the EU to achieve continuous improvement of quality of life both for current and for future generations, through the creation of sustainable communities able to manage and use resources efficiently and to tap the ecological and social innovation potential of the economy, ensuring prosperity, environmental protection and social cohesion.

(European Council, 2006: 3)

The seven key challenges are:

- climate change and clean energy
- sustainable transport
- sustainable consumption and production
- conservation and management of natural resources
- public health
- social inclusion, demography and migration
- global poverty and sustainable development challenges.

Each key challenge is described in terms of an overall objective, specific operational objectives and targets, and a list of actions to be pursued. In addition, the SDS is underpinned by the four key objectives and the ten policy guiding principles. The key objectives are: environmental protection, social equity and cohesion, economic prosperity, and meeting our international responsibilities. As an aside, the discussion of environmental protection contains no explicit reference to living within environmental limits. The description of economic prosperity contains a reference to an eco-efficient economy which provides high living standards (European Council, 2006: 4). It is not clear how the goals of an eco-efficient economy equate to those of a sustainable economy. Nor is it clear whether such an objective promotes sustainable development.

The ten policy guiding principles are as follows:

- promotion and protection of fundamental rights
- solidarity within and between generations
- open and democratic society
- involvement of citizens
- involvement of businesses and social partners
- policy coherence and governance
- policy integration
- use best available knowledge
- precautionary principle
- make polluters pay.

These guiding principles correspond to the underlying values of a dynamic European model of society and serve as a basis for the EU SDS (Eurostat, 2009: 30).

To further complicate matters, the renewed EU SDS also highlights certain crosscutting policies which contribute to the knowledge society, namely education and training, and research and development. It advocates the use of economic instruments in implementing the Strategy while calling for integrated financing mechanisms, and proposes actions towards communication, dissemination and stakeholder involvement.

The processes surrounding the renewed EU SDS are impressive. The Strategy introduces a formal governance cycle whereby the December European Council reviews progress and priorities every two years. The Commission is requested to support this review by submitting a progress report on the implementation of the SDS in the EU and the Member States, analysing both the present situation and proposing orientations and actions for the future. Measuring progress towards sustainable development is an integral part of the EU SDS, and it is Eurostat's task to produce a monitoring report every two years based on the EU set of sustainable development indicators (Eurostat 2009: 7). The Commission's progress report then draws on conclusions in the Eurostat monitoring reports.

In its first stocktaking, the Commission published a progress report that reaffirmed that the Strategy's key challenges remained valid. As much of what the EU does is at the strategic, as opposed to operational, level of governance, coordination between strategies can be problematic. Various stakeholders have found it difficult to understand why there are several crosscutting priority strategies at EU level, including for example, the Lisbon Strategy for Growth and Jobs, the Climate Change and Energy Package, the Integrated Maritime Policy and the EU SDS (European Commission; 2005: 451).

To illustrate, the key objective of the Lisbon process is for the EU to become, by 2010, 'the most competitive and dynamic knowledge-based economy in the world, capable of sustaining growth with more and better jobs and greater social cohesion' (European Parliament, 2000: para. 5). The link between the Lisbon process and the EU SDS has continually been problematic and was a major issue of a public consultation on the EU SDS launched by the European Commission in July 2004. Many contributors indicated 'that the two strategies could not be in harmony, while others stress the need to bring them more into line with each other' (European Commission, 2005: 451). The complementary nature of the EU SDS and the Lisbon Strategy were set out in the renewed EU SDS (Eurostat, 2009: 79). Most recently, the Commission has concluded that:

> By addressing the overarching long-term goal of the EU, the EU SDS forms the overall framework within which the Lisbon Strategy, with its focus on growth and jobs, provides the motor of a more dynamic economy. While the EU SDS is primarily concerned with quality of life, intra- and inter-generational equity and coherence between all policy areas, including external EU relations, it recognizes the role of economic development in facilitating the transition towards a more sustainable society. The Lisbon Strategy thus makes an essential contribution to the overarching objective of sustainable development by focusing primarily on actions and measures aimed at increasing competitiveness and economic growth, and enhancing job creation.
>
> (Eurostat, 2009: 29–31)

The Commission, in its latest review, recommends that to ensure more efficient monitoring and enforcement by Member States, mechanisms used in the Lisbon Strategy could also be used to monitor the implementation of the EU SDS. They would include jointly identified objectives, measuring instruments (indicators, guidelines), benchmarking (comparison of Member States' performance) and emulation to replicate and scale up best practices. Measures in support of both strategies, with visible positive results on growth, jobs and the environment, could be identified. Mainstreaming eco-innovation, resource efficiency and green growth could be a leading theme (European Commission, 2009: 14).

The UK strategies and framework

UK strategic action on sustainable development precedes that of the EU. The UK was one of the first countries to respond to the Brundtland report in July 1988. Its response, *A Perspective by the United Kingdom on the Report of the World Commission on Environment and Development*, states: 'there can be no quarrel with the [Brundtland principles] as a general definition. The key point is how to translate it into practice, how to measure it, and how to assess progress towards its achievement' (DOE, 1988).

In 1989, the Government produced a progress report on implementing sustainable development. This report, *Sustaining Our Common Future*, was a first attempt to set out policy aims and measures for the UK specifically directed towards achieving sustainable development (DOE, 1989). The ideas in this report were taken up in 1990 in the UK's first comprehensive environment strategy: the white paper, *This Common Inheritance: Britain's Environmental Strategy*, which mentioned sustainable development, but only indirectly in Chapter 4 (DOE, 1990). Following the Rio summit, in October 1992, the Government called for a national debate on sustainable development and began a wide-ranging consultation process. The Department of Environment (DOE) and the Scottish, Welsh and Northern Ireland Offices all published open letters inviting views on the nature of sustainable development and on the possible framework for the national strategy. A three-day seminar was held with a wide range of stakeholders and a consultation paper was published in July 1993 which set out the main topics for the strategy. It was sent to over 6000 organizations and over 500 responses were received. *Sustainable Development: The UK Strategy* (the 1994 strategy) was published in January 1994 (UK Government, 1994: 7). A summary of the responses was included as an annex to the strategy and included fairly popular concerns that were not carried through into the strategy, such as those relating to timescale and the pursuit of economic growth.

One of the key successes to come out of the Strategy was the introduction of the UK Roundtable on Sustainable Development, which brought together representatives of the main sectors or groups, and the Government's Panel on Sustainable Development to give authoritative and expert advice to Government. Both the Roundtable and the UK Panel acted as advisory bodies to Government and produced very useful critical reports on government progress towards sustainable development, ultimately leading the way for the creation of the UK Sustainable Development Commission (SDC).

Over time, this strategy was criticized for ignoring many of the social justice issues raised in the Brundtland report. It was also criticized for a lack of concrete targets, an action plan and review of processes (DETR, 1998). A key criticism of the Strategy was its silence on the Government's priorities and that it set the Government virtually no targets for action. There were indicators to measure progress, but these were not linked to policy objectives and there were far too many of them. Perhaps most importantly, the 1994 strategy lacked a clear vision. The closest it came to providing a definition of sustainable development was to state that: 'Most societies aspire to achieve economic development to secure rising standards of living, both for themselves and for future generations. They also seek to protect and enhance their environment, now and for their children. Reconciling these two aspirations is at the heart of sustainable development' (UK Government, 1994: para. 3.1). Consistent with other developed countries for that period, it opted for a very weak approach to sustainable development which continued to favour high economic growth as the key measure of progress.

As a result, much of the Government's action lacked a focus. Moreover, the emphasis on trade-offs meant that sustainable development became synonymous with 'environmental protection'. Whereas before the 1994 Strategy, things were done on a purely economic basis, after the Strategy there needed to be some consideration given to the effects on the environment. As the terms 'environment' and 'sustainable development' were used interchangeably, arguably this led to sustainable development being marginalized to the 'environmental' parts of government (Ross, 2003).

After coming to power in 1997, the Labour Government announced its intention to prepare a new strategy. A consultation document *Opportunities for Change* was published in February 1998, along with a summary leaflet. Supplementary documents on specific aspects of sustainable development, such as tourism, biodiversity and a new set of headline indicators, were also produced that year. Over a thousand responses were received to *Opportunities for Change* itself and another 4,500+ to the summary leaflet. Interestingly and disappointingly, compared to the Conservatives before it, the Labour Government chose to include in the strategy itself only those responses which supported its approach.

In the 1999 strategy (DEFRA, 1999), the Labour Government expanded the definition of sustainable development to include social concerns while still pursuing high economic growth as an objective (para. 1.9): 'What is sustainable development? At its heart is the simple idea of ensuring a better quality of life for everyone, now and for generations to come' (para. 1.1); 'For the future we need ways to achieve economic, social and environmental objectives at the same time, and consider the longer term implications of decisions' (para. 1.10). The new strategy explicitly set out four main aims: social progress which recognizes the needs of everyone; effective protection of the environment; prudent use of natural resources; and maintenance of high and stable levels of economic growth. It also set out seven priorities for the future, which relate to investing in people, social exclusion, transport, improving cities and towns, energy efficiency, waste, and achieving sustainable development internationally. It then set out ten principles to guide government policy, including putting people at the centre, taking a long-term perspective, taking account of costs and benefits, and the precautionary principle. The strategy was much shorter than its 1994 predecessor and written in a more accessible way. Its ten chapters were much more generalized: the need for change; producing a strategy; progress and priorities; guiding principles and approaches; sending the right signals (government action); a sustainable economy (note this strategy still advocates high economic growth); building sustainable communities; managing the environment and resources; international cooperation and development, and action; and future reporting. The strategy introduced several very important tools to the UK process. First, predating the strategy itself, was the establishment of a special crosscutting House of Commons Select Committee, the Environmental Audit Committee, whose remit is to monitor government progress towards sustainable development and report to Parliament. Second, it announced the creation of the UK SDC as an expert body to monitor progress on sustainable development and to build consensus on action to be taken by all sectors to accelerate its achievement (DEFRA, 1999: paras. 5.2, 5.24). This role over time was expanded from critical friend to sustainable development watchdog. Interestingly, in this strategy the Government promised that whenever it created a new public body, it would consider whether to include sustainable development in its remit. It also promised to renew the scope for including sustainable development as an objective of existing departments and public bodies (DEFRA, 1999: para. 5.4). These commitments were largely ignored in the subsequent years. Furthermore, the 1994 strategy introduced headline indicators, but these still remained detached from the overall policy set out in the strategy (DEFRA, 1999).

The government produced annual reports on progress for this strategy and these were reviewed by the newly established House of Commons Environmental Audit Committee, the SDC and others. Target setting improved but was still far from satisfactory. The strategy was criticized for watering down the environmental side of sustainable development in favour of social concerns. This was particularly true in its implementation, where traditional environmental tools now were expected to consider social concerns and yet new units and mechanisms were also being established which were entirely focused on social concerns (Ross, 2003). Moreover, the new definition caused confusion, as evidenced by Lord Whitty's remarks during the debates on the Local Government Act 2000:

> The three-pronged strategy is one that is reflected in other legislation and in the key subsection of this legislation . . . I should have hoped that sustainable development would be understood more clearly and more comprehensively than, regrettably, it is. For the purposes of this legislation I believe that some clarity is achieved by making reference to all three [prongs – economic, social, environmental].[3]

Moreover, due to devolution, different parts of the strategy applied either to all of the UK or to only a part or parts of the UK. It was not at all obvious what, for example, applied only to England, what applied to England and Wales and what applied to the whole of the UK (EAC, 2004; SDC, 2004; DEFRA, 2004; SDCS, 2008).

By 2004, it had become evident to policymakers in the UK that the ecological changes being experienced were, or would soon be, creating unacceptable consequences and that the weak version of sustainability popular among governments and business was not working. As Bosselmann (2008: 53) later observes, the attempt to roll three types of sustainability (ecological, economic and social) into one overarching concept of sustainability had left it pointing in multiple directions without any central meaning.

The SDC and others around the world were calling for sustainable development to be 'the central organising principle of government' (Bosselmann, 2008, ch. 6; SDC, 2009: 2; Dernbach, 2009: 27–39). The Government and the devolved administrations were keen to have a new approach to sustainable development which addressed these concerns and reflected the new constitutional reality in the UK under devolution. In 2004, the DEFRA as the lead UK government department published *Taking it On: Developing a UK sustainable development strategy together – A consultation paper* (DEFRA, 2004). Once again the consultation process was extensive and conducted using a wide range of media. In 2005, *One future – different paths: The UK's shared framework for sustainable development* was published theoretically jointly by all the administrations in the UK (HM Government *et al.*, 2005). It is important to note that in 2005, Northern Ireland was being run by direct rule, so the Framework was not actually published by the devolved government in Northern Ireland. This may be one reason for Northern Ireland's reluctance to fully engage with the Framework (see the discussion below).

The Framework is structured around: a shared understanding of sustainable development; a common purpose outlining what the UK is trying to achieve; the guiding principles needed to achieve it; sustainable development priorities for UK action at home and internationally; and indicators to monitor the key issues on a UK basis.

The Framework sets out its goal for sustainable development: 'to enable all people throughout the world to satisfy their basic needs and enjoy a better quality of life without compromising the quality of life of future generations' (HM Government *et al.*, 2005: 7). It then sets out a new common approach to sustainable development based on five principles: living within environmental limits, ensuring a healthy and just society, achieving a sustainable economy, promoting good governance, and using sound science responsibly (HM Government *et al.*, 2005: 8; Scottish Executive, 2005; National Assembly for Wales, 2004, Northern Ireland Office, 2006).[4] The aim of seeking high economic growth is gone. This change, combined with the explicit acknowledgement of the Earth's environmental limits, demonstrates a deeper commitment to ecological or strong sustainability.

The Framework has been well received. There are, however, some difficulties. For example, it is not apparent that all of its indicators are specifically linked to the specific aims in the Framework. Furthermore, there is some concern that the flexible nature of the arrangement is giving the devolved administrations in particular too much discretion in relation to how they use the Framework as a template for their own constituencies. While faster progress such as that described below in Wales should be encouraged, experience in Scotland and Northern Ireland (also described below) show that, arguably, the Framework could be more forceful about its minimum requirements in relation to each of the priorities, the targets and their timescales. The Framework's lack of legal or political clout has also led to it being virtually ignored by incoming devolved governments and, most recently, the post-2010 UK coalition Government. While flexibility is important to ensure governments can put their own twist on sustainable development, allowing change for change's sake and sustainably illiterate policy and decision making is counterproductive.

The Framework was to act as a template for the more specific strategies produced by each of the administrations. On the same day as the publication of the Framework, the UK administration published the 2005 strategy, which deals with reserved (or UK-wide) issues and those issues which, following devolution, only pertain to (mainly) England (DEFRA, 2005). The 2005 strategy is a bigger strategy than its predecessor and includes more detailed actions. Its structure is also different. Chapter One sets out the development and vision behind the new strategy. Chapter Two sets out how the government aims to help people make better choices by introducing a comprehensive behaviour change model for policymaking, to be applied in all priority areas. One of the key elements of the new approach is the need to engage people close to home. Chapter Three focuses on the 'One planet economy', for the first time, discussing the need for sustainable consumption and production as opposed to increasing economic growth at any cost. Chapter Four is dedicated to what is described as 'the greatest threat': climate change and energy. Despite this description, it does not dominate the strategy, and dealing with climate change is expressed as action towards sustainable development. Chapter Five details actions directed at protecting natural resources and enhancing the environment, while Chapter Six addresses the social concerns surrounding both the creation of sustainable communities and a fairer world. The final chapter sets out the monitoring and review mechanisms aimed at ensuring it happens (DEFRA, 2005).

The 2005 strategy sets out clear actions, some of which were long overdue. For example, it increases the powers of the SDC so that the Government is no longer reporting on its own progress. Instead a strengthened SDC would act as the independent 'watchdog' of government progress (DEFRA, 2005: 154). It also finally agreed to mainstream sustainable development in the Service through the 'Professional Skills In Government' programme and embedding sustainable development into the curriculum of the National School of Government, launched in the first half of 2005 (DEFRA, 2005: 155–6). Key commitments also included: researching environmental limits and environmental inequalities; taking account of natural systems as a whole, through the use of an ecosystems approach; strengthening UK and international measures to improve the environmental performance of products and services, including improved product design; a continued drive to improve resource efficiency and reduce waste and harmful emissions across business sectors, aided by the new 'Business Resource Efficiency and Waste' programme; a new push to influence consumption patterns, including proposals for new advice for consumers and new commitments on sustainable procurement in the public sector to make the UK a leader within the EU by 2009. Very importantly, the Government reiterates its commitment to achieving the UN's 0.7 per cent target for overseas development assistance as a proportion of gross national income (DEFRA, 2005: 141).

The 2005 strategy does have direction. It sets out clear principles and priorities, and then details these with commitments and targets. It also allocates responsibility. At the end of every chapter there is an explicit statement of the responsibilities for individual government departments and agencies. Things are far from ideal but there is no doubt that the 2005 strategy is more mature than its predecessor.

Since devolution in 1998, responsibility for many of the aspects of sustainable development has been devolved to institutions in Scotland, Northern Ireland and Wales. The system is asymmetrical and power is distributed differently for each (see Chapter 2). The devolved administrations were actively involved in the production of the *Shared Framework for Sustainable Development* and are responsible for producing their own strategies for sustainable development, largely using the Framework as a template and adding detail in relation to their own priorities and competences (Scottish Executive, 2005; National Assembly for Wales, 2004; Northern Ireland Office, 2006).[5] Interestingly, the political landscape has been much more dynamic in Wales and Scotland and this has had an effect on the extent to which the Framework's template has been accepted, used and developed.

By 2010, the UK *Shared Framework* was fast becoming out of date. The devolved administrations had published new strategies which deviated from the Framework. New discussions were needed to promote a consistent vision across the UK, whereby everyone is working together towards broadly similar objectives. Moreover, the arrival of a new government at Westminster also means that it is time for a new strategy. It was hoped that one would be announced sometime in early 2011, but that did not happen.

The Welsh strategies

When the UK Parliament established the National Assembly for Wales (Assembly) under the Government of Wales Act 1998, it included a requirement to produce a scheme of sustainable development.[6] Similar duties were not included in the Scotland and Northern Ireland settlements, as these created parliaments with legislative power, and it was thought that imposing such a duty would be contrary to the spirit of devolution. Importantly, the Welsh provisions need to be distinguished as they were, at least formally, imposed on the Assembly and later the Welsh Assembly Government (WAG), rather than being introduced by the institutions themselves. That said, the WAG is proud that sustainable development is a core principle within its founding statute (WAG, 2009: 8).

The Government of Wales Act 2006 s. 79 requires the Welsh Ministers to produce a scheme setting out how they propose, in the exercise of their functions, to promote sustainable development, and to report annually on how all functions were carried out.[7] Every four years, the Assembly is to report on the effectiveness of the proposals (WAG, 2008). The provisions are confined to these procedural obligations. There is no definition of sustainable development, nor does the Act impose a substantive duty on the key Welsh institutions.[8] Moreover, the procedures are very vague. For example, the Welsh Ministers must consult such persons as 'they consider appropriate'.[9] These minimal procedures have led to the Welsh institutions being quicker than the other devolved administrations to incorporate sustainable development into their policies and the exercise of their functions, to review their progress regularly and to respond accordingly (CAG Consultants, 2003; Flynn *et al.*, 2008).

The first scheme, entitled *Learning to Live Differently*, was published in November 2000 (National Assembly for Wales, 2000), well ahead of anything in the other devolved administrations. Indeed, even its replacement, published in March 2004, *Starting to Live Differently*, which was accompanied by a 'Sustainable Development Action Plan' published in October 2004 (National Assembly for Wales, 2004), preceded the UK *Shared Framework* by several months. As required under the Government of Wales Act, the Assembly, and subsequently, the Welsh Ministers, produced the required effectiveness reports on the first two sustainable development schemes. Both reports, produced by independent consultants, strongly commended the commitments to sustainable development made by the Welsh institutions, but pointed to difficulties in driving those commitments through to delivery (CAG Consultants, 2003; Flynn *et al.*, 2008). The SDC in 2005 also criticized the Welsh institutions for starting well but not having ambitious commitments, failing to join up the delivery of commitments, and failing to embed sustainable development across the Welsh public sector (SDC, 2006: 3–5).

In 2007, the WAG published *One Wales: A Progressive Agenda for Wales* (*One Wales*), consisting of 228 commitments which the Welsh Assembly Government was working towards to 2011. These commitments are set out in chapters on the following topics: strong and confident nation; healthy future; prosperous society; living communities; learning for life; fair and just society; and sustainable environment and rich and diverse culture. Quarterly updates on progress on each of the 228 commitments in *One Wales* are provided through the 'One Wales Delivery Plan' (WAG, 2007).

The most recent review, conducted in 2008 by Flynn and others, included not only the 2004 scheme, but also *One Wales*. The review tested both, using a thematic framework which asked if the programmes did the following: articulate what sustainable development looks like; acknowledge risks, conflicts, incentives and trade-offs; provide a consistent and meaningful message; challenge existing partnership approaches; and ensure effective engagement and delivery and measure tangible change (Flynn *et al.*, 2008). The review concluded that:

> There was overwhelming evidence from the interviews and documentary analysis that WAG provide inconsistent or in many cases, no *meaningful* messages on sustainable development in their policy, guidelines and financial arrangements . . . It was felt that the One Wales document was a missed opportunity, and that it should have emphasized the SD Scheme and its importance in underpinning all activity – not just the environmental objectives of Government.
>
> (Flynn *et al.*, 2008: 15)

The purpose of the statutorily required review is to inform the next strategy and, in 2008, *A Draft Scheme for Sustainable Development* was produced for consultation. The WAG received over 90 responses. In addition, the WAG held events in Swansea, Llandudno and Aberystwyth where individuals and groups were invited to provide detailed comments.

The most recent scheme, *One Wales: One Planet*, is the most ambitious of any of the UK strategies to date (WAG, 2009). It sets out the Assembly Government's vision of a sustainable Wales, whereby sustainable development is to be the overarching strategic aim of all the WAG's policies and programmes, across all ministerial portfolios. The WAG believes sustainable development should be a real organizing principle, relevant to all sectors of society. It demands joined-up government with a focus on the long term and on serving the citizen, directly supporting the aims already set out in the Wales Spatial Plan and for Local Service Boards across Wales. The Scheme stays true to the UK Framework in as much as it confirms its five core principles, but goes further, explicitly setting out an indicative route map of the journey that the WAG will need to take to use only their fair share of the Earth's resources. For example, all policymaking is to be underpinned by two core principles (involvement and integration), and six supporting principles (reducing Wales' eco-footprint,[10] consideration of full costs and benefits, precaution, polluter pays, proximity, and distinctiveness). The two core principles must be central to all key decisions about an organization's policies and programmes. The six supporting principles should be appropriately and proportionately applied according to the particular issue in question. Not all supporting principles will be relevant to each decision (WAG, 2009: 26–7). Moreover, the Scheme uses only five headline indicators to follow its progress: sustainable resource use – Wales's ecological footprint; sustaining the environment – percentage of Biodiversity Action Plan species and habitats recorded as stable or increasing; a sustainable economy – gross value added (GVA) and GVA per head; a sustainable society – percentage of the population in low-income households; and finally, a measure of the wellbeing of Wales, which is under development (WAG, 2009: 19).

Importantly, the scheme explicitly states that it is not separate from the *One Wales* agenda, which was a criticism in the Flynn *et al.* review. It provides a unifying vision and set of operational principles that is to thread through, support and drive all of the WAG's policies and programmes to holistically deliver sustainable development. Whilst the vision, the definition of sustainable development and the underpinning principles of sustainable development will remain constant, the WAG acknowledges the need for flexibility to reflect new policies and ensure continued progress towards its vision (WAG, 2009).

One of the unique challenges for Wales is that, often, it does not have the legislative competence to introduce the necessary changes. Primary legislation continues to be made at Westminster. Flynn *et al.* conclude that increased legislative power is vital if Wales is to fully meet its aspirations (2008: 15).

The Scottish strategies

In sharp contrast to Wales, the Scotland Act 1998 does not include an obligation in relation to the production of a scheme for sustainable development. Instead, in March 1999, the Secretary of State for Scotland's Advisory Group on Sustainable Development set out ten action points for the Scottish Parliament. The first of these was that 'Priority should be given by the Parliament to put sustainable development at the heart of its policy making, to ensure the social inclusion of all Scots, to ensure economic viability and environmental responsibility' (Advisory Group on Sustainable Development, 1999). Unfortunately, by October 2001, a report by WWF Scotland made it very clear that sustainable development in Scotland was not being given priority:

> Overall, notwithstanding some positive rhetoric and one or two very positive steps, there has been little action by the Scottish Executive to secure the radical change which is essential if progress is to be made. There is no Scottish strategy, and no effective machinery of government for sustainable development in Scotland. Surprisingly, and pre-dating devolution, the approach has ignored and not matched progress elsewhere in the UK. Devolved Scotland – far from forging ahead – is lagging behind.
>
> (Birley, 2001)[11]

Indeed, the Scottish Parliament and Scottish Executive went about their work for six years without producing a strategy. The first two coalition Governments produced 'Programmes for Government', which contained many 'green' initiatives, but prior to the publication of the first Scottish strategy in late 2005 there was very little general understanding of sustainable development in Scotland (Ross, 2006: 8). During that time, the Scottish Executive produced some evidence of strategic thinking on sustainable development and some basic indicators.[12] There were also general statements such as the 'Liberal–Labour Partnership Agreement' (Scottish Labour Party and Scottish Liberal Democrats, 2003) and the Scottish Executive's statement on sustainable development, *Meeting the Needs* (Scottish

Executive, 2002a). The result was that while many impressive initiatives were taken during that time – the special cabinet sub-committee on sustainable development with external expert members is particularly notable – the effect was inconsistent, piecemeal, misunderstood and often counterproductive (Ross, 2006: 29).

When *Choosing Our Future: Scotland's Sustainable Development Strategy* finally appeared in December 2005, it closely followed the Framework as a template (Scottish Executive, 2005). Interestingly, although some consultation took place, the new strategy was not subjected to a strategic environmental assessment (SEA). Technically, the SEA was not required, as the new Act, the Environmental Assessment (Scotland) Act 2005 (asp 15), was not in force. However, given the then Government's strong commitment to SEA and its very explicit extension of the coverage of this EU directive to include strategies, this omission highlighted the lack of joined-up thinking within that administration. The first two chapters of the Strategy focus on the vision set out in the Framework and putting them in context for Scotland. The Scottish Strategy is more committed to economic growth, but not at any cost. It has individual chapters for travel, wellbeing, food, communities, environmental justice, natural heritage and resources, waste, Scotland's global contribution, the built environment, education, making it happen and working together. Each chapter ends with actions for the future. In *Choosing Our Future,* four priorities were set for Scotland (Scottish Executive, 2005): climate change and energy; sustainable consumption and production: natural resource protection and environmental enhancement; and sustainable communities. Later, the Strategy states that 'The business case for sustainability is simple. Smarter use of resources does not just make good economic sense; it is absolutely essential for our long-term survival' (Scottish Executive, 2005: para. 3.11). Throughout the Strategy, environmental objectives and actions are listed ahead of social and economic goals, thus reinforcing a vision based on limits rather than trade-offs.

Choosing Our Future quickly became a historic document. Understandably, although unfortunately, given the need for long-term planning, after the Scottish National Party's success in the Scottish Parliament's election in May 2007, it replaced the previous government's sustainable development strategy with its own *Economic Strategy* and national performance indicators, along with the single objective of 'increasing sustainable economic growth' (Scottish Government, 2007a; Scottish Government, 2010). The approach in many respects is very modern. A key innovation for the Scottish Government is that the indicators have been completely embedded in the Government's approach to governance. The Scottish vision for success for Scotland is described and measured in four parts which support and reinforce each other:

- The Government's purpose (sustainable economic growth) and associated targets
- Five strategic objectives that are the focus of actions
- 15 national outcomes describing what the Government wants to achieve
- 45 national indicators to track progress.

The *Economic Strategy* lists its five strategic objectives as: wealthier and fairer, smarter, healthier, safer and stronger, and greener. It then identifies five strategic priorities it considers to be critical to economic growth: learning, skills and wellbeing; supportive business environment; infrastructure development and place; effective government; and equity.

A related programme 'Scotland Performs' aims to measure and report on the Scottish Government's progress towards its purpose of increasing sustainable economic growth. To do so, it uses seven purpose targets, relating to economic growth, productivity, participation, population, solidarity, cohesion and sustainability (Scottish Government, 2007b: 43–7). As Scotland Performs uses slightly different terminology from the Strategy, it is not clear how these specifically relate to the programme set out in the Strategy itself. Scotland Performs then sets out 15 national outcomes to better articulate the Government's overall purpose (Scottish Government, 2008a), which describe the kind of Scotland the Government aspires to, and 45 national indicators covering key areas of health, justice, environment, economy and education to measure progress (Scottish Government, 2008b).

As discussed above, the *Economic Strategy* has a much clearer structure than its predecessor. However, the change did little to improve the public's understanding of sustainable development, especially since it took two years for the Scottish Government to even try to realign itself with the rest of the UK by explaining how its unique approach could still fit within the UK Framework (Scottish Government, 2010). As this was done through the main planning policy document, it does not necessarily mean that the interpretation can be extrapolated more generally to all areas. Moreover, the explanation does not sit easily with the UK Framework and only serves to add confusion. In paragraph 33 of Scottish Planning Policy, the Government notes that planning authorities should take a positive approach to development, recognizing and responding to economic and financial conditions in considering proposals that could contribute to economic growth (Scottish Government, 2010: para. 33).

Elsewhere, it lends its support to the five principles set out in the Framework and contends that 'Sustainable economic growth means building a dynamic and growing economy that will provide prosperity and opportunities for all, while respecting the limits of our environment in order to ensure that future generations can enjoy a better quality of life too' (Scottish Government, 2010: para. 36). Moreover, the purpose targets in Scotland Performs include increasing GDP growth rate and increasing the population. Worse still, the sustainability targets actually only relate to emissions. None of this is consistent with the vision set out in the UK Framework and in many respects is a step back towards a much weaker approach to sustainable development.

Perhaps most worrying is the complete lack of public involvement in the process. The *Economic Strategy* appeared out of the blue, with no public consultation process at all. SEA is required by primary legislation for all strategies in Scotland and this would have guaranteed some public consultation. However, the Scottish Government decided this was unnecessary. The

Government's answers to certain parliamentary questions posed at the time by members of the Green Party did raise questions about the reasoning behind this decision:

> Robin Harper (Lothians) (Green Party): 'The cabinet secretary's answer is entirely consistent with that given by his colleague, Fiona Hyslop, on 21 November: that conducting an environmental assessment of the strategy would be too "difficult and time-consuming". The Cabinet Secretary for Finance and Sustainable Growth should be familiar with the Environmental Assessment (Scotland) Act 2005, which exempts from environmental assessment only financial plans or programmes. It is clear that that exemption does not apply to "The Government Economic Strategy". Will he point me to the provision in the Act that says that strategic environmental assessments of strategy documents are not required if they would be too time-consuming or difficult to conduct?'
>
> (Scottish Parliament, 2007, column 4426)

Given the lack of alternative consultation, this failure is significant. Overall however, the Strategy is capable of improving the sustainability of Scotland. It has a clear vision, with clear actions, targets and indicators.

Northern Ireland strategies

Northern Ireland has lagged behind the rest of the UK in relation to the sustainable development agenda. It was not until 2006 that its first strategy, a *Sustainable Development Strategy for Northern Ireland: First Steps towards Sustainability* was published, and notably this was while devolution was still suspended (Northern Ireland Office, 2006). This was a full year behind the publication of the *Shared Framework*. The Strategy was subsequently endorsed by the Office of the First Minister and Deputy First Minister which produced a plan of implementation for the strategy.

Unsurprisingly, given it was produced under suspension, the Strategy closely resembled the UK Framework. It differed, however, in three respects. The draft strategy was subject to an extensive consultation process, and a direct outcome of the consultation was the addition of a further principle: promoting opportunity and innovation. This is, in itself, quite an interesting addition. The strategy expands on this new principle, explaining: 'It is about seeing sustainable development as an area of risk which, when managed effectively, can create opportunities to innovate and enhance reputation that are fundamental to long-term success' (Northern Ireland Office, 2006: 19). This explicit recognition of the risk involved was clearly designed to appeal to the innovators and opportunists of this world.

The need for sustainable development to become integrated into the Comprehensive Spending Review, future spending reviews and subsequently into relevant Public Service Agreements (PSAs) in Northern Ireland was identified as key in helping to ensure that the Government contributes to the delivery of the objectives and targets identified in the strategy. The Northern Ireland Government also agreed to review the current remit of the SDC and the need for an independent watchdog function, along with consideration of the establishment of a sustainable development forum and its roles.

The Office of the First Minster and Deputy First Minister (OFMDFM) published an 'Implementation Plan' (OFMDFM, 2006) in November 2006, which developed, in more detail, the strategic targets contained in the first Strategy. In many respects, the first Strategy reads like a background paper, rather than a strategy. It goes through the history of sustainable development internationally, in the EU and in the UK, and lists the challenges facing the Earth and Northern Ireland. Moreover, the Implementation Plan failed to really get off the ground. For example, no indicators to measure progress against targets were ever produced.

In essence, neither of the parties in power, the Democratic Unionist Party and Sinn Féin, was that interested in sustainable development, and it was not until October 2009 that the Executive finally approved the opening of the public consultation phase of the draft of its own Sustainable Development Strategy. The phase went on until 15 January 2010. Thus in sharp contrast to Scotland – which had failed to consult on either of its strategies, yet produced full programmes for action – Northern Ireland had consulted a great deal and produced little in terms of action.

The new Strategy, entitled *Everyone's Involved*, was published in May 2010 (Northern Ireland Executive, 2010). The stated aim of the new Strategy is 'to identify and develop actions that will improve the quality of life for ourselves and for future generations' (Northern Ireland Executive, 2010: 1). It sets out seven commitments, most of which are vague. For example, Commitment One: 'In the development of new strategies and policies, we will require departments to incorporate comprehensive "sustainability scans" as one component of their Impact Assessment process, which will provide SMART evidence of the inclusion of sustainability criteria' (Northern Ireland Executive, 2010: 5).

The 2009 consultation document made no reference at all to the UK *Shared Framework*. However, following the consultation, the new Strategy, like its predecessor, ended up using the UK Framework's principles for sustainable development, along with promoting opportunity and innovation. It also then has six priority areas for action (Northern Ireland Executive, 2010: 14–16):

- Building a dynamic, innovative economy that delivers the prosperity required to tackle disadvantage and lift communities out of poverty
- Strengthening society so that it is more tolerant, inclusive and stable and permits positive progress in quality of life for everyone
- Driving sustainable, long-term investment in key infrastructure to support economic and social development
- Striking an appropriate balance between the responsible use and protection of natural resources in support of a better quality of life and a better quality environment

- Ensuring reliable, affordable and sustainable energy provision and reducing our carbon footprint
- Ensuring the existence of a policy environment which supports the overall advancement of sustainable development in and beyond Government.

These clearly deviate significantly from those in the UK Framework and do not put ecological sustainability or living within the Earth's limits at the core of sustainable development. In each priority area, a number of strategic objectives have been identified. It is against these strategic objectives that progress towards the achievement of the sustainable development vision is to be measured (Northern Ireland Executive, 2010: 16).

The NI Executive published *Focus on the Future*, its 'Implementation Plan', in April 2011, which sets out actions for the achievement of each objective (Northern Ireland Executive, 2011: 21). The Plan repeats the hierarchical approach in the strategy. It is structured in two ways and in two parts. The first part sets out the actions within the Plan on a department-by-department basis. Lead departments have been identified for each of the 32 strategic objectives, and these departments will be responsible for overseeing progress against targets and communicating their findings to the OFDFM. The second part sets out for each strategic objective every action contributing to its achievement (Northern Ireland Executive, 2011: 7). The Plan commits the Executive to develop a set of indicators which will be used by the OFDFM to report annually on overall progress (Northern Ireland Executive, 2011: 15).

Impressively, both of the Northern Ireland strategies and the Implementation Plan have been shaped and greatly strengthened through discussion and public consultation. A stakeholder group with a membership of over 40 representatives from all sectors of Northern Ireland society, including the UK Government's independent adviser on sustainable development from the SDC, was involved in helping to influence and develop the direction of the first strategy. Indeed, it was the stakeholder group that proposed extending these with the addition of two further specific Northern Ireland priority areas: 'Governance for Sustainable Development' and 'Learning and Communication', and one further specific Northern Ireland guiding principle – 'opportunity and innovation'.

Northern Ireland is unique in the UK, in that responsibility for the production and review of the Strategy and Implementation Plan is at the highest level. The OFMDFM is to provide strong leadership to ensure delivery of this Strategy. Although this is impressive, it is not a decision that was made by the devolved Government, but, instead, was made at the instigation of the Northern Ireland Secretary of State, Peter Hain, during direct rule. As a department run by two political parties with different political priorities and aspirations, it is impressive that the second strategy was also produced by the OFMDFM. Clearly, this requires close cooperation and partnership working with other departments.

Overall, the new Strategy is designed as a framework document. Despite it being overly wordy for this purpose, it does show progress from the previous Strategy. The Northern Ireland Executive still appears attached to the idea of economic growth as the panacea for all ills, but on occasion, this is qualified as an objective which is limited to reducing poverty. The Implementation Plan, the targets set in it, the relationship of these with the Programme for Government and the PSAs, and the Investment strategy are vital in terms of actually implementing the Strategy. As such, the new Strategy is very dependent on other things happening – the Implementation Plan took a long time to arrive and a new indicator set is still being produced. Indeed, the Strategy itself does not contain a timetable for the production of the indicators. While, on paper, there appears to be some progress, it is painfully slow. Commitments and targets need to be accompanied by timetables to be meaningful. It is disappointing that the Strategy still fails to define a clear role for the SDC (or a similar body) in Northern Ireland, as the benefits achieved by doing so in the UK, Scottish and Welsh strategies have been significant.

Thus, in Northern Ireland, unlike in Scotland, there has been an enormous amount of public consultation, but it is unfortunate that, in many respects, this has slowed progress significantly. The necessary implementation tools following the first Strategy were never put in place and indeed, Northern Ireland has yet to have a set of sustainable development indicators in place, yet alone any monitoring of these. This failure to deliver is affecting the actual delivery of sustainable development and one hopes that the timetable for putting the new implementation plan and indicators in place is adhered to more strictly.

Analysis and conclusion

In research studies covering the strategies of several countries, the UK strategies tend to do quite well. Swanson *et al.* (2004) used six governance elements in their study of the national sustainable strategies of 20 countries and the EU. First, they considered the nature of the strategy and government coordination, looking at the relevance and comprehensiveness of the strategy and departmental involvement. As all the UK (and EU) strategies use a thematic approach, they do cover most aspects of sustainable development and are capable of acting as logical frameworks for decision making. Next, Swanson *et al.* examined the placement of overall responsibility for the strategy. The head of state was responsible in only six of the 21 jurisdictions. In the UK, it is only in Northern Ireland where responsibility for the strategy rests at the highest level. Only four of the 21 jurisdictions had a legislative underpinning for their strategic process. In the UK, it is only Wales that currently has this requirement.

The fourth governance element they examined was the link between the strategy and planning and budget processes. Only one of the 21 jurisdictions had fully integrated these. The UK was one of the nine jurisdictions where the links were tangential and still being developed through spending reviews. The fifth element examined was the formality and breadth of stakeholder involvement. The review above shows mixed results in this respect. As the UK and Welsh administrations seem to be getting the balance right between consultation and delivery, it is unfortunate to see Scotland and Northern Ireland erring at the two extremes. The final element considered in the Swanson *et al.* study was the extent to which the strategy contained links to local levels through guidance or sub-national coordination. Again, the UK Framework approach fared well in this last element (Swanson *et al.*, 2004).

In a separate work, Swanson and Pinter observe that:

> the UK SDS (2005) continues to be one of the good practice examples from a strategy co-ordination perspective. Not only is it comprehensive, it also involves multiple levels of government in the development of the strategy and therefore speaks to each level. The strategy includes a comprehensive framework intended to guide policy across the UK government. As well as nationally articulated strategy, individual departments are asked to develop their own sustainable development strategies within the context of the more far-reaching UK Strategy.
>
> (Swanson and Pinter, 2007: 34)

The UK strategies are not without fault and, importantly, certain key definitional issues continue to inhibit progress. At present, it is difficult to decide where those both inside and outside the Government are to find the current meaning of sustainable development. An obvious answer for the UK courts reviewing a UK statute or policy is to rely on the current definition set out in UK Government policy. However, there is no obligation on public bodies to use the one set out in the current Strategy. Definitions, principles and objectives for sustainable development can be found in documents and policy at almost every level of Government and for many different sectors, as well as in secondary sources including most dictionaries (Ross, 2008: ch. 8). Moreover, different legislation points decision makers to different places, and at present the guidance provisions are not in any standard form and, in many instances, the legislature has actually tailored them to the needs of the particular regime (Ross, 2008). Some of the guidance is limited to that specifically addressed to that particular agency,[13] while elsewhere, any ministerial guidance is relevant.[14] In other statutes the guidance is limited to that specifically relating to sustainable development (Ross, 2008: ch. 8).[15]

The imprecise nature of sustainable development does have implications. While some flexibility and contextualization has proven to be very useful, imprecise terms introduce a lack of consistency both internally – within a regime or public body, and externally – between regimes or public bodies. There may be a lack of continuity in the meaning of the term over time and this may result in confusion as to the meaning and expectations, both for those implementing the legislation and for those subject to it. Finally, imprecision may give the executive (a public body) too much discretion and take power away from the judiciary and the legislature.

If central government could ensure that the same definition and approach are being consistently used throughout the public sector and if decision makers were required to refer to the same guidance (or in the context here, strategy), then consistency would be possible. This idea is pursued in detail in Chapters 12 and 13.

Devolution is also clearly a cause of inconsistency. As noted by Porritt (2009: 46), 'so far, rather than there being a sense of collective endeavour for SD alongside the diversity of approaches, there is a strong impression that they [the devolved administrations] are energetically pursuing their own agendas without much reference to Whitehall, and vice versa'. Thus, while the Welsh experience shows the benefits of flexibility and allowing certain parts of the country to forge ahead with the sustainability agenda, the Scottish and Northern Ireland experiences also demonstrate the vulnerability of policy-based approaches to electoral 'short termism'. The fact remains that it is the UK that must comply with EU law and the targets and obligations agreed at international level. The devolved administrations cannot act purely in their own self-interest in relation to sustainable development. The benefits of the *Shared Framework* – such as a negotiated and shared vision which crosses political and administrative boundaries and joint ownership of that vision – have been recognized outside the UK (Swanson and Pinter, 2007: 56). A new shared framework needs to be negotiated to lay down a consistent template for the interpretation of sustainable development across the UK, which sets appropriate boundaries within which the devolved and UK Governments can operate. There ought to be stricter controls to ensure compliance with the vision set out in the Framework at all levels and within all parts of Government.

Furthermore, other mechanisms need to be more clearly aligned to the vision and objectives set out in the Strategy so that it genuinely provides a framework or template for decision making. The CSD observed that, 'A national sustainable development strategy is a tool for informed decision-making that provides a framework for systematic thought across sectors and territory' (Division for Sustainable Development, UNDESA, 2002, Executive Summary). Swanson and Pinter (2007: 47, 58) note that the UK NSDS is still not sufficiently linked to existing government planning, reporting and budgeting processes. Research by Blair and Evans into the progress made by UK local government on sustainable development confirms this point:

> For sustainability to be mainstreamed, the frameworks of corporate management, the processes and specific tools (targets and indicators), audit, review and inspection procedures all need to be appropriately aligned and geared to a common sustainability set of criteria. Currently this is not the case. In the absence of some universally applied minimum stewardship standards and approaches, a local authority could be delivering exactly what its community wishes, with total democratic legitimacy, but which might contravene any sense of environmental or social justice.
>
> (Blair and Evans, 2004: 41)

Indeed, given the importance of other mechanisms being linked to the Strategy, most of the difficulties and criticisms surrounding the other mechanisms would be resolved if the criticisms directed at the development, use and review of the Strategy itself were addressed.

Meadowcroft, however, is careful to put the role of the Strategy in perspective. He makes an important distinction between formal strategy processes and strategic decision making for sustainable development:

> If the ideal formal strategy process is not understood to subsume all strategic action for sustainable development, the expectations for the strategy processes themselves can be somewhat more modest. From this perspective, they can be seen as making as contribution to 'strategic public management' or 'reflexive governance' without being conceptualized as the 'be all' and 'end all' of these processes.
>
> (Meadowcroft, 2007)

Clearly other tools are also necessary and these are the subject of chapters 6–10 below.

Ideally then, every decision needs to use sustainable development as a template, and sustainable development should be a 'whole systems' concept, whereby it provides the forum or 'table' to which important and more concrete objectives and values can be brought (Ross, 2010a). This is not limited to the production of a strategy or its review. The role of a strategy in this process is to provide guidance as to how sustainable development operates in any given decision-making process in order to ensure that certain objectives and values have influence in the decision-making process (Ross, 2009; 2010a).

This chapter, like many of those that follow, ends with the call for sustainable leadership. As discussed in the next chapter, leadership is the most essential criteria for delivering real change. As the CSD concludes:

> Sound leadership and good governance is necessary for effective strategy development. This is key to guaranteeing that the policy and institutional changes that the strategy entails are affected, the necessary financial resources committed and institutions assume full responsibility for implementation of the strategy in their respective areas.
>
> (Division for Sustainable Development, UNDESA, 2002: 17)

Notes

1 Capital comprises the stock of man-made capital (machines and infrastructure together with the stock of knowledge and skills) and human capital, as well as the stock of natural capital including natural resources (renewable and non-renewable), biological diversity, habitat, clean air, water, and so on. We can pass on less of the environment so long as we offset this loss by increasing the stock of roads and machinery or other man-made capital (Pearce, 1993: 15). The weak sustainability interpretation of sustainable development still requires that the depletion of natural resources that are in fixed supply – non-renewable resources – should be accompanied by investment in substitute sources (Pearce, 1993: 15–16). For a slightly stronger view, see Bowers (1997: 194).

2 The 1999 strategy advocates the three prongs – social, economic and environment, and high economic growth is still one of four objectives (DEFRA, 1999).

3 See the Local Government Act 2000 ch. 22 s. 2, which provides: (1) Local authorities are to have power to do anything which they consider is likely to achieve any one or more of the following objects – (a) the promotion or improvement of the economic well-being of their area; (b) the promotion or improvement of the social well-being of their area, and (c) the promotion or improvement of the environmental well-being of their area (Lord Whitty, House of Lords Debates, Local Government Bill, Column 1482, 25 January 2000).

4 *Sustainable Development Strategy for Northern Ireland: First Steps Towards Sustainability* (Northern Ireland Office, 2006) was produced while devolution was still suspended. The OFMDFM has produced an Implementation Plan for the Strategy.

5 Note that Wales has a statutory duty to produce a sustainable development scheme under the Government of Wales Act 2006 ch. 32 s. 79 (previously the Government of Wales Act 1998 ch. 38 s. 121).

6 The Government of Wales Act 1998 s. 121.

7 The Government of Wales Act 2006 s. 79 replaces s. 121 of the 1998 Act to reflect the subsequent separation of power between the WAG and the Assembly.

8 In the 2006 Act Schedule 2, clause 8(2) there is very weak substantive obligation imposed on the Assembly Commission (which is the contracting arm of the legislature) that 'in the exercise of the functions of the Assembly Commission due regard must be had to the principle of promoting sustainable development'.

9 The 2006 Act s. 79(3).

10 The Ecological Footprint measures the amount of biologically productive land and water area required to produce the resources an individual, population or activity consumes and to absorb the waste it generates, given prevailing technology and resource management.

11 The follow-up report is slightly less critical. See Birley (2002).

12 These include specific documents such as *Building a Sustainable Scotland: Sustainable Development and the Spending Review 2002* (Scottish Executive, 2002b) and *Sustaining Our Working Environment* which sets out what the Executive was doing to reduce the environmental impact of its operations and so contributes to sustainable development with clear targets (see Chapter 7 for more detail). There are also sectoral strategies that address sustainable development objectives or issues, including *Forward Strategy for Agriculture*, *A New Strategy for Scottish Tourism*, and *The Social Inclusion Strategy*. For a detailed consideration of the extent to which sustainable development issues are integrated into these and other strategies, see CAG Consultants (2004: 16).

13 The Environment Act 1995 ch. 25 s. 31, s. 40.

14 The Planning and Compulsory Purchase Act 2004 ch. 5 s. 39(3).

15 The Clean Neighbourhoods and Environment Act 2005 ch. 16 s. 88(9). A unique form of words is found in the Local Government in Scotland Act 2003 asp 1 s. 2 where '[regard is to be had] (a) to any guidance provided by the Scottish Ministers for local authorities on the performance of those duties; . . . (b) to what are, whether by reference to any generally recognized, published code or otherwise, regarded as proper arrangements'. So while only guidance issued specifically to the local authorities is relevant, regard may also be had to certain published codes and, interestingly, these codes may come from elsewhere such as an international body. In the event of a conflict, s. 2 provides that the specific ministerial guidance is to take precedence.

References

Advisory Group on Sustainable Development (1999) *Scotland the Sustainable? 10 Action Points for the Scottish Parliament*, Edinburgh: Advisory Group on Sustainable Development.

Alder, J. and Wilkinson, D. (1999) *Environmental Law and Ethics*, London: Macmillan.

Beder, S. (2006) *Environmental Principles and Policies: An Interdisciplinary Introduction*, London: Earthscan.

Birley, T. (2001) *Reality Check: A Review of Scottish Executive Activity on Sustainable Development: Report to WWF Scotland*, Aberfeldy: World Wildlife Fund.

Birley, T. (2002) *Reality Check 2002: A Review of Scottish Executive Activity on Sustainable Development-Report to WWF Scotland*, Aberfeldy: World Wildlife Fund.

Blair, F. and Evans, B. (2004) *Seeing the Bigger Picture*, Newcastle: Sustainable Development Commission.

Blowers, A. (1992) 'Planning a sustainable future: Problems, principles and prospects', *Town and Country Planning*, 61(5): 132–5.

Bosselmann, K. (2008) *The Principle of Sustainability: Transforming Law and Governance*, Aldershot: Ashgate.

Bowers, J. (1997) *Sustainability and Environmental Economics: An Alternative Text*, Harlow: Longman.

CAG Consultants (2003) *How Effectively has the National Assembly for Wales Promoted Sustainable Development?*, Report to the Welsh Assembly Government.

CAG Consultants (2004) *Is the Scottish Executive Structured and Positioned to Deliver Sustainable Development?*, 10th Report, vol. 2, Edinburgh: Environment and Rural Development Committee.

Department for Transport, Scottish Executive, Welsh Assembly Government (2009) *Transport Statistics for Great Britain 2009*, 35th edition, London: Department for Transport.

Department of Energy and Climate Change (DECC) (2010) *Average Surface Temperature: 1772–2009*, DECC, http://www.decc.gov.uk/assets/decc/statistics/climate_change/1_20100312122831_e_@@_gafg0l.xls, accessed 12 August 2010.

Department of the Environment (DOE) (1988) *A Perspective by the United Kingdom on the Report of the World Commission on Environment and Development*, London: DOE.

DOE (1989) *Sustaining Our Common Future*, London: DOE.

DOE (1990) *This Common Inheritance: Britain's Environmental Strategy*, Cm 1200, London: DOE.

DEFRA (1999) *A Better Quality of Life: A Strategy for Sustainable Development for the United Kingdom*, London: DEFRA.

DEFRA (2004) *Taking it On: Developing UK Sustainable Development Strategy Together: A Consultation Paper*, London: DEFRA.

DEFRA (2005) *The UK Strategy for Sustainable Development: Securing the Future*, London: DEFRA.

Department of Environment, Transport and the Regions (DETR) (1998) *Sustainable Development: Opportunities for Change Consultation Paper on a Revised UK Strategy*, London: DETR.

Dernbach, J. (2008) 'Navigating the U.S. Transition to sustainability: Matching national governance challenges with appropriate legal tools', *Tulsa Law Review*, 44: 93–120.

Dernbach, J. (2009) *Agenda for Sustainable America*, Washington, DC: Environmental Law Institute.

Division for Sustainable Development, UNDESA (2002) 'Guidance in preparing national sustainable development strategy: Managing sustainable development in the new millennium', Background paper no. 13, DESA/DSD/PC2/BP13, Rome: Department of Economic and Social Affairs.

Dobson, A. (1995) *Green Political Thought*, London: Routledge.

Environmental Audit Committee (EAC) (2004) *The Sustainable Development Strategy: Illusion or Reality? Thirteenth Report of Session 2003–4*, HC 624–1, London: EAC.

European Commission (1993) *Towards Sustainability: A European Community Programme of Policy and Action in Relation to the Environment and Sustainable Development*, Luxembourg: Directorate General for Environment, Nuclear Safety and Civil Protection.

European Commission (2001) *A Sustainable Europe for a Better World: A European Union Strategy for Sustainable Development*, Brussels: European Commission.

European Commission (2005) *Summary of the Public Consultation for the Review of the European Sustainable Development Strategy*, Brussels: European Commission.

European Commission (2009) *Mainstreaming Sustainable Development into EU policies: 2009 Review of the European Union Strategy for Sustainable Development*, Com 400, Brussels: European Commission.

European Council (2006) *Review of the EU Sustainable Development Strategy: Renewed Strategy*, Brussels: European Council.

European Parliament (1999) *Helsinki European Council: Presidency Conclusions*, Luxembourg: European Parliament.

European Parliament (2000) *Lisbon European Council: Presidency Conclusions*, Luxembourg: European Parliament.

Eurostat (2009) *Sustainable development in the European Union: 2009 monitoring report of the EU sustainable development strategy*, Luxembourg: Office for Official Publications of the European Communities.

Flynn, A., Marsden, T., Netherwood, A. and Pitts, R. (2008) *Final Report: The Sustainable Development Effectiveness Report for the Welsh Assembly*, Cardiff: Welsh Assembly Government.

Freeman, J. (1999) 'Private parties, public function and the real democracy problem in the new administrative law?', in D. Dyzenhous (ed.) *Recrafting the Rule of Law*, Oxford: Hart.

French, D. (2005) *International Law and Policy of Sustainable Development*, Manchester: Manchester University Press.

Grainger, A. (2004) 'Introduction', in M. Purvis and A. Grainger (eds) *Exploring Sustainable Development: Geographical Perspectives*, London: Earthscan.

Hardi, P. and Zdan, T. (eds) (1997) *Assessing Sustainable Development: Principles in Practice*, Winnipeg: International Institute for Sustainable Development.

Helm, D. (2000) 'Objectives, instruments and institutions', in D. Helm (ed.) *Environmental Policy Objectives, Instruments and Implementation*, Oxford: Oxford University Press.

HM Government, Scottish Executive, Welsh Assembly Government, Northern Ireland Office (2005) *One future – different paths: The UK's shared framework for sustainable development*, London: DEFRA.

HM Treasury (2011) *Budget 2011*, HC 836, London: HMSO.

MacNeill, J. (1989) 'Strategies for sustainable economic development', *Scientific American*, 261(3): 154–65.

Meadowcroft, J. (2007) 'National sustainable development strategies: Features, challenges and reflexivity', *European Environment*, 17(3): 152–63.

National Assembly for Wales (2000) *Learning to Live Differently: The Sustainable Development Scheme of the National Assembly for Wales*, Cardiff: National Assembly for Wales.

National Assembly for Wales (2004) *Starting to Live Differently: The Sustainable Development Scheme of the National Assembly for Wales*, Cardiff: National Assembly for Wales.

Northern Ireland Executive (2010) *Everyone's Involved: Sustainable Development Strategy*, Belfast: Northern Ireland Executive.

Northern Ireland Executive (2011) *Focus on the Future – Sustainable Development Implementation Plan 2011–2014*, Belfast, OFMDFM.

Northern Ireland Office (2006) *Sustainable Development Strategy for Northern Ireland: First Steps Towards Sustainability*, Belfast: Northern Ireland Office.

Office of the First Minister and Deputy First Minister (OFMDFM) (2006) *A Positive Step: Northern Ireland: A Sustainable Development Implementation Plan*, Belfast: OFMDFM.

Pearce, D. (1993) *Blueprint 3: Measuring Sustainable Development*, London: Earthscan.

Porritt, J. (2009) 'The standing of sustainable development in government', http://www.jonathonporritt.com/pages/2009/11/the_standing_of_sustainable_de.html, accessed 12 April 2010.

Porritt, J. (2011) *'The Greenest Government Ever'? One Year On: A Report to Friends of the Earth*, London: FOE.

Rees, W.E. (1996) 'Revisiting carrying capacity: Area-based indicators of sustainability', *Population and Environment*, 17(3): 192–215.

Ross, A. (2003) 'Is the environment getting squeezed out of sustainable development?', *Public Law*, Summer: 249–59.

Ross, A. (2006) 'Sustainable development in Scotland post devolution', *Environmental Law Review*, 8: 6–32.

Ross, A. (2008) 'Why legislate for sustainable development? An examination of sustainable development provisions in UK and Scottish statutes', *Journal of Environmental Law*, 20(1): 35–68.

Ross, A. (2009) 'Modern interpretations of sustainable development', *Journal of Law and Society*, 36(1): 32–54.

Ross, A. (2010a) 'It's time to get serious: Why legislation is needed to make sustainable development a reality in the UK', *Sustainability*, 2: 1101–27.

Ross, A. (2010b) 'Sustainable development indicators and a putative argument for law: A case study of the UK', in D. French (ed.) *Global Justice and Sustainable Development*, Leiden: Martinus Nijhoff.

Salmon, P. (2003) 'Sustainable development in New Zealand', *RMB*, 5: 13.

Scottish Executive (2002a) *Meeting the needs . . . Priorities, Actions and Targets for Sustainable Development in Scotland*, Edinburgh: Scottish Executive Environment Group.

Scottish Executive (2002b) *Building a Sustainable Scotland: Sustainable Development and the Spending Review 2002*, Edinburgh: Scottish Executive.

Scottish Executive (2005) *Choosing our Future: Scotland's Sustainable Development Strategy*, Edinburgh: Scottish Executive.

Scottish Government (2007a) *The Government's Economic Strategy*, Edinburgh: Scottish Government.

Scottish Government (2007b) *Scottish Budget Spending Review 2007*, Edinburgh: Scottish Government.

Scottish Government (2008a) 'National Outcomes' http://www.scotland.gov.uk/About/scotPerforms/outcomes, accessed 30 August 2010.

Scottish Government (2008b) 'Strategic Objectives' http://www.scotland.gov.uk/About/scotPerforms/objectives, accessed 30 August 2010.

Scottish Government (2010) *Scottish Planning Policy,* Edinburgh: Scottish Government.

Scottish Labour Party and Scottish Liberal Democrats (2003) *A Partnership for a Better Scotland: Partnership Agreement,* Edinburgh: Scottish Government.

Scottish Parliament (2007) *Meeting of the Parliament: Thursday 13 December 2007, Session 3,* Edinburgh: Scottish Parliament.

Secretariat of the Convention on Biological Diversity (2006) *Global Biodiversity Outlook (GBO-2),* Montreal: Convention on Biological Diversity.

Stern, N. (2007) *The Economics of Climate Change: The Stern Review,* Cambridge: Cambridge University Press.

Streurer, R. and Martinuzzi, A. (2005) 'Towards a new pattern of strategy formation in the public sector: First experiences with national strategies for sustainable development in Europe', *Environment and Planning C: Government and Policy,* 23(3): 455–72.

Sustainable Development Commission (SDC) (2004) *Shows Promise. But Must Try Harder: An Assessment by the Sustainable Development Commission of the Government's Reported Progress on Sustainable Development over the Past Five Years,* London: SDC.

SDC (2006) *Sustainable Development in Wales: From Pioneer to Delivery,* London: SDC.

SDC (2009) *Where Are We Now: A Review of Progress on Sustainable Development,* London: SDC.

Sustainable Development Commission Scotland (SDCS) (2008) *Sustainable Development: A Review of Progress by the Scottish Government,* Edinburgh: SDCS.

SDCS (2009) *Sustainable Development: Third Annual Assessment of Progress by the Scottish Government,* Edinburgh: SDCS.

Swanson, D. and Pinter, L. (2007) 'Governance strategies for national sustainable development strategies', in OECD, *Institutionalizing Sustainable Development,* Paris: OECD.

Swanson, D., Pinter, L., Bregha, F., Volkery, A. and Jacob, K. (2004) *National Strategies for Sustainable Development: Challenges, Approaches and* Innovations in Strategic and Co-ordinated Action, Winnipeg and Eschborn: IISD and Deutsche Gesellschaft für TechnischeZusammenarbeit.

Thirion, S. (2008) 'Involving citizens in defining and measuring well-being and progress', Part II, in *Well-being for All: Concepts and Tools for Social Cohesion,* (Trends in Social Cohesion 20) Strasbourg: Council of Europe Publishing.

UK Government (1994) *Sustainable Development: The UK Strategy,* London: HMSO Cm 6467.

United Nations (UN) (2002) *Plan of Implementation of the World Summit on Sustainable Development,* A/CONF.199/20/Res.2, New York: UN.

UN Development Programme (UNDP) (2009) *Human Development Report 2009: Overcoming Barriers: Human Mobility and Development,* Geneva: UNDP.

UN Environment Programme (UNEP) (2002) *Global Environment Outlook, GEO 3: Past, Present and Future Perspectives,* London: Earthscan.

UNEP (2007) *Global Environment Outlook, GEO 4: Environment for Development,* Nairobi: UNEP.

UN General Assembly (UNGA) (1992a) *The Rio Declaration on Environment and Development,* A/CONF.151/26 Vol. 1, New York: UN.

UNGA (1992b) *Agenda 21,* A/CONF.151/26 Vol. 1, New York: UN.

Welsh Assembly Government (WAG) (2007) *One Wales: A Progressive Agenda for the Government of Wales* – An agreement between the Labour and Plaid Cymru Groups in the National Assembly, Cardiff: WAG

WAG (2008) *Sustainable Development Annual Report 2007–2008,* Cardiff: WAG.

WAG (2009) *One Wales: One Planet: The Sustainable Development Scheme of the Welsh Assembly Government*, Cardiff: Welsh Assembly Government.

World Commission on Environment and Development (WCED) (1987) *Our Common Future*, Oxford: Oxford University Press.

World Wildlife Fund (WWF), Zoological Society of London and Global Footprint Network (2008) *Living Planet Report 2008*, Gland: WWF.

5 Clear commitment and leadership

This chapter explores the instances of leadership and lack of leadership for the sustainable development agenda in the UK. It is important to distinguish between leaders and leadership. A 'leader' is either a post holder who was elected or appointed to lead something, or a person who actually shows leadership. The post holder is looked to as the source of leadership, but may or may not perform this role well. In contrast, leadership may be an exercise by anyone from any part of an organization or group, and even when an appointed leader exists, others may exercise leadership (Parkin, 2010: 94). This chapter deals predominantly with the leadership exercised by political and government leaders. However, it also evaluates the mechanisms which not only allow alternative sources of sustainable development leadership to emerge within government and be supported but also act to challenge the unsustainable leadership of our political leaders.

The chapter begins by emphasizing the importance of effective leadership for a successful shift towards true sustainable development, the obstacles to that shift and highlights the tools that not only provide evidence of leadership but also act to minimize the effects of political whim and a lack of leadership. For the purposes of analysis, leadership for sustainable development is then examined under four headings: obvious commitment and responsibility at the highest level of government; leadership embedded into the main workings of government; support for leadership at all levels through training, advice and responsibility; and, finally, protection from a lack of leadership through priorities, targets with timetables, obligations and procedures with clear lines of accountability.

The discussion below is not exhaustive, but it does cover some of the UK's successes and failures in promoting leadership in the quest for sustainable development. Some tools have been more effective than others. Some effective tools have been discontinued. The reality is that politics is messy and, as such, the evidence of leadership for sustainable development is patchy, cyclical and often inconsistent. Moreover, subsequent leaders may prefer to use different tools to communicate, promote and coordinate their vision of sustainable development, perhaps simply for the sake of change. The UK's institutional characteristics, such as the primacy of government departments, prime ministerial authority and the implications of asymmetrical devolution in the different parts of the UK are also analyzed in the context of leadership.

Importance of effective leadership for sustainable development

Effective leadership in sustainable development often means making decisions that may be unpopular in the short term but necessary in the long term. Such leadership is required throughout society. It is needed in business and the markets, in education, technology, the arts and popular culture, and in the political and administrative arms of government. The Organisation for Economic Cooperation and Development (OECD) checklist maintains that 'Clear government commitment to sustainable development goals, leadership, and communication of this commitment, are essential to support the development of a concrete strategy and subsequent action' (OECD, 2002: 5). In its study of 19 countries and the EU, Swanson *et al.* (2004: 7) concluded that 'Leadership is perhaps the most critical aspect of strategic management. Through a consultative process, it provides the vision for development activities and services'. As Hardi and Zdan explain:

> Committed, even inspired, leadership is critical. In any given situation, a country, business, region, citizens group, or administration, may require a convincing push toward doing assessments. This may originate from external forces, such as public demands or dissatisfaction. However, it is always more effective when it begins with internal stimulus: strong leadership and long-term vision.
>
> (Hardi and Zdan, 1997: 155)

Research in the UK backs this up. In her review of statutory sustainable development duties in the UK, Cussons (2006: 16) reported that the view among public bodies was that 'the single most important factor determining an organization's approach to sustainable development was considered to be management leadership'. Her study of 12 UK organizations (which included government departments, agencies and local authorities) revealed a number of cases where organizations 'considered they had gone considerably further than any legal interpretation of their duty would require them to do, because they had been driven by a management with a strong understanding of and commitment to sustainable development' (Cussons, 2006: 16).

Obstacles to leadership for sustainable development

Firstly, leaders find it difficult to act for long-term benefits when the pressure for short-term gains is so strong and so immediate. As noted by Salim:

> Government leaders however, are chosen by a democratic process influenced by political forces. In developing countries when income is low and political campaigns expensive, collusion between government leaders, political parties and business conglomerates becomes increasingly realistic. This makes the government rather weak and reluctant to encounter and act as a countervailing

power against big corporations and those with money; guns and physical strength. It also means that governments, especially in "soft states" become part of the problem as indicated by government's inability to correct market failures.

(Salim, 2007: 28)

While perhaps to a lesser extent, Salim's comments also ring true for many developed countries.

Another hurdle is that it is likely the case that effective leadership for sustainable development will only be provided if those with a strong understanding of sustainable development are elected. This means that, first, committed individuals stand for election, the electorate understands the importance of electing someone committed to sustainable development and then proceeds to do so. Alternatively, those already elected could learn the importance of sustainability on the job. Even if such a politician did see the light, the shift is difficult, as sustainable development may run counter to their electoral promises. According to Porritt (2009: 21) 'It may be true that voters today are indeed more short-termist and self-interested than previous generations. "What has the future ever done for me?" may well be a familiar knee-jerk response from voters invited to balance the interests of their own generation with those of generations to come'. Porritt, however, also sees the alternative reality that it could just be that many citizens are longing for honest debate and tough-minded leadership about the challenges of overcoming unsustainable trends in production and consumption patterns.

A further problem for both political leaders and leaders more generally relates to management and leadership styles. Often, the focus for both management and leadership is to address the immediate and practical needs of the particular organization. This type of transactional leadership is premised on 'getting the job done' and is preoccupied with power and position. It is mired in daily affairs, is short-term and 'hard data'-oriented. It focuses on tactical issues; follows and fulfils role expectations by striving to work effectively within current systems; and supports structures and systems that reinforce the bottom line, maximize efficiency and guarantee short-term profits. In contrast, the move towards sustainable development requires changes in the way things are done or a transformation. Transformational leadership is based on our search for meaning, is preoccupied with purposes, values, morals and ethics, transcends daily affairs, and is oriented on long-term goals without compromising human values and principles. It designs and redesigns jobs to make them meaningful and challenging, and aligns internal structures and systems to reinforce overarching values and goals (Parkin, 2010: 103). Some political leaders are at least aware of this requirement. For example, a Junior Minister in Northern Ireland's Office of the First Minister and Deputy First Minister (OFMDFM), Robin Newton, described sustainable development as 'a powerful and transformative force and we must harness this force in a positive way to build a better future for our families – after all, our families are our future' (Newton, 2010).

Parkin notes that 'As the twenty-first century progresses, the trend will certainly be towards critical problems slowed or hastened by our ability to solve some of the wicked ones' (2010: 113). Wicked problems are complex and uncertain, with no clear solutions. Critical problems are so bad and urgent, that they need a command-and-adjust response. The need to address climate change is fast moving from a wicked problem to a critical one.

Thus, in order to deal with the realities described above, leadership for sustainable development will require both the softer skills implied by transformation and the hard transactional skills associated with tightly run organizations (Parkin 2010: 104).

Leadership for sustainable development – the essentials

What does leadership for sustainable development actually entail? Swanson *et al.* (2004: 7) note that for leadership to be effective it 'must be grounded in the fundamental principles of sustainable development, that is, it must represent both existing and future generations, and it must understand the interdependency among economic, social and environmental systems'. These are not consistent with the aims and incentives of either our political leadership or our management structures.

The research on the requirements of sustainable development leadership is fairly consistent. The OECD (2002: 5) maintains that achieving a clear commitment and leadership implies addressing the following questions:

- Is there a clear commitment at the highest level for the formulation and implementation of sustainable development objectives and strategies?
- Is this commitment effectively communicated to the various sectors of the government machinery and across levels of government?
- When gaps exist between the administrative and political agendas, are specific efforts made to bridge (or fill) them?
- Is leadership expressed through a sequence of priorities over time?
- Is government maintaining a sense of urgency, despite the longer-term nature of the issues related to sustainable development?
- Are pioneer activities of selected agencies and local communities encouraged, rewarded and disseminated?

Similarly, Swanson *et al.* (2004: 7) describe that the challenges presented to leaders by sustainable development are: choosing approaches for the strategy process; demonstrating commitment and focus; including the intergenerational principle of sustainable development; and addressing the linkages between economic, social and environmental sustainability. Thus, leaders need to understand and be committed to the long-term aims of sustainable development.

The two sets of criteria set out above have been reduced, for the purposes of analysis in this chapter, to four admittedly overlapping headings: obvious commitment and responsibility for sustainable development at the highest level of government; leadership on sustainable development embedded into the main workings of government; support for sustainable leadership at all levels through training, advice and responsibility; and, finally, protection from a lack of leadership through priorities, targets with timetables, obligations and procedures with clear lines of accountability. These are examined in detail in the context of the UK administrations, below.

Commitment and responsibility at the highest level of government

State responsibility for the many aspects of sustainable development is divided between levels of government in the UK and elsewhere. As explained by the Commission on Sustainable Development (CSD): 'The political process involves ensuring the existence of a strong political commitment from the top leadership as well as from local authorities of a country' (Division for Sustainable Development, UNDESA, 2002: 2). Indeed, McNeill (2007) agrees that leadership for sustainable development by Heads of State and local governments is crucial. He observes that in Canada, it was one of the provincial governments that led the sustainable development field for a number of years because of the personal commitment and drive of the Head of Government (MacNeill, 2007: 22).[1] In the UK, while energy policy is largely a matter reserved to the UK Government, education and nature conservation are largely devolved matters, dealt with separately for the different parts of the UK, while waste management and development control are the responsibility of local authorities. The UK Sustainable Development Commission (SDC) has, on more than one occasion, noted the more unified leadership and drive for sustainability that the devolved administrations have been able to create in Scotland and Wales, and the first steps made in Northern Ireland (SDC, 2004: 21). Moreover, many significant innovations have come from local authorities.

This section explores the priority afforded to sustainable development by leaders in the UK, the devolved administrations and local authorities. It then examines the extent to which real responsibilities for sustainable development rest with those in the highest positions of leadership. The section ends with some good and not so good examples of how leaders in the UK have communicated their views and actions on sustainable development to those both inside and outside government.

The priority afforded to sustainable development by leaders

Essentially, the real key to leadership in sustainable development is where leaders rank it in the list of priorities for the top level of government. As discussed elsewhere, there are alternative perspectives. Sustainable development may be considered solely in the context of the environment or resource management. It may be subsumed under the agenda to address climate change. Sustainable development may simply be considered one of the government's many objectives. For example, many of the UK statutes include a duty in relation to sustainable development. However, this duty is often a secondary objective which is only to be pursued after the main objectives have been met (Ross, 2006). As discussed in Chapters 2 and 4, there is an increasing recognition that these approaches, based on weak sustainability (see Chapter 4), have not led to sustainability. 'Short-termism' has prevailed, with little or no consideration given to the Earth's limits, the needs of future generations and indeed, the needs of the poorer members of the present generation. Parkin opines that leaders' reluctance towards stronger, more long-term visions of sustainability stems from three factors. First, leaders are trapped by an economy that depends on ever-increasing consumption for success; second, we have an impoverished imagination about what policy is needed to make the shift to sustainable (for example, low carbon, pollution, waste) lifestyles, and third, the fear that the cost of rectifying current and historic inequities will be very great. Using only the UK's share of the Earth's resources would require significant sacrifices by its population (Parkin, 2010: 32–6).

Alternatively, sustainable development could be the central organizing principle of government. Jackson concludes that:

> The idea of an economy whose task is to provide capabilities for flourishing within ecological limits offers the most credible vision to put in its place. But this can only happen through changes that support social behaviours and reduce the structural incentives to unproductive status competition.
>
> (Jackson, 2009: 91)

Porritt (2009: 6) maintains that 'The economy drives everything else. Perhaps it shouldn't be that way, but it is. Everything else falls into place, including the full repertoire of "environmental protection measures", if a country's economy is being driven forward in a genuinely sustainable way'.

It is likely that this stronger vision of sustainable development would need to be first developed in a strategic document which then could be used to compel change in the Treasury and elsewhere, inside and outside government.

This approach is possible in the UK and, as discussed in Chapter 4, Welsh leaders have set out strong ambitions for sustainable development in the Welsh scheme for sustainable development, entitled *One Wales: One Planet: The Sustainable Development Scheme of the Welsh Assembly Government (One Wales: One Planet)* (WAG, 2009b). The scheme specifically sets out sustainable development as the overarching strategic aim of all Welsh Assembly Government (WAG) policies and programmes across all ministerial portfolios, and confirms that sustainable development will be the central organizing principle of the WAG, as well as the steps to be taken to embed this approach. Uniquely, it sets an explicit long-term aim for Wales to use only its fair share of the Earth's resources (WAG, 2009b: 9). The First Minister of Wales, Carwyn Jones, in his St David's Day speech on 1 March 2010, emphasized how proud he was that sustainable development was at the heart of the WAG's decision-making process (WAG, 2010). In 2007, the previous First Minister for Wales, Rhodri Morgan, stated: 'We are committed to sustainable development' (WAG, 2007).

Some local authorities are also heading in the right direction. The Mayor of London, Boris Johnson announced that:

> London's ten Low Carbon Zones are now officially 'live', championing the latest energy-busting technologies, trialling innovative ways to go green and helping people save money. Not only will this have a hugely positive impact on our environment but it is stimulating new industries to create job opportunities.
>
> (Johnson, 2010b)

The emphasis of the Scottish First Minister is decidedly on a weak approach to sustainability which retains economic growth as the priority. In his speech to the Scottish Parliament outlining the Programme for Scotland 2009/10, First Minister Alex Salmond stated that the purpose of the Scottish Government has always been 'to focus Government and public services on creating a more successful country, with opportunities for all of Scotland to flourish, through increasing sustainable economic growth' (Salmond, 2009a). However, this is tempered by the leadership's serious commitment to addressing climate change. The Scottish ministers have imposed on themselves a duty under the Climate Change (Scotland) Act 2009 s. 35, to set out specific measures for reducing greenhouse gas emissions to meet Scotland's ambitious statutory targets. In the report, the Scottish Government reiterates that:

> The public sector, including the Scottish government itself, must become a leader in the adoption of low carbon, energy efficient technology and practice . . . Government employees flew half a million miles less in 2008–09 than the previous year and we are encouraged to use video-conferencing as an alternative to travel wherever possible.
>
> (Scottish Government, 2010: 73)

The situation across the UK Government is mixed. According to Porritt:

> Inconsistent political leadership on sustainable development has allowed certain Whitehall departments to remain aloof from any shared responsibility for securing more sustainable outcomes across government. For instance, both the Department for Business, Industry and Skills and the Department for Transport have remained largely resistant to any serious engagement with sustainable development practice, and have successfully defended leadership styles and cultures of practice that have been hostile at worst, and lukewarm at best, to cross-government endeavours on sustainable development. They have relied on an evidence base and on ways of developing new policy interventions that are no longer fit for purpose, given what we now have to do to achieve a very low-carbon, ultra-efficient economy.
>
> (Porritt, 2009: 2)

Moreover, the Conservative-Liberal Democrat coalition Government elected to Westminster in 2010 failed to include sustainable development amongst the economic priorities set out in its programme for government (Cabinet Office, 2010). The environmental measures listed are all very specific, dealing with matters such as tree planting, hunting, whaling and fuel poverty (Cabinet Office, 2010: 17–18). While the word 'sustainable' is used a few times in the document in relation to growth, banking, lending, food production, transport and travel, there is a lack of vision in relation to ecological limits or intergenerational equity. It is particularly disappointing, since the Liberal Democrats have a good track record in this area. The second partnership agreement between Labour and the Liberal Democrats in Scotland promised 'a Scotland that delivers sustainable development; that puts environmental concerns at the heart of public policy and secures environmental justice for all of Scotland's communities'. The environment was presented as a recurring theme and this became known as the agreement's 'strong environmental thread' which was symbolized in the document by an asterisk in the shape of a 'tree' (Scottish Labour Party and Scottish Liberal Democrats, 2003). This influence is not apparent at UK level.

Responsibility at the highest level

The CSD emphasizes that in its view, 'it is also very clear that top level leadership is most important' (Division for Sustainable Development, UNDESA, 2002: 2). As J. MacNeill, Secretary General of the World Commission on Environment and Development (WCED) and chief architect and leader author of *Our Common Future* (the Brundtland Report) (WCED, 1987) explains, 'it is the Head of Government – the President or the Prime Minister who set the goals of his or her administration and the broad policy directions that will be followed to achieve them' (MacNeill, 2007: 21).

Rhetoric at the top level of government is not enough, and the acceptance of responsibility for sustainable development provides much greater evidence of commitment. One of the perceived downfalls of President Barack Obama's leadership following the explosion and subsequent oil spill in the Gulf of Mexico in 2010 was the public's view that he was not taking responsibility for what was happening in relation to the US response (*Independent*, 2010).

In 2006, the OECD (2006: 7) recommended that responsibility for national strategies should be placed in the office of the Prime Minister or equivalent, claiming that institutionalizing sustainable development, whether through national strategies or other means, will not happen – and certainly not in any significant way – if the person at the top is not determined to make it happen or if that individual fails to sustain that determination long enough to see it through. A classic example of the Prime Minister undoing the good work done elsewhere by government was when, on the day after the new Secretary of State for Climate Change, Ed Miliband, announced a legally binding pledge to cut Britain's greenhouse gas emissions by 80 per cent by 2050, covering all sectors of the economy, including shipping and aviation (*Independent*, 2008a), the then Prime Minister

Gordon Brown was threatening petrol companies with an inquiry under competition laws if they refused to pass on lower oil prices to motorists (Grice, 2008). The previous week, the Government backed plans to allow the expansion of Stansted Airport to handle an extra 10 million passengers a year and increase the number of flights from 241,000 to 264,000 (*Independent*, 2008b). By continuing to provide secure supplies of cheap oil and gas, there is little incentive to anyone to consume less fuel or switch to alternative fuels or alternative transport.

For this reason, the level of leadership that is responsible for the production of the sustainable development strategy is particularly telling. MacNeill (2007: 21) observes that 'I have never quite understood how a departmental strategy could be effective in the absence of a national strategy; nor how a national strategy can be effective if it is not driven from the very top'. Further, Meadowcroft (2007: 158) argues that while sustainable development 'requires specialized champions . . . as long as it remains the preserve of environment ministers it will remain on the sidelines of the decision-making that most directly influences the development trajectory'.

In their evaluation of national sustainable development strategies (NSDSs), Swanson *et al.* (2004) found that a key UK downfall is that responsibility for the sustainable development strategy rests with a single department, the Department of Environment, Food and Rural Affairs (DEFRA), instead of resting with the very top level of authority – the Prime Minister or the Cabinet Office.

Leadership on the NSDS at the highest level is very possible. In Norway, Germany, Finland, the Czech Republic, the Slovak Republic and Portugal, responsibility for the strategy lies at the top, in the office of the President or Prime Minister (Swanson *et al.*, 2004: 43). This can be done directly by the Prime Minister's office or by using high-level committees or councils chaired by the head of state. Meadowcroft reasons that 'core politico-administrative agencies (such as the cabinet office, or the office of the prime minister) must take an active interest – establishing across-government priorities, identifying complementarities and managing trade-offs, and driving the achievement of critical goals' (Meadowcroft, 2007: 158). Moreover, this form of leadership already exists in the UK. Although Northern Ireland may lag behind the rest of the UK in its progress towards sustainable development, responsibility for sustainable development and the production of the sustainable development strategy in Northern Ireland lies firmly at the highest level within the Office of the First Minister and Deputy First Minister (OFMDFM). As Robin Newton, Junior Minister in the OFMDFM, explains: 'The NI Executive is supportive of, and committed to, leadership in sustainability, that is why it has made sustainability one of the key crosscutting themes in the Executive's Programme for Government' (Newton, 2010).

There is some evidence of the previous UK Government reluctantly starting to introduce responsibility for sustainable development into its higher levels of leadership. Following the recommendation by the Environmental Audit Committee (EAC) in its 2007–2008 report, that one minister should have overall responsibility for sustainability operations, the Government announced that the sustainability of government is one of the Cabinet Secretary's four corporate priorities (EAC, 2009a: para. 50). This is, however, still a long way from the Prime Minister's Office.

Finally, if sustainable development is treated as an economic goal rather than an environmental one, then the role of strong leadership from the Treasury in this type of approach should not be underestimated. The CSD emphasizes the influence of finance ministers and advocates that: 'There must be effective engagement and close involvement of the Ministry of Finance and Planning in the strategy development process right from the beginning' (Division for Sustainable Development, UNDESA, 2002: 2). MacNeill is more specific about the role of the minister of finance, noting that:

> The budget determines more than any other single statement of government policy, whether development will move in directions that are sustainable or unsustainable . . . Thus, it is the Minister of Finance who makes the most significant statement of policy affecting sustainable development in any given year. And his statement is followed closely by those of energy, agriculture, industry and other ministers – in other words – the ministers who command big budgets.
>
> (MacNeill, 2007: 21)

As discussed in Chapter 7, there are a number of examples of linking financial measures to sustainability criteria in the UK, but these remain ad hoc. One good example is that the Scottish Government has published a carbon assessment of the Scottish Budget 2010–2011, the first such appraisal undertaken anywhere, along with the Climate Change Delivery Plan and Carbon Assessment of Transport (SDCS, 2009: 41). While refinement of the methodology will be required, this represents a significant contribution to the development of effective machinery for addressing carbon in government. At UK level, Porritt notes that:

> there has been no sustained, consistent leadership from Treasury, and that constant indifference (and occasional hostility) has cascaded through the rest of Whitehall and beyond, signalling that while SD is important, it is not fundamental to policy-making. This has been seriously damaging. The importance of the interventions noted above shows what might have been achieved had the Treasury consistently backed the vision and principles set out in the Government's own SD Strategy. Unfortunately, I fear that a large number of officials inside the Treasury don't even know that the Government has got a Sustainable Development Strategy.
>
> (Porritt, 2009: 20–1)

Communicating leadership both inside and outside government

It is not enough to be a silently committed leader. It is essential that this commitment is communicated to the wider public and, very importantly, to those within government. The objectives of this communication vary. The main objective may simply be to pacify activists by saying the right things and then doing nothing about it. At other times, especially during periods of crisis or uncertainty, the communication may be predominantly symbolic. This often is an important aspect of leadership. For instance, the aim of a particular speech may be to show that the leader is aware of the issue, that it is important to them, but that they are still working out how to approach or tackle it. In other instances, the communication is designed to show leadership by demonstrating to followers the way forward, report on progress or account for success or failure. Communication for any of these purposes can take a variety of forms.

The way the leadership uses and treats the term 'sustainable development' itself in speeches, policy and legislation is very telling. Lord Whitty's remarks during the debates on the Local Government Act 2000 are telling:

> The three-pronged strategy is one that is reflected in other legislation and in the key subsection of this legislation . . . I should have hoped that sustainable development would be understood more clearly and more comprehensively than, regrettably, it is. For the purposes of this legislation I believe that some clarity is achieved by making reference to all three [prongs].[2]

This led Jonathon Porritt, the SDC Chairman, to observe:

> So we find ourselves in a classic vicious circle. Politicians argue that using the language of sustainable development can only turn people off, and will therefore only get in the way of genuinely good – and often sustainable – things they want to do. And yet, with the language of sustainable development still absent from high-level political talking or used in a partial or misleading way, it is not altogether surprising that the public doesn't get it yet . . . It is simply unacceptable [to] have politicians arguing that the public will not be receptive to a concept that no one has taken the trouble to explain to them. Ministers at the most senior level need to grasp the nettle and take the argument out to them.
>
> (Porritt, 2002: 46–7)

The consistency of the message is vital for progress towards sustainable development. If the leader uses environment and sustainable development interchangeably or sends mixed messages, then the public and the rest of the public service have very little guidance as to what the main aims are.

Taking a leadership role at an international summit or conversely, failing to attend such a summit, sends clear messages about the priorities of a leader. In 2002, John Prescott, the then Deputy Prime Minister, and Margaret Beckett, the then Environment Minister, headed the UK delegation to the Johannesburg World Summit on Sustainable Development, until Tony Blair arrived (BBC, 2002). Against the backdrop of former US President George Bush's refusal to participate in the emission reduction scheme of the UN Framework Convention on Climate Change (UNFCCC), the decision by US President Barack Obama to personally attend the second week of talks at the UNFCCC Conference of the Parties in Copenhagen in December 2009 was highly symbolic (BBC, 2009).

Certainly, speeches and debates, as well as the forum they are given, provide evidence of the commitment to a particular agenda by a given leader. In November 1989, former UK Prime Minister Margaret Thatcher dramatically hauled the issue of climate change on to the world stage, addressing the UN General Assembly and the world's media, dedicating over 4,000 words to it and ensuring that climate change was recognized as a looming global crisis (Thatcher, 1989). Mrs Thatcher was the first world leader to publicly take the issue seriously. In her speech, she stressed that 'It is life itself – human life, the innumerable species of our planet – that we wantonly destroy. It is life itself that we must battle to preserve' and further highlighted the 'prospect of irretrievable damage to the atmosphere, to the oceans, to earth itself' (Thatcher, 1989). Throughout the speech, Thatcher, as one might expect, took care to emphasize that efforts to deal with the crisis must not be allowed to hinder economic growth. However, while she emphasized that economic growth is necessary 'in order to generate the wealth required to pay for the protection of the environment' she qualified the statement by underscoring that 'but it must be growth that does not plunder the planet today and leave our children to deal with the consequences tomorrow' (Thatcher, 1989; Anonymous, 2009: 46–8). An anonymous article in *Affect* notes, however, that two days prior to giving this passionate speech, Thatcher had demonstrated her commitment to the free market (at the expense of the environment), at the UNFCCC Noordwijk Ministerial Conference in the Netherlands, where the UK blocked a proposal to reduce carbon dioxide emissions by 20 per cent by 2005. The article points out that her conduct set an enduring standard, adhered to over the two decades since, for political inaction masked by elaborate rhetoric (Anonymous, 2009: 49).

Efforts made by the leaders in the devolved governments to attend talks at European and international levels are also significant. For example, Jane Davidson, WAG Minister for Environment, Sustainability and Housing, represented all the regional governments and Wales at the preliminary talks in Barcelona before the Copenhagen Summit (WAG, 2009a) This shows initiative and commitment.

Obviously, no mention of sustainable development at all can also be highly symbolic, but not in a positive way. The Prime Minister, David Cameron, has said very little about sustainable development since coming to power focussing instead on 'sustainable growth'. In May 2011 the UK Government was criticised in an open letter from 15 organisations of losing its way on environmental issues and the 'green economy' (Batty, 2011). In a report criticizing the progress of the Scottish Executive on sustainable development, the World Wildlife Fund in 2002 noted that there had been no public indication of interest in sustainable development by those holding the post of First Minister; no First Minister had taken part in the two annual parliamentary debates on the topic; and none had made a single major speech on the subject (Birley, 2001: 20). In February 2002, Jack

McConnell, Scotland's third First Minister in four years, became the first to set out his thinking on environmental policy in a speech emphasizing that:

> a government with a wide, strong and deep commitment to the environment is not accomplished by putting it in the title of one department. Environmental problems affect urban and rural Scotland. And every part and layer of government can affect the environment. And every department, every agency, every public, private and voluntary body can help change.
>
> (McConnell, 2002: para. 41)

Several subsequent speeches retained traces of the sustainable development theme (McConnell, 2004a, 2004b). As indicated earlier, his Scottish National Party (SNP) successor, Alex Salmond, has regularly spoken about combating climate change and renewable energy, yet it appears to always be in the context of economic growth and not other sustainable development issues/limitations. Indeed, while the First Minister is clearly a leader in the climate change agenda, this is not carried over to the more general context of sustainability. In his speech entitled 'Choosing Scotland's Future' in January 2010, he spoke of developing a low-carbon economy which would tackle climate change, but first and foremost would be 'creating real wealth' for Scotland (Salmond, 2010b). In contrast, and on a more positive note, whilst not the top level of Scottish leadership, Scottish Environment Secretary Richard Lochhead has at least shown interest in sustainable development issues, referring to the limits of the Earth's natural resources: 'Scotland is embarking on the zero-waste journey to protect our environment and help our economy. We can't go on as business as usual because we can't afford to and because resources are finite' (Lochhead, 2010).

The speeches of Northern Ireland Environment Minister Edwin Poots often appear as trying to convey a new set of values on his listeners in line with sustainable development. For example, when speaking at the Futuresource 2010 conference, a major exhibition and conference for the sustainable waste, recycling and resource management sector, Mr Poots emphasized that:

> The reality is that we cannot continue to dump our waste in large holes in the ground, without thought for the materials and energy that can be recovered, or for its impact on our environment . . . Aspiring to zero waste means changing behaviours, it means reducing what we use, reusing and recycling goods and materials, maximizing the use of resources. It also means thinking creatively and innovatively to produce a sustainable, dynamic economy.
>
> (Poots, 2010a)

Similarly, in his speech at the 2010 Biodiversity Conference, Mr Poots noted that:

> Biodiversity is quite simply the variety of life on earth and is essential for sustaining the natural living systems that provide us with food, fuel, health,

wealth and other vital services and resources . . . We are part of this system and we need to focus on the challenge of safeguarding our natural environment, both at a global and local level.

(Poots, 2010b)

Jane Davidson, WAG Minister for Environment, Sustainability and Housing regularly gives speeches which are examples of a leader communicating vision and action on sustainable development. In speaking to Assembly Members on the introduction of a charge for single-use carrier bags, she stated 'I have long said that carrier bags represent a waste of resources' and explained that she hoped to come to an agreement with retailers whereby the net receipts of the charge would go to environmental projects (Davidson, 2009a). Speaking in September 2009 on the announcement of Wales's first low-carbon town, Ms Davidson noted that 'By becoming Wales's first low-carbon town, Aberdare will now be at the forefront of bringing about a new way of living within our resources, whilst also ensuring communities and businesses can succeed and grow' (Davidson, 2009b).

Porritt (2009) hypothesizes that sustainable development may be an easier concept to operationalize at the sub-national level. In his review of the standing of sustainable development in government in the UK, he notes that 'the new devolved system has opened up political space for innovation in Scotland and Wales, and that there has been a potentially helpful break with "path dependence"' (Porritt, 2009: 46). This allows the leaders in the devolved administrations to be more proactive. Thinking idealistically, it may be the case that strong sustainable development leadership in one UK administration may put pressure on others to follow suit. Indeed, sustainable development may be an area within the remit of the devolved administrations where they can draw a contrast with the UK Government, or actually do something innovative. More cynically, one could also argue that the devolved administrations can safely sound radical about issues like sustainable development while being unable to deliver, as the key drivers, such as energy, are still the UK Government's responsibility.

The same is true in relation to leadership at the highest level of local authority government. Boris Johnson, the Mayor of London, speaking about climate change and renewable energy, said:

To improve our quality of life, care for our planet and save money from our pockets, we need to adapt our homes and workplaces, moving London to an energy-efficient future. This has a host of broader benefits including the creation of new jobs and industries. This cannot be tackled only with top-down solutions from politicians but through a collective response.

(Johnson, 2010a)

This particular passage could be symbolic rhetoric except that it was accompanied by a list of actions and commitments (see earlier reference to Johnson, 2010b).

Blair and Evans in their 2004 report on sustainable development within local governance concluded that, 'However strong the rhetoric for sustainable development within policy, the practice reveals a lack of political commitment at all levels to take tough decisions but also seize opportunities for innovation and special community leadership role' (Blair and Evans, 2004: 26). The fact remains, however, as noted by Porritt (2009: 52) in his final report, that much of the progress made in local authorities:

> in SD in general and climate action in particular has been found to depend on 'wilful individuals' who have managed to innovate in spite of constraints . . . Capacity has also been limited by lack of resources, confusion, lack of leadership from the top in many councils, and poor skills for 'doing SD'.
>
> (Porritt, 2009: 52)

Thus, among local authorities, like the other levels of government, there are examples at both ends of the spectrum.

Embedding sustainable development into high-level workings of government

Joined-up policies like sustainable development require visible leadership from the political centre that is effectively transposed to individual departments or directorates through ministers. As discussed later (in Chapter 7), in the UK not only are many powers devolved to the Scottish, Welsh and Northern Ireland administrations, but even within the UK Government itself, power is allocated to the Secretaries of State who head up government departments. As elected members of the ruling government, Secretaries of State should ensure their departments adhere to overall government policy however, this fragmentation of actual power has led to individual departments developing their own ways of working and their own priorities (see Chapter 7). The OECD (2002: 5) notes that 'stronger political leadership is needed to shape the debate on how to take sustainable development forward' and 'this leadership has, in turn, to address problems that result from "silo" thinking, from a reluctance to cede decision-making authority, and from "short-termism"'.

Thus, a conundrum exists. As observed by Kavanagh and Richards (2001: 17), 'Joined-up government relies on prime ministerial authority rather than a well-established institutional base and new cultural values. In theory, it is possible for departments spontaneously to join up. In practice, the stimulus usually comes from elsewhere – the centre'. For each of the UK administrations, this means that not only must the Prime/First Minister show a firm commitment, but that this must then be communicated, understood and put into action by the Cabinet, all ministers and then by the senior public service.

Transformational leadership strategies demand that internal structures and systems are aligned and realigned to reinforce overarching values and goals and not simply focus on the daily chores at hand (Parkin, 2010: 103). Thus, coordination requires the development of mechanisms and structures which facilitate discussion, sharing of information and joint decision making in line with a clear vision of sustainable development. Several high-level coordination tools have been introduced for sustainable development in the various administrations in the UK, however, they have also fallen victim to the political preferences of new leaders. Most of these are discussed in Chapter 7. However, four tools have relevance to leadership for sustainable development: the use of the special cabinet or other ministerial committees; the use of official committees; the allocation of responsibility to senior public servants across government; and opportunities for coordination between levels of government.

Cabinet and other ministerial committees

Three of the four of the UK administrations have seen the value of having high-level ministerial and cabinet committees whose remit it is to promote sustainable development. However, it is only the Welsh committee that has stood the test of time, and cabinet committees seem to have lost favour with more recent administrations in the UK and Scotland.

As early as 1990, the Conservative Government under Prime Minister Margaret Thatcher established an Environment Cabinet Committee to pursue cross-departmental environmental coordination, as well as an inter-ministerial network of 'Green ministers' to provide leadership within individual departments for 'the greening government agenda' (see Chapter 7). In 1997, the then Labour Prime Minister Tony Blair retained both committees but raised the profile of the renamed Cabinet Committee on Environment and Sustainable Development (ENV) by appointing the Deputy Prime Minister to its chair.[3]

Following recommendations by the EAC, the ENV's remit became more explicit: 'to consider environmental policies and coordinate those on sustainable development'. After the June 2001 election, the remit was strengthened further: 'to consider environmental policies and monitor and keep under review those on sustainable development' (DEFRA, 2001: 6). Further recommendations from the EAC led to energy being added to the remit in 2005 (EAC, 2003: para. 73).

A second high-level committee, the Green Ministers Committee (GMC) was originally established to provide leadership, support and some monitoring of the greening government agenda. The GMC had real potential to change culture across the public sector, as it was made up of ministers from each department and therefore had access into every department (Ross, 2005: 27–49; CAG Consultants, 2004: 9). In 2001, the GMC was upgraded to a formal subcommittee of ENV to be known as ENV(G). The new status was supposed to be 'an important step forward and recognition that Green ministers have an important role to play in driving forward sustainable development in Government' (DEFRA, 2001: 45, para. 7.7).

The ENV received two reports from the Green ministers each year – an annual report dealing with the environmental performance (and later sustainable development) in government itself, and a more general annual report on the UK Strategy (DEFRA, 2001, 2002, 2004).

A cabinet committee dedicated to the sustainable development agenda should have been a useful means of encouraging cross-governmental leadership and support. Nevertheless, in 2000, the Deputy Prime Minister, as Chair of the ENV, felt the need to write to all chairs of Cabinet Committees to remind them of the role of the ENV and to encourage them to involve the ENV whenever sustainable development issues arose (HM Government, 2000: para. 2). While an impressive act of sustainable leadership by the Deputy Prime Minister, the incident also highlights how difficult it is to encourage coordination between departments and ministers in pursuit of a common crosscutting theme.

A key difficulty with both UK Cabinet Committees was that due to cabinet secrecy, there was no way of knowing if, when or how often the ENV met, let alone what it discussed or decided, as no records of the meetings were made public. Secrecy also meant it was very difficult to assess whether the ENV was doing anything at all.

The EAC, in an early report, commented on this loss:

> There are some benefits in the transformation of the Green Ministers Committee into a formal Cabinet sub-Committee. It carries more clout, in particular with regard to target setting where it is now able to set targets for all departments. By contrast the status of targets set by the former Green Ministers Committee was always somewhat unclear. The downside of the transition is that the workings of ENV(G) are now covered by the Cabinet code of secrecy, and therefore nothing can be disclosed – not even the number of times it has met.
>
> (EAC, 2003: para. 72)

Indeed, secrecy may have contributed to the downfall of both UK committees. Under Gordon Brown's leadership, the ENV Committee was abandoned and the related Ministerial Committee on Energy and Climate Change downgraded to a sub-committee. The exact timing of the disappearance of the GMC or ENV(G) is more of a mystery. In 2006, the GMC was still in existence (EAC, 2006). Yet, in 2009, in her answer to a parliamentary question, Tessa Jowell, then Minister for the Cabinet Office, stated that:

> There is currently no 'Green Ministers' Cabinet Committee. Issues relating to energy and the environment would generally be dealt with through ED (Environment and Energy) Committee, or its parent Committee, the Economic Development Committee . . . Information relating to the proceedings of Cabinet Committees, including when and how often they meet, is generally not disclosed, as to do so could harm the frankness and candour of internal discussion.[4]

Thus, even the demise of the ENV was subject to cabinet secrecy.

Both UK high-level committees were valuable and the loss has been significant. In the EAC report for 2008–2009, Andrew Lee for the SDC notes that:

There needs to be much clearer ministerial engagement in this agenda, particularly for example with the sustainable development ministers working across government departments and . . . that bringing the sustainable development ministers together with a 'real substantive agenda' could make a real difference in building some championing at ministerial level across departments of what could be achieved.

(EAC, 2009a: para. 53)

Scotland also had a successful Cabinet Sub-committee on Sustainable Scotland. In January 2000, the Ministerial Group on Sustainable Scotland was formed to take forward the environmental and sustainable development commitments contained in the Labour–Liberal Democrat Partnership Agreement and the Coalition's Programme for Government. In 2002, it was upgraded to a Cabinet Sub-committee and until 2005, met quarterly. As a show of leadership, the First Minister chaired the Sub-committee and the Ministers of Environment and Rural Development, Finance, Communities and Enterprise and Lifelong Learning were members. It also uniquely had three external appointees as members. The external experts improved the Sub-committee's knowledge base and this was an example of involving stakeholders more directly. A potential downfall of the Scottish Sub-committee, compared to the UK GMC, was that it did not have a direct link to every executive department, which restricted its efforts in coordination. The Sub-committee's remit was to: identify priorities for action on sustainable development; decide on issues of timing and implementation relating to action to be taken forward on each portfolio; determine how the resources agreed by Cabinet should be used; monitor the overall Executive performance in relation to its environmental commitments; support Cabinet colleagues in embedding sustainable development and environmental justice in their policies and programmes; and report annually to Cabinet (CSCSS, 2003). After 2002, the Sub-committee could take policy decisions directly, rather than having to refer them to the Cabinet for approval.

Whereas cabinet secrecy remains paramount at the UK level, the reports of minutes from the Scottish Sub-committee meetings were available on the internet. The reports show that the Sub-committee made a significant contribution to sustainable development in Scotland by, for example, agreeing a mechanism for monitoring sustainable development commitments in the Programme for Government, as well as monitoring commitments made in the Spending Review 2002 (CSCSS, 2002, 2003). When it came to power in 2005, the SNP dismissed the need for such a committee. Instead, in 2009, it introduced a high-level committee of officials but this does not have the seniority or power of a ministerial committee (see below). The SDC, in its final annual report, reiterated its request that the Scottish Government look afresh at the role of the Cabinet Sub-committee on Sustainable Scotland used by the last administration and consider whether such a model may again be appropriate (SDCS, 2010: 23).

The only Cabinet committee still in existence is in Wales. The Committee on Sustainable Futures is chaired by the Minister for Environment, Sustainability and Housing, although the Deputy First Minister is a member. It provides ministerial oversight and determines priority actions on tackling the causes of climate change and adapting to the impacts of climate change. It is specifically charged with overseeing the delivery of the *One Wales: One Planet* commitment to an annual 3 per cent reduction in emissions. The Committee provides strategic direction and ensures cross-departmental cooperation, including cooperation with relevant UK Government Departments and the UK Committee on Climate Change, as appropriate, to deliver commitments which extend across ministerial portfolios and it is supported in its work by the Climate Change Commission for Wales. Moreover, it is expected to examine other major policy developments, such as the Sustainable Development Scheme and the reduction of Wales's ecological footprint, as well as providing a joint ministerial focus on major investment projects and initiatives, insofar as they present opportunities for demonstrating positive action on climate change and wider sustainable development (WAG, n.d.).

The Committee's agendas, minutes and supporting documentation are all published on the its website. The minutes and papers of one meeting held on 4 October 2010 provide ample evidence of the value and contribution such a committee makes towards supporting leadership in sustainable development. At the meeting, the Minister for Environment, Sustainability and Housing (the Chair) provided the Cabinet Committee with an oral update on the future of the SDC, following the UK Government's announcement of its decision to withdraw financial support. The Chair reported that she was committed to seeking independent advice on sustainable development, which would continue to draw on the best practice from the UK, Europe and wider afield, to inform the Assembly Government when taking policies forward. This commitment had also received the support of the Assembly during the Plenary debate on the Sustainable Development Annual Report. The Chair provided the Cabinet Committee with a report on the work underway to embed sustainable development and climate change in the Department for Environment, Sustainability and Housing. Ministers indicated that it was important to demonstrate what was happening in terms of delivery and the Cabinet Committee highlighted the value of risk assessments and noted the current work underway in relation to flood and coastal erosion for managing climate change impacts in the future. The Cabinet Committee also considered a paper, which set out the progress made on embedding sustainable development as the central organizing principle for Government and considered how the process could be accelerated. It was agreed that it was useful to provide practical examples of where sustainable development had been embedded successfully (WAG, n.d.).

Thus, evidence exists in the UK, Scotland and Wales that this type of specialist cross-government ministerial committee provides and supports high-level political leadership for sustainable development. The value is significant in terms of coordinating policy, sharing best practices, reinforcing sustainable development as a priority, and educating new ministerial members.

Official-level coordination

The OECD (2002: 5) maintains that 'developing leadership and capacity through-out public sector organizations is . . . essential'. It states that this is especially difficult because of the possibility of 'conflict among various interests both in the public and private sectors' (OECD, 2002: 5). Moreover, as Daintith and Page (1999) observe in the UK, 'departmental primacy has been the central organizing principle of the executive branch. The permanent head of department is responsible to the minister for its overall organization, management and staff-ing'. As a result, control tends to be developed and enforced within individual departments. Each department works towards its own objectives in its own way and the centre has remarkably little influence on public sector behaviour (Daintith and Page, 1999: 381). For cross-departmental initiatives like sustain-able development, new institutional mechanisms are needed to facilitate and encourage coordination of effort.

High-level committees of senior officials are vital for coordination in government, especially in relation to joined up and transformational policies like sustainable development, and these have been used in the UK for some time now. The original GMC (ENV(G)) was supported by committee ENV(O) to carry things through to the operational level of departments (DEFRA, 2001). The delivery of the UK Sustainable Development Strategy and its com-mitments is overseen by the Sustainable Development Programme Board (SDPB), which is made up of high-ranking UK Government officials from key departments, and chaired by DEFRA. A lower-level Sustainable Development Policy Working Group also meets before the SDPB to discuss the same issues in order to brief the senior officials who sit on the SDPB (DEFRA, 2011: para. 6.5).

Under the SNP, the Scottish Government has two such committees. First the internal 'Leading By Example High Level Group on Environmental Performance' is to provide the necessary drive and profile to bring about a significant change in the Scottish Government and core agencies' approach to environmental per-formance. More innovative is the 'High Level Group – Sustainable Scotland' which brings together leaders to provide strategic policy capacity and leadership on key sustainability issues. The Group is chaired by Scotland's sole Permanent Secretary, and not only includes senior civil servants, but also representatives of civil society to take advantage of their collective knowledge, different perspectives and practical experience, and to work together on sustainability, particularly the broad area of sustainable consumption. It meets around four times a year, with a remit to:

- Provide strategic policy input into the high-level sustainability challenges Scotland faces
- Champion sustainability, promoting leadership and delivery within the sec-tors and organizations represented, including through communicating on sustainability issues to wider audiences

- Provide leadership on public sector environmental performance
- Advise and comment on progress towards National Outcomes for respective sectoral interests.

The Group has met regularly and its minutes are published so its actions can be reviewed and monitored. In its final annual report, the SDC commented that while stakeholders welcomed that this High Level Group was chaired by the head of the civil service and that it had external members from the public sector, NGOs and business, concern was expressed that it had little influence on policy and was not able to look in depth at issues facing government and help develop sustainable solutions. The SDC has argued that the Group needs a clearer role within government, ought to have the power to ensure greater accountability for delivery of sustainable development within and outside government, and should be given a more active role in monitoring corporate performance (SDCS, 2010: 22).

Responsibility of high-level public servants

Networking by senior public servants is just window dressing if they do not have responsibility for sustainable development or face consequences for failing to meet certain obligations. Responsibility brings with it an incentive to succeed, which in turn, can be an incentive to lead. In the UK administrations, permanent secretaries (the highest level of senior management in government) now have included in their personal performance management contracts, responsibility for how their departments are performing on the UK Sustainable Development in Government (SDiG) and Sustainable Operations on the Government Estate (SOGE) targets (EAC, 2009b). So far, the impact has been limited: 'The inclusion of sustainability goals in the personal objectives of permanent secretaries was an important gesture. There is little evidence to suggest that this had any effect on departments' efforts to achieve sustainability' (EAC, 2009a: para. 49). It is likely to take time, however, for these obligations – and importantly, the consequences of failing to meet them (see below) – to be fully appreciated by all permanent secretaries.

An alternative approach exists in Scotland under the Climate Change (Scotland) Act 2009 s. 44, which places duties on all Scottish public bodies (including the Scottish Government) in relation to climate change. These duties include a duty to, in exercising its functions, act to contribute to the Act's emission reduction targets in a way it considers sustainable. The heads of these public bodies then must direct their minds to this obligation and account for any successes or failures to Parliament, the public and, in the past, the SDC.

Coordination between levels of government on sustainable development

Devolution separates the powers of the state between the centre and the devolved institutions. Thus, while for example, energy and much of transport are powers reserved to the UK Government, environmental protection, local government and town and country planning are devolved matters. The legislatures in Scotland, Northern Ireland (and in certain circumstances, Wales) can pass primary legislation on these matters and their governments are charged with administering the laws in these areas. These areas are interlinked, and leadership for sustainable development requires the different levels of government to work together. Sustainable development requires coordination of all parts of the UK, not only in its relations with other countries in the international and EU arenas, but to ensure that progress is genuinely being made and any improvements made in one part of the country are not being undone by action in another part of the country. The high point for UK-wide coordination for sustainable development has to be the joint production in 2005 of the UK-wide *One future – different paths: The UK's shared framework for sustainable development* (HM Government *et al.*, 2005), which is a clear example of the UK's central and devolved administrations in the UK working together for a common aim. Unfortunately, this level of coordination in the sustainable development agenda has been less evident in recent years (see Chapter 4). In 2011 the UK Shared Framework is overdue for replacement and it will be interesting to observe the leadership dynamics at work between the very different administrations in London, Edinburgh, Cardiff and Belfast in producing its successor. One positive move is that the Joint Ministerial Committee between the UK and devolved administrations has become significantly more active post-2009 and thus, there clearly is a desire on the part of the administrations to address related reserved and devolved issues together. More co-ordination is possible. The North South Ministerial Council between the Northern Ireland Executive and the Republic of Ireland have annual plenary and sectoral meetings (including environment, health, tourism and transport) which address key issues requiring co-ordinated action (NSMC, 2011).

Supporting leadership with training and expert advice

Sustainability leadership requires leaders to have the knowledge necessary to make sustainable choices and often the responsibility to do so. Essentially, leaders need to understand why this is important and often need incentives to take on the sustainability agenda

But committed leaders in sustainable development do not just wander into political arenas, let alone be elected. The key is that elected leaders need to be educated, supported, persuaded and, if necessary, compelled to govern in a sustainable fashion. As such, leadership for sustainable development needs to be supported by training for sustainable development and expert advice based on the best knowledge available.

Training

One way of supporting leadership in sustainable development is to provide training for ministers and civil servants. The details of this training in the

National School of Government and for ministers are set out in Chapters 4 and 6 of this volume. Other examples also exist. In the Government's 2005 strategy for delivering sustainable development, the strategy set out: 'the need to enable, encourage and engage people and communities in the move towards sustainability; recognizing that the government needs to lead by example' (HM Government, 2005: 26). The Government also undertook to: start a 'Sustainable Communities Module' for local authority leaders and chief executives; improve skills and encourage sustainable procurement in local government; and introduce training on awareness and understanding of sustainable communities to local authority middle managers (HM Government, 2005: 41).

One of the difficulties with any training on leadership for sustainable development is how students then transpose what they have learned into their day-to-day lives, especially when faced with the inevitable response of 'it's unrealistic' (Parkin, 2010: 2, 260). Parkin's response is that we need to train what she calls 'positive deviants', who are people who do the right thing for sustainability, despite being surrounded by 'the wrong institutional structures, the wrong processes and stubbornly uncooperative people' (Parkin, 2010: 1). She advocates tackling these hurdles to sustainability leadership by using powers of persuasion, imagination and example, and argues that positive deviance can be exercised at any level of an organization (Parkin, 2010: section 3). Thus, leaders not only need to receive training on what sustainable development is and the tools available for its implementation, but also on how to mobilize action, especially in times of conflict or uncertainty.

As mentioned earlier, in reality, effective leadership for sustainable development at the highest political levels needs a very strong commitment. This is most likely to be found in leaders who already had a strong understanding of sustainable development before their election and whose manifestos are consistent with its goals.

Expert advice

Once elected, however, all political leaders are offered advice from a wide range of sources. Experts can be used to support sustainable development leadership in a variety of ways. Good leadership demands good information. The details of knowledge management tools used in the UK and the benefits of involving a wide range of stakeholders in policy and decision making are addressed in Chapter 6. The use of experts in training is explored in Chapters 4 and 6. As discussed earlier, non-governmental experts also added value to the Scottish Government on its Cabinet Sub-committee and to its high-level committee of officials. Experts have also been used by the UK Government in specialist task forces to advise ministers on certain sustainable development issues (DEFRA, 2005: 154). For example, in 2003, the Secretary of State for Environment, Food and Rural Affairs established a Sustainable Development Task Force, comprising ministers and key stakeholders, whose remit was to advise on delivery of World Summit on Sustainable Development commitments and the development of this new strategy. In 2009 the Ministerial Third Sector Task Force on Climate Change, the Environment and Sustainable Development was introduced to bring together ministers (from DEFRA, DECC, the Office of the Third Sector, and Communities and Local Government) and representatives from the third sector. It aims to identify specific actions that Government and the third sector can take together to tackle climate change, environmental issues and sustainable development more broadly.

Prior to its demise in 2010, the SDC provided valuable support for leadership in sustainable development both in relation to cross-governmental general advice on big policy issues such as the targets in the Climate Change Act, international relations and the production of the national strategies. The SDC also, however, provided a more focused leadership effort. For example, it entered into a partnership with the Department for Children, Schools and Families (DCSF) to build capacity for sustainable development within the DCSF and to affect the delivery of policy across the school sector and beyond. An SDC Adviser was 'embedded' in DCSF from 2005 to help policy teams understand the impact of their policies on sustainability and, crucially, how sustainability can make their own policies more effective. This developed into joint leadership on sustainability across the school sector and wider DCSF policy on children and young people. By 2010, three SDC Advisers worked within the Department supporting its major policy directorates. A *National Framework for Sustainable Schools* was published in May 2006 after extensive consultation with schools, young people, business and third sector organizations. The Framework has developed into a significant force in the schools sector, despite not being separately funded, not being a legal imperative and not having its own pot of money to promote it. The force behind it comes from partners and stakeholders who see the leadership from DCSF and the SDC as giving them the licence and a shared agenda to work with schools (DCSF, n.d.).

Each of the UK administrations also has specialist units on sustainable development to provide internal advice to officials on technical matters such as policy appraisal, procurement and greening operations. The benefits and limits of these units are discussed in detail in Chapter 7.

Using clear priorities, targets, timetables and monitoring to support leadership for sustainable development and protect against poor leadership

Leadership of any kind is not static and changes all the time for many reasons. Indeed, Kavanagh and Richards (2001: 1, 17) warn that high-level commitment is a necessary but not sufficient requirement, because the leader may lose influence or lose interest and an integrated approach to sustainable development needs leadership at all levels. Salim notes that 'sustainable development requires a genuine checks and balances system that is supported by a triangle of equal partnerships between governments, corporations and relevant groupings of civil society to exert corrections in the market as well as remedy governance failures' (2007: 28).

As discussed earlier, there is real pressure on leaders to opt for the short-term quick fix of the challenges directly involving or facing them and their electorate, while sustainable development requires a much longer-term vision and considers the entire global community. Dernbach (2002–2003: 99) observes that 'political and other leaders come and go, but properly established targets and timetables remain in place'. He notes that goals are a management tool for focusing the efforts of administrative agencies, corporations and other organizations, and even national governments and the international community. Goals become the basis around which budgets are developed and implemented, personnel are hired and allocated, programmes are created, modified, or harmonized, and rewards and punishments meted out. He adds that 'an agreement to a target and timetable is ordinarily a commitment to achieve it and by demonstrating greater commitments, targets and timetables are a way of providing additional credibility to decision makers when they claim to be interested in moving toward sustainability' (Dernbach, 2002–2003: 101, 102). All of the UK administrations now use targets to focus the efforts of their political and administrative leaders, the wider public sector and beyond. The UK and Scottish Governments have imposed legal obligations on themselves to reduce greenhouse gas emissions by 80 per cent by 2050 (Climate Change Act 2008; Climate Change (Scotland) Act 2009), the Northern Ireland administration aims to source 40 per cent of its electricity from renewable sources by 2020 (Northern Ireland Assembly, 2010), and the Edinburgh City Council is aiming for zero waste to be sent to landfills, with a target of 75 per cent being recycled by 2020 (City of Edinburgh Council, 2010). The extent to which these targets are enforceable in court is debatable and, in many respects, their legal enforceability is secondary to the symbolic messages they send.

Although the importance of review is discussed in Chapter 10, at this stage it is important to acknowledge its role in reinforcing good leadership. Accountability measures include parliamentary question time, calls to appear before certain committees, naming and shaming, and media attention. Arguably, judicial accountability is possible, but much harder.

Niestroy (2007) notes that Parliaments, like other parts of the public sector, require new mechanisms for coordination and improving policy coherence since parliamentary committees mostly follow this sectoral organization. The UK's EAC, which is tasked with more overarching responsibilities, is a notable exception (Niestroy, 2007: 73). The EAC has been very effective. It has been reporting on sustainable development in government since 1998. Many of its recommendations have been taken on board by Government, including those relating to leadership. Following the recommendation by the EAC in its 2007–2008 report, that one minister should have overall responsibility for sustainability operations, the Government announced that the sustainability of government is one of the Cabinet Secretary's four corporate priorities (EAC, 2009a: para. 50). In the 2007–2008 reporting period, 16 per cent of government agencies did not report their performance. In response to this, the EAC stated: 'We deplore the continuing failure of a significant portion of Executive Agencies to report their performance against their Sustainable Operations on the Government Estate targets' (EAC,

2009a: paras. 41–5). The Government has also been regularly called to account for its decisions. In 2010, the EAC conducted a full inquiry into the embedding of sustainable development in Government and specifically the UK Coalition's decision to cease funding the work of the SDC (EAC, 2011).

As indicated earlier, all permanent secretaries now have objectives relating to their department's performance against the SOGE targets for 2008–2009 and the EAC has threatened to invite permanent secretaries who do not meet their targets to explain their performance in person to the Committee (EAC, 2009a: paras. 47–9).

Conclusion

Sustainable development requires a cultural change across departments and across levels of government, both in terms of integration and in terms of new priorities and goals. Dernbach notes that:

> the conceptual framework provided by sustainable development is not the same as the political commitment needed to achieve it. Nor does the merit of the framework depend on the extent to which it has been successful in persuading people and organizations over the past decade to adopt it. Like all major changes sustainable development will require time and concerted effort to come to fruition in the real world.
>
> (Dernbach, 2002–2003: 136)

A further difficulty is aptly put by Schout and Jordan: 'all this begs the question of what comes first, the chicken of political leadership or the egg of administrative instruments to translate it into practice?' (Schout and Jordan, 2008: 63). The reality is that we need both to happen concurrently now.

First, we need our political leaders to be willing to take up the challenge and become 'positive deviants'. Our leaders are faced with mounting short-term pressures, yet, must address long-term challenges. But we are running out of time. There is no time to wait for a collective shift towards sustainability with the requisite international treaties and immediate institutional reforms to mainstream sustainability. Parkin calls for a:

> very positive revolution: against everything that leads back to behaviours that caused the ecological (and economic) breakdown in the first place and a stampede towards a future that puts improving the quality of life for people and the environment as the primary purpose of everything we do.
>
> (Parkin, 2010: 2)

However, this 'deviance' needs to be supported and mainstreamed as soon as possible by institutional structures, as well as through training, advice and grassroots pressure. The value of high-level cabinet committees to provide the leadership for the agenda and reinforce this through a network of green ministers with ministerial representation from every department and a further network of green civil servants working down from the permanent secretaries themselves would support this change. This approach works because a clear line of responsibility exists between the centre and the departments. It needs to be further supported by the appropriate training for leaders at all levels and across administrations, using the joint committee structures. Sustainable development goals must also be protected from a lack of leadership through clear targets with timetables, legal obligations with real consequences and direct lines of accountability. Opportunities to communicate about sustainable development must be developed and maintained through high-level committees and intergovernmental groups, as well as partnerships. Innovations in sustainable development should be rewarded and protected from the pressures the electoral system brings.

A key aspect of transformational leadership is this ability to get the most out of one's followers and, indeed, encourage leadership amongst them. As Porritt (2009: 21) observes, 'there is a large body of advocates for SD in business that is simply getting on with valuable work that could be accelerated and expanded with consistent political leadership'.

Thus, although they are important stakeholders in the implementation process for sustainable development, our political leaders are not necessarily the most important ones. The next chapter addresses two other key criteria for the effective delivery of sustainable development. Given the unpredictable leadership for sustainable development of our leaders, it is especially imperative to involve stakeholders in the push towards sustainability and to use knowledge responsibly and manage it effectively.

Notes

1 The reference is to the province of Manitoba and its leader from 1999 to 2009, Premier Gary Doer.
2 See the Local Government Act 2000 ch. 22 s. 2 which provides: (1) Local authorities are to have power to do anything which they consider is likely to achieve any one or more of the following objects – (a) the promotion or improvement of the economic well-being of their area; (b) the promotion or improvement of the social well-being of their area, and (c) the promotion or improvement of the environmental well-being of their area. Lord Whitty, House of Lords Debates, Local Government Bill, Column 1482, 25 January 2000.
3 House of Commons Debates, Written Answers, 35, column 542, 31 July 1997.
4 House of Commons, Column 311W, 10 November 2009.

References

Anonymous (2009) 'Review of Margaret Thatcher's 1989 address to the UN General Assembly', *Affect*, 1: 46–50.
Batty, D. (2011) 'David Cameron in danger of breaking green pledge, warn green groups', *Guardian* 14 May.
Birley, T. (2001) *Reality Check: A Review of Scottish Executive Activity on Sustainable Development: Report to WWF Scotland*, Aberfeldy: World Wildlife Fund.

Blair, F. and Evans, B. (2004) *Seeing the Bigger Picture*, Newcastle: Sustainable Development Commission.

BBC (2002) 'Prescott enters summit fray', *BBC online*, 28 August, http://news.bbc.co.uk/1/hi/uk_politics/2220790.stm, accessed 22 May 2011.

BBC (2009) 'Obama switches climate change visit to end of summit', *BBC Online*, 4 December, http://news.bbc.co.uk/1/hi/8396591.stm, accessed 22 May 2011.

Cabinet Office (2010) *The Coalition: Our Programme for Government*, London: Cabinet Office.

Cabinet Sub-Committee on Sustainable Scotland (CSCSS) (2002) *Annual Report*, London: CSCSS.

CSCSS (2003) *First Report of Meeting held 5 November 2003*, London: CSCSS.

CAG Consultants (2004) *Is the Scottish Executive Structured and Positioned to Deliver Sustainable Development?*, 10th Report, vol. 2, Edinburgh: Environment and Rural Development Committee.

City of Edinburgh Council (2010) Waste Strategy 2010–2025.

Cussons, S. (2006) *Review of Statutory Sustainable Development Duties*, London: Department for Environment, Food and Rural Affairs.

Daintith, T. and Page, A. (1999) *The Executive in the Constitution: Structure, Autonomy and Internal Control*, Oxford: Oxford University Press.

Davidson, J. (2009a) 'Charge on single use carrier bags to come into force by 2011', Press Release, 3 November, Cardiff: Welsh Assembly Government.

Davidson, J. (2009b) 'Aberdare to lead green energy drive as first low carbon town in Wales', Press Release 14 September, Cardiff: Welsh Assembly Government.

Davidson, J. (2010) 'Minister calls on Wales to celebrate fair trade fortnight', Press Release 23 February, Cardiff: Welsh Assembly Government.

Department for Children, Schools and Families (DCSF) (n.d.) http://www.teachernet.gov.uk/sustainableschools/, accessed 4 January 2010.

Department of Environment, Heritage and Local Government (n.d.) 'Plastic bags', http://www.environ.ie/en/Environment/Waste/PlasticBags/, accessed 15 August 2010.

Department of Environment, Food and Rural Affairs (DEFRA) (2001) *Greening Government: Third Annual Report*, London: DEFRA.

DEFRA (2002) *Sustainable Development in Government: First Annual Report 2002*, London: DEFRA.

DEFRA (2003) *Sustainable Development in Government: Second Annual Report 2003*, London: DEFRA.

DEFRA (2004) *Achieving a Better Quality of Life – Review of Progress towards Sustainable Development: Government Annual Report 2003*, London: DEFRA.

DEFRA (2005) *The UK Strategy for Sustainable Development: Securing the Future*, London: DEFRA.

DEFRA (2011) 'Written Evidence to the Environmental Audit Committee for its inquiry Embedding sustainable development across Government, after the Secretary of State's announcement on the future of the Sustainable Development Commission' (ESD 30), http://www.publications.parliament.uk/pa/cm201011/cmselect/cmenvaud/writev/esd/esd30.htm, accessed 20 May 2011.

Dernbach, J. (2002–2003) 'Targets, timetables and effective implementing mechanisms: Necessary building blocks for sustainable development', *William & Mary Environmental Law and Policy Review*, 27: 79–136.

Division for Sustainable Development, UNDESA (2002) 'Guidance in preparing national sustainable development strategy: Managing sustainable development in the new millennium', Background Paper No. 13, DESA/DSD/PC2/BP13, Rome: Department of Economic and Social Affairs.

The ENDS Reports (1999) 'Green Ministers' first report', *The Ends Reports*, 294: 7.

Environment and Rural Development Committee (2004) *10th Report,* Vol. 1, SP Paper 206, Edinburgh: Scottish Parliament.

Environmental Audit Committee (EAC) (2003) *Greening Government 2003 Thirteenth Report 2002–03,* HC 961, London: House of Commons.

EAC (2006) *Sustainable Development Reporting by Government Departments Seventh Report 2005–2006,* HC 1322, London: EAC.

EAC (2009a) *Greening Government: Sixth Report of Session 2008–2009,* HC 503, London: House of Commons.

EAC (2009b) *Greening Government: Government's Response to the Committee's Sixth Report of Session 2008–2009: Seventh Special Report of Session 2008–2009,* HC 1014, London: House of Commons.

EAC (2011) *Embedding Sustainable Development across Government, after the Secretary of State's Announcement on the Future of the Sustainable Development Commission: First Report of Session 2011,* HC 504, London: EAC.

Grice, A. (2008) 'Brown: Petrol firms must lower fuel prices or face OFT inquiry', *Independent,* 17 October.

Hardi, P. and Zdan, T. (eds) (1997) *Assessing Sustainable Development: Principles in Practice,* Winnipeg: International Institute for Sustainable Development.

HM Government (2000) *The Government's Response to the Environmental Audit Committee's Report on The Greening Government Initiative: First Annual Report from the Green Ministers Committee,* London: HMSO.

HM Government (2005) *Securing the Future: Delivering UK Sustainable Development Strategy,* London: DEFRA.

HM Government, Scottish Executive, Welsh Assembly Government, Northern Ireland Office (2005) *One future – different paths: The UK's shared framework for sustainable development,* London: DEFRA.

Independent (2008a) 'Britain to pledge legally-binding emissions cut', *Independent,* 16 October, http://www.independent.co.uk/environment/climate-change/britain-to-pledge-legallybinding-emissions-cut-963363.html, accessed 22 May 2011.

Independent (2008b) 'Government green light for Stansted expansion', *Independent,* 9 October, http://www.independent.co.uk/news/uk/home-news/government-green-light-for-stansted-expansion-955874.html, accessed 22 May 2011.

Independent (2010) Leading article 'Deep implications of the Gulf of Mexico oil spill', *Independent,* 28 May, http://www.independent.co.uk/opinion/leading-articles/leading-article-deep-implications-of-the-gulf-of-mexico-oil-spill-1984895.html, accessed May 2011.

Jackson, T. (2009) *Prosperity without Growth: Transition to a Sustainable Economy,* London: Sustainable Development Commission.

Johnson, B. (2010a) 'Mayor calls for Londoners' ideas to help tackle climate change', 9 February, Greater London Authority.

Johnson, B. (2010b) 'London's energy-busting Low-Carbon Zones go live', 19 March, Greater London Authority.

Kavanagh, D. and Richards, D. (2001) 'Departmentalism and joined-up government: Back to the future?', *Parliamentary Affairs,* 54: 1–18.

Lochhead, R. (2010) 'Zero Waste Plan', Edinburgh: Scottish Government.

MacNeill, J. (2007) 'Leadership for sustainable development', in OECD, *Institutionalizing Sustainable Development,* Paris: OECD.

McConnell, J. (2002) First Minister's Speech, Edinburgh, 18 February, http://www. spokes.org.uk/oldsite/firstministerspeech.htm, accessed 23 August 2010.

McConnell, J. (2004a) Lecture at Sabhal Mor Ostaig, Skye.

McConnell, J. (2004b) First Minister's Speech on Renewable Energy.

Meadowcroft, J. (2007) 'National sustainable development strategies: Features, challenges and reflexivity', *European Environment*, 17(3): 152–63.

Newton, R. (2010) 'World's first Sustainable Ocean Summit launched in Belfast', Belfast: Northern Ireland Executive.

Niestroy, I. (2007) 'Sustainable development governance structures in the European Union', in OECD *Institutionalizing Sustainable Development*, Paris: OECD.

North South Ministerial Council (NSMC) (2011) Environment Sectoral Formal Joint Communique, Paper NSMC ENV 1(11)JC, Armagh, NSMC Joint Secretariat.

Northern Ireland Assembly Committee for Enterprise, Trade and Investment (2010) Official Report 18 November, http://www.niassembly.gov.uk/record/committees2010/ ETI/101118_RenewableEnergyInquiry.htm, accessed 11 January 2011.

Organisation for Economic Co-operation and Development (OECD) (2002) *Improving Policy Coherence and Integration for Sustainable Development: A Checklist*, Paris: OECD.

OECD (2006) *Good Practices in the National Sustainable Development Strategies of OECD Countries*, Paris: OECD.

Parkin, S. (2010) *The Positive Deviant: Sustainability Leadership in a Perverse World*, London: Earthscan.

Poots, E. (2010a) 'Poots speaks at high profile international conference and trade fair', 15 June, Belfast: Northern Ireland Executive.

Poots, E. (2010b) 'Environment minister celebrates the protection of our natural environment', 21 April, Belfast: Northern Ireland Executive.

Porritt, J. (2002) *Achieving a Better Quality of Life: Government Annual Report 2001*, London: DEFRA.

Porritt, J. (2009) 'The standing of sustainable development in government', http://www. jonathonporritt.com/pages/2009/11/the_standing_of_sustainable_de.html, accessed 12 April 2010.

Ross, A. (2003) 'Is the environment getting squeezed out of sustainable development?', *Public Law*, Summer: 249–59.

Ross, A. (2005) 'The UK approach to delivering sustainable development in government: A case study in joined-up working', *Journal of Environmental Law*, 17(1): 27–49.

Ross, A. (2006) 'Sustainable development in Scotland post devolution', *Environmental Law Review*, 8: 6–32.

Salim, E. (2007) 'The paradigm of sustainable development', in OECD *Institutionalizing Sustainable Development*, Paris: OECD.

Salmond, A. (2009a) Programme for Scotland 2009/10, Edinburgh: Scottish Parliament.

Salmond, A. (2009b) 'Working towards a low carbon economy', Edinburgh: Scottish Government.

Salmond, A. (2010a) Speech at Sustainable Scotland Summit, June.

Salmond, A. (2010b) 'Green investment can build prosperity', 13 January, Edinburgh: Scottish Government.

Salmond, A. (2010c) 'Renewable energy agreement', 16 July, Edinburgh: Scottish Government.

Schout, A. and Jordan, A. (2008) 'Administrative instruments', in A. Jordan and A. Lenschow (eds) *Innovation in Environmental Policy: Integrating the Environment Sustainability*, Cheltenham: Edward Elgar.

Scottish Government (2010) *Low Carbon Scotland: The Draft Report on Proposals and Policies: Scotland – A Low Carbon Society.*

Scottish Labour Party and Scottish Liberal Democrats (2003) *A Partnership for a Better Scotland: Partnership Agreement,* Edinburgh: Scottish Government.

Sustainable Development Commission (SDC) (2004) *Shows Promise. But Must Try Harder: An Assessment by the Sustainable Development Commission of the Government's Reported Progress on Sustainable Development over the Past Five Years,* London: SDC.

Sustainable Development Commission Scotland (SDCS) (2009) *Sustainable Development: Third Annual Assessment of Progress by the Scottish Government,* Edinburgh: SDCS.

SDCS (2010) *Fourth Annual Assessment of Progress by the Scottish Government,* Edinburgh: SDCS.

Swanson, D., Pinter, L., Bregha, F., Volkery, A. and Jacob, K. (2004) *National Strategies for Sustainable Development: Challenges, Approaches and Innovations in Strategic and Co-ordinated Action,* Winnipeg and Eschborn: IISD and Deutsche Gesellschaft für TechnischeZusammenarbeit.

Thatcher, M. (1989) Speech to United Nations General Assembly (Global Environment) 8 November 1989, http://www.margaretthatcher.org/speeches/displaydocument. asp?docid=107817, accessed 11 January 2011.

United Nations (UN) (2002) *Plan of Implementation of the World Summit on Sustainable Development,* A/CONF.199/20/Res.2, New York: UN.

Welsh Assembly Government (WAG) (2007) 'Wales adopts the three "Ws" to tackle climate change', 6 December, Cardiff: WAG.

WAG (2009a) 'Regional Governments must not be excluded from a new deal on climate change', 5 November, Cardiff: WAG.

WAG (2009b) *One Wales: One Planet: The Sustainable Development Scheme of the Welsh Assembly Government,* Cardiff: WAG.

WAG (2010) 'First Minister sends St David's Day greetings around the world', 1 March, Cardiff: WAG.

WAG (n.d.) Sustainable Futures Cabinet Committee, http://194.174.16.149/about/ cabinet/cabinetsubcommittees/cc/;jsessionid=JyZpTQNBvWNC9M5pZC7hPDpSfZh 2shhNlhn0B04DmvhRSlCJVptJ!680693219?lang=en, accessed 26 July 2011.

World Commission on Environment and Development (WCED) (1987) *Our Common Future,* Oxford: Oxford University Press.

6 Stakeholder involvement and efficient knowledge management

This chapter explores – together – the next two Organisation for Economic Co-operation and Development (OECD) criteria for effective implementation of sustainable development: stakeholder involvement and efficient knowledge management. It is clear that governments alone cannot deliver sustainable development and the support of individuals, businesses, the voluntary sector and the wider public sector is needed. At the same time, the science (including economics and other social sciences) being used to underpin our decision making is becoming increasingly complicated and is often uncertain. Moreover, different perspectives bring different viewpoints. Achieving all of this within a timely, cost-effective and certain manner is essential for good governance and for sustainable development.

This chapter begins by exploring notions of good governance and the reasoning behind involving stakeholders and the wider public in decision making. It then examines the need for research and sound science, and the limits of science, as well as the need to ensure not only that these are explained and understood by stakeholders and the public, but also that the views, experiences and perspectives of stakeholders and the public are incorporated into decision-making processes. The chapter then reviews some of the mechanisms used in the UK for involving stakeholders and the wider public, and for managing knowledge. This review adopts an illustrative approach, focusing on examples of good practice while at the same time acknowledging that these are often ad hoc and can be contrasted with instances where the practice has been poor, ill-conceived, misunderstood, or resulting in ineffective decisions and policies. The chapter ends with a call for stakeholder involvement and knowledge management being explicitly incorporated into an iterative and holistic approach to sustainable development. This approach is explored more fully in Chapter 13.

Good governance, stakeholder involvement and knowledge management

The OECD emphasizes that: 'Good governance and sound public management are preconditions for the implementation of sustainable development policies' (OECD, 2002: 2). Consistent with this view, the UK Government and devolved administrations' joint Strategic Framework, *One future – different paths: The*

UK's shared framework for sustainable development sets out a clear commitment to using good governance which involves 'Actively promoting effective, participative systems of governance in all levels of society – engaging people's creativity, energy, and diversity' (HM Government *et al.*, 2005: 8).

Modern good governance has the capacity to adapt to new events, scientific developments, and differing and changing perspectives. In other words, policy and decision-making processes need to be participative, self-critical, iterative and flexible. This type of approach is present in adaptive management strategies whereby decision makers and implementers are constantly monitoring and learning about the effects of their actions, correcting errors, improving their understanding and making adjustments (Lee, 1993: 7, 9). This is particularly important for sustainable development because of the difficult intellectual, policy and political challenges of integrating environment into decision making. Effective adaptive management strategies demand stakeholder and public involvement and efficient knowledge management for reasons set out below.

Stakeholder and public involvement

Traditionally, the public participates in the democratic process by voting and holding ministers to account via members of Parliament. This form of representative democracy has been strengthened recently through reforms to the electoral system and improved access to information to enable the electorate to make more educated choices (Oliver, 2003: 34).[1] Oliver (2003: 35) observes that the democratic process also involves more direct citizen participation in government, such as the opportunity to put one's views forward, as well as rights to: be consulted; make representations; receive responses; and access information. These processes can take many forms and result in varying degrees of influence on the final decision.

Under various international agreements, the UK has committed itself to involving the public more in decision making.[2] The OECD, the Commission on Sustainable Development and the UK Sustainable Development Commission (SDC) all emphasize the importance of effective stakeholder involvement and efficient knowledge management for sustainable development (OECD, 2002: 6; Division for Sustainable Development, UNDESA, 2002; SDC, 2004).

Stakeholders are defined for the purposes of this chapter as those persons directly involved or affected by policies or decisions. They may include the regulated, the regulator, an owner of land, the relevant community (including a global community at times), non-governmental organizations representing affected interests, local or competing businesses, users of services and recipients of benefits or disadvantages. Where possible, this chapter includes the wider public in the definition of stakeholders, but it is occasionally necessary to distinguish between stakeholders and the wider public, as the reasons for their involvement sometimes differ.

Stakeholders who are directly involved or affected by policies or decisions need to be involved in order to 'ensure the participation of decision-makers to secure a firm link to adopted policies and resulting action' (Hardi and Zdan, 1997, 3). Oliver notes that:

> participation, in the sense of consultation and being listened to on the part of those affected by possible policy changes, may result in better-prepared and thought out proposals being implemented . . . Involving affected parties means they are more likely to understand the reasoning behind certain decisions and thus, increase acceptability of decisions and in turn the likelihood of them being implemented.
>
> (Oliver, 2003: 34–5)

Arguably, as many as possible of the directly affected stakeholders ought to be involved. Principle 8 of the Bellagio Principles provides that 'assessment of progress toward sustainable development should first obtain broad representation of key grassroots, professional, technical and social groups, including youth, women, and indigenous people – to ensure recognition of diverse and changing values' (Hardi and Zdan, 1997).

Many of the same benefits are true in relation to involving the wider public:

> without broad participation, it is impossible to reflect the diverse and changing nature of values held across society, and chosen courses of action will respond to the short-term needs of a particular interest group rather than being founded in the aspirations of a cross-section of society.
>
> (Hodge and Hardi, 1997: 18)

For this reason, it is often wise to treat the wider public as stakeholders. Hardi and Zdan maintain that fundamental to sustainable development is:

> the realization that the range of stakeholders must assume responsibility for and participate in resolution of the many human and ecological problems now before us. Involving them in decision-making processes governing conditions that affect them, they will be more likely to assume responsibility and act.
>
> (Hodge and Hardi, 1997: 18)

Finally, participating in decisions about one's future is a good in itself. Participation allows people to feel in control of their lives, and this has been found to be an essential component of human wellbeing (Thirion, 2008).

Efficient knowledge management

Efficient knowledge management seeks to address the difficulty in trying to make the very complicated, complex and unpredictable nature of sustainable development accessible to stakeholders with different backgrounds and objectives. As noted by the OECD:

Scientific knowledge should be the basis for raising awareness in different constituencies and increasing the visibility of the sustainable development concept within and outside government (including in the media). However, since conclusive scientific evidence will not be available for many of the decisions to be made, it is crucial to ensure that sufficient debate occurs to confront values, perceptions and views, in order to take decisions that are more universally acceptable.

(OECD, 2002: 3)

This requires governments to judge their interventions in the policy debate appropriately. To this end, the OECD maintains that governments should: fund research based on a range of paradigms and options including 'dissident opinions'; stipulate that scientific institutes should reflect broader societal concerns, where appropriate; and organize public discussion guided by concrete scenarios on conflicting information and knowledge (OECD, 2002: 5).

Similarly, the Bellagio Principles set out explicitly that the assessment of progress towards sustainable development should ensure that the methods and data used are accessible to all and make explicit all judgements, assumptions and uncertainties in data and interpretations (Hardi and Zdan, 1997: 3). Moreover, the assessment should be designed to address the needs of the audience and sets of user. The Bellagio Principles also require the provision of institutional capacity for data collection, maintenance and documentation (Hardi and Zdan, 1997: 4). The importance of knowledge management is recognized in the UK. Indeed, all of the UK administrations committed themselves to using sound science responsibly in the UK Government and Devolved Administrations joint Strategic Framework, *One Future – Different Paths* (HM Government *et al.*, 2005: 8), which involves ensuring that policy is developed and implemented on the basis of strong scientific evidence, whilst taking into account scientific uncertainty (through the precautionary principle) as well as public attitudes and values.

Efficient knowledge management in the context of good governance and the better regulation agenda

It is essential to counterbalance all this data collection and participation against the importance of actually making decisions and policies in a timely and cost-efficient fashion to provide certainty and security within the system. Essentially, knowledge needs to be managed efficiently. For some time, the UK has signed up to the 'Better Regulation' agenda which is aimed at the reduction of the costs and administrative burden (red tape) on businesses and on regulators associated with regulation, without reducing the regulations' effectiveness (Better Regulation Task Force, 2005; Gunningham, 2009). The objective is to increase gross domestic product (GDP) by reducing the costs of regulation to business. The objectives are to be achieved by, for example, simplifying the administrative process attached to the granting of permits, making the outcomes of such processes more predictable, and ensuring that the decision-making process is not unduly lengthy (Anderson, 2009). The danger is highlighted by Kirk and Blackstock in their review of the use of public participation in modern environmental permitting regulations in both England and Scotland:

> the standard permit processes are designed to meet the Better Regulation Agenda, have thus altered the meaning of 'better quality decisions' in this context. Rather than the idea of improving the range of information and values on which decisions are based by drawing on public knowledge and expertise, better quality decisions in the context of standard permits appears to mean quicker, more consistent decisions.
>
> (Kirk and Blackstock, 2011)

Hence, the challenge for efficient knowledge management is to find or generate quality information within the needed timeframe, sift through it to find the information needed for the particular purpose, and share that information among a wide variety of stakeholders and the wider public in a meaningful way so that policy and decision making is informed, timely and as certain as possible. Various means of resolving this dilemma are explored at the end of this chapter.

The link between stakeholder involvement and efficient knowledge management

The OECD checklist is very clear about the link between stakeholder participation and effective knowledge management:

> the complexity and unpredictability of the long-term effects of most issues related to sustainable development imply that, for most policy decisions to be made, conclusive scientific evidence is not always available . . . [Thus] for many of the decisions to be made, it is crucial to ensure that sufficient debate occurs to confront values, perceptions and views, in order to take decisions that are more universally acceptable.
>
> (OECD, 2002: 5)

This means governments need to accompany their opportunities for stakeholder involvement with improved scientific data, arbitration processes for managing conflicting knowledge, opportunities for free debate, scenarios to show alternatives and mechanisms for accurately disseminating information to a wider audience.

As such, the two criteria (stakeholder involvement and efficient knowledge management) are studied together here. In many instances, knowledge management tools also act to inform certain stakeholders, and vice versa. Thus, while the two criteria are distinct, many mechanisms studied in fact contribute to both.

This chapter focuses on some good practice examples in the UK and EU of involving stakeholders and the wider public, as well as of promoting efficient knowledge management. More specifically, the mechanisms are very loosely grouped into: those used to generate quality information from experts, stakeholders and the wider public; those used to effectively communicate information to stakeholders and the wider public; those used to share and exchange information among decision makers, stakeholders and the wider public, such as consultations; and finally, those used to create genuine partnerships in decision making. The focus in this chapter is on participation and knowledge management in sustainable development decision and policy making. The chapter does not explore the endless opportunities under the many relevant environmental, social and economic regimes, although some of these, such as environmental impact assessment, are discussed in Chapter 7. Moreover, the contribution made by the public and stakeholders in reviewing and monitoring policy and decisions about sustainable development and as key sources of accountability is discussed later, in Chapter 10.

Many of the mechanisms discussed in each grouping will also fulfil other roles. For example, partnerships used in decision making also clearly share information among the partners, and may also generate information. As will be seen, excellent examples are present from around the UK and at EU level and yet, often this good practice is not regularly followed or embedded into the everyday activities of government.

Generating quality information

Expert research

The OECD stipulates that funding quality research into the range of sustainable development options, from a wide range of perspectives, is essential for the implementation of sustainable development. The EU renewed strategy emphasizes that:

> Research into sustainable development must include short-term decision support projects and long-term visionary concepts and has to tackle problems of a global and regional nature . . . There is still a strong need for further research in the interplay between social, economic and ecological systems, and in methodologies and instruments for risk analysis, back- and forecasting and prevention systems.
>
> (European Commission, 2009: 19)

One of the key objectives of the EU Seventh Framework Programme for Research and Technological Development for the period 2007–2013 (FP7) is to contribute to sustainable development. In 2007 and 2008, around 44 per cent of the total budget devoted to cooperative research was allocated to sustainable development-related projects. Two of the Joint Technology Initiatives established under FP7, the 'Clean Sky' and 'Hydrogen and Fuel Cells' initiatives, are also linked to sustainability. The total EU contribution amounts to €1.3 billion.

Moreover, in the European economic recovery plan, the European Commission (EC) proposed three major public–private partnerships around three key issues for sustainability: 'green cars', 'energy-efficient buildings' and 'factories of the future' (European Commission, 2009: 12).

Similarly in the UK, the higher education funding councils have explicitly targeted their hotly contested research funding towards sustainable development research, particularly in the STEM (science, technology, engineering and maths) disciplines (HEFCE, 2010).

Public and stakeholder perceptions and views – surveys

Scientific and other discovery, innovation and development are only one part of the data-collection process. Information is also needed from stakeholders about how the system works, why it is not working, how it could be improved and what those in the system expect in terms of outcomes, as well as from themselves. Moreover, information is needed about public opinion, values, understanding, perceptions and wishes.

The views of close stakeholders may be different from those of the wider public and it is equally important that these views become known. The Sustainable Development Commission in Scotland (SDCS), as part of its annual review of the Scottish Government's progress towards sustainable development, regularly undertook its own stakeholder surveys. For example, in 2008 it conducted an online survey of members of the Scottish Sustainable Development Forum, Scottish members of the Commission's Panel and other stakeholders. The results were used to inform the review more widely. The survey produced valuable information essential for effective decision making and policymaking on sustainable development. The survey showed concern amongst respondents that the Scottish Government is focusing too heavily on economic growth to the detriment of social and environmental factors. One-fifth of people who responded did not think the sustainable development principles were influencing delivery then and did not expect them to do so in the future. The survey, however, also revealed that 75 per cent of respondents believed Scotland's priorities and actions for sustainable development are about the same as, or ahead of, the rest of the UK (SDCS, 2009: 10).

In the same way, public perceptions and attitudes are often unknown or buried in, for example, more general public attitudes surveys, and yet, arguably, all government decision making and policymaking is done in the name of the public's interest. Finding this data involves careful survey work. The UK Government has regularly commissioned surveys of public attitudes and behaviours toward the environment since 1986. Post-devolution, these have focused on England, and more recently other surveys, such as those on wellbeing, have also been commissioned. The environment survey in 2009 was commissioned jointly by the Department of Environment, Food and Rural Affairs (DEFRA) and the Energy Saving Trust to provide a representative picture of what people in England think and behave, across a range of issues relevant to the environment. It consisted of 2,009 face-to-face interviews in people's homes in England. Compared to 2007, there has been a small increase in the proportion of people willing to do things to help the environment – most people said they had some knowledge of climate change, and knowledge of the term 'carbon footprint' has increased. Around half of people saw 'being green' as not being a minority lifestyle, and most people agreed that there is an environmental challenge and that it is not too late to do something about it (compared to 30 per cent two years ago) (DEFRA, 2009: 2).

Communication

The public in the UK have powerful process rights of access to information through the Access to Environmental Information Regulations, Freedom of Information Acts and through the UK's adoption of the Aarhus Convention on Access to Information, Public Participation in Decision Making and Access to Justice in Environmental Matters.[3] Historically, such information has been disseminated to the public using public notices, reports, registers, advertisements and further information provided to stakeholders using more directed methods such as neighbour notification. These methods are all still used, particularly in regulatory regimes, but there is also an increasing reliance on electronic measures, direct campaigns and training.

Regardless of the means used, the information needs to be capable of being used by stakeholders and members of the public. Unfortunately, the initial data produced by the experts and derived from public surveys is often too detailed and technical to be understood by stakeholders or the general public and therefore needs to be adapted and targeted to specific audiences for specific purposes.

The discussion below highlights several excellent examples exist of innovation in improving the dissemination of information in useful and comprehensible ways.

Websites

The internet has provided opportunities for innovation and many of the good practice examples involve creative use of websites. For example, Thinksustainable was launched in April 2005 by DEFRA, alongside *The UK Strategy for Sustainable Development: Securing the Future* (the 2005 strategy), as a package to provide a coordinated approach to embedding sustainable development in government. This package includes communicating clear messages and behaviours through, for example, campaigns, tools and events. A package of 'sustainable development tools' has been developed to help government policymakers as well as those working on projects and programmes to consider how their work impacts on sustainable development. It includes an interactive policy tool, called 'Stretching the Web', a film, titled *The Bigger Picture*, and a game called 'Stockwatch' (DEFRA, n.d.).

Cynnal Cymru – Sustain Wales was set up by the Welsh Assembly Government (WAG) as an independent, not-for-profit organization which promotes sustainable development and provides practical information to help people live more sustainably (Cynnal Cymru – Sustain Wales, n.d.: 1). Following the closure of the SDC, at the end of March 2011, the WAG appointed a new Commissioner for Sustainable Futures to provide advice to the Assembly Government and leadership for sustainable development across Wales. Cynnal Cymru, are to support this new Commissioner, enabling the views and experiences of the wider community in Wales to be shared with him and fed into his advice to government.

Sustain Wales keeps up to date with the latest scientific evidence base, and communication is central to its role. It provides a range of web-based and published resources that inform, inspire and engage stakeholders across Wales to take positive action for sustainable development. The website itself contains a huge array of materials. For example, it contains the details of 12 new case studies which link to the sectoral engagement work around the sustainable development scheme. It also includes academic research and examples of good practice. Among Sustain Wales's other communication successes are regular e-bulletins sent to stakeholders, 12 policy updates prepared and distributed, and a 'Green List' of real sustainability contributors for Wales, developed and published via media such as the internet. Given its strong emphasis on communication, Sustain Wales contributes to many of the categories in this chapter. (Cynnal Cymru – Sustain Wales, n.d.)

Meetings and engagement

Sometimes it is more effective to deal with individuals on a face-to-face basis. Again, Sustain Wales provides excellent examples of how meetings can be used to engage stakeholders. Using sector-specific language, Sustain Wales undertakes targeted engagement campaigns which raise awareness of the urgent need to act on climate change and facilitate greater engagement with WAG's *One Wales: One Planet: The Sustainable Development Scheme of the Welsh Assembly Government* (WAG, 2009). For example, Sustain Wales held three sectoral engagement events to explore how different sectors can help deliver the scheme. One such campaign targeted women's networks in Wales to encourage women to take positive action in the home and their communities. Its 'Sustainable Home' display was taken to two exhibitions to promote sustainability messages to women. Another campaign, directed at mental health networks in Wales, focused on reducing food waste as an area for practical action by client groups (Cynnal Cymru – Sustain Wales, n.d.: 9–12). Sustain Wales also took a visual exhibition of leadership for sustainable development and climate change to at least six community/art/business venues across Wales between September and March 2009 and to a major overseas exhibition (the Smithsonian Folk-life Festival) in July 2009.

Education and training

Meaningful stakeholder and public involvement needs those involved to understand the challenges confronted, their role in overcoming those challenges and specific actions they can take that will really make a difference. Passively providing access to information, no matter how accessible and well presented, is not enough, nor is simply providing information to individuals on request. Sometimes, the new challenges, new ways of doing things and the values underpinning these need to be taught to the wider public or to certain specific stakeholders. As such, training and education are a key part of stakeholder involvement and knowledge management.

The Sustain Wales campaigns discussed above are also excellent illustrations of how tools can educate the public on various sustainability issues. All the administrations in the UK regularly use targeted radio, television and advertising campaigns to educate the public on a range of sustainability issues such as energy efficiency, biodiversity concerns (such as declines in the honey bee and red squirrel populations), coping with winter weather, obesity, consumer debt and smoking.

As mentioned in Chapter 4, sustainable development has now been mainstreamed into the training of the civil service, and courses are offered on leadership, procurement and sustainable development in government by the National School of Government (National School of Government, n.d.: 20, 41, 70). Once again, Sustain Wales is also heavily involved in training at all levels and in all sectors. It provides ministerial briefings, focusing on its work and findings related to engagement and behaviour change. These briefings used to be in addition to the work of the SDC which, until 2011 acted as the Government's sustainable development policy advisers. Sustain Wales also contributes to sustainable development training for civil servants (Cynnal Cymru – Sustain Wales, n.d.: 16–18).

Sharing information between decision makers, stakeholders and the public

Some of the examples of education and training above also encourage two-way dialogue, whereby valuable information is also passed on to those doing the training. This section examines two kinds of tools that, by design, are specifically aimed at achieving this two-way dialogue: networks and consultation processes.

Networks

The European Sustainable Development Network (ESDN) is an informal network of public administrators and other experts dealing with sustainable development strategies in Europe. In 2002, public administrators in charge of national sustainable development strategies (NSDSs) from several EU Member States met for the first time for a workshop-like exchange of experiences in the Netherlands. These events have now become annual conferences. Since 2003, membership has broadened to include the coordinators of NSDSs and the national coordinators of EU environmental integration and sustainable development policies, experts from the EC, representatives from various National Councils for Sustainable Development, and national members of the Sustainable Development Working Group of the European Environment and Sustainable Development Advisory Councils. These annual conferences facilitate an exchange of experience and knowledge in various ways and have resulted in an informal network of sustainable development strategy coordinators and other sustainability experts (ESDN, n.d.). The EC has since advocated a strong role for the ESDN. Among other things, the ESDN should facilitate the exchange of good practices and experiences, gather views on specific priority themes and issues to be discussed by Member States, and mainstream sustainable development issues, vertical integration and coherence between the EU, national and sub-national levels of policymaking (European Commission, 2009: 28).

Sustain Wales collaborates with partners, such as Science Shops Wales, Cardiff University, the University of Wales and other institutions to ensure that relevant research-based information informs their work on areas of shared interest, including behavioural change, leadership for sustainable development, social enterprise, resource scarcity and climate change science (Cynnal Cymru – Sustain Wales, n.d.: 4).

In Scotland, the Sustainable Development Forum was set up in June 2002 to bring people together to work towards a sustainable Scotland by: promoting debate; involving interested parties; raising awareness and understanding; promoting good practice; and making recommendations for action. It is an independent body with no direct influence on Executive policy but is expected to liaise with the Executive across all areas of its work. The Forum meets twice a year and much of its work is conducted by means of online discussion groups. In the past, the Forum has examined topics such as education, media and communication, economics for sustainability, social capacity building, and policy integration. Membership is publicly advertised and open to all. Its actual influence is difficult to measure due to the advisory nature of its role.

The benefits of central and local governments working together are well documented, and all parts of the UK have networks with local government. For example, the coordination of activities in Scotland under Local Agenda 21 is now undertaken by the Sustainable Scotland Network (formerly the Scottish Local Agenda 21 Network). This group includes representatives from all local councils and encourages networking and discussion on the implementation and monitoring of policies and projects on sustainable development. The Network has recently been strengthened by the appointment of a Development Officer.

Consultation processes

Consultation involves seeking the views of stakeholders and/or the wider public so that those views can be taken into account in the decision-making process. The extent to which those views are taken into account varies enormously. Good consultation not only improves stakeholder involvement, it also improves public awareness. Ideally, it should occur early in the policymaking or decision-making process. Given the wide-ranging areas of work of government, there are many varied types of consultation. In most cases, the consultation exercises aim to provide opportunities for all those who wish to express their opinions of a proposed area of work to do so in ways that inform and enhance that work. Consultation exercises may seek views in a number of different ways, such as written papers, public meetings, focus groups, questionnaire exercises or online discussion forums.

The amount of consultation and the quality of that consultation vary enormously, even within each of the UK administrations. Some of the best examples of consultation in the context of sustainable development are discussed in detail in Chapter 4, in relation to the production of the UK sustainable development strategies. Consultation for each of the UK strategies has been extensive. Prior to the production of the first UK strategy produced in 1994, the Department of Environment and the Scottish, Welsh and Northern Ireland Offices all published open letters inviting views on the nature of sustainable development and on the possible framework for the national strategy. A three-day seminar was held with a wide range of stakeholders, and a consultation paper was published in July 1993 which set out the main topics for the strategy. It was sent to over 6,000 organizations and over 500 responses were received. *Sustainable Development: The UK Strategy* was published in January 1994 (UK Government, 1994: 7). A summary of the responses were then added as an annex to the Strategy which included concerns that were not carried through into the Strategy, such as those relating to timescale and the pursuit of economic growth.

In contrast, Scotland has consulted very little on its strategies for sustainable development. Consultation is a crucial part of strategic environmental assessment (SEA) and the Scottish Government extended the SEA directive to include strategies, arguably like *The Government's Economic Strategy* (the *Economic Strategy*) (Scottish Government, 2007). This decision was not made while the SNP was in government but it did not vote against it. However, the *Economic Strategy* appeared out of the blue, with no public consultation process at all. The reasons given by the Cabinet Secretary for Finance and Sustainable Growth, John Swinney MSP in his response to a question posed by the Green Party is contrary to the decision to extend SEA coverage:

> The Government has taken the view that the economic strategy provides a framework for several subsequent decisions that the Government may or may not take, all of which will be subject to strategic environmental assessment as appropriate. The Government has judged that focusing environmental assessment on detailed and specific initiatives, policies and programmes would be more meaningful and manageable. That would give a more meaningful account of the individual environmental impact, rather than the more generic impact, which is therefore more difficult to quantify, of 'The Government Economic Strategy'.
>
> (Scottish Parliament, 2007, column 4426)

Conversely, there is a danger of consulting too much and consequently, getting very little done. Some evidence of this failing is present in Northern Ireland's strategic processes to date and, as of the autumn of 2010, Northern Ireland had yet to produce a set of indicators for any strategy (Chapter 4).

Consultation on sustainable development goes beyond consulting on the strategies. Decisions on individual projects may trigger an obligation to consult or seek representations through, for example, the planning acts or environmental assessment. Changes to legislation will also trigger an obligation to consult. Typically, consultations in the UK involve a written paper inviting answers to specific questions or more general views about the material presented. For example, and somewhat ironically given the previous example, the Scottish Executive produced a written consultation paper about the details of the regulations to implement the Directive on Strategic Environmental Assessment and later produced a separate consultation paper on the principles of the Bill which extends SEA beyond the scope of the Directive. There was also a major conference in Edinburgh and seminars in Glasgow and Aberdeen to raise awareness about SEA and to stimulate debate. These seminars were publicized on the Scottish Executive SEA website. Copies of all the responses received to the consultation exercises are placed in the Scottish Executive library. The views and suggestions detailed in the consultation responses are analyzed and used as part of the decision-making process.

Partnership in decision making and policymaking

In some instances, stakeholders and the public need to be much more actively involved in decisions, especially where these have a direct effect on their lives. Partnership between levels of government is vital for the effective delivery of certain services where responsibilities are shared between levels of government. For example, *Achieving our Potential: A Framework for Addressing Poverty and Inequality,* which was prepared jointly by the Scottish Government and the Convention of Scottish Local Authorities (CoSLA), highlights the benefits of a coordinated approach to tackling difficult problems. It is based around action in four key areas:

* Reducing income inequalities
* Introducing longer-term measures to tackle poverty and the drivers of low income
* Supporting those experiencing poverty or at risk of falling into poverty
* Making the tax credits and benefits system work better for Scotland.

The Framework above complements other joint initiatives with CoSLA, such as the Early Years Framework and Equally Well. Its actions include work by community planning partners to tackle poverty and disadvantage. It is being supported by the £435 million Fairer Scotland Fund (Scottish Government, 2008; SDCS, 2009: 39).

One of the biggest successes in involving a large group of stakeholders in decisions which directly affect their lives has been with schoolchildren under the Eco-Schools programme which has been rolled out across the UK. Eco-Schools is an international award programme that guides schools towards sustainability by providing a framework to help embed sustainability principles into the heart of school life. Once registered, schools follow a simple seven-step process to address a variety of environmental themes, ranging from litter and waste, to healthy living and biodiversity. In November 2010, over 15,000 schools in England, over 3,500 schools in Scotland, over 1,500 of the schools in Wales and over 650 schools in Northern Ireland were registered in the Eco-Schools programme, and 1,222 schools in England, around 1,200 schools in Scotland, 233 in Wales and over 180 in Northern Ireland awarded the prestigious Green Flag (Eco-Schools, n.d.; Eco-Schools Scotland, n.d.; Eco-Schools WAG, n.d.; Eco-Schools Northern Ireland, n.d.).

Partnerships involving non-state actors also exist. For example, the Association of Directors of Public Health (UK) since 2007 has led a collaborative partnership initiative to call on decision makers to take action on active travel by:

- Committing 10 per cent of transport budgets to cycling and walking initiatives
- Setting a 20 mph default speed limit in residential areas
- Creating safe and attractive walking and cycling conditions
- Improving driver training and better enforced traffic laws
- Setting ambitious official targets for increases in walking and cycling.

By 2008, the initiative had over 70 partners, covering a wide variety of interests and including: Age Concern; the SDC, the Royal College of Nursing; Royal College of Physicians; Royal Institute of British Architects; Northern Ireland Cycling Initiative; Strathclyde Partnership for Transport; and Play Wales. In 2009, the funding for active travel represented around 1 per cent of the transport budget and to do what the partnership suggested would require a significant reallocation of transport funds. As of 2011, this had not occurred (see below) (SDCS, 2009: 21).

Challenges

Increased public participation and stakeholder involvement can lead to better decision making. However, several important caveats to this statement are needed. Some highlight potential areas where participatory regimes fall down while others refer to the constraints that necessarily are imposed on wide participation.

First, the participation mechanisms must be appropriate. As observed by Poustie (2004: chs 11, 12), formal participation mechanisms may not be very successful at reaching all those affected, especially those in disadvantaged communities or without access to information technology. Over-reliance on the internet, for example, may exclude certain groups and even fall foul of age or disability discrimination laws. Indeed, participation exercises often fail to generate any public interest. As noted by Rowan Robinson *et al.*, it is not so much that the public is apathetic in these instances, as passive. Members of the public often do have a view that they are willing to express when directly asked, but they may be less willing to reply to a general call for views as this does not trigger their immediate interest. It could also be that they do not believe that they have sufficient expertise to comment on a particular matter (Rowan Robinson *et al.*, 1996: 38). These are issues that many of the campaigns and engagement tools, such as those used by Sustain Wales and discussed above, are directly designed to overcome.

Second, it is essential that the mechanisms used in the name of stakeholder involvement and effective knowledge management are genuine, as opposed to what Arnstein (1969: 217) describes as manipulation or tokenism. For example, consultation processes following a decision are not genuine as the consultations could not have possibly influenced the decision-making process. Education and training which are entirely one-sided and fail to give participants the opportunity to question techniques or objectives are similarly not genuine, and are described by Arnstein as therapy (1969: 217). The Scottish Government's consultations on its *Economic Strategy* and subsequent related policies are clear illustrations of consultation in name only.

As such, the information and decision-making powers need to be properly managed. Wide participation is sometimes not desirable. As discussed above, the Better Regulation agenda, for example, sets out other significant good governance requirements which often conflict with wide participation, including the timeliness of decision making, certainty in decision making and ensuring clear lines of responsibility and accountability. Choosing the appropriate approach is not easy.

Sometimes, it is only necessary to inform or educate the public, while at other times, the public needs to be more actively involved and their views fed into the decision-making process more directly. Erring either way can cause problems. Where views are very persuasive, the participation exercise can actually be a form of co-decision, which may be ideal. The danger here is that the actual (and often statutory) decision makers may wrongfully delegate their decision-making power to one or more stakeholders. Unauthorized delegation of this kind can, in the UK, make the decision open to challenge by judicial review (Bradley and Ewing, 2007: 733).

The reverse is the more common problem, whereby the participation exercise is simply a hoop that decision makers need to go through and makes no difference at all to the ultimate decision. This can occur due to late consultation, a failure to give any responses to consultation or ignoring the work of a partnership in favour of a unilateral decision. In these instances the involvement is simply token, in that it does not really involve the views of stakeholders. It may improve the amount of information available to the decision maker but often, if the decision is already made, it does not even achieve that objective.

A further danger is that so much time is spent consulting and involving stakeholders, that no decisions are made and nothing gets done. In Northern

Ireland, there is recognition that initial consultation is not enough and the Executive needs to start making real decisions and taking real action. The 2010 Northern Ireland Strategy notes:

> We have consulted extensively in developing this document and listened to the views of stakeholders, but that is not enough. We need stakeholders (individuals, community groups, businesses and organizations) to take steps in driving delivery. We are now looking to those stakeholders, and to those working inside and outside of Government, to contribute to the attainment of the targets set within our Implementation Plan and support the priority areas for action.
>
> (Northern Ireland Executive, 2010)

A third challenge is that it is possible for the public or stakeholders, if empowered with decision-making capabilities, to ignore sustainability altogether and choose unsustainable options. As explained by Jacobs, French (2005: 33) notes that at its most extreme, empowerment potentially undermines the very focus of sustainable development. 'Does sustainability now mean . . . whatever emerges from appropriately participative and multi-stakeholder socio-political processes whether or not these are ecologically sustainable?' (Jacobs, 1999: 35). The question has been addressed at the project and national levels, and iterative mechanisms devised to allow both top-down and bottom-up decision-making processes to coexist and support one another. Research by Reed *et al.* found that:

> By empirically testing indicators developed through participatory research, it is possible to retain community ownership of indicators whilst improving accuracy, reliability and sensitivity. It may also be possible to develop quantitative thresholds through reductionist research that can improve the usefulness of sustainability indicators. By combining quantitative and qualitative approaches in this way, it is possible to enhance learning by both community members and researchers.
>
> (Reed *et al.*, 2006: 414)

Thus, combined top-down, bottom-up approaches are possible, but these take time and require careful planning and support.

Fourth, Oliver (2003: 48) warns that with some forms of participatory democracy or collective decision making, 'if things go wrong it may not be clear whose fault, if anyone's, the mistake was'. Thus, if we are going to change the mechanisms of decision making to include stakeholders or even multiple government actors, this change must also be reflected in the accountability mechanisms (Ross, 2005; Performance and Innovation Unit, 2000). This is discussed in more detail in Chapter 10.

Finally, leaders must understand the contribution wide participation and efficient knowledge management makes to the implementation of sustainable development. Poor leadership can easily undo much of the good work achieved by stakeholder involvement and efficient knowledge management. For example, despite the EU's ambitious research agenda, according to Eurostat data, the share of gross domestic expenditure on research and development in GDP in the EU decreased between 2000 and 2007 from 1.85 per cent to 1.83 per cent. This indicator shows a move away from the EU target of 3 per cent by 2010 (Eurostat, 2009).

Similarly, poor leadership has undone much of the good work by the collaborative partnership on active travel led by the Association of Directors of Public Health (UK). The initiative sought support from the highest level of government, including a significant reallocation of transport funds. Yet, in its draft budget for 2010–2011, the Scottish Government failed to signal its commitment to active travel by not increasing the active travel funding within the transport budget, signifying a gap between the Scottish Government's aims and its financial commitments (SDCS, 2009: 21).

Thus, there are plenty of examples of good practice of stakeholder and public involvement and efficient knowledge management occurring in the UK and devolved administrations to deliver sustainable development. Unfortunately, these are often ad hoc instances, reliant on individuals and unsupported by review or monitoring mechanisms. There are also examples of participation in name only or participation which falls on the deaf ears of policymakers. Stakeholder involvement and efficient knowledge management need to be included in the holistic, iterative and reflexive mechanisms put in place to deliver the aims in the national sustainable development strategy and should be based on the substantive principles contained in the strategy. They also need to be supported by review mechanisms and, where necessary, legal obligations which ensure certain procedures are followed, regardless of any changes in the whims of leadership. These conclusions are further developed in Chapter 13.

Notes

1 See, for example, the Scotland Act 1998 ch. 46 ss. 1–8.
2 For example, UNGA (1992a: Principle 10); UNECE (1998: Articles 6–8).
3 These include among others: the Access to Environmental Information Regulations 2004 (SI 3391) Freedom of Information (Scotland) Act 2002 asp13; UNECE (1998).

References

Anderson, S. (2009) *The Anderson Review: The Good Guidance Guide: Taking the Uncertainty Out of Regulation*, London: Better Regulation Executive.

Arnstein, S. (1969) 'A ladder of citizen participation', *Journal of the American Institute of Planners*, 35(4): 216–24.

Association of Directors of Public Health (and partners) (2008) *Take Action on Active Travel*, Bristol: Sustrans.

Better Regulation Task Force (2005) *Regulation – Less is More: Reducing Burdens, Improving Outcomes* (BRTF Report) 'Executive Summary', London: BRTF.

Bradley, A.W. and Ewing, K.D. (2007) *Constitutional and Administrative Law*, 14th edition, Harlow: Pearson.

CAG Consultants (2004) *Is the Scottish Executive Structured and Positioned to Deliver Sustainable Development?*, 10th Report, vol. 2, Edinburgh: Environment and Rural Development Committee.

Cynnal Cymru – Sustain Wales (n.d.) *Work Plan 2009–2010*, http://www.sustainwales.com/home/downloads/90406_-_Final_Work_Plan_2009_-_2010.pdf, accessed 5 September 2010.

Davidson, S., Martin, C. and Treanor, S. (Ipsos MORI) (2009) *SEABS'08: The Scottish Environmental Attitudes and Behaviours Survey 2008*, Edinburgh: Scottish Government.

Department of Environment, Food and Rural Affairs (DEFRA) (2005) *The UK Strategy for Sustainable Development: Securing the Future*, London: DEFRA.

DEFRA (2009) *2009 Survey of Public Attitudes and Behaviours towards the Environment*, London: DEFRA.

DEFRA (n.d.) 'thinksustainable', http://www.defra.gov.uk/sustainable/think/, accessed 7 September 2010.

Division for Sustainable Development, UNDESA (2002) 'Guidance in preparing national sustainable development strategy: Managing sustainable development in the new millennium', Background Paper No. 13, DESA/DSD/PC2/BP13, Rome: Department of Economic and Social Affairs.

Eco-Schools (n.d.) http://www.eco-schools.org.uk/, accessed 19 November 2010.

Eco-Schools Northern Ireland (n.d.) http://www.eco-schoolsni.org/default.aspx, accessed 19 November 2010.

Eco-Schools Scotland (n.d.) http://www.ecoschoolsscotland.org/page.asp?pg=10, accessed 19 November 2010.

Eco-Schools Wales (n.d.) http://www.eco-schoolswales.org/home.asp, accessed 20 May 2011.

Environment and Rural Development Committee (2004) *10th Report*, Vol. 1, SP Paper 206, Edinburgh: Scottish Parliament.

European Commission (2009) *Mainstreaming Sustainable Development into EU policies: 2009 Review of the European Union Strategy for Sustainable Development*, Com 400, Brussels: European Commission.

European Council (2006) *Review of the EU Sustainable Development Strategy: Renewed Strategy*, Brussels: European Council.

European Sustainable Development Network (ESDN) (n.d.) http://www.sd-network.eu/, accessed 21 December 2010.

Eurostat (2009) *Sustainable development in the European Union: 2009 monitoring report of the EU sustainable development strategy*, Luxembourg: Office for Official Publications of the European Communities.

French, D. (2005) International Law and Policy of Sustainable Development, Manchester: Manchester University Press.

Gunningham, N. (2009) 'Environmental law regulation and governance: Shifting architectures', *Journal of Environmental Law*, 21(2): 179–212.

HM Government, Scottish Executive, Welsh Assembly Government, Northern Ireland Office (2005) *One future – different paths: The UK's shared framework for sustainable development*, London: DEFRA.

Hardi, P. and Zdan, T. (eds) (1997) *Assessing Sustainable Development: Principles in Practice*, Winnipeg: International Institute for Sustainable Development.

Higher Education Funding Council for England (HEFCE) (2010) 'Allocation of funding for additional new entrants and efficiency activities in 2010–11 through the University Modernisation Fund', Circular 2010-08, London: HEFCE.

Hodge, R.A. and Hardi, P. (1997) 'The Need for Guidelines: the Rationale Underlying the Bellagio Principles for Assessment', in P. Hardi and T. Zdan (eds) Assessing Sustainable Development, *Principles in Practice*, Winnipeg: IISD.

Jacobs, M. (1999) 'Sustainable development as a contested concept', in A. Dobson (ed.) *Fairness and Futurity: Essays on Environmental Sustainability and Social Justice*, Oxford: Oxford University Press.

Jenkins, V. (2002) 'Learning from the past: Achieving sustainable development in the reform of local government', *Public Law*, Spring: 130–51.

Kirk, E.A. and Blackstock, K.L. (2011) 'Enhanced decision making: Balancing public participation against better regulation in British environmental permitting regimes', *Journal of Environmental Law*, 23(1): 97–116.

Lee, K.N. (1993) *Compass and Gyroscope: Integrating Science and Politics for the Environment*, Washington, DC: Island Press.

National School of Government (n.d.) *Programmes 2010–2011: Learning and Innovation for Efficient Public Services*, http://www.nationalschool.gov.uk/downloads/Programmes2010.pdf, accessed 26 July 2011.

Northern Ireland Executive (2010) *Everyone's Involved: Sustainable Development Strategy*, Belfast: Northern Ireland Executive.

Oliver, D. (2003) *Constitutional Reform in the UK*, Oxford: Oxford University Press.

Organisation for Economic Co-operation and Development (2002) *Improving Policy Coherence and Integration for Sustainable Development: A Checklist*, Paris: OECD.

Performance and Innovation Unit (2000) *Wiring it up: Whitehall's Management of Cross-Cutting Policies and Services*, London: Cabinet Office.

Poustie, M. (2004) *Environmental Justice in SEPA's Environmental Protection Activities: A Report for the Scottish Environment Protection Agency*, Edinburgh: Scottish Environment Protection Agency.

Reed, M.S., Fraser, E.D.G. and Dougill, A.J. (2006) 'An adaptive learning process for developing and applying sustainability indicators with local communities', *Ecological Economics*, 59(4): 406–18.

Ross, A. (2005) 'The UK approach to delivering sustainable development in government: A case study in joined-up working', *Journal of Environmental Law*, 17(1): 27–49.

Ross, A. (2006) 'Sustainable development in Scotland post devolution', *Environmental Law Review*, 8: 6–32.

Rowan Robinson J., Ross, A., Walton, W. and Rothnie, J. (1996) 'Public access to environmental information: A means to what end?', *Journal of Environmental Law*, 8(1): 19–42.

Scottish Executive: National Statistics (2002) *Public Attitudes to the Environment in Scotland Research Findings*, No. 24/2002, Edinburgh: Scottish Executive.

Scottish Government (2007) *The Government's Economic Strategy*, Edinburgh: Scottish Government.

Scottish Government (2008) *Achieving our Potential: A Framework to tackle Poverty and Income Inequality in Scotland*, Edinburgh: Scottish Government.

Scottish Government (2009) *Scottish Ministerial Code: A Code of Conduct and Guidance on Procedures for Members of the Scottish Government and Junior Scottish Ministers*, Edinburgh: Scottish Government.

Scottish Parliament (1999) SPOR, vol. 1, no 8, column 367ff.

Scottish Parliament (2007) *Meeting of the Parliament: Thursday 13 December 2007, Session 3*, Edinburgh: Scottish Parliament.

Sustainable Development Commission (2004) Shows Promise, But Must Try Harder. An Assessment by the Sustainable Development Commission of the Government's

Reported Progress on Sustainable Development over the Past Five years, London: SDC.

Sustainable Development Commission Scotland (SDCS) (2009) *Sustainable Development: Third Annual Assessment of Progress by the Scottish Government*, Edinburgh: SDCS.

Sustainable Scotland Network (n.d.) 'Sustainable Scotland Network', http://www.sustainable-scotland.net, accessed 7 September 2010.

Thirion, S. (2008) 'Involving citizens in defining and measuring well-being and progress', Part II, in *Well-being for All: Concepts and Tools for Social Cohesion* (Trends in Social Cohesion 20), Strasbourg: Council of Europe Publishing.

UK Government (1994) *Sustainable Development: The UK Strategy*, London: HMSO.

UN Economic Commission for Europe (UNECE) (1998) *Convention on Access to Information, Public Participation in Decision Making and Access to Justice in Environmental Matters*, 25 June, Aarhus: UN.

UN General Assembly (UNGA) (1992a) *The Rio Declaration on Environment and Development*, A/CONF.151/26 Vol. 1, New York: UN.

UNGA (1992b) *Agenda 21*, A/CONF.151/26 Vol. 1, New York: United Nations.

Welsh Assembly Government (WAG) (2009) *One Wales: One Planet: The Sustainable Development Scheme of the Welsh Assembly Government*, Cardiff: WAG.

Welsh Assembly Government (n.d.) 'Waste Awareness Wales', http://www.wasteawarenesswales.org.uk/ecoschools.html, accessed 19 November 2010.

7 Mechanisms – institutional and policy integration

This chapter examines the UK's progress towards environmental policy integration (EPI) and the broader ideal of 'putting sustainable development at the heart of government'. It begins by considering the role of government in the implementation of sustainable development and the need for cooperation and coordination among government actors. The chapter then reflects on the traditional character and organization of the UK public sector and how this can act as an obstacle to joined-up or integrated government. It then examines the importance of integrating environmental protection matters into all decision making for sustainable development and how this differs from the similar aim of integrating sustainable development into decision making. The chapter follows the evolution of specific initiatives aimed at securing integration in governance, including: those aimed at operations and the 'greening' of the government estate including procurement; those aimed at policy and decision making such as action plans, strategic environmental assessment (SEA), sustainability appraisals, impact assessments and pre-legislative scrutiny of bills; those focused on providing a source of expertise, including sustainable development units and the UK Sustainable Development Commission (SDC); and finally, those focused on finance, such as spending reviews, public sector agreements and specialized funds. The chapter concludes by emphasizing the need for evident leadership and accountability in relation to these tools, as well as the role of indicators and other means for monitoring and review.

The role of government in the implementation of sustainable development

Governments at all levels have had to develop an understanding of the term 'sustainable development' and consider how to implement it in their respective territorial jurisdictions – regions, countries and localities.

While it is popular to consider sustainable development as a shared objective whereby everyone – businesses, governments, individuals and so on – can make a difference, the impact of government activity or, more broadly, the public sector as a whole on the overall quality of the environment and more generally, towards sustainable development must not be underestimated. The UK Government employs over 515,000 staff housed in thousands of buildings across the UK and in other countries (Civil Service, n.d.). If these buildings are not energy- and resource-efficient, the impact on the environment will be significant. Moreover, governments make decisions that affect how the rest of us behave and it is through policy that a real influence is felt. In the UK, public expenditure usually stands as roughly 36–37 per cent of gross domestic product (GDP), although for 2009 and 2010 spending shot to 47 per cent of GDP, and while some of this expenditure was for operations, most was used to implement policy decisions which influence the behaviour of others (HM Treasury, 2011: 11). To use an extreme example, it is governments which decide when to go to war, what weapons to use and what areas should be targeted for destruction. A more everyday example is whether the school curriculum should include an appreciation of sustainable development as an educational objective.

The effect of government activity on the environment was among the issues raised in *Our Common Future* (the Brundtland Report) (WCED, 1987) in 1987: 'the major central economic and sectoral agencies of governments should now be made directly responsible and fully accountable for ensuring that their policies, programmes, and budget support development that is ecologically as well as economically sustainable' (WCED, 1987: 314). Furthermore, the Rio Declaration, the product of the 1992 UN Conference on Environment and Development, stated: 'In order to achieve sustainable development, environmental protection shall constitute an integral part of the development process and cannot be considered in isolation from it' (UNGA, 1992: Principle 4).

Similar aims are evident at European Community level. The Consolidated version of the Treaty on the Functioning of the European Union emphasizes the importance of EPI in Article 11: 'Environmental protection requirements must be integrated into the definition and implementation of the Union policies and activities, in particular with a view to promoting sustainable development'.[1]

To genuinely achieve this, individual departments and agencies would need to reassess their objectives and priorities and in many instances, alter the way they operate.

Moreover, having a clear strategy is necessary but not sufficient. As asserted by Meadowcroft:

> it is helpful to keep in mind the distinction between a national sustainable development strategy process on the one hand, and the broader practice of strategic decision making and policy implementation for sustainable development on the other. The first refers to a formal process – to the development, implementation and periodic review of an explicit strategy. The second denotes a much wider process of taking and implementing decisions which are of strategic significance for sustainable development. . . Important decisions will inevitably be made at different times, by different groups and in different forums, and one cannot expect that these will necessarily be integrated into a single bureaucratic process associated with the periodic

preparation of a formal strategy . . . Government activity is complex and multi-faceted . . . Hence the importance of ensuring that an understanding of sustainable development informs behaviour across all of government, including in contexts that will remain only loosely connected to the formal strategy process.

(Meadowcroft, 2007: 157)

The process is formidable. The Canadian Commissioner of the Environment and Sustainable Development in his Annual Report 2000, for example, states that:

The pursuit of sustainable development is complicated by the fact that responsibility for it is widely shared between departments, between governments and with other partners. Typically, a number of organizations are responsible for one aspect of the issue or another but none is responsible for the whole. They need to work together to develop and implement a co-ordinated approach. But managing these working relationships has proved difficult.

(Canadian Commissioner of the Environment and Sustainable Development, 2000: para. 2)

Before examining some mechanisms in detail, this chapter considers the nature of the UK public sector generally and how its traditions have been extended into the workings of the devolved administrations. The extent to which both the UK and devolved administrations have been able to override these traditions with more modern ways of working are then explored in the context of sustainable development.

The traditional character and organization of the UK public sector

A key obstacle hindering integration is the way governments organize themselves. The Brundtland Report recognized how the traditional form of government organization described above hinders efforts towards sustainable development: 'Those responsible for managing natural resources and protecting the environment are institutionally separated from those responsible for managing the economy. The real world of interlocked economic and ecological systems will not change: the policies and institutions must' (WCED, 1987: 9).

The challenge is very evident in the UK, where today, traditional responsibility for certain government functions is divided between the UK central government and each of the devolved administrations. Devolution is asymmetrical, so central government is responsible for more functions in certain parts of the country (most notably England) than for others (most notably Scotland). Within each administration, functions are historically divided in a similar way among various parts of government, most commonly into departments. Each department is headed by a minister who is chosen by the Prime Minister (or First Minister) from members of the relevant legislature. The doctrine of ministerial responsibility means that the minister is ultimately responsible for all activity in his or her department and is answerable to legislature and to the public for his or her department. The Prime Minister or First Minister meets with ministers in the Cabinet where overall government policy is determined. The Prime Minister or First Minister exercises a certain amount of pressure over ministers and can remove them from their posts, but ultimate responsibility remains with individual ministers. Ministerial responsibility is also essential to protect the anonymous nature of the civil service. Officials are career civil servants and are kept secure from political changes. This means expertise is not necessarily lost with a change of government, but it also means that systems within departments become firmly entrenched. As Daintith and Page (1999: 381) conclude, 'departmental primacy has been the central organizing principle of the executive branch . . . The corollary of departmental primacy was an essentially decentralized system of internal control for the operation of which the ministerial head of each department was responsible to Parliament'. Ministers are accountable to the legislature directly through questions and debates in the legislature as well as being subject to scrutiny by the relevant legislative committee. As a result, control tends to rely on self-discipline, and each department works towards its own objectives in its own way and the centre has remarkably little influence on public sector behaviour. Hence, the culture of different departments may be quite distinct.

Following criticism that the UK public sector was relatively over-centralized and monolithic, inward-looking and too removed from the needs of service users, the Conservative Governments of the 1980s and early 1990s introduced a variety of measures designed to improve efficiency and responsiveness. The subsequent Labour Government did the same but also introduced measures seeking to promote joined-up policymaking and multi-agency responses to tackle the so-called 'wicked issues' like crime, truancy, social exclusion and sustainable development which straddled traditional departmental responsibilities (Ling, 2002: 618). Autonomous departments dealing with discrete areas are not conducive to such coordination (Ling, 2002: 618). The traditional departmental system discouraged ideas that considered the long term and cut across organizational boundaries to get to the root of a problem (Prime Minister and Minister for Cabinet Office, 1999: ch. 2, para. 5), as the incentives to achieve the organizational aim were greater than those intended to foster more central objectives (Ling, 2002: 618). For example, at one time, the value added tax (VAT) on fuel was less than the VAT on energy conservation materials, despite the government's commitment to promoting energy efficiency (British Government Panel on Sustainable Development, 1997: para. 14).

The devolved administrations subsequently inherited this system and initially largely followed its rules. However, proportional representation has resulted in an increased likelihood of coalition and minority governments and this in turn has influenced the approach taken to governing in Wales and Scotland in particular. More recently, and as described below, the leaders in Wales and Scotland have chosen to be more innovative in the size of their respective cabinets and the allocation of responsibilities among ministers.

The need for integration in the implementation of sustainable development

With the benefit of hindsight, the original description of EPI set out in the Brundtland Report is ambitious, calling on the major central economic and sectoral agencies of governments to be made directly responsible and fully accountable for ensuring that their policies, programmes and budget support development that is ecologically and economically sustainable (WCED, 1987: 314). It has been argued that this approach would turn the policy status quo on its head, so that in future, environmental protection would involve a much more holistic and, above all, proactive search early on in the policy process for opportunities to prevent damage from occurring (Jordan and Lenschow, 2008: 4). Like interpretations of sustainable development based around ecological sustainability, this approach affords the environment 'principled priority' in decision making (Laffery and Hovden, 2003: 9). The practical reality however, is that similarly to sustainable development, two broad understandings of EPI have emerged – one weak and one strong. Weak EPI occurs when the sectors simply take environmental considerations 'into account' without giving them any special priority. The core sectoral policies remain untouched, although some new routines may be added which increase the amount of information available to policymakers (Jordan and Lenschow, 2008: 11). For example, there may be a requirement to conduct an environmental assessment for certain types of planning applications, but so long as regard is paid to assessment, the decision maker can decide however he or she wants. In contrast, strong EPI corresponds more to placing environmental considerations at the heart of decision making in other sectoral policies, and where contradictions arise between environmental and sectoral policies, priority is given to the former rather than the latter. This vision of EPI is essential for securing ecological sustainability and in turn, stronger forms of sustainable development.

Initially, the integration principle focused on integrating environmental concerns into decision making. This concern has received wide acceptance, and action has been taken to address this silo government at all levels. For example, the Treaty on the Functioning of the European Union in Article 11 provides that 'Environmental protection requirements must be integrated into the definition and implementation of the Union policies and activities, in particular with a view to promoting sustainable development'.[2] The EU has acted on this commitment by introducing measures such as SEA of plans and programmes by public bodies.[3]

More recently, the integration principle has broadened to include all aspects of sustainable development and most importantly, a concern about ecological limits and intergenerational aspects. The Organisation for Economic Co-operation and

Development (OECD) has stated that in order for public management systems to respond to the challenges presented by sustainable development, specific initiatives are needed 'by government to better integrate economic, environmental and social goals within the mandate of each existing institution' (OECD, 2002a: 2). A lack of effective coordination between sectors and across the various levels of government is therefore one of the major challenges. Furthermore, 'coherence is still lacking between the key choices made by the public sector and those made by the private sector' (OECD, 2002a: 3).

Within the UK, the concept of 'greening government' really first took in 1997 when the New Labour Government announced it was 'committed to putting concern for the environment at the heart of policymaking, so that it is not an add-on extra, but informs the whole of government' (Labour Party, 1997). Among other things, to take this forward, the Government upgraded the Green Ministers' Committee (GMC) to a Cabinet Committee (see Chapter 5) and established a Sustainable Development Unit located in the Department of the Environment, Transport and the Regions as a pan-governmental resource.

Since then, all of the administrations in the UK have introduced a wide range of mechanisms designed to integrate either environmental protection or sustainable development or both into government decision making, including measures such as cabinet sub-committees, integrated policy appraisal, greening operations through sustainable development in government (such as procurement), reporting obligations and the creation of special advisory sustainable development units (DEFRA) 2002a, 2003; Scottish Executive 2003, 2004a). The extent to which these have been effective varies (Ross, 2003; Environment and Rural Development Committee, 2004a; CAG Consultants, 2004; Ross, 2005). The remainder of this chapter is devoted to exploring some of the mechanisms aimed at improving the integration of environmental concerns into the activities of government and those with the broader aim of integrating sustainable development into the activities of government. For the purpose of this chapter, the integration tools are categorized as those addressing the organization and functions of government, those aimed at the operations of government, those directed at policymaking activity, and those which use the finances of government for integration. It also explores the opportunities in place for ensuring that government decision makers have access to strong advice, training and expertise for all of these activities. It is impossible to review all of the devices used by the four administrations in this regard, so instead, specific examples are used to highlight certain aspects of some of the more important tools.

Changes to the organization and function of government for sustainable development

As discussed in Chapter 5, in order for sustainable development to become the organizing principle of governance or even the lesser aim of being integrated into government activities, there needs to be visible leadership from the centre that is effectively transposed to departmental level. Kavanagh and Richards (2001: 17) observe that 'Joined-up government relies on prime ministerial authority rather than a well-established institutional base and new cultural values. In theory, it is possible for departments spontaneously to join up. In practice, the stimulus usually comes from elsewhere – the centre'.

Chapter 5 explored the role of individual leaders at different levels of government and the value of training and allocating clear responsibilities to individuals to promote and support leadership. Yet, individual leadership alone is not enough. It is unlikely that joined-up government can be properly established and maintained when departments continue to hold resources, authority and dominate policymaking and delivery. Peter Mandelson's belief that a 'super minister' without portfolio based in the Cabinet Office could tackle 'wicked issues' such as housing or drug abuse faltered, because ministers acquire power from the size, status and functions of their departments (Mandelson and Liddle, 1996: 245). Departments are not neutral organizations. Each has its own culture and modus operandi. What is needed is cultural change within and across departments. As discussed in Chapter 5, cabinet and other high-level committees can reinforce leadership for sustainable development. There is no need to repeat the discussion on cabinet and other high-level committees here, but it is vital to recognize their significant value in coordinating efforts to integrate environmental concerns into all government action. Instead, the focus here is on how the actual organization of government and the allocation of government functions can encourage and support coordination. These institutional changes are necessary for progress on improving sustainable development at all levels of government activity – operations, policymaking and even government finance.

The organization of government

As discussed above, the traditional ways the UK has chosen to govern itself do not easily support crosscutting policies or joined-up working. Thus, sustainable development and the integration of sustainable development into the heart of government activity require institutional change.

An example of too many departments being involved in a sustainability project is the UK (English) implementation of the Strategic Environmental Assessment Directive (Council Directive 2001/42/EC) on the assessment of certain plans and programmes on the environment.[4] The process was led by the Office of the Deputy Prime Minister (ODPM). As discussed below, Department for Environment, Food and Rural Affairs (DEFRA) leads on environmental appraisals within the integrated policy appraisal (IPA) process. Even at a late stage in the implementation process (July 2004) there was little evidence of the two departments coming together and deciding how the SEA Directive and IPA should interact. The IPA website was silent on SEA and, likewise, the SEA website made no mention of IPA (Ross, 2005: 46).

Similarly, the complex governing arrangements in Northern Ireland have clearly hindered opportunities for integration. As described by Porritt:

> many would say that Northern Ireland is significantly 'over-governed' . . . There are 11 government departments, with key sustainable development functions widely dispersed. One department is responsible for climate change policy, but energy and economic development sit in another, transport in a third. Building regulations are located in a different department from housing policy, and both are separate from the government's design policy on the built environment. In addition, the problems of 'variable geometry' have been exposed all too visibly in Northern Ireland. For example, the ambitions of the UK Climate Change Act have largely been ignored. While Scotland, Wales and, indeed, Ireland have all introduced exacting emissions reduction targets, there are no new commitments in Northern Ireland.
>
> (Porritt, 2009: 44–5)

In contrast, there are several very good examples of how departmental reorganization can improve integration. The first examples involve merging traditionally separate and often conflicting responsibilities into a single department or agency. For example, the Department of Energy and Climate Change (DECC) was created in October 2008 to bring together energy policy (previously with the Department for Business, Enterprise and Regulatory Reform, which is now the Department for Business, Innovation and Skills) and climate change mitigation policy (previously with DEFRA). DECC exists to take the lead in tackling climate change, which is a massive threat to the global environment, and in ensuring that the UK has access to secure, clean, safe and affordable energy. Its creation reflects the fact that climate change and energy policies are inextricably linked – two-thirds of the UK's emissions come from its energy use. Decisions in one field cannot be made without considering the impacts in the other. Similarly, Marine Scotland, which was created in 2009, is responsible for marine policy and planning, renewable energy and fisheries. This is clearly an attempt to develop a more coherent and integrated approach to resolve tensions between conflicting interests, while effectively delivering a healthy marine environment, sustainable fish stocks and aquaculture and the necessary expansion of marine renewables (SDCS, 2009: 47).

The second type of institutional reorganization is more radical. When the Scottish National Party came to power in 2005, it removed all the departmental boundaries to create a single Scottish Government. The Government is now organized around five directorates which are responsible for progressing the five core strategic objectives of the Government: wealthier and fairer Scotland, healthier Scotland, safer and stronger Scotland, smarter Scotland and greener Scotland. The organization of the Welsh Assembly Government (WAG) is also explicitly focused on joined-up delivery. However, the approach is more complicated than that used in Scotland. The WAG is organized around seven directorates: Economy and Transport; Sustainable Futures – Rural Affairs, Heritage and Environment; Health and Social Services; Local Government and Public Service Delivery; Education, Lifelong Learning and Skills; Finance; and People, Places and Corporate Services. Each of these administrations has allocated overall responsibility for their administration in the hands of only one permanent secretary and this also has a coordinating effect.

Allocation of functions

In order for government to prioritize integrating sustainable development into its activities, functions like producing a sustainable development action plan, training civil servants or monitoring progress need to be clearly allocated to certain individuals or bodies. There also needs to be consequences for a failure to deliver. Without these features, priority will not be given to integrating sustainable development into the activities of government. For example, the National Health Service (NHS) Scotland's Chief Executive set out a requirement for NHS Boards in Scotland to nominate a board-level Champion for Sustainability and to develop and implement a Sustainability Action Plan based on the NHS Strategy (Health and Finance Directorate, 2009). Another example is that from 2007–2008 onwards, all UK permanent secretaries are accountable for their department's overall progress under the Sustainable Operations of the Government Estate framework and for ensuring that key staff in their departments have performance objectives and incentives that drive the implementation of the Sustainable Procurement Action Plan, linked to performance objectives for delivering efficiency savings (DEFRA, n.d.). Integration is promoted by clearly allocating responsibility for sustainable development (albeit only in relation to operations) to high-level personnel across the UK public sector.

For the allocation of responsibility to be effective as a means of cultural change, there needs to be consequences for non-compliance. These do not often exist, but the Environmental Audit Committee of the House of Commons (EAC) has made it very clear that it intends to call those permanent secretaries with poor records to account in person for any poor performance (EAC, 2009b: paras. 47–9).

Advice and training

All of the UK administrations need support and expertise for their work on sustainable development. This expertise needs to be available from both internal and external sources. The administrations have specialist units with the necessary expertise to conduct research into sustainable development, develop policy and process initiatives, review progress and offer advice and training. These units are all housed in the department or directorate responsible for producing the sustainable development strategy.

For example, the UK Sustainable Development Unit (SDU) based in DEFRA was introduced in 1997 as an inter-departmental resource to promote the sustainable development agenda, provide advice and guidance to departments on the full range of greening government issues (environmental appraisal, technical advice), and provide support for the GMC. Despite the SDU appearing to have the hallmarks of such a crosscutting unit, it has, for a variety of reasons, failed to achieve that standing. In 1998, the EAC observed that 'the Unit has been enlarged but still seems to suffer from some lack of status, perhaps being seen more as an administrative arm of the Green Ministers' Committee rather than an active, problem solving Unit pushing forward the Government's agenda' (EAC, 1998b: para. 18). Indeed, the *Modernising Government* White Paper does not address the work of the Unit in tackling an important crosscutting policy. Research for DEFRA on crosscutting issues found that initially, the Unit was stretched widely, without the authority enjoyed by its equivalent in the social policy field, the Social Exclusion Unit (EAC, 1998b: para. 18).

The location of this crosscutting unit is just as indicative of the government's priority for sustainable development as who produces the strategy. It is DEFRA which produces the strategy and the SDU is located in DEFRA. As discussed in Chapter 4, research shows that strategies are best produced at the highest level as a responsibility of the Prime Minister or Deputy Prime Minister. Similarly, research shows that to have an impact, crosscutting units like the SDU need to be based in the Prime Minister's Office or the Cabinet Office to have a truly integrating effect. The rationale for keeping the SDU in the relevant 'environment' department was put forward by the then Environment Minister who had clearly confused environmental protection and sustainable development:

> I understand the argument for mainstreaming it [the SDU] like some of the other crosscutting units . . . We remain dominated by economics and to some extent increasingly by social targets, but the environment is a bit marginalized. For that reason, there is some benefit in retaining it in a big, powerful Department that has the capacity to keep pressing.[5]

Surely, if this was the case and the SDU was in fact, the 'environment' unit it should probably have been renamed. Moreover, if this was the case, there would also be an argument for establishing a genuine SDU within the centre to coordinate the activities of all the units and departments involved in sustainable development.

In January 2002, the EAC (2002: para. 30) reiterated its concern about the location of the SDU and declared that the failure to move it to the Cabinet Office following the post-election reorganization of government departments was a missed opportunity.

In terms of delivering joined-up government or sustainable development in government, the work of the SDU is difficult to uncover. It does not have its own website and although it does now publish in its own name, it is clearly a 'behind the scenes' operator. The EAC has continuously encouraged the SDU to build a distinctive role for itself in driving forward the sustainable development agenda through authorship of relevant guidance and monitoring of departmental performance (EAC, 1998b: para. 18).

In relation to operations, further expertise and advice is provided by the Centre of Expertise in Sustainable Procurement (CESP) which was established within the Office of Government Commerce (OGC) in 2008 to provide leadership and support to central government bodies on their environmental sustainability. The 2010 Budget announced an extension to the remit of the Government's Chief Sustainability Officer and of CESP to provide leadership, challenge and support to the wider public sector on energy efficiency, working with existing delivery bodies to ensure a coordinated approach to sustainable procurement. Following the election in 2010, the OGC is part of the Cabinet Office (OGC, n.d.).

Unfortunately, the record shows that internal crosscutting units often are limited in their capacity to actually drive reform in the UK public sector. There are three reasons for this. First, regardless of where a crosscutting unit is located, strong leadership is absolutely essential to ensure its success. Daintith and Page note that:

> the units and their policies depend for their influence upon the consensus in their favour within the Cabinet system, at the highest political levels of the executive, a consensus which may need to be sustained, or even imposed by the political leadership and power of the Prime Minister.
>
> (Daintith and Page, 1999: 385)

Second, the units and their respective functions must also be accepted by the departments, as that is where the power lies in the UK public sector. Finally, traditional departmental select committees and ministerial responsibility cannot effectively scrutinize these units, and so the question of their accountability is unresolved. Even a crosscutting unit like the SDU – which was backed up by two high-level ministerial committees and at least initially, scrutinized by the EAC, a specialist issue-based select committee – seems to be struggling for acceptance, influence and power.

There are also several bodies which work closely with government and which are, to varying extents, at arm's length from government. Up until 2011, when the UK coalition Government decided to stop its funding, the most important of these was the SDC: the UK Government's independent adviser on sustainable development, with a duty in Whitehall to report on the Government's own sustainability performance. The SDC provided informed, evidence based advice to the UK and devolved governments on finding solutions to problems which helped it to meet its commitment to sustainable development, as well as on developing the attitudes, skills and knowledge in government needed to make the best decisions for today and the future. It also held these governments to account on its progress towards sustainability.

Other bodies also exist. For example, in Wales, advice and expertise is provided by Cynnal Cymru – Sustain Wales which is an independent, not-for-profit organization that promotes sustainable development and provides practical information to help people live sustainably. In the context of integration, it contributes to sustainable development training for civil servants to increase their capacity and leadership on sustainable development. Operating at the boundary between government, business and civil society, Sustain Wales is uniquely positioned to assimilate the views of each group and generate communication between them that will result in positive action for sustainable development (Cynnal Cymru – Sustain Wales, n.d.). Since the closure of the SDC at the end of March 2011, the WAG has appointed its own Commissioner for Sustainable Futures who will provide advice to the Assembly Government and leadership for sustainable development across Wales. Cynnal Cymru is to provide support for the new Commissioner enabling the views and experiences of the wider community in Wales to be shared with the Commissioner and fed into his advice to government (Cynnal Cymru – Sustain Wales, n.d.)

Civil servants also need to understand what EPI or integrating sustainable development actually means, why it is so important and what action is needed to make it happen. As such, training is essential. In the UK, the public sector is shared among the administrations in Great Britain (England, Scotland and Wales), and Northern Ireland has its own separate public sector. Civil servants from each of the Great Britain administrations receive very similar training, largely provided by the National School of Government which has facilities in Sunningdale (Berkshire), London and Edinburgh. Much of the same training is offered to Northern Ireland civil servants. Thirteen of the courses offered at the National School of Government explicitly include training on sustainable development (National School of Government, 2010a). Two of the key aims of the School's Core Learning Programme for senior civil servants and ministers are: to promote the highest standards in policy development and implementation by driving consistent approaches, common standards, and common language – a shared understanding across government; and to 'join up' government by creating professional communities (National School of Government, 2010b).

Integration into operations

Over time, it has become obvious that some aspects of 'greening government' and later 'sustainable development in government' are proving more difficult to implement than others. Indeed, by the time the greening government initiative had transformed into 'sustainable development in government', the emphasis had been firmly shifted to the operational side of government activity. Moves to put the environment (and later sustainable development) actually into the heart of decision making have continued to prove elusive (see below). In contrast, integrating environmental protection and/or sustainable development into the running of the government estate and its operations has proven far easier. It is here where each of the administrations, but most especially the UK Government, has made the most progress by, among other things, reducing its waste, energy consumption and water use, and changing its procurement practices.

Over time, the UK Government's approach to sustainable development in government has become more refined, with more and more ambitious targets subject to stricter timetables (DEFRA 2002b, 2004, 2006b). These relate entirely to government operations including procurement, and provide no guidance as to policymaking.

The processes are continually being reported upon and reviewed. A review of the 2006 Sustainable Operations on the Government Estate (SOGE) process found it to be effective but limited, as it only applied to non-departmental public bodies on a voluntary basis, contained unambitious targets, and elicited a general feeling that the process was not delivering results fast enough.

The current Sustainable Development in Government (SDiG) framework was agreed in 2010, and replaces the SOGE targets upon their expiry in 2010/11. The SDiG framework will apply new tougher outcome-focused targets which will run from a 2010/11 baseline to 2016/17 (with carbon budgets operating from a 2012 baseline) and apply to more of the Government estate. It covers the UK-based estates and operations of all English central Government departments and their Executive Agencies, as well as non-ministerial departments and Executive Non-Departmental Public Bodies (NDPB) (subject to minimum criteria). All Regional Development Agencies are included. The targets do not apply to the devolved administrations and apply to all Executive NDPB only if they have more than 1000m^2 in floor space and more than 250 full-time equivalent staff. An Executive NDPB is established in statute and carries out administrative, regulatory and commercial functions, employs its own staff and is allocated its own budgets (DEFRA, n.d.).

The SDiG targets have been set in line with the themes of *The UK Strategy for Sustainable Development: Securing the Future* (the 2005 strategy) (DEFRA, 2005), namely: climate change and energy; sustainable consumption and production; natural resource protection; and sustainable communities. Each begins with a long-term aspiration and is then followed by targets of varying specificity. Essentially, it is a broad programme covering all aspects of the UK Government's operations and estate.

A key aim of the SDiG framework is to compel Government to reduce its greenhouse gas emissions and ensure that the estate is resilient to the impacts of the changing climate. Under the new framework, Government has set itself a target to reduce its greenhouse gas emissions by 34 per cent by 2020 (from 1999/2000 levels), up from 30 per cent in the SOGE. The SDiG framework also includes challenging targets on waste reduction and recovery, more efficient use of water, promoting the protection and enhancement of biodiversity, and positive engagement with the community. In support of these targets, Departments should among other things: work towards an accredited certified environmental management system (that is, ISO 14001, EMAS or British Standard BS 8555); only procure buildings in the top quartile of energy performance; and adopt a whole-organization approach to carbon management, such as the Carbon Trust's Carbon Management Programme or equivalent.

Sustainable procurement holds an enhanced place in the SDiG framework, encouraging Government to use its considerable purchasing power to positively influence suppliers and reduce the impact of the supply chain on the environment (DEFRA, n.d.).

The OGC is responsible for providing leadership, challenge and support on Government delivery against the SOGE and SDiG frameworks. It publishes the 'Government's Delivery Plan Update on Progress' against the targets every six months, together with an annual report on performance (OGC, 2010). Detailed guidance on the SOGE targets is also available on the OGC website and will be accompanied by guidance on the new SDiG targets. The SDC, as the Government's independent watchdog until 2011, published an annual SDiG Report, assessing Government operations and procurement practices. The Report sets out how well the Government is meeting its targets and highlights future challenges for Government (SDC, 2010).

The SDiG is a good model and is one area where the UK Government is ahead of the devolved administrations. The SDC strongly advocated that the SDiG framework be replicated in the devolved administrations, as it provides several advantages: independent scrutiny of progress, which is a vital part of a good governance model; detailed recommendations for improvement and capacity building; a proven performance management model which drives further performance improvements; a potential to roll-out to the wider public sector; and finally, the ability to benchmark against Whitehall departments and ideally, the other devolved administrations (SDCS, 2009: 49).

Following recommendations by the SDC, the Scottish Government is investigating the possibility of operating a similar SDiG framework. In its annual report on the Scottish Government's progress towards sustainable development, the SDC found the Scottish Government to be behind the UK Government in relation to operations. While joining the Carbon Trust Carbon Management Programme and reducing the amount of waste arising, overall performance in some key areas of estate management was poor in 2007/08. Of particular concern was the increase in greenhouse gas emissions from both buildings and transport over the previous year. Given the Government's commitment to leadership through the Climate Change (Scotland) Act 2009, this situation must be turned around. No progress was made in 2010 against the water target and the achievement of the reductions needed by 2011 must be in doubt (SDCS, 2009: 49).

Wales is closer to formalizing its SDiG framework with the assistance of the SDC. In Wales, the environmental performance of Government has been measured against the Green Dragon Standard since 2003. As of 2009, the WAG has adapted this to the broader SDiG framework used by the UK Government.

The 5th Annual Report on environmental performance across the WAG's in-house business operations and core administrative estate covers the period 1 April 2008 to 31 March 2009 (WAG, 2009a). Throughout the Report, specific reference is made, where relevant, to offices included in the Assembly Government's Green Dragon Level 5 Certificate. The organization manages its environmental performance by an environmental management system equivalent to ISO 14001, established via the Green Dragon Environmental Standard 2006. It encompasses any policy or business operation impacting on in-house environmental performance. This system enables sustainable approaches to be incorporated into everyday business.

The WAG's performance is reported against objectives and targets set at the beginning of the year. In the 2008/09 Report, many of these have been met or exceeded. However, some areas of performance have not met expectations. For example, 83 per cent of everyday paper consumption was from recycled paper, a decrease against the 2007/08 figure of 89 per cent. Emissions from business travel increased by 1.4 per cent compared to 2007/08, to 3,570 tonnes, although initiatives including improved conferencing technology and reviews of travel plans had been introduced (WAG, 2009a: 2, 3).

For the first time, in 2009, the Green Dragon Report was subjected to external scrutiny by the SDC. *One Wales: One Planet: The Sustainable Development Scheme of the Welsh Assembly Government* requires the SDC to assess and report on the WAG's operations across its administrative estate (WAG, 2009b). The SDC assessment of the WAG's performance against Green Dragon targets showed some progress and some problems. For example, the WAG was very likely to outperform the pan-UK Government's performance on recycling and has achieved a recycling rate of 59 per cent of waste arising (relative to 2006/07) and 85 per cent of electricity supply contracts are now green tariffs, providing 73 per cent of electricity consumed in all offices. Unfortunately, while the increase in carbon dioxide emissions from buildings has been reversed and overall carbon dioxide emissions from the WAG's administrative estate are decreasing (down 4 per cent in the 2011 reporting year, compared to the previous year), emissions from road vehicles used for WAG business increased by 1.4 per cent in 2008/09 compared to 2007/08, and this represents insufficient progress if the WAG is to meet its target of a 30 per cent reduction in emissions by December 2010 (based on a 2006/07 baseline) (SDCW, 2009). The real indicator of progress was the fact that the SDC assessment took place, and this was a significant new contribution that the Commission was providing for Wales.

Although Northern Ireland has no SDiG framework in place, in its most recent strategy, the Government states that as part of its leadership role in sustainable development, government is committed to managing the impacts of its own business and estate. To help do this, all departments produced action plans in late 2006 and early 2007 (OFMDFM, n.d. a). The Northern Ireland Executive has approved guidance on integrating equality of opportunity and sustainable development into public sector procurement. The guidance provides practical advice on how to take account of equality and sustainable development when procuring goods, works and services. This guidance will be kept under review to promote good practice (Northern Ireland Executive, 2010: 31).

A key conclusion in this discussion is that even in the UK where the SDiG process is now sophisticated and iterative, there are key areas where things are either getting worse or no progress is being made. What this demonstrates very clearly is the limits of a purely procedural approach. Without leadership and some compelling factors to change the culture of the public sector, progress will be limited. Moreover, the contribution of the SDC in reviewing and monitoring the SDiG process has been instrumental in encouraging and coercing departments to change their habits. The loss of the SDC will be felt in this area, and by allowing governments to avoid any detailed scrutiny, could very likely undo much of the progress made to date.

Integration into policymaking

Despite its name, the SDiG focuses primarily on government operations and ignores policymaking. Policymaking is: 'the process by which governments translate their political vision into programmes and actions to deliver "outcomes" – desired changes in the real world' (Prime Minister and Minister for Cabinet Office, 1999: ch. 2, para. 1). Policymaking is the real challenge facing government, and injecting change into policymaking is a substantial ask. Currently, tools used for ensuring public bodies 'contribute to the achievement of sustainable development' can be grouped under five categories. As discussed earlier, this is a rather woolly aim, and for the purposes of this chapter, it is proposed that this means acting in accordance with the relevant sustainable development framework and strategy. The five categories of policy tools are: institutional changes to support sustainable development; sustainable development action plans, individually for separate departments and agencies and more joined-up action plans aimed at challenges such as climate change; policy appraisal tools, such as integrated policy appraisal, SEA and sustainability assessments; pre-legislative scrutiny of legislation; and the use of substantive legal duties. The first three are dealt with below. A full discussion on the value of substantive legal duties follows in the next chapter on the use of legislation. A review of the tools available to drive the necessary shifts in the finances of government are related and discussed in the next section.

Sustainable development action plans

The 2005 strategy (DEFRA, 2005), requires all central government Departments and their Executive Agencies to produce Sustainable Development Action Plans (SDAPs) and report on progress regularly. This requirement is a key means of ensuring that government strategy is 'converted into action' across the whole of government, and that the public sector becomes a leading exponent of sustainable development (DEFRA, 2005: 10). A SDAP sets out the strategic actions that an organization intends to take to integrate sustainable development into its decision making and everyday operations. It can also be produced by multiple bodies in relation to a particular concern or challenge such as transport or climate change. The SDC produced guidance on producing the SDAPs which, among other things, suggested that departments: organize their SDAPs by policy, operations, procurement and people; ensure all their actions are SMART (specific, measureable, accountable, realistic and time related); and focus on outcomes rather than outputs (SDC, 2008).

For most organizations, this means outlining the actions that will build a sustainable development approach to the policies they produce or deliver, people they work with, goods and services they procure, and the operations they manage. Most departments published their first SDAP in 2006. The third set of action plans covers up to 2012.

The 2005 strategy also explicitly empowers the SDC to act as the Government's watchdog for sustainable development, which includes scrutinizing and reporting on Government's performance on sustainable development. The SDC reported twice on the progress of departments and the reports show huge variation between departments.

The individual directorates of the Scottish Government are not obliged to produce SDAPs. This is probably consistent with the Scottish Government's holistic approach to governance. An action plan in the form of the National Performance Framework does exist for the whole Government, which sets out clear targets and timetables and is reviewed annually by the SDC (see Chapter 4).

Northern Ireland strategies always refer to an implementation plan. The previous strategy's implementation plan was never adopted and the Executive, in 2010, seemed to be consulting forever on the new plan. In April 2011, the NI Executive published *Focus on the Future*, its 'Implementation Plan' that sets out actions for the achievement of each objective (Northern Ireland Executive, 2010: 21). The Plan repeats the hierarchical approach in the strategy. It is structured in two ways and in two parts. The first part sets out the actions within the Plan on a department by department basis. Lead departments have been identified for each of the 32 strategic objectives and these departments will be responsible for overseeing progress against targets and communicating this to the OFDFM. The second part sets out for each strategic objective every action contributing to its achievement (Northern Ireland Executive, 2011: 7). The difficulty is that, without indicators, monitoring progress is very difficult. The Plan, however, commits the Executive to develop a set of indicators to be used by the OFDFM to report annually on overall progress (Northern Ireland Executive, 2011: 15). While there is some evidence to show progress, in this area it is clear that Northern Ireland still significantly lags behind the rest of the UK in actually producing tools to aid the delivery of sustainable development.

The WAG is under an obligation to produce an action plan for its sustainable development scheme ('the Welsh Action Plan'). In their 2006 review, Flynn and Marsden noted certain particular features of the Welsh Action Plan which limit its impact. Three are worth noting as they are common downfalls of many action plans First, Flynn and Marsden found that many of the targets in the Welsh Action Plan were unambitious. Whilst there was a sense from some interviewees that they could have gone further in the commitments that they entered into, there was also a recognition that since the action plan was a political document that the minister would report on, it was sensible to have targets that could be achieved (Flynn and Marsden, 2006: 21). Second, if there was a move towards more integrated working to achieve thematic targets or goals, there is a widespread feeling among WAG staff that people could not contribute because they do not have the time or the resources. In other words, it simply was not a sufficient (political) priority. Third, Flynn and Marsden (2006) observed that there is confusion in the Action Plan as to what constitutes *real actions*, as opposed to further plans, consultations and task groups. As a result, the Action Plan's priorities were not sufficiently wide and encompassing to engage multiple partners and stakeholders in bringing about the necessary changes needed, neither were they sufficiently deep in their reach to connect with particularly relevant policy programmes within and beyond the Assembly. For example, in relation to promoting sustainable communities, rather than tying actions more specifically to the relevant plans and policy programmes, six detached actions were specified, all of which involved further progress on the plans and policies themselves. Indeed, Flynn and Marsden (2006: 29) note that there was little detail on how communities will or could become more sustainable, and of how or when this might be more achieved.

All the UK administrations and the EU have also commissioned action plans for dealing with specific issues or concerns relating to sustainable development. These plans include both short-term and long-term targets with explicit dates and annual contributions. They allocate responsibility for certain activities and often provide opportunities for consultation on proposals within the plans. For example, targeted crosscutting action plans and programmes are a key feature of the EU approach to implementing sustainable development and the action plans include significant legislative, policy and financial initiatives.

For example, the EU Green Transport Package addresses the greening of transport, the internalization of external costs and the abatement of noise from railways. It also included a proposal on internalization charges for lorries. In April 2009, a regulation setting binding targets for carbon dioxide emissions from new passenger cars was adopted. The 'Sustainable Consumption and Production and Sustainable Industrial Policy' Action Plan aims to improve the environmental performance of products, boost demand for more sustainable goods and production technologies, and foster innovation. This Action Plan was accompanied by proposals for a recast of the Ecodesign and Energy Labelling Directives and the revision of the Eco-label and Eco-Management and Audit Scheme Regulations. Retailers play a key role in influencing consumer choices, and a forum has been established with the aim of reducing the environmental footprint of the retail sector and better informing consumers (European Commission, 2009: 7).

In Scotland, an Environmental and Clean Technologies (ECT) Action Plan has been developed by the Scottish Environment Protection Agency, Scottish Enterprise, Highlands and Islands Enterprise and the Scottish Funding Council. It aims to join up public sector support for companies wanting to develop green technologies, moving away from the current ad hoc nature of investment (ECT Strategic Partnership, 2009).

Thus, action plans add a great deal to the rhetoric and vision set out in strategies and can genuinely promote the coordinated responses required for EPI and sustainable development. However, the actions need to be real actions as opposed to simply further plans or consultations which can easily be used to give the impression of action without actually producing any.

Assessment and appraisals

Policy, like specific projects, needs to be appraised to determine its potential impact on various regions, economies, sectors, people and the environment. The UK Government has long advocated the use of environmental assessment as an integral part of the policymaking process in each department. Environmental assessment is a process for the early identification and assessment of the likely significant environmental effects, positive and negative, of certain projects. However, the UK Government's track record for actually doing the appraisals has been weak (EAC, 1998b, 2002, 2003, 2009b).

More recently, requirements to conduct sustainability appraisals have been introduced. These are processes that encourage some or all sustainable development objectives to be integrated into policies, programmes, projects, activities and decision making at an early stage. They are designed to help identify potential environmental, social and economic effects and issues as early as possible, allowing alternative solutions or mitigation measures to be explored. Alternatively, positive effects and opportunities for performance enhancement can also be identified and promoted. These methods allow sustainability and environmental issues to be considered in a systematic, transparent and auditable way (DEFRA, 2006b).

Sustainability appraisal and SEA are two of several types of appraisal or assessment that public sector bodies are required to conduct. Others include regulatory impact assessments, equal opportunities assessments and rurality assessments. The difficulty is that with so many different forms of appraisal, public sector bodies need some coordinated means of screening their policies for significant impacts to ensure all areas are considered and, where necessary, to ensure that more detailed appraisals are undertaken. The use of SEA, sustainable appraisal and broader appraisal tools (IA) are discussed below.

Strategic environmental assessment

The Strategic Environmental Assessment Directive (Council Directive 2001/42/EC) on the assessment of certain plans and programmes on the environment was agreed by EU Member States in June 2001 and came into force in July 2004.[6] While this Directive applies only to plans and programmes, it probably also increases the attention afforded higher policy level decision making, since decisions made at this level are likely to become more exposed to appraisal.

SEA, in the context of the Directive, is a process for the early identification and assessment of the likely significant environmental effects, positive and negative, of certain programmes and plans developed by the public sector (including private companies which undertake functions of a public nature under the control or direction of Government). SEAs are required for specified plans and programmes in the fields of agriculture, forestry, fisheries, energy, industry, transport, waste and water management, telecommunications, tourism, town and country planning, and land use 'which set the framework for future development consent' for projects subject to the 1997 Directive on environmental assessment. Also covered are those plans and programmes determined to require assessment under the 1992 Directive on habitats because of their likely effects on wildlife sites. Other plans and programmes which set the framework for development consent of projects must also be subject to SEA, but only if Member States determine that they are likely to have significant environmental effects. Among other things, the Directive does not apply to strategies or plans and programmes solely concerned with national defence, civil emergency or financial or budget plans and programmes. Member States may also exempt plans and programmes which 'determine the use of small areas at local level' or are minor modifications to existing plans or programmes, where they decide that these will not have significant effects. The Directive sets out the criteria for 'significant effects'.

SEA applies at a broad level rather than to individual projects/developments that might arise under any particular strategy, programme or plan, and complements environmental impact assessments on individual projects.[7] It allows the cumulative effects of potential developments to be taken into account at an early stage and for alternative approaches to be considered before any decision is taken. Transparency of decision making is crucial to the SEA process, including public consultation and publication of the assessment. Broadly, the SEA process involves: preparing an environmental report (as defined); carrying out consultations; taking into account the environmental report and the results of the consultation in decision making; providing information on the decision; and post-decision monitoring.

The Directive has been implemented in the UK separately for England, Scotland, Wales and Northern Ireland, along with some cross-border measures. The administrations in England, Wales and Northern Ireland have decided to maintain the Directive's original scope, and in this form, the Directive covers plans and programmes, such as development plans under town and country planning laws and waste management plans under the Waste Directive.[8]

In contrast, the Environmental Assessment (Scotland) Act 2005 goes beyond the requirements of the Directive[9] to extend SEA's application to public sector strategies which are defined as strategies 'which are subject to preparation or adoption (or both) by a responsible authority at national, regional or local level; or which are prepared by a responsible authority for adoption through a legislative procedure'.[10] The Act also extends the application of SEA to all public sector strategies, programmes and plans likely to have significant environmental effects, regardless of whether they are required by legislative, regulatory or administrative means or whether they set a framework for future development consents.[11] Interestingly, as highlighted in Chapter 4, the Scottish Government has been reluctant to subject its own strategies to the SEA process. Notably, *The Government's Economic Strategy* (Scottish Government, 2007) was not accompanied by an SEA because, to quote the Cabinet Secretary for Finance and Sustainable Growth John Swinney:

> The Government has taken the view that the economic strategy provides a framework for several subsequent decisions that the Government may or may not take, all of which will be subject to strategic environmental assessment as appropriate. The Government has judged that focusing environmental assessment on detailed and specific initiatives, policies and programmes would be more meaningful and manageable. That would give a more meaningful account of the individual environmental impact, rather than the more generic impact, which is therefore more difficult to quantify, of 'The Government Economic Strategy'.[12]

Sustainability appraisals

'Sustainability appraisal' is a single appraisal tool that provides for the systematic identification and evaluation of the economic, social and environmental impacts of a proposal. Sustainability appraisals are used in various contexts in the UK including: by departments for activities relating to their operations and estates under the SDiG framework for office moves and so on (DEFRA, 2006b). The Ministry of Defence (MoD) has produced a 'Sustainability Appraisal Handbook' containing the toolkit to assist its project managers, decision makers and contractors in the integration of potential environmental, social and economic issues into their activities and to specify the further assessment of the identified impacts and subsequent redesign or mitigation measures. Although the MoD policy commitment to appraisal applies across the whole department, the Handbook is designed primarily for programmes, projects, activities and decisions that could affect the built estate. The guidance provides that the sustainability appraisal should: take a long-term view of the expected social, economic and environmental effects of a proposed plan; check that sustainability objectives are turned into sustainable planning policies; reflect global, national, regional and local concerns; and form an integral part of all stages of plan preparation.

In the context of town and country planning in the UK, sustainability appraisals evolved in the 1990s from the environmental appraisal of development plans by local planning authorities. In England and Wales Section 39 of the Planning and Compulsory Purchase Act 2004 now requires a sustainability appraisal to be carried out on development plan documents and supplementary planning documents as part of the Local Development Framework. Similarly, the Planning etc. (Scotland) Act 2006 has placed a new focus on how the National Planning Framework and Development Plans will contribute to sustainable development. A sustainability appraisal is used by planning authorities to assess whether proposed plans and policies meet sustainable development objectives. Sustainability appraisal in this context is similar to a SEA, but includes assessment of social and economic inputs, in addition to environmental inputs. Thus, development plans in the UK could be subjected to both a SEA and a sustainability appraisal.

The relationship between SEA and broader sustainability appraisals is an issue. While the primary concern of SEA is protection of the environment, sustainability appraisals balance the environment against other objectives.

In the initial Scottish Executive draft guidance on SEA for Development Plans, it was envisaged that some planning authorities may wish to extend the environmental assessment of the development plan to cover socio-economic issues. It notes that already, many of the assessments of Scottish development plans have been accompanied by full sustainability appraisals so that there is a growing amount of experience in this type of assessments (SEDD, 2003). The guidance indicated that an environmental assessment should comply with the SEA directive and it is up to individual planning authorities to decide if they wish to exceed its minimum requirements (SEDD, 2003). Sheate *et al.* conclude that:

> SEA and SA [sustainability appraisal] should, therefore, be seen as complementary to each other. The actual relationship between SEA and SA will depend upon the preferred interpretation of sustainable development. If a 'balanced' view is taken SEA will no doubt be seen as existing below SA in the assessment tier. If a stronger environmental view is taken then SEA may be seen as a preferable alternative to SA, or at the very least as a means of strengthening wider sustainability appraisal where it brings baseline information together with objectives led assessment.
>
> (Sheate *et al.*, 2003: 16)

In England, initially the ODPM (2003: para. 2.8) seemed to prefer the 'balanced' view described above as: 'the present guidance gives some indication of how an SEA can form part of a Sustainability Appraisal which also examines the social and economic effects of a plan'.

Another issue is how sustainability appraisal relates to other broader appraisal tools, such as integrated policy appraisal or, as it is now known in the UK, 'impact assessment'. As is discussed below, the broad tool used at UK level has recently undergone some substantial changes to accommodate sustainability appraisals and, based on the explanation below, it is fair to say that while the two are distinct, at least at the UK level, they also generally complement each other.

Impact assessment/integrated policy appraisal

Both the 1999 white paper, *Modernising Government* and *A Better Quality of Life: A Strategy for Sustainable Development for the United Kingdom* (the 1999 strategy), committed the UK Government to produce and deliver an integrated system of impact assessment and appraisal tools in support of sustainable development, covering impacts on business, the environment, health and the needs of particular groups in society (Prime Minister and Minister for Cabinet Office, 1999: ch. 2, para. 12; DEFRA, 1999).

In 1999, a key document produced in relation to integrated policy appraisal was a comprehensive guidance note – a checklist to provide guidance with screening

(Cabinet Office, 1999). The checklist provided that policy proposals be considered in relation to particular government objectives, key issues and data relating to modernizing government and sustainable development. Sustainable development was presented as an overriding objective along with that of modernizing government at the beginning of the checklist. The list then identified more specific policy areas, many of which are encompassed by sustainable development: scientific evidence, risk, environmental appraisal, rural proofing, equal treatment and health. The result was that each of these aspects of sustainable development was raised individually and discussed. Sustainable development appeared to be one of the processes or tools for bringing all the issues together and ensuring a balanced and sustainable decision-making process (Ross, 2003: 258).

In 2002, the checklist was replaced by the Cabinet Office Strategy Unit's new IPA tool (Cabinet Office Strategy Unit, 2002). The IPA is designed to assist policymakers 'screen' for the potential impacts of their proposals by providing access to the most up-to-date guidance. While the old checklist genuinely appeared to support the idea of sustainable development as a coordinating objective of government, this was less evident in the IPA where, along with many of its component parts, sustainable development is simply listed as one of 15 possible impacts (Sheate *et al.*, 2003: 15).

The EAC (2003: para. 44) noticed these difficulties: 'this tool is at present little more than a reminder to departmental staff that they must consider and, where relevant, carry out various other forms of appraisal' (EAC, 2003: para. 45).

More recently, the IPA has been replaced by impact assessment. The impact assessment process encourages policymakers to start with the premise that it is always desirable to identify and, as far as possible, assess the impacts of a policy proposal. The UK Better Regulation Executive (BRE) Impact Assessment Guidance describes an impact assessment as:

> A *tool* used by policymakers to assess and present the likely costs and benefits (monetised as far as possible) and the associated risks of a proposal that might have an impact on the public, private or civil society organisations, following Green Book's appraisal and evaluation techniques. A continuous process, consistent with the policy appraisal cycle, as set out in the Green Book, to help policymakers to fully think through the reasons for government intervention, to weigh up various options for achieving an objective and to understand the consequences of a proposed intervention.
>
> (BRE, 2010a: 2)

The BRE has compiled a one-stop 'Toolkit for Impact Assessment' for policymakers. Impact assessments are used to show the impacts (costs and benefits) of government policy on firms, individuals and government. Within the Toolkit is a revised Sustainable Development Specific Impact Test to help policymakers articulate sustainability issues more clearly within the impact assessment process (BRE, 2010b; Price and Durham, 2009).

The specific 'Sustainable Development Impact Assessment' is number 'A6.10'. It is listed after specific impact assessments for equality, health and wellbeing, competition, greenhouse gas and wider environmental impacts (BRE, 2010b: 76). It is good to see that each of these areas has their own specific impact assessment. In this regard, it is sensible that the sustainable development impact assessment is last. However, upon reading the toolkit it is not clear what the sustainable development impact assessment adds, or how it relates to the other impacts.

Further details are set out on the DEFRA website and are more explicit as to the added value of the sustainable development test. Essentially the SD test should be applied when first considering an issue and throughout the policy development process as appropriate. The results of the test can show ministers whether or not the options are compatible with sustainable development. The test provides a framework within which to combine information about Sustainable and Development Impacts with information from the rest of the IA about the balance of monetised and nonmonetised costs and benefits. Stage one of the test refers back to other IA including the wider environmental impact test extending its analysis to account for impacts beyond ten years and certain social aspects.

Stage two combines the results of Stage one with the results of the IA. Where it is calculated that the balance of monetized and non-monetized costs and benefits result has a net positive impact on society but there are SD-related issues, then:

- In the event of impacts on an environmental limit, accounting for advice from the responsible department, you should consider whether any necessary changes or additions to the policy affect the conclusion of the IA.
- In the event of significant long-term impacts, you should present this clearly to ministers, alongside any mitigating actions where appropriate, in order to allow them to decide whether or not the strength of the net benefits implied by the IA result is sufficient to outweigh any negative long-term impacts. (DEFRA, 2010)

This uses the 'capitals' approach recommended in the latest review, whereby impacts on environmental assets and social impacts are explicitly considered, even when they are hard to value (Price and Durham, 2009). Breaches of environmental limits in legislation will have to be explicitly highlighted in advice to ministers, and the responsible department will have to be informed so that measures can be sought to try and mitigate these impacts. It is also clear that policies with long-term impacts in the future may not be valued correctly in conventional cost-benefit analysis in impact assessments, and therefore, the new test introduces a requirement to graphically display large impacts falling in the future (DEFRA, 2010).

The result is that wider environmental concerns and health and wellbeing are taken into account – once for the sustainable development impact and then again separately, along with the sustainable development impact in the final decision-making process. The value added of the separate sustainable development assessment appears to be to ensure that decision makers are given clear evidence of the impacts on any environmental limits including the effects of changes and additions, as well as any significant long-term effects and possible mitigating actions. Unfortunately, without a clear vision, the policy direction remains muddled and the impact assessments, while providing information, fail to give a sense of priority.

In its third annual review in 2009, the SDC noted that the Scottish Government is developing an integrated assessment framework which will evaluate interventions for their economic, social and environmental costs and benefits (SDCS, 2009). The Commission hoped to engage with Government in the development of this framework and clarify how it links to the existing processes of sustainability appraisal and SEA (SDCS, 2009: 15).

The Welsh Integration Tool (WIT) is designed as an integrated appraisal mechanism to be used by officials when developing policies and evaluating projects. It was developed with the WAG by Forum for the Future. The WIT requires decision makers to answer a number of standard appraisal questions, such as what is being proposed, why and what are the potential risks. What it then adds is a set of questions about how a policy will contribute to a set of WAG objectives. It works as an integrative tool in two ways. First, it encourages officials to see how their work contributes to broader goals. Second, appraisal is a group activity involving individuals from outside the source of the policy, so again, it encourages thinking beyond departmental boundaries. The Tool has been promoted internally and externally and has generally been well received. Flynn and Marsden (2006: 62) found that:

> the Tool represents a considerable effort of time and resources to improve decision making and as such appears to have gained considerable legitimacy within the Assembly. As yet, though, there is little to show as to what it has achieved or that it has made any impact at senior political or managerial levels.
>
> (Flynn and Marsden, 2006: 62)

In Northern Ireland, all new strategies and policies are to be subject to a 'sustainability scan' as part of the impact assessment process, using the Northern Ireland Civil Service Policy Toolkit to enable departments to balance the social, economic and environmental dimensions of sustainable development (OFMDFM, n.d. b). The new Northern Ireland Strategy includes a commitment to review and consult on the effectiveness of their current policymaking guidance to reflect the objectives expressed throughout the Strategy (Northern Ireland Executive, 2010: 28). On a very positive note, the strategy emphasizes that 'A key part of the impact appraisal process which is often neglected is the scanning or scoping process. That is, the process whereby a decision is taken as to whether or not an appraisal or assessment is needed'. It recognizes the importance of this process and its first commitment is that: 'In the development of new strategies and policies, we will require departments to incorporate comprehensive "sustainability scans" as one component of their Impact Assessment process, which will provide SMART evidence of the inclusion of sustainability criteria' (Northern Ireland Executive, 2010).

Pre-legislative scrutiny

Uniquely in the UK, the Scotland Act 1998 requires the legislative competence of any bill to be assessed before it is introduced to Parliament and again before it receives Royal Assent.[13] In addition, the Standing Orders of the Scottish Parliament require every Executive-promoted bill to be accompanied by a policy memorandum setting out the bill's policy objectives, the alternative approaches considered, the consultation undertaken and an assessment of the effects of the bill on equal opportunities, human rights, island communities, local government, sustainable development and other matters considered relevant.[14] The policy memorandum provides an opportunity to argue the case for the bill and provides the basis for debate and discussion in the relevant committee.

A review of all of the sustainable development statements contained in policy memoranda from 1999 to April 2005 revealed no significant pattern and overall, the quality has remained variable. In 1999–2000, nine of the eleven policy memoranda accompanying bills claimed their bills had no impact on sustainable development, yet arguably, most subject areas can easily impact on sustainable development. However, regardless of a greater familiarity with the concept, the 'no impact' figure has remained high. Since 2001, between 38 per cent and 86 per cent of policy memoranda claimed their bills had no impact. Surprisingly, these 'no impact' bills encompass areas such as fur farming, dog fouling, local government, criminal justice, the abolition of feudal tenure, education and training, and standards in schools (Ross, 2006: 20).

At the other end of the spectrum, when the Executive perceived a bill to have a significant impact on sustainable development, the specific impacts were addressed comprehensively. As early as 2000, the policy memorandum accompanying the National Parks (Scotland) Bill included a widespread description of its potential impact on all aspects of sustainable development. In two later instances, the policy memoranda gave very detailed explanations of how each bill would address all aspects of sustainable development, making specific references to provisions in the bill. In both cases, the general statement on sustainable development was supported by separate statements on economic, social and environmental factors (Ross, 2006: 20).

Between the two extremes, the statements were very patchy. Some included a vague observation that the bill addressed all aspects of sustainable development. More often, the statement gave rough examples of the bill's contribution to all aspects of sustainable development. Policy memoranda post-2001 appear more likely to emphasize how a bill may contribute to social sustainability, and post-2003, more references are made to the Scottish Executive/Government policy on sustainable development, combined with a tendency to grasp at straws with respect to environmental impacts (Ross, 2006: 21). A review by Reid (2010) shows no significant change in this erratic use of the sustainable development statements in pre-legislative memoranda. For example, pre-legislative statements ought to have affected the subsequent parliamentary debates on bills, but there is little evidence of this happening. A study commissioned by the Environment, Resources and Development Committee revealed that while the Committee and Parliamentary discussions on bills failed to address all sustainable development issues, they did touch on many relevant ones, even when these were not mentioned in the policy memorandum. That said, the issue was rarely deliberately addressed and, instead, the discussions usually only strayed into a topic (Environment and Rural Development Committee, 2004b: 42–3).

Changes are needed to ensure that the sustainability impacts of legislation are identified as early as possible. This could be achieved by first employing something like a sustainability appraisal and then using its results to ensure that the policy memorandum is as comprehensive as possible. This would assist Parliament and committees in having a better understanding of the actual impacts of a bill.

Integration in finance and budgeting

As observed by Meadowcroft (2007), 'money is a key resource for government, an important mechanism of internal control and a tool for influencing societal behaviour'. The importance of integrating sustainable development into the finances of government is explained by MacNeill (2007: 21): 'The budget determines more than any other single statement of government policy, whether development will move in directions that are sustainable or unsustainable'.

Government finance has been divided into three for the purposes of analysis here: encouraging sustainable development through taxation; supporting sustainable development through investment; and including sustainable development in the design of budgeting processes.

Encouraging sustainable development through taxation

The tax system can be used to alter behaviour by taxing certain environmental 'bads' thus making alternatives more economical. The raising of environmental revenues through environmental taxes first appeared in earnest in 1987 through a tax differential on leaded petrol to encourage drivers to shift to vehicles using other types of fuel. Subsequently, green taxation has been extended to, among other things, automatic annual tax increases on vehicle fuel (the fuel levy), indirect tax on domestic fuel, lower vehicle excise rates for smaller cars and lorries, a tax on aggregates (quarrying), a ban on leaded petrol, a tax on waste going to landfill, and the climate change levy, which is a tax on non-domestic energy use. Essentially, as the Government explains in its 2009 response to an EAC report:

where the Treasury refers to environmental taxes it means the climate change levy, aggregates levy and landfill tax – those taxes that were introduced primarily to have an environmental impact. Each of these taxes was introduced alongside a cut in National Insurance Contributions as part of the shift from 'goods' to 'bads'.

(EAC, 2009a: 8)

To date, the benefits of taxation have been mixed. On a positive note, leaded petrol cars have been phased out and the landfill tax has led to increased recycling facilities being offered by local authorities. Problems exist on the purposes of some of the taxes, because when the economy is struggling or oil prices increase, the Government has yielded to pressure and suspended the fuel duty escalator (Jordan *et al.*, 2003: 187). In 2004, the SDC concluded that the use of environmental taxation is one area where the government has failed to put the environment into the heart of government (SDC, 2004: 21).

One difficulty relates to the purpose of environmental taxation. Such taxes could potentially have a dual impact. First, as discussed above, they can be used to alter behaviour in favour of more environmentally benign alternatives. They could also be used to support more positive initiatives by using the revenue they generate to pay for sustainable development initiatives (like public transport). Successive UK Governments have resisted hypothecating revenues in this way to particular spending programmes as it 'imparts inflexibility in spending decisions and can lead to a misallocation of resources, with reduced value for money for taxpayers'. As such Government's spending priorities are not in general, determined by the way in which the money is raised (EAC, 2009a: 8).

Investments, grants and subsidies to support sustainable development

One way government finance acts to support sustainable development is through the use of specialist funds. The funding can be directed at other (often lower) levels of government, companies, communities or individuals.

At EU level, cohesion policy is being used to provide incentives to national, regional and local governments of Member States. The EU invests in action to promote sustainable development by integrating sustainable development initiatives into national and regional development strategies. In the period 2007–13, €105 billion, or 30 per cent of the total €347 billion allocation for Cohesion Policy Funds, will be spent on the environment. Cohesion policy also promotes the development of policy mechanisms, such as the programming approach and multi-level governance, that support sustainable development within programme management structures and encourage regions to pursue sustainable development (European Commission, 2009: 12).

In 2008, the Scottish Government launched a £27.4 million fund to support community level action to cut carbon emissions in line with Scotland's ambitious targets set in the Climate Change (Scotland) Act 2009. Over 160 community projects have been funded, ranging in scale from bids of just a few hundred pounds to carry out community surveys, to million pound-plus projects aiming to achieve significant levels of behaviour change. For example, Zero Carbon Dunbar 2025, aims to involve the whole community in transforming Dunbar into a zero-carbon, sustainable community by 2025, by cutting carbon emissions by 10 per cent each year with a short-term goal of cutting 2.5 tonnes of carbon dioxide per household. This is mainly to be achieved by engaging with house-holders to achieve significant behaviour change in relation to energy use in the home. A drop-in advice centre on the High Street of Dunbar offers home energy surveys which emphasize the benefits to householders of tackling fundamentals such as insulation and organizes follow-up visits to support people in keeping to commitments made (SDCS, 2009: 45).

Conversely, it is important to ensure that subsidies are not going towards unsustainable activities. To assist in limiting this, the EC aimed to put forward a roadmap for the reform by 2008/09, sector by sector, of subsidies that have considerable negative effects on the environment and are incompatible with sustainable development, with a view to gradually eliminating them (European Commission, 2009: 24). While the wait for the roadmap is ongoing, some progress has been made in relation to case studies using OECD criteria (Valsecchi *et al.*, 2009).

Green budgeting, spending reviews and public service agreements

Green budgeting actually encompasses a wide range of activities involving a diverse range of actors, institutions and instruments. The process of developing expenditure priorities, formally adopting the budget, implementing the spending programmes, monitoring and evaluating their effectiveness and raising revenue, could all be said to form part of a budgetary life cycle (Wilkinson *et al.*, 2008: 70). In the UK, all of the administrations throughout the past 30 years or so have used the budgetary process to meet environmental protection objectives and thus, integrate environmental protection concerns into financing decisions. The main tools currently being used are spending reviews and public service agreements in various forms. Other possibilities, such as those using an eco-systems management approach, whereby the costs of certain ecosystem services are included in the costs of the activity, are still in development. These are discussed in turn below.

The spending review is a key tool in the finance armoury of each of the administrations. In the UK, the spending review operates as a biannual detailed examination of portfolio budgets, whereby spending plans and targets are set for the next three-year period. The outcome of the spending review forms part of the budgeting process and is reflected in the planned budget alloca-tions for those 'forward' financial years covered by the most recent spending review. These can potentially provide an opportunity to reorient government towards a sustainable development agenda and encourage integration and coordination.

It was the Labour Government which introduced a two-yearly cross-departmental process of reviewing spending, whereby all UK departments had to bid to the Treasury for their upcoming spending allocations. The aim is to align future spending programmes with the Government's core priorities (EAC HC 92, session 1998/99, para. 2). As part of the process, the Treasury agreed public service agreements with each department, which stipulate specific policy targets. The spending review has also been used to foster integration. For example, in the 1998 and 2000 reviews, departments were asked to consider sustainable development in their spending plans (EAC HC 92, session 1998/99, para. 11; HC 70 session 2000/01, appendix). In the 2002–2004 reviews, a more systematic sustainable development reporting process was introduced to support each department's bid for funding (Russel and Jordan, 2008: 253).

The actual performance of the UK's spending review process does not appear to have been a great success. Even when departments were required to produce a sustainable development report (as in the 2002 review), their quality was poor. Indeed, many seemed to be written long after the main spending priorities had been decided (Russel and Jordan, 2008: 257). In 2004, this requirement to produce separate reports was reduced to a voluntary activity. The Treasury argued that the sustainable development considerations should be integrated into individual department's submissions (Russel and Jordan, 2008: 257).

There is also some dispute regarding the value of public service agreements. They were also mentioned in the 2005 strategy as a means of enforcing the government's accountability commitments. Yet, the EAC has commented on the small number of environmental targets in the public service agreements produced as part of the 2002 and 2004 reviews. In the 2004 review, only ten of the 124 departmental targets were environmental and six were the responsibility of DEFRA. Although public service agreements are supposed to explain who is responsible for the delivery of individual targets, they are often framed in such imprecise and unenforceable terms, that they are effectively little more than weak mission statements (Russel and Jordan, 2008: 257).

The UK coalition Government took a different approach to the 2010 spending review, taking the view that the complex system of public service agreements relied too heavily on rigid targets. Instead, the Government asked departments to publish business plans that show the resources they need to protect key frontline services and deliver on their objectives. To ensure that resources are prioritized within tighter budgets, departments were to prioritize their main programmes against a tough set of criteria to ensure value for money in public spending. The criteria are: is the activity essential to meet Government priorities?; does the Government need to fund this activity?; does the activity provide substantial economic value?; can the activity be targeted to those most in need?; how can the activity be provided at lower cost?; how can the activity be provided more effectively?; can the activity be provided by a non-state provider or by citizens, wholly, or in partnership?; can non-state providers be paid to carry out the activity according to the results they achieve?; and can local bodies, as opposed to central Government, provide the activity? (HM Treasury, 2010).

Unfortunately, the process now makes no mention at all of any sustainable development objective.

The potential of the whole spending review process to really contribute to the implementation of sustainable development is more evident from an analysis of the 2002 Scottish Spending Review, whereby sustainable development was among the priorities set for the Spending Review.[15] Departments produced draft aims, objectives and targets for their portfolios, along with a detailed assessment of what the spending in their area would achieve. In relation to sustainable development, departments were expected to demonstrate the extent to which their proposals would, for example, lead to reductions in resources use or reduce the need for travel (for example by improved logistics and planning and the use of advanced technologies).

The statements prepared for each portfolio were then examined by the now defunct Cabinet Sub-committee on Sustainable Scotland. Commentary from the Sub-committee was referred back to departments and used to refine the statements and the aims, objectives and targets. The revised statements were returned to the Sub-committee so that its views could be taken into account by the Cabinet when making the final decisions on the Spending Review. The approach generated some major commitments to sustainable development in Scotland across the Executive (Scottish Executive, 2002), including:

- increasing the amount of waste collected by local authorities which is recycled or composted to 25 per cent
- developing education for sustainable development across the curriculum, including initiatives like the Sustainable Secondary Schools Initiative and Eco-Schools
- working with the Enterprise Networks to promote growth in clean technology sectors, including renewable energy and energy efficiency; resulting in the production of the Green Business Strategy.

As a follow-up to its role on the Spending Review, the Cabinet Sub-committee would monitor and review progress on the targets contained in the sustainability statements (CSCSS, 2002: para. 12). It also deliberated its role in the 2004 spending review process (CSCSS, 2004). This circular process clearly integrates and monitors sustainable development in relation to the spending plans of departments and, while some improvements could be made, is a useful internal coordinating mechanism. Since the disbanding of the Cabinet Sub-committee it is not clear who has taken on this responsibility. Another danger in Scotland is that there is no objective external review of the process to highlight its successes and problems and suggest where improvements could be made. This gap does not exist at the UK level as the EAC regularly scrutinizes the spending review process.

Assessing the certain impacts of the budget

More recently, some basic attempts have been made to assess not just the sustainability impacts of an administration's entire budget, but its carbon impact.

The Scottish Government has published the carbon assessment of the Scottish Budget 2010–2011, the first such appraisal undertaken anywhere, along with the Climate Change Delivery Plan and Carbon Assessment of Transport. While refinement of the methodology will be required, these represent significant contributions to the development of effective machinery for addressing carbon in Government (Scottish Government, 2009).

Valuing eco-systems services

Arguably, to really make government finance sustainable in the sense of being ecologically and economically sound, account needs to be taken of the costs and benefits to the environment of a particular decision. In July 2011, HM Treasury and Department for Work and Pensions published a Green Book discussion paper on valuing social impacts such as health, family and community stability, educational success and environmental assets which cannot be inferred from market prices, where it acknowledges that the valuation of such non-market impacts should not be ignored in decision making. (Fujiwara and Campbell, 2011; HM Treasury, n.d.).

In recent years, attempts have also been made to quantify key benefits including nutrient recycling, food production, water regulation, waste treatment and cultural benefits. Systems could be put in place to provide compensation for the loss of such ecosystem services. For example, compensation would be paid by a developer of a golf course for the loss of wetlands. More difficult would be trying to charge businesses and individuals for the use of certain ecosystem services. An industry would have to pay not only for the use of clean water, but also for the detrimental effect this would have on the ecosystem. At present, there remain many scientific, economic and legal hurdles which would need to be addressed before this type of system could be used in the UK, although research has been commissioned throughout the UK to bring this about (Reid, 2011; Christie *et al.*, 2011).

Conclusion

The integration of environmental protection and, more broadly, sustainable development into the activities of government in some respects is one of the easier asks of the OECD criteria. There are a wide range of tools and these can often be introduced without having to expressly set out allegiance to a particular 'vision' of sustainable development, especially one which runs counter to the traditional pro-growth model. However, given the piecemeal success described above it is clear that it is not that simple.

Ideally, integration emerges spontaneously as actors realize their interdependence in particular areas and take steps to address this. Schout and Jordan (2008: 53) note that this view sees hierarchical coordination from above or allocating specific coordinating roles as unnecessary and as adding extra layers of bureaucracy. Coordination from this viewpoint takes place by bargaining and interaction between the relevant actors. However, as Schout and Jordan explain reliance on bureaucratic politics does not tend to work in relation to environmental protection for three main reasons. First, environmental quality is a public good so there is little incentive for actors to routinely take environmental protection into account. Second, officials in sectoral ministries will not enter into conflict over environmental matters, as they do not see these as relevant or important enough to fight over. The result is that economic aspects continue to dominate decision making. Another difficulty is that environmental concerns tend to be allocated to weak ministries, compared to other sectoral ministries. Finally, asking sectors to take the environment into account is also unlikely to have an enduring impact, as it requires ministries to act in ways which often deviate away from direct achievement of their main objectives (Schout and Jordan, 2008: 53).

These three issues can be overcome using the right tools. For example, the creation of mega departments like the Department of Energy and Climate Change, and the use of crosscutting units, and ministerial and other high-level committees to deal with specific issues, both within and between administrations, encourages working across organizations.

The OECD maintains that having a variety of integration elements to pursue coordination at different levels is a necessary but not sufficient condition for greater integration (OECD, 2002b). The UK has many mechanisms and yet, often, they do not work well in combination. So, for example, no SEA was conducted on the Scottish Government's *Economic Strategy* and, as detailed in Chapter 9, too many of the sustainable development indicators are unrelated to specific aims in the relevant strategy. Furthermore, an effective supply of information on possible policy overlaps or spill-overs is very important to the success of an administratively based EPI system like that used in the UK. There needs to be more opportunities for information to flow between departments and administrations and for that information to be relayed down the organizations (Russel and Jordan, 2008: 264).

It is also clear that the traditional working of the UK public sector and those processes encapsulated in the term 'departmentalism' can easily stop integration initiatives in their tracks. Departmental officials must be given incentives to engage with environmental integration initiatives in order to think beyond their department's core sectoral interests. Adding SDiG targets to the performance goals for all Permanent Secretaries is a move in the right direction, but these could be further integrated into many more job descriptions, together with obligations to be involved in environmental coordination initiatives on a daily basis (Schout and Jordan, 2008: 265).

In the UK, it is safe to say that some integration methods have been more successful than others. The UK administrations have had only very limited success at integrating environmental and sustainable development factors into policymaking. This is consistent with the findings of Jacob *et al.* (2008: 42) who found that 'most countries seem to prefer to develop policy objectives and frameworks that flag the importance of EPI without developing operational structures and procedures that significantly alter the distribution of power among the various actors involved or decisively change the prevailing political and administrative routines of policymaking'. Jacob also notes that 'the harder and more consequential instruments that make the environment a main concern for all sectoral policymakers are adopted less frequently and with far less enthusiasm' (Jacob *et al.*, 2008: 42). Indeed, even when the UK has introduced harder mechanisms such as SEA, impact assessment and pre-legislative scrutiny, these have been seldom or restrictively used and have all failed to make headway towards putting sustainable development or environment into the heart of government policymaking. Instead, these seem to have been more about making the right noises at times when the environment or sustainable development were high on the political agenda.

The UK's progress in relation to 'greening' its budgetary cycle has been more mixed. Some progress is being made, especially in relation to the climate change mechanisms such as the climate change levy and investment in low-carbon technologies. However, experiments involving the introduction of sustainable development into the budgetary processes, such as through the spending reviews, have been short-lived and quickly watered down.

The fact that many of the instruments are deployed in a superficial and ad hoc manner, with little attention paid to diagnosing underlying problems, seems to support the theory that there is an undeniable tendency to deploy the 'easier' instruments (missions statements, weak teams, specification of task, and so on), than some of the more 'difficult' ones (rules, specification of outputs, and so on) (Schout and Jordan, 2008: 65). Moreover, the analysis here suggests that even when these more 'difficult' mechanisms exist for policy integration, they may not stand the test of time, as where it is possible, especially in difficult times, new governments will remove the instigators of real change (such as the SDC) to protect conventional economic and, often, short-term objectives.

However, there is one large exception to this general conclusion. Several 'harder mechanisms' have been successfully introduced in relation to the operations of government and workings of the government estate. The SDiG programme in particular has set ever-increasing targets, introduced tough reporting and review processes, and, in many areas, delivered real results. The fact that the UK's success has been held up to the other administrations to encourage them to follow suit also demonstrates the value of imparting information across administrations. The UK needs to apply its knowledge on integration in operations and apply it to policy.

Once again, the issue of leadership arises. Effective integration must be based on a system of mutual inter-dependence between the bottom and the top. Leadership from the top is needed to override departmental sectoral interests and yet the leadership needs to be compelled into action through pressure and scrutiny from environmental groups, public bodies, the wider public and, possibly, the courts.

The mechanisms described in this chapter have all been policy or institutional in nature. The next chapter deals with the role of law and legal obligations to promote sustainable development and, in many instances, support the mechanisms set out here. Law, as a means of making social policy binding, may even offer solutions to some of the challenges to policy integration described above.

Chapter 10 then deals with monitoring and accountability, and the importance of changes in the accountability structures to reflect integrated responsibilities and roles should not be underestimated. If the component parts are jointly accountable to the same body, then this may force them to cooperate with one another and the centre. In fact, pressure from the outside may be the most effective incentive to work together.

Notes

1 Consolidated versions of the Treaty on European Union and the Treaty on the Functioning of the European Union, *Official Journal of the European Union* (OJ) (2008), C 115.
2 Consolidated versions of the Treaty on European Union and the Treaty on the Functioning of the European Union (OJ) (2008), C 115.
3 Directive 2001/42/EC on the assessment of certain plans and programmes on the environment (OJ) (2001), L 197/30.
4 Directive 2001/42/EC on the assessment of certain plans and programmes on the environment (OJ) (2001), L 197/30.
5 House of Commons Debates, column 176WH, 18 January 2010.
6 Directive 2001/42/EC on the assessment of certain plans and programmes on the environment (OJ) (2001), L 197/30.
7 Directive 85/337/EEC on the assessment of the effects of certain public and private projects on the environment (OJ) (1985), L 175, as amended by Directive 97/11/EC (OJ) (1997), L 73.
8 See the Environmental Assessment of Plans and Programmes Regulations 2004 (SI 2004, No. 1633); the Environmental Assessment of Plans and Programmes (Wales) Regulations 2004 (WSI 2004, No. 1656); and the Environmental Assessment of Plans and Programmes Regulations (Northern Ireland) 2004 (SR 2004, No. 280). None of these go beyond the remit of the Directive.
9 The Environmental Assessment (Scotland) Act 2005 asp 15.
10 The Environmental Assessment (Scotland) Act 2005 s. 4(1).
11 The Environmental Assessment (Scotland) Act 2005 ss. 5, 6.
12 Meeting of the Parliament, 13 December 2007, answer to question S30 p 4426, Scottish Parliamentary Corporate Body, Edinburgh, http://www.scottish.parliament.uk/Apps2/Business/ORSearch/ReportView.aspx?r=4762&mode=pdf, accessed 24 May 2011.
13 The Scotland Act 1998 ch. 46 ss. 31–6.
14 Standing Orders of the Scottish Parliament 3rd Edition (4th Revision) (June 2009) Chapter 9.3.3 – note increasing numbers of Committee and Members bills are accompanied by policy memoranda.
15 The others were health, education, crime, transport and jobs and closing the opportunity gap.

References

Better Regulation Executive (BRE) (2010a) *Impact Assessment Guidance*, Version 1.0, URN: 10/898, London: BRE.
BRE (2010b) *Impact Assessment Toolkit*, Version 1.0, URN: 10/901, London: BRE.
British Government Panel on Sustainable Development (1997) *Third Report*, London: DOE.

CAG Consultants (2004) *Is the Scottish Executive Structured and Positioned to Deliver Sustainable Development?*, 10th Report, vol. 2, Edinburgh: Environment and Rural Development Committee.

Cabinet Office (1999) *Policymakers Checklist: Using Impact Assessment and Appraisal – A Toolkit*, London: Cabinet Office.

Cabinet Office Strategy Unit (2002) *Impact Assessment and Appraisal Guidance Checklist for Policymakers*, London: Cabinet Office.

Cabinet Sub-Committee Sustainable Scotland (CSCSS) (2002) Annual Report 2002, http://www.scotland.gov.uk/Resource/Doc/921/0002369.doc, accessed 26 July 2011.

CSCSS (2004) *Report of meeting held 10 March 2004*, http://www.scotland.gov.uk/Resource/Doc/921/0002369.doc, accessed 26 July 2011.

Canadian Commissioner of the Environment and Sustainable Development (2000) 2000 May Report of the Commissioner of the Environment and Sustainable Development, Ottawa: Office of the Auditor General of Canada, http://www.oag-bvg.gc.ca/internet/English/parl_cesd_200005_e_1137.html, accessed 27 July 2011.

Centre for Management and Policy Studies (2001) *Better Policymaking*, London: CMPS.

Civil Service (n.d.) http://www.civilservice.gov.uk/about/index.aspx, accessed 21 January 2011.

Christie, M. *et al.* (2011) Economic Valuation of Benefits of Ecosystems Services delivered by the UK Biodiversity Action Plan, London, DEFRA.

Cynnal Cymru – Sustain Wales (n.d.) *Work Plan 2009–2010*, http://www.sustainwales.com/home/downloads/90406_-_Final_Work_Plan_2009_-_2010.pdf, accessed 5 September 2010.

Daintith, T. and Page, A. (1999) *The Executive in the Constitution: Structure, Autonomy, and Internal Control*, Oxford: Oxford University Press.

Department of Environment, Food and Rural Affairs (DEFRA) (1999) *A Better Quality of Life: A Strategy for Sustainable Development for the United Kingdom*, London: DEFRA.

DEFRA (2002a) *Sustainable Development in Government Annual Report*, London: DEFRA.

DEFRA (2002b) *Framework for Sustainable Development on the Government Estate*, London: DEFRA.

DEFRA (2003) *Sustainable Development in Government Annual Report*, London: DEFRA.

DEFRA (2004) *Framework for Sustainable Development on the Government Estate*, London: DEFRA.

DEFRA (2005) *The UK Strategy for Sustainable Development: Securing the Future*, London: DEFRA.

DEFRA (2006a) *Sustainable Operations on the Government Estate*, London: DEFRA.

DEFRA (2006b) 'Mandate Detail', http://www.defra.gov.uk/sustainable/government/gov/estates/mandate-detail.htm, accessed 5 September 2010.

DEFRA (2006c) *Procuring the Future: Sustainable Procurement Action Plan*, London: DEFRA.

DEFRA (2010) 'Sustainable Development Impact Assessment', http://www.defra.gov.uk/corporate/policy/guidance/sd-impact/, accessed 28 May 2010.

DEFRA (n.d.) Sustainable Development in Government website, http://sd.defra.gov.uk/progress/soge/performance-data-2010/target-areas/perm-sec-objectives/, accessed 24 May 2011.

Environment and Rural Development Committee (2004a) *10th Report*, Vol. 1, SP Paper 206, Edinburgh: Scottish Parliament.

Environment and Rural Development Committee (2004b) *10th Report*, Vol. 2, SP Paper 206, Edinburgh: Scottish Parliament.

Environmental Audit Committee (EAC) (1998a) 'EAC of the House of Commons', Press Release 03/97–98, London: House of Commons.

EAC (1998b) *Sixth Report 1998–99*, HC 426, London: House of Commons.

EAC (2002) *First Report 2001–02*, HC 67, London: House of Commons.

EAC (2003) *Thirteenth Report 2002–03*, HC 961, London: House of Commons.

EAC (2009a) *Fourth Special Report Pre-Budget Report 2008: Government Response to the Committee's Third Report 2008–2009*, HC 563, London: House of Commons.

EAC (2009b) *Greening Government: Sixth Report of Session 2008–2009*, HC 503, London: House of Commons.

ECT Strategic Partnership (2009) *Environmental and Clean Technologies Action Plan 2009/10*, Edinburgh: Scottish Government.

European Commission (2009) *Mainstreaming Sustainable Development into EU Policies: 2009 Review of the European Union Strategy for Sustainable Development*, Com 400, Brussels: European Commission.

European Council (2006) *Review of the EU Sustainable Development Strategy: Renewed Strategy*, Brussels: European Council.

Flynn, A. and Marsden, T. (2006) *Aiming Higher: Assessing the Sustainable Development Plans and Actions of the Welsh Assembly in terms of its Commitments in the UK wide strategy: A Report to the Sustainable Development Commission*, Cardiff: Cardiff School of City and Regional Planning.

Fujiwara, D. and Campbell, R. (2011) Valuation Techniques for Social Cost-Benefit Analysis: Stated Preference, Revealed Preference and Subjective Well-Being Approaches – A Discussion of Current Issues, London, HM Treasury, DWP.

Health and Finance Directorate (2009) *Sustainable Development Strategy for NHS Scotland*, CEL 15 (2009), Edinburgh: Scottish Government.

HM Treasury (2010) *Budget 2010*, HC 61, London: HM Treasury.

HM Treasury (2011) *Budget 2011*, HC 836, London: HM Treasury.

HM Treasury and Public Services Productivity Panel (2001) *The Role of External Review in Improving Performance*, London: HM Treasury.

Jacob, K., Volkery, A. and Lenschow, A. (2008) 'Instruments for environmental policy integration in 30 OECD countries', in A. Jordan and A. Lenschow (eds) *Innovation in Environmental Policy: Integrating the Environment for Sustainability*, Cheltenham: Edward Elgar.

Jordan, A. and Lenschow, A. (2008) 'Integrating the environment for sustainable development: An introduction', in A. Jordan and A. Lenschow (eds) *Innovation in Environmental Policy: Integrating the Environment for Sustainability*, Cheltenham: Edward Elgar.

Jordan, A., Wurzel, R., Zito, A. and Bruckner, L. (2003) 'Policy innovation or "muddling through"? "New" environmental policy instruments in the United Kingdom', *Environmental Politics*, 12(1): 179–200.

Kavanagh, D. and Richards, D. (2001) 'Departmentalism and joined-up government: Back to the future?', *Parliamentary Affairs*, 54(1): 1–18.

Labour Party (1997) *In trust for tomorrow: Labour Party Manifesto*, London: Labour Party.

Laffery, W. and Hovden, E. (2003) 'Environmental policy integration: Towards an analytical framework', *Environmental Politics*, 12(3): 1–22.

Ling, T. (2002) 'Delivering joined-up government in the UK: Dimensions, issues and problems', *Public Administration*, 80(4): 615–42.

MacNeill, J. (2007) 'Leadership for sustainable development', in OECD, *Institutionalizing Sustainable Development*, Paris: OECD.

Mandelson, P. and Liddle, R. (1996) *The Blair Revolution: Can New Labour Deliver?*, London: Faber & Faber.

Meadowcroft, J. (2007) 'National sustainable development strategies: Features, challenges and reflexivity', *European Environment*, 17(3): 152–63.

Mulgan, G. and Lee, A. (2001) *Better Policy Delivery and Design*, London: Performance and Innovation Unit.

National School of Government (2010a) 'Programmes', http://www.nationalschool.gov.uk/programmes/keyword.asp?id=299, accessed 5 September 2010.

National School of Government (2010b) 'Core Learning Programme', http://www.nationalschool.gov.uk/csclp/index.asp, accessed 5 September 2010.

Northern Ireland Executive (2010) *Everyone's Involved: Sustainable Development Strategy*, Belfast: Northern Ireland Executive.

Northern Ireland Executive (2011) *Focus on the Future, Sustainable Development Implementation Plan for 2011–2014*, Belfast: Northern Ireland Executive.

Office of the First Minister and Deputy First Minister (OFMDFM) (n.d. a) 'Sustainable Operations on the Government Estate', http://www.ofmdfmni.gov.uk/index/economic-policy/economic-policy-sustainable-development/sustainable-development-sustainable-operations.htm, accessed 5 September 2010.

OFMDFM (n.d. b) http://www.ofmdfmni.gov.uk/index/improving-public-services/policylink/policy-toolkit.htm, accessed 24 May 2011.

Office of Government Commerce (OGC) (2010) 'Government Delivery', http://www.ogc.gov.uk/sustainability_programme_progress.asp, accessed 30 August 2010.

OGC (n.d.) 'What's new', http://www.ogc.gov.uk/index.asp, accessed 5 September 2010.

Office of the Deputy Prime Minister (ODPM) (2003) *The Strategic Environmental Assessment Directive: Guidance for Planning Authorities*, London: ODPM.

Organisation for Economic Co-operation and Development (OECD) (2002a) *Improving Policy Coherence and Integration for Sustainable Development: A Checklist*, Paris: OECD.

OECD (2002b) *Environmental Performance Reviews: the UK*, Paris: OECD.

Porritt, J. (2009) 'The Standing of sustainable development in government', http://www.jonathonporritt.com/pages/2009/11/the_standing_of_sustainable_de.html, accessed 12 April 2010.

Price, R. and Durham, C. (2009) *Review of Economics of Sustainable Development*, London: Government Economic Service and DEFRA.

Prime Minister and Minister for Cabinet Office (1999) *Modernising Government*, Cm 4310, London: HMSO.

Reid, C.T. (2010) 'Environment and sustainable development', in E.E. Sutherland, K.E. Goodall, G.F.M. Little and F. Davidson (eds) *Law Making and the Scottish Parliament: The Early Years*, Edinburgh: Edinburgh University Press.

Reid, C.T. (2011) 'The Privatisation of Biodiversity? Possible New Approaches to Nature Conservation Law in the UK', *Journal of Environmental Law*, 23, doi10.1093/JEL/eqr005.

Ross, A. (2003) 'Is the environment getting squeezed out of sustainable development?', *Public Law*, Summer: 249–59.

Ross, A. (2005) 'The UK approach to delivering sustainable development in government: A case study in joined-up working', *Journal of Environmental Law*, 17(1): 27–49.

Ross, A. (2006) 'Sustainable development in Scotland post-devolution', *Environmental Law Review*, 8: 6–32.

Russel, D. and Jordan, A. (2008) 'The United Kingdom', in A. Jordan and A. Lenschow, *Innovation in Environmental Policy: Integrating the Environment for Sustainability*, Cheltenham: Edward Elgar.

Schout, A. and Jordan, A. (2008) 'Administrative instruments', in A. Jordan and A. Lenschow (eds) *Innovation in Environmental Policy: Integrating the Environment for Sustainability*, Cheltenham: Edward Elgar.

Scottish Executive (2002) *Building a Sustainable Scotland: Sustainable Development and the Spending Review*, Edinburgh: Scottish Executive.

Scottish Executive (2003) *Sustaining Our Working Environment Annual Report 2002/2003*, Edinburgh: Scottish Executive.

Scottish Executive (2004a) *Sustaining Our Working Environment Annual Report 2003/2004*, Edinburgh: Scottish Executive.

Scottish Executive (2004b) *Strategic Environmental Assessment A Consultation on the Proposed Environmental Assessment (Scotland) Bill*, Paper 2004/12, Edinburgh: Scottish Executive.

Scottish Executive Development Department (SEDD) (2003) *Interim Planning Advice Environmental Assessment of Development Plans*, Edinburgh: David Tyldesley & Associates, Scottish Executive Social Research.

SEDD (2004) *Planning Circular 2/04 Strategic Environmental Assessment for Development Planning: the Environmental Assessment of Plans and Programmes (Scotland) Regulations 2004*, Edinburgh: SEDD.

Scottish Government (2007) *The Government's Economic Strategy*, Edinburgh: Scottish Government.

Scottish Government (2009) Carbon Assessment of the 2010–2011 Draft Budget, Edinburgh, Scottish Government http://www.scotland.gov.uk/publications/2009/09/17102339/0 accessed 14 September 2011.

Sheate, W.R., Dagg, S., Richardson, J., Ashemann, R., Palerm, J. and Steen, U. (2003) 'Integrating the environment into strategic decision making: Conceptualizing policy SEA', *European Environment*, 13(1): 1–18.

Sustainable Development Commission (SDC) (2004) *Shows Promise. But Must Try Harder: An Assessment by the Sustainable Development Commission of the Government's Reported Progress on Sustainable Development over the Past Five Years*, London: SDC.

SDC (2008) *Driving Change Sustainable Development Action Plans Guidance for Government Organizations*, London: SDC.

SDC (2010) *Becoming the 'Greenest Government Ever'*, London: SDC.

Sustainable Development Commission Scotland (SDCS) (2009) *Sustainable Development: Third Annual Assessment of Progress by the Scottish Government*, Edinburgh: SDCS.

Sustainable Development Commission Wales (SDCW) (2009) *Sustainable Development in Government Wales 2009*, Cardiff: SDCW.

UN General Assembly (UNGA) (1992) *The Rio Declaration on Environment and Development*, A/CONF.151/26 Vol. 1, New York: UN.

Valsecchi, C., ten Brink, P., Bassi, S., Withana, S., Lewis, M., Best A., Oosterhuis, F., Dias Soares, C., Rogers-Ganter, H. and Kaphengst, T. (2009) *Environmentally Harmful Subsidies: Identification and Assessment* (Final report for the European Commission's DG Environment), Brussels: Institute for European Environmental Policy.

Welsh Assembly Government (WAG) (2009a) *Green Dragon Standard Environmental Report 2008–2008*, Cardiff: WAG.

WAG (2009b) *One Wales: One Planet: The Sustainable Development Scheme of the Welsh Assembly Government*, Cardiff: WAG.

Wilkinson, D., Benson, D. and Jordan, A. (2008) 'Green budgeting', in A. Jordan and A. Lenschow (eds) *Innovation in Environmental Policy: Integrating the Environment for Sustainability*, Cheltenham: Edward Elgar.

World Commission on Environment and Development (WCED) (1987) *Our Common Future*, Oxford: Oxford University Press.

8 Mechanisms – the role of legislation[1]

Clearly, the move towards sustainable development requires public sector bodies to alter their behaviour to consider the various aspects of sustainable development and, among other things, become more integrated and open in their decision making. If such a change is needed to actually deliver sustainable development, then it is tempting to compel that change by legislating. Legislation can be used to formalize both procedural processes and substantive duties in relation to environmental policy integration and, more broadly, sustainable development. It can also be used to entrench a particular vision of sustainable development or various related principles in a more constitutional sense.

The first appearance of the word 'sustainable' in the sense of environmental sustainability in a UK statute was in the Natural Heritage (Scotland) Act 1991.[2] Since then, 'sustainable' and 'sustainable development' have slowly become increasingly common terms in UK legislation. Yet, while many countries, such as New Zealand, have used legislation to drive their sustainable development agenda forward at a comparatively early stage (Bosselmann and Grinlinton, 2002; Curran, 2004: 267),[3] the UK's initial approach to the sustainable development agenda was largely non-legislative (Ross, 2005: chs 4, 7). Indeed, in 2000, the Government dismissed the need for legislation, stating that sustainable development could be placed at the heart of an organization by policy directions from the executive or by the inclusion of non-statutory aims and objectives (DETR, 2000: paras. 5.2, 5.4). There is also a view that the needs of sustainable development are often better served by specific provisions rather than any general overarching duty or objective. As the Environment and Rural Development Committee of the Scottish Parliament reported, 'although these "catch all" sustainable development clauses have a place in legislation, if there are clearly identifiable sustainable development issues raised by a Bill, these will be more effectively addressed directly, rather than mopped up in a single phrase' (CAG Consultants, 2004: 43). This is the case in the UK and there are many instances of legislation that makes no explicit reference to sustainable development, yet clearly is aimed at addressing certain sustainable developmnt issues. For example, amendments to the Town and Country Planning (Scotland) Act 1997 s. 72 impose certain obligations on local authorities to include greenhouse gas emission policies in development plans through the installation and operation of low- or zero-carbon generating technologies.[4] Clearly, this potentially will have a huge impact on sustainable development, despite no mention of it in the provision.

Moreover, in a review of the UK Parliament's use of sustainable development duties published in 2002, Jenkins concluded that while none of the duties created legal obligations, they could have significant value as statements of policy (Jenkins, 2002: 601). Thus, there is merit in legislating using sustainable development language for even just for symbolic reasons. However, such legislation could do much more and could be used to explicitly allocate responsibility, and promote, or indeed institutionalize, integrated working or crystallize a particular vision.

Since 1999, references to sustainable development have become much more commonplace in statutes of both the UK and Scottish Parliaments. In 2008, Ross reported that 0.4 per cent (two out of 455) of the UK statutes enacted from 1991 to 1998 referred to sustainable development. In contrast, 4.7 per cent (12 out of 255) of UK statutes and 11 per cent (10 out of 91) of Scottish statutes enacted from 1999 to 2005 referred to sustainable development (Ross, 2008: 37). Three possible reasons for the increase are worth noting. First, the UK tends to use legislation to crystallize environmental policy once it has been tested and is more widely accepted. Over the last decade, sustainable development has proven its resilience as a policy tool and now can be more formally recognized. For example, sustainable development has been a key policy objective of the planning systems both north and south of the border for many years, but was only included in a relevant statute in England and Wales in 2004 and in the Scottish equivalent in late 2006.[5] Second, much of the sustainable development agenda falls within the competence of the devolved administrations, and Ross found that a greater percentage of Scottish statutes refer to sustainable development (Ross, 2008: 37). One reason for this is that some of the areas devolved to the Scottish Parliament – environment, local government and planning – are more associated with the concept, than reserved matters such as immigration, abortion or foreign affairs. However, it also shows an increased willingness on the part of the Scottish administration to use the term in its legislation. Following the success of the Green Party in the second post-devolution election in Scotland, party leaders evidently perceived that a sound environmental record would appeal to the electorate, and the second partnership agreement between Labour and the Liberal Democrats has a very obvious environmental or 'green' thread running through it (Scottish Labour Party and Scottish Liberal Democrats, 2003). Indeed, the Scottish Parliament has made sustainable development a primary objective for some statutory regimes.[6] It has also gone some way towards introducing a general sustainable development duty whereby a public body, in exercising its functions, must act in a way that it considers most sustainable.[7] Similarly, while there are not many individual references to sustainable development in Northern Ireland legislation, the Assembly has introduced a general substantive duty on all its public bodies to contribute to the achievement of sustainable development and the term has appeared in a few measures of the Welsh Assembly.[8] Finally, although not one of the European Community's core environmental principles,[9] sustainable development has been elevated in status to one of the Community's general aims and this is reflected in its legislation.[10] This, in turn, has influenced the content of UK primary legislation.[11]

This chapter examines the use of the term 'sustainable development' in Acts of the UK, Scottish and Northern Ireland Parliaments. Although the powers of the Welsh Assembly have increased to permit the adoption of 'measures', and are likely to increase further, as of the Spring of 2011, it has not enacted its own primary legislation. The chapter begins by describing the slow increase in the use of sustainable development in legislation and the different ways it is used in legislation. There are numerous specific statutory obligations that relate to sustainable development, which have been imposed on individuals or groups of public sector bodies. The focus of this chapter is on these provisions, examining in detail their form, strength and limits, and how they can be monitored, reviewed and enforced both inside and outside the courts. The chapter concludes that over and above any symbolic value, in many instances, the provisions also have legal significance. The formulations vary and while some are simply a material consideration to be used in decision making, those that set out mandatory requirements such as reporting do create binding legal rules. Furthermore, there are a few examples of where the duty or objective is set out as a clear legal rule that could be interpreted as providing a framework for decision making. The chapter ends by considering the value of more generally applicable legislative obligations in, for instance, a specific sustainable development statute. This conclusion is developed more fully in Chapter 13.

Definitional issues

As discussed earlier in this volume, while there is a general agreement in the academic community that sustainable development is a good thing, there remains no consensus on the exact meaning of the term. The most common definition of sustainable development: 'Development that meets the needs of the present without compromising the ability of future generations to meet their own needs' (the Brundtland definition) (WCED, 1987: 43), is attractive because it offers a comprehensive and consensual approach which is able to bring together different and conflicting interests. Even within the UK, the Brundtland definition has been expressed to mean different things ranging from a trade-off between the environment and economic development (DEFRA, 1994: 7), to a complex concept which involves five guiding principles: living within environmental limits, just society, sustainable economy, good governance and sound science (HM Government *et al.*, 2005: 8).

Given the range of possible meanings, it could be considered helpful for legislators to provide a definition of sustainable development for the purposes of a particular statute. None of the statutes studied makes any genuine attempt to define the term.[12] The decision regarding whether or not to include a definition has been the subject of a number of debates on the floor and in Committees of both the UK and Scottish Parliaments. At the Committee stage of the Planning and Compulsory Purchase Bill, the Minister, Tony McNulty explained the difficulty faced by legislators:

> As some Opposition Members have clearly shown, albeit tortuously, it is inappropriate to include a definition in the Bill. So we shall leave the phrase in, unless, rather than making law in statute, as we are doing, we are running a rather fun sixth-form debating society.[13]

The more precise legislation is, the easier it is for courts to interpret and enforce it in a way that is consistent with what the legislature intended. A common criticism against the use of vague or unenforceable terms is that they undermine the role of law in protecting individual rights (Brandl and Bungert, 1992: 92). However, as Rubin (1989: 374) explains, in a modern state, contemporary legislation serves a range of purposes including: creating direct prohibitions, regulatory controls and administrative agencies; conferring benefits on groups or individuals; issuing guidance; conferring grants of jurisdiction and statutory duties; imposing enforcement and implementation procedures; and facilitating private arrangements. Some legislation is simply symbolic, expressing the political authorities' awareness of an issue and that something needs to be done about it (Mader, 2001: 122).

The imprecise nature of sustainable development does have implications. Imprecise terms introduce a lack of consistency both internally within a regime or public body and externally among regimes or public bodies. There may be a lack of continuity in the meaning of the term over time and this may result in confusion as to the meaning and expectations for both those implementing the legislation and those subject to it. Finally, imprecision may give the executive (a public body) too much discretion and take power away from the judiciary and the legislature.

Each of these concerns has arisen to some extent in the specific case of sustainable development. These are discussed in detail below. Two of the difficulties (inconsistency and confusion) can be described as teething problems, which have, over time, been mitigated, but the others have proven to be more pervasive.

The first teething difficulty arose when the Natural Heritage (Scotland) Act 1991 became the first statute in UK history to impose on an agency, Scottish Natural Heritage (SNH), a mandate which included the term 'sustainable'. The general aims and purposes of SNH include an obligation 'to have regard to the desirability of securing that anything done whether by SNH or any other person, in relation to the natural heritage of Scotland is undertaken in a manner which is sustainable'. The Act provided no definition of 'sustainable' and at that time, there was no UK Government guidance as to its meaning. Consequently, SNH had to define the term for its own purposes (SNH, 1993). Given the concept's holistic nature and the need for integrated solutions as a matter of public policy, it would not be particularly useful for every agency to develop its own definition and approach to sustainable development. In the end, SNH's approach provided the model for the first UK-wide strategy for sustainable development produced by the Conservative Government in 1994. However, as discussed below, not all of the statutes direct decision makers to the strategy and this failure aggravates the inconsistent interpretation and application of sustainable development in the UK.

The second teething problem seems to coincide with a shift in the Government's definition of sustainable development. As previously noted, in the Conservative's 1994 strategy, sustainable development was simply a trade-off between the environment and economic development (DEFRA, 1994). The Labour Government, in *A Better Quality of Life: A Strategy for Sustainable Development for the United Kingdom* (the 1999 strategy), significantly altered the UK concept to include a social dimension (DEFRA, 1999: para. 1.10). There was a fear in Government that the term was incomprehensible to the wider public and several UK and Scottish statutes either deliberately avoided using the term and instead, relied on its component parts or alternatively, used the term but also included its component parts.[14] So, for example, the Local Government Act 2000 in s. 4(1) provides that 'Every local authority must prepare a strategy . . . for promoting or improving the economic, social and environmental wellbeing of their area and contributing to the achievement of sustainable development'. The concerns however seem to have been temporary and by 2001, both the UK and Scottish Parliaments had enacted legislation referring to sustainable development.

A further definitional issue arises when the ordinary rules of statutory interpretation regarding undefined terms are applied to the term 'sustainable development'. There is jurisprudence that states that words in an Act of Parliament are to have the same meaning they had at the date when the Act was passed (unless some subsequent Act has declared that some other construction is to be adopted or has altered the previous statute).[15] This is particularly problematic in the context of sustainable development, as the definition is constantly evolving. In interpreting the Environment Act 1995, it is not desirable to refer back to the 1994 definition of sustainable development. An alternative approach is set out by Lord Steyn in *R v Burstow and Ireland*.[16] Lord Steyn refers to Victorian draftsman Lord Thring, who encouraged drafting so that an Act of Parliament is 'always speaking'. Lord Steyn states that if a statute is of the 'always speaking' type, it must be interpreted in the light of the best current scientific appreciation.[17] Given the scientific nature of the term 'sustainable development', there is a strong argument in favour of it being of the 'always speaking variety'.

Assuming the courts are willing to apply the current meaning of sustainable development, where would they be able to it find it? Definitions, principles and objectives for sustainable development can be found in documents and policy at almost every level of government and for many different sectors, as well as in secondary sources including most dictionaries. An obvious answer for the UK courts reviewing a UK or devolved statute is to rely on the current definition set out in UK or devolved Government policy. The danger with this approach is that from a constitutional perspective, it may undermine the separation of powers between the legislature, the executive and the judiciary. First, it takes legislative power away from Parliament and passes it to the executive and then, if the court feels this is the only interpretation available to it, it also usurps the power of the judiciary to freely interpret and apply the law.[18] In *Wilson v First County Trust (no. 2)*, the House of Lords dealt with these issues in the context of the Parliamentary papers and confirmed that while the courts could consult Parliamentary debates as background, it is a fundamental error of principle to confuse what a minister may have said with the will and intention of Parliament as a whole and, that even when clear and unambiguous, ministerial statements should be treated as background to the legislation rather than authoritative indications of statutory meaning.[19]

With regard to the term 'sustainable development', Ross (2008: 43) observes that a legislative solution has been found to circumvent these difficulties to a certain extent. Parliament still provides no definition, but all of the statutes she studied included requirements to have regard to ministerial guidance in exercising the 'sustainable development' objective or duty.

This approach is beneficial in that central government can ensure that the same definition and approach are being consistently used throughout the public sector. Constitutionally, another benefit of this approach is that it means the definition and principles behind sustainable development are not set in stone, but at the same time, they are not left to chance. It also addresses the criticism of attributing the Government's view to the whole of Parliament by giving Parliament's consent to do so (Ross, 2008: 43).

Similar issues have existed in the UK for the past 60 years in relation to the term 'planning'. There has been no definition of 'planning' provided in any of the planning statutes since 1947. The term has been broadly defined by the executive and the courts and, over time, there has been some evolution in its meaning to reflect broader social, economic and political changes. As observed by Collar (1999: 10):

> Throughout the years, writers have suggested a variety of objectives, which have altered as the planning system has developed . . . However the flexibility of the land use planning system has the advantage of being able to adjust to new philosophies and ideas as they arise, such as the concept of sustainable development, whereby planners may be seen as trustees of the environment for future generations.[20]

Thus, the courts and the executive have been able to administer and interpret the planning statutes for over 50 years without a definition of planning, so working with the term 'sustainable development' in the same way is not so extraordinary.

That said, the experience with land use planning is not directly transferable to sustainable development. The term 'planning' is largely only used in one sense and one context. Moreover, its meaning at any given time is largely accepted and comes from one source, that being the government guidance on planning. In contrast, the term 'sustainable development' is used in a wide range of contexts, the guidance provisions are not in any standard form and, in many instances, the legislature has tailored them to the needs of the particular regime. Some of the guidance is limited to that specifically addressed to that agency,[21] while elsewhere, any ministerial guidance is relevant.[22] In other statutes, the guidance is limited to that specifically relating to sustainable development.[23] The reference to guidance in the statute introduces a process for determining the meaning of the term. In this way, the constitutional concerns are lessened as the content of the guidance itself then acts to limit the public body's discretion by providing the detail as to the executive's current policy on sustainable development. The type and extent of the power Parliament has delegated to the executive differ depending on the formulation of the provision. However, as shall be discussed in the conclusion to this chapter and again in Chapter 13, this differentiated approach to guidance may run counter to the actual implementation of sustainable development and a more consistent reference to specific guidance (for example, the relevant sustainable development strategy) may be more desirable.

The sustainable development provisions

In the UK, sustainable development sometimes appears as a purpose for a particular agency or for a regime as a whole. More often, it is used to impose a duty on a particular public body or group of public bodies. The provision may also introduce certain procedural requirements in relation to either the content of or processes for guidance, regulations, reports or strategies.

While for the purpose of analysis, each of the categories is dealt with separately below, it is important to emphasize that the various legislative forms are interrelated. The purpose of an agency may influence the way it exercises its functions, duties and powers. For example, the Marine and Coastal Access Act 2009 in s. 2(1) provides that 'it is the duty of the Marine Management Officer [to secure that its functions are so exercised . . .] (a) with the objective of making a contribution to the achievement of sustainable development'. Thus, the duty is defined through the objective. Similarly, under the Sustainable Energy Act 2003 s. 1, the Secretary of State 'must in each calendar year publish a report (sustainable energy report) on the progress made in the reporting period towards its 'sustainable energy aims'. Here, the aims are supported by a procedural requirement.

Importantly, none of the provisions establish sustainable development as a 'legal principle' and there is general consensus that sustainable development has not achieved the status of an enforceable legal principle in either EU or UK law (De Sadeleer, 2005: 311; and see below, Chapter 12). Winter (2004: 13–14) helpfully explains the difference between legal principles and objectives (or policies or non-legal principles) in the context of environmental law. He observes that if a principle is contained in a law or sub-legal norm, it will have legal effect if the legislator intended it to have such effect. In contrast, policies, ideals and objectives may be mentioned in law, but if so, are not meant to be binding.[24] These are identifiable by being either set out expressly as tasks or ideals or, alternatively,[25] will be indeterminate due to vague language (Macrory, 2004).

So for example, clearly, the duty imposed on SNH in the Natural Heritage Scotland Act 1991 'to have regard to the desirability of securing that anything done whether by SNH or any other person, in relation to the natural heritage of Scotland is undertaken in a manner which is sustainable' is so diluted that it can only be interpreted as a rather vague objective.

Attempts have been made in relation to other subjects (notably nature conservation) to rationalize the use of different formulations to create some sort of hierarchy of obligations, starting perhaps with aims and objectives, and then moving down through purpose, functions, duties and then powers (Roberts, 2004: 212). Like studies in other contexts, Ross confirms that there is no obvious hierarchy of terms with respect to the use of the term 'sustainable development' in statutes (Ross, 2008).

Some aims, however, are very powerful, others much less so – and the same is true of duties. The different formulations can create very different legal impacts. Some of the provisions are almost purely symbolic, some are simply material considerations to be taken into account in the decision, some could possibly create a legal rule dictating how a decision is to be made and others create a mandatory procedural requirement. As a result, each provision needs to be examined on its own, referring to any related provisions in order to establish its overall impact.

Aims and purposes

Historically, very few UK statutes include a clause setting out their purpose or any objectives for the public bodies they create. Instead, the purpose is something which needs to be deduced by those implementing the legislation and those enforcing it, either through the language of the statute, the explanatory notes or references to parliamentary debates.[26] Some recent Acts contain a section setting out the purpose or purposes of the legislation which is a substantive part of the Act. As discussed above, sustainable development is not sufficiently precise to be considered a legal principle per se but it does show up as a purpose or objective.

Sustainable development appears either as an overall aim of the particular public body or of the regime as a whole in several statutes in various forms. The first appearance of the phrase 'sustainable development' in a UK statute is in the Environment Act 1995 which sets out aims for both the Environment Agency (the Agency) for England and Wales and the Scottish Environmental Protection Agency (SEPA) that are similar but different and equally convoluted. The Agency is given sustainable development as a specific aim, while SEPA's aims are to be set out in guidance from the Scottish ministers.[27] Section 4(1) creates a complicated and relatively unclear system of priority by placing limitations on the pursuit of the sustainable development aim. It provides that:

> it shall be the principal aim of the Agency (subject to and in accordance with the provisions of this Act or any other enactment and taking into

account any likely costs) in discharging its functions so to protect or enhance the environment, taken as a whole, as to make the contribution towards attaining the objective of achieving sustainable development mentioned in subsection (3) below.

The complexity of this provision means using it to challenge the Agency inside or outside court would be very difficult.

In contrast, the purposes set out in the Regional Development Agencies Act 1998 are clear. Section 4(1) provides that:

a regional development agency shall have the following purposes:

(a) to further the economic development and the regeneration of its area,
(b) to promote business efficiency, investment and competitiveness in its area,
(c) to promote employment in its area,
(d) to enhance the development and application of skills relevant to employment in its area,
(e) to contribute to the achievement of sustainable development in the United Kingdom where it is relevant to its area to do so.

While the wording is clear, the Act provides no means for prioritizing among its different purposes. It is also an example of a formulation which sets out some of the components of sustainable development separately as purposes, and then essentially repeats itself by also including sustainable development as one of the primary purposes (Jenkins, 2002: 592). As explained by the Parliamentary Under-Secretary of State for the Environment, Transport and the Regions:

The purposes of the RDAs [Regional Development Agencies] are not mutually exclusive . . . We have made no attempt to rank them in terms of importance or to define each purpose completely separately. Sustainable development can be looked at in two ways. It is one of the five purposes of the RDAs and will inform the agencies' actions on the other four purposes where sustainable development is involved. It will also enable the agency to act independently on sustainable development even where such action would not fall under any of the other four purposes. The provision was drafted as an enabling factor.[28]

The more recent Climate Change Act 2008 is clearer about priority. Powerfully, the objectives, proposals and policies for both the carbon budgets and in the Programme for Adaptation to Climate Change must be 'such as to contribute to sustainable development'.[29]

There are some instances where the statute is silent about its purpose but sustainable development can be implied as a primary or secondary purpose of the regime or public bodies from the duties or powers created under the Act.

Often in these cases, the power or duty may be described using the purpose. For example, the International Development Act 2002 provides in s. 9(1) that 'each of the statutory bodies mentioned in Schedule 1 may enter into and carry out agreements for the purpose of . . . (a) furthering sustainable development in one or more countries outside the United Kingdom'. Here the power to enter into agreements is limited to certain purposes.

A duty may also be framed as meeting an objective. The Planning and Compulsory Purchase Act 2004 in relation to development planning provides in s. 39(2) that 'The person or body must exercise the function with the objective of contributing to the achievement of sustainable development'. This is supported by Planning Policy Statement 1 which requires all plans to be subject to a sustainability appraisal.

Duties

Sustainable development appears most commonly as a duty on one or more agencies or ministers to act in a certain way. These provisions vary enormously, but all use mandatory language, whereby the public body must at least direct its mind in some way to the concept. Any discretion is introduced through the use of vague language and qualifications and, importantly, tends to relate to the weight to be attached to the concept. The duties vary significantly in relation to their clarity, strength, the extent to which they are qualified by other provisions and, inevitably, in their overall effect (Ross, 2008: 48).

Clarity

The initial sustainable development duties were opaque. Under the Environment Act 1995 s. 31(1), the guidance issued to SEPA by the Scottish ministers 'must include guidance with respect to the contribution which, having regard to SEPA's responsibilities and resources, the Scottish Ministers consider it appropriate for SEPA to make, by the performance of its functions, towards attaining the objective of achieving sustainable development'.

The provision is mandatory but each of the phrases 'contribution', 'having regard to SEPA's responsibilities and resources'; 'considers appropriate' gives discretion to the decision maker and substantially weakens the provision's potential. Indeed, combined, it would be very difficult to show that SEPA or the Scottish ministers had failed to comply with the provision in any given circumstance.

As is shown below, subsequent drafters seem to have found much clearer formulations. However, some variance does exist and a standard form is still a long way off.

Strength

The provisions also vary in intensity. The strongest duty possible would be a duty to achieve sustainable development. Given the definitional issues surrounding the term, this would be a tall order and none of the statutes go that far. Instead they are couched with phrases which add layers of discretion.

The following list covers most of the formulations used in the UK and starts with the weaker provisions and ends with the stronger provisions. Emphasis is added to highlight the phrases which add discretion:

- *is to encourage the fundable bodies to contribute (so far as reasonably practicable for them to do so)* to the achievement of sustainable development (Further and Higher Education (Scotland) Act 2005 s. 20)
- shall *have regard to the desirability of securing* that anything done . . . is undertaken in a manner which is sustainable (Natural Heritage Scotland Act 1991 s. 1(1))
- *is to have regard to the desirability* of achieving sustainable development (Further and Higher Education (Scotland) Act 2005 s. 20)
- *must have regard to national policies and advice relating to sustainable development contained in guidance* (Clean Neighbourhoods and Environment Act 2005 s. 88(9))
- must, in exercising functions . . . *take into account the need to do so in a way that contributes* to the achievement of sustainable development (Climate Change (Scotland) Act 2009 s. 92)
- shall exercise its powers *in the way it considers best calculated to contribute* to the achievement of sustainable development (Greater London Authority Act 1999 s. 30(5)(b); Railways Act 1993 s. 4(1)(bb) (as amended by the Transport Act 2000 s. 224); Water Industry Act 1991 s. 27A(12), s. 2(3) (as amended by the Water Act 2003))
- shall exercise its powers *in the way best calculated to contribute* to the achievement of sustainable development (Transport Act 2000 s. 207(2)(b); Water Industry (Scotland) Act 2002 s. 51; Water Environment and Water Services (Scotland) Act 2003 s. 2(4); Northern Ireland (Misc Prov) Act 2006 s. 25)
- must act *in the way best calculated to further* the achievement of sustainable development (Marine (Scotland) Act 2010 s. 3)
- must exercise the function *with the objective of contributing to (or furthering)* the achievement of sustainable development (Planning and Compulsory Purchase Act 2004 s. 39(2); Planning etc. (Scotland) Act 2006 s. 2) Planning Act (Northern Ireland) 2011 s. 5(1)
- shall discharge its duties *in a way which contributes to* the achievement of sustainable development (Local Government in Scotland Act 2003 s. 1(5))
- must act in exercising its functions *in a way that it considers is most sustainable* (Climate Change (Scotland) Act 2009 s. 44(1)).

All of the duties contain some discretion. In his classic study, Davis (1970: 25) notes that discretion is a tool that is indispensable for individualization of justice, but uncontrolled and unnecessary discretionary power can be dangerous. While some of the earlier duties seem to give unlimited discretion,[30] the later duties tend to be worded so as to confine or structure the discretion in a certain way.

Those rules which create limits on discretionary power act to confine it, while those rules which specify what the administrator is to do within the limits structure the discretionary power (Davis, 1970: 25). For example in the Planning and Compulsory Purchase Act 2004 s. 39(4), the sustainable development objective is specifically limited to the public bodies' development planning functions and not extended to their development control functions. This confines the discretion and was the subject of much debate during the Bill's passage.[31] Those provisions which require regard to ministerial guidance or where the decision maker is obliged to balance several duties or objectives act to structure discretion.

The more discretion a provision allows, the weaker the obligation becomes. The strength of the duties described above varies enormously. Unsurprisingly, the first appearance of the word 'sustainable' in a UK statute appears at the weaker end. The Natural Heritage (Scotland) Act 1991 provides that SNH shall 'have regard to the desirability of securing that anything done whether by SNH or any other person, in relation to the natural heritage of Scotland is undertaken in a manner which is sustainable'. Courts have held that 'to have regard to' does not mean 'slavishly adhere to'.[32] The term 'desirability' serves to further dilute the strength of the provision. Moreover, something may be considered desirable but not as desirable as another result so it will receive little or no weight. In 1991, however, this provision gave a significant endorsement to the sustainable development agenda and it is hugely symbolic for that reason (Ross *et al.*, 1995). While generally, as will be discussed below, the provisions over time are becoming stronger, this is not always the case. The Climate Change (Scotland) Act 2009 s. 92 imposes a particularly obtuse duty on Scottish Ministers and the advisory body who 'must, in exercising functions . . . take into account the need to do so in a way that contributes to the achievement of sustainable development'.

Other provisions do use mandatory language and arguably create stronger obligations. For example, the Land Reform (Scotland) Act 2003 s. 51(3) provides that ministers shall not consent [to a proposal by a community to buy land] 'unless the community have given their approval and Ministers are satisfied . . . (c) that what the community body proposes to do with the land is compatible with furthering the achievement of sustainable development'. This formulation sets out how the Scottish ministers are actually to make the decision as a legal rule. Dworkin (1977: 24) explains that 'rules are applicable in an all or nothing fashion. If the facts a rule stipulates are given, then either the rule is valid . . . or it is not, in which case it contributes nothing to the decision'. Furthermore, when principles [defined here to include policies] intersect, the decision maker resolving the conflict must take into account the relative weight of each. Rules do not have this dimension (Dworkin, 1977: 27). Using this logic, s. 51(3) creates a legal rule.

Some formulations are much more complicated. A common phrase is 'shall exercise its powers *in the way best calculated to contribute* to the achievement of sustainable development'.[33] This formulation still sets out how decisions are to be made as a legal rule but it is couched with discretionary language which means other factors will influence the decision. To quote Richard Page (South West Hertfordshire) in the Committee stage of the Energy Bill, 'I contribute to flag days by buying a flag for various charities, but I hardly think that my contribution will be absolutely vital to achieving their aims'.[34] This does not prohibit these from being considered legal rules. Dworkin notes that:

> words like 'reasonable' . . . and 'significant' . . . make the application of the rule which contains it depend to some extent upon principles or policies lying beyond the rule, and in this way makes that rule itself more like a principle. But they do not quite turn the rule into a principle, because even the least confining of these terms restricts the kind of other principles and policies on which the rule depends.
>
> (Dworkin, 1977: 28)

Rules then may be formulated to allow the balancing of opposing concerns with the scope of the rule (Winter, 2004). De Sadeleer (2005: 311) describes these as rules of indeterminate content and argues that such a rule may be created so long as it appears in a normative text, and is formulated in a sufficiently prescriptive manner.

The Greater London Authority Act 1999 provides a good example of a duty which creates a policy objective to be balanced with other objectives and another duty which arguably creates a rule. Section 30(1) gives the Authority the power to do anything to further its principal purposes.[35] The Act then creates two different approaches for decision making and both rely on sustainable development. Under s. 30(4), which deals with the determination of whether and how to exercise the power, the duty imposed on the Authority is 'to have regard to the achievement of sustainable development'. Thus, sustainable development is simply an aspirational goal that is deliberately framed to be a material consideration in making the decision. In contrast, s. 30(5), which deals with the actual exercise of the powers, imposes a duty on the Authority to act in the way it considers best calculated to contribute to the achievement of sustainable development subject to a reasonableness test. This formulation creates a rule which describes a framework for the decision-making process. In many ways this replicates, in statutory form, policy initiatives such as sustainability appraisal. A discussion on how the courts may interpret these different formulations, drawing on the UK experience with other environmental provisions, is below.

Thus, there is no standard form of sustainable development duty, and both strong and weak provisions are common. Some phrases may simply reflect differences in drafting style, although most of these provisions have received a fair amount of pre-legislative scrutiny and phrases have been added, dropped or amended at various stages of the legislative process. Several provisions have been tailored to a particular agency or regime. Generally, the more recent statutes tend to create stronger and clearer sustainable development duties. Finally, it is also very important to remember that some of the strongest provisions for delivering sustainable development may not even mention the phrase itself.

Qualifications

In order to reveal the potential impact of these duties and objectives, it is often important to look beyond the immediate provision to ensure it is not further qualified by a separate provision that, as mentioned above, can also be used to limit discretion. For example, there may be other duties that need to be balanced against the duty. The statute may also include some means of prioritizing duties.

Previous studies into environmental and conservation provisions have found that, in general, the stronger a duty apparently is, the more likely it is to be qualified in some way (Roberts, 2004: 211). This pattern has not emerged for the sustainable development duties and objectives. Some of the weak provisions are not qualified, but others are. While the majority of the stronger provisions are qualified, there are a few very strong provisions that remain unqualified (Ross, 2008: 52).

The weak provisions in the Natural Heritage (Scotland) Act 1991 s. 1(1) are unqualified. While there is no discretion left to the decision makers as to whether they can take sustainable development into consideration, there is no need for any further qualification. It is possible for the decision makers 'to have regard to the desirability of securing that anything done . . . is undertaken in a manner which is sustainable' and give it very little weight and do something completely contrary to it.

In contrast, the similar weak provision in the Further and Higher Education (Scotland) Act 2005 is qualified. Section 20 provides that the relevant public body is to '(a) *have regard to the desirability* of achieving sustainable development and (b) in particular *encourage* the fundable bodies to contribute *(so far as reasonably practicable for them to do so)* to the achievement of sustainable development'. This duty is subject to the Scottish Further and Higher Education Funding Council's main duties which relate to the funding of education and research.

There are, however, also examples at the other extreme, where strong provisions in relation to sustainable development remain unqualified. The Planning and Compulsory Purchase Act 2004 s. 39(2) provides that those bodies involved in development planning in England and Wales must exercise the function with the objective of contributing to sustainable development. The Land Reform (Scotland) Act 2000 repeatedly requires the Scottish ministers to be satisfied that the sustainable development implications of any community and crofting community bodies established under it, as well as any proposals by such bodies to purchase land, meet certain sustainable development criteria.[36] These two Acts establish sustainable development as a primary duty for their respective public bodies and it has priority over any other duties or objectives.

Thus, the legislatures are becoming more confident about introducing stronger duties in relation to sustainable development. However, while others exist, the provisions above are the exception, as most of the other strong duties are accompanied by significant qualifications. While several Acts have provisions which state that functions are to be exercised in the way best calculated to contribute to the achievement of sustainable development, there is no uniform approach to qualification. The Marine (Scotland) Act 2010 s. 3, for example, adds 'so far as consistent with the proper exercise of their functions'. Thus, two seemingly identical provisions in different statutes may have very different potential impacts due to the differences in their qualifications.

A common reason for the variety is that the qualifications are the result of the legislative process and have been tailored to the needs of the particular regime or agency. For example, during discussions on the Water Bill, the Minister explains why sustainable development is not a primary objective of the regulator:

> The authority is an economic regulator. Sustainable development is an important part of that. No one disagrees with that argument – I fully sub-scribe to it – but we must get the correct balance between its functions: its economic function of price setting and the important function of sustainable development and its promotion.[37]

The Transport Act 2000, in s. 207(2), provides that '(2) *in exercising its functions in accordance with subsection (1)* the Authority shall act in the way best calculated . . . (b) to contribute to the achievement of sustainable development'. The applicability of subsection (2) is limited by subsection 1 which provides that 'the Authority shall exercise its functions *with a view to furthering its purposes and shall do so in accordance with any such strategies as it has formulated with respect to them* (except when exercising the function of reviewing those strategies)'. Thus, the sustainable development duty is subject to the overall purposes of the Authority and any of its strategies (not just a sustainable development strategy). The converse is also true, and the sustainable development duty, in turn, provides an additional limitation on how the Authority is to exercise its functions.[38]

The Water Industry Act 1991, as amended by the Water Act 2003, sets out in s. 2, not only a long list of duties, but also a clear system of priority between two sets of duties. Subsection (2A) sets out a list of primary duties for the Secretary of State and the Authority, including a duty to consumers. Section 2(3) then provides that '*Subject to subsection (2A) above*, the Secretary of State or, as the case may be, the Authority shall exercise and perform the powers and duties mentioned in subsection (1) above in the manner which he or it considers is best calculated' . . . to do several things including at '(e) to contribute to the achievement of sustainable development'.

Importantly, s. 2 is formulated as a very complicated single legal rule. The effect of this is that, despite their wordings, the individual duties (including the sustainable development duty) then simply become objectives to be balanced in applying the rule. The qualification for subsection (2A) assists the agency when it is faced with conflicting duties and sends a clear direction as to priority. Sustainable development is clearly one of the secondary duties. Unfortunately,

s. 2 provides no guidance to the Authority as to how to prioritize the four primary duties nor is there any prioritization among the five secondary duties.

In all these circumstances, it is helpful to take a pluralist perspective whereby conflict is seen as endemic in any social system and to accept that conflict is not necessarily bad. The challenge is to manage the conflict using the appropriate mechanisms (Roberts, 2004: 207–8).

Pluralism in the context of sustainable development can be viewed in three different ways. First, as described above, within a statute, sustainable development may be one objective that needs to be balanced against other objectives, such as value for money.

Second, the conflicts internal to the term sustainable development and its imprecise nature mean that it can be manipulated to support or refute different policy outcomes based on different objectives and the amount of weight attached to them. One decision may be sustainable because it attaches more weight to economic considerations over social or environmental ones, while another decision may favour environmental factors. As noted by Lee (2005: 27), 'The complexity and profound ambiguity of sustainable development means that in the absence of continued debate, rather than providing progressive impulses in environmental regulation, sustainable development could instead provide a moral cloak for "business as usual"'. This coincides with findings of the In House Policy Consultancy (IHPC) that 'a significant number of organisations with the same duties have also responded with varying degrees of rigour to their duty' and that the duties need to be supported by education and training and scrutiny mechanisms (Cussons, 2006: 15). This supports the view expressed earlier and developed in Chapter 13 that a consistent approach to guidance referring to the relevant sustainable development strategy may be desirable.

Finally, if the qualifications are kept to a minimum, then some of the more recent formulations of the sustainable development duty may create a legal rule which can provide a framework for decision making. In these cases only the policies and concepts referred to in the rule may be used to influence an agency's decision making generally or a particular type of decision.[39] These two final points emphasize the importance of a clear vision and leadership. They also demonstrate that these provisions can only make a significant impact on the actual delivery of sustainable development if they are predicated on a robust and ecologically responsible vision (Chapter 12) and an approach to sustainable development set out in a single source (Chapter 13).

Targets

One way of giving greater legitimacy to substantive duties is to phrase them as 'targets'. Targets set clear goals that are capable of being acted upon. Recently, there has been an increase in the use of duties and targets in UK statutes, especially in areas such as fuel poverty, climate change and biodiversity. For example, the Climate Change Act 2008 s. 1(1) provides: 'It is the duty of the Secretary of State to ensure that the net UK carbon account for the year 2050 is at least 80% lower than the 1990 baseline'. The enforceability of these targets in court is questionable however, and one has to question what might be achieved by bringing an action against the government for failing to meet established targets.

To date, there have been no sustainable development provisions which are set out as targets. Indeed, it is hard to see how a target for sustainable development could be set that would attract the same sort of public attention as those for climate change or biodiversity. Sustainable development reflects a holistic view that is difficult to express as a single indicator or target.

However, targets do have a role in any legislative approach to sustainable development, both as precise deadlines for producing documentation and as benchmarks for specific sustainable development indicators that are essential to drive forward progress. More indirectly, specific climate change, biodiversity, fuel, poverty and other targets could be used as evidence to assess progress towards sustainable development.

Procedural requirements – formalization

While in one sense, a 'duty to consider' is a procedural requirement in that it imposes a process on a decision maker, the procedural requirements referred to in the context of this section are those which formalize a process: requirements to produce or follow something in written form, or requirements to provide notice, publish or consult. These formalized procedural obligations in relation to sustainable development vary in form, and include: provisions which give the minister the power to produce regulations, directions or guidance on sustainable development; obligations which set out the process and content of a strategy, report or scheme relating to sustainable development; and procedures whereby if the substantive sustainable development requirement is not fulfilled, the body or instrument is not valid. Some of these provisions could operate as legal rules in the form of mandatory requirements which relate to sustainable development.

Lee and Abbot observe that:

> as a mode of regulation, proceduralisation is in part a wholly appropriate response to the well-known challenges to the authority in regulation. Its attempts to improve the legitimacy of environmental decision-making become increasingly urgent, given the contemporaneous and possibly countervailing response of moving to the market for environmental regulation.
>
> Lee and Abbot (2003: 108)

Proceduralization is particularly useful in relation to a concept like sustainable development whose substantive meaning is imprecise. The procedures act to limit the discretion inherent in sustainable development, but they need to be more than a box-ticking exercise and must encourage reflection on the substantive objectives behind the procedures. Several of the procedural requirements studied can also act as monitoring or enforcement mechanisms to ensure compliance with either substantive requirements or other procedures. These accountability and review procedures provide the necessary link between the procedures and substantive compliance. They also can ensure that discretion is being exercised without arbitrariness or illegality.

The procedural requirements can be framed as either duties or powers and are discussed below under two subheadings: guidance, directions and regulations; and reports and strategies.

Guidance, directions and regulations

Guidance, directions and regulations are all forms of administrative rules. These rules are important tools, both for confining discretionary power and for structuring it (Davis, 1970: 97).

As discussed above in relation to the definition of sustainable development, the power to produce guidance is common in UK statutes and is usually accompanied by an obligation on the relevant agency to have regard to that guidance. The Environment Act 1995 s. 4(3) provides that:

> the guidance given under subsection (2) above must include guidance with respect to the contribution which, *having regard to the Agency's responsibilities and resources, the Ministers consider it appropriate for the Agency to make, by the discharge of its functions, towards attaining the objective of achieving sustainable development.*

The qualifications give the ministers a great deal of leeway in the timing and content of the guidance. However, the Agency must then have regard to guidance.

A few provisions give ministers the power to produce binding regulations relating to sustainable development. For example, the Building (Scotland) Act 2003 s. 1(1) provides that:

> the Scottish Ministers may, for any of the purposes of . . . (c) furthering the achievement of sustainable development . . . make regulations ('building regulations') with respect to the design, construction, demolition and conversion of buildings and the provision of services, fittings and equipment in or in connection with buildings.

Regulations can be used to ensure reporting obligations are publicized, monitored and reviewed. The Local Government in Scotland Act 2003 s. 13(1) provides that it is the duty of a local authority to make arrangements for reporting to the public the outcome of the performance of its functions. The Scottish ministers may make regulations governing the reporting obligations of the local authority and such regulations 'may include provisions for a statement setting out . . . an account of how what it did contributed to the achievement of sustainable development'.[41] This ensures some consistency in the process, content and quality of information in the local authority reports (Cussons, 2006, Annex D: 32).

Finally, the minister may also be given the power to issue directions which are binding on those to whom they are given. The Water Environment and Water Services (Scotland) Act 2003 provides in s. 2(6) that 'the Scottish Ministers may give directions (whether general or specific) and guidance . . . and SEPA and the responsible authorities must comply with any such directions and have regard to any such guidance'. Thus, over and above the guidance, the Scottish ministers can exert an additional means of control and actually compel compliance using a direction. Similarly, the Buildings (Scotland) Act 2003 gives the Scottish ministers the power to direct a local authority to take action if they believe the local authority is not enforcing the regulations.[42]

Strategies and reports

Provisions requiring ministers or other public bodies to produce a strategy, scheme, plan or report on sustainable development have the benefit of being easily enforced and complied with, since the report is either produced on time, in the specified form, containing the correct content and so on, in the correct way, or it is not. The question is where and who is best placed to monitor and enforce compliance. A failure to comply with a statutory procedure can be grounds for judicial review as it may mean that the agency has, for example, acted *ultra vires*. As will be discussed below, this can be a slow, costly and far from effective means of enforcement. Alternative bodies, such as central government, external auditors, the Sustainable Development Commission, parliamentary committees, the media and interest groups may be better placed to secure compliance (Ross 2006: 6; Cussons, 2006, Annex D: 32). Some statutes are silent about enforcement and monitoring but in many cases, it is the statute itself that actually includes the provisions to establish these arrangements. The benefits of these provisions are set out below.

For example, the Local Government Act 2000 s. 4 provides that 'every local authority must prepare a strategy . . . for promoting or improving the economic, social and environmental well-being of their area and contributing to the achievement of sustainable development in the UK'. Unfortunately, the provision provides no obvious indication as to what happens to the strategies once they are produced and there are no real consequences arising from a failure to produce a strategy except a challenge under judicial review. The IHPC study reported anecdotally that compliance with this requirement was mixed (Cussons, 2006, Annex C: 26). In order to be useful, these strategies need to be comparable, disseminated effectively and monitored.

In sharp contrast, under the Transport (Scotland) Act 2005, there are several compliance-based procedures. Under s. 5(1), it is the duty of each Transport Partnership to draw up a strategy for transport within its region. Section 5(2) provides that its transport strategy 'shall include provision about . . . (d) how transport in the region will be provided, developed, improved and operated so as . . . (iii) to be consistent with the principles of sustainable development and to conserve and enhance the environment'. The Act establishes a procedure for the production of the strategies and there are clear consequences for failure to produce a strategy. Section 7 sets out requirements on the review, modification and renewal of regional transport strategies and provides that a Transport Partnership (a) shall keep its transport strategy under review; or (b) may modify its transport strategy or draw up a new one. Furthermore, if the Transport Partnership fails to do either (a) or (b), the Scottish ministers can force them to do so, using a direction.[43]

Probably the most influential of the reporting obligations are those found in the Government of Wales Act 2006 s. 79(1)[44] which provides that 'The Welsh Ministers must make a scheme ("the sustainable development scheme") setting out how they propose, in the exercise of their functions, to promote sustainable development'. Section 79(7) then provides that:

> in the year following that in which an ordinary general election is (or, apart from section 5(5), would be) held, the Welsh Ministers must (a) publish a report containing an assessment of how effective their proposals (as set out in the scheme and implemented) have been in promoting sustainable development, and (b) lay a copy of the report before the Assembly.

The first of these effectiveness reports, published by independent consultants in 2003, strongly commended the commitments to sustainable development made by the Assembly, but pointed to difficulties in driving those commitments through to delivery (CAG Consultants, 2003). Subsequently, in March 2004, a revised Scheme was laid before the Assembly that strengthened and generalized the commitments in the original Scheme and a separate Action Plan was produced, setting out how these commitments would be put into effect (WAG 2004a, 2004b). As discussed in Chapters 4 and 13, these procedures have continued to encourage improvements being made in Wales's substantive commitment to sustainable development.

Procedures can also be used to reinforce strong substantive obligations. The Land Reform (Scotland) Act 2003 s. 38(1) provides that:

> Ministers shall not decide that a community interest is to be entered in the Register unless they are satisfied . . . (b) that . . . (ii) the land is sufficiently near to land with which those members of that community have a substantial connection and that its acquisition by the community body is compatible with furthering the achievement of sustainable development.

In this case, a failure to meet the strong substantive provisions relating to the main purpose of community bodies and interests is supported by serious procedural implications in company and land law. Fox (2007: 47) reported that by

March 2006, there had been five cases where the Scottish ministers had refused to register the community interest in the Register of Community Interests in Land Charges because the community body had failed to show that its purpose was for sustainable development or that its Memorandum, Articles, membership or constitution were compatible with the Act. In fact, this had been the most common ground of rejection.

In both cases, the procedures are significant because they create consequences for failure to meet either substantive or procedural obligations. These consequences have little to do with the courts, but instead rely on other controls – in the first instance, independent appraisal, legislative scrutiny, interest groups and the media and in the second instance, the executive, company and property law.

While some good UK examples exist, notably the Government of Wales Act 1998, the Scottish Parliament appears to have been more proactive at including procedural requirements to enforce and monitor sustainable development obligations in its statutes than its UK counterpart, thus increasing the potential impact of the obligations.

The legal significance of the provisions – enforceability in court

None of the statutes studied creates criminal or administrative offences in relation to sustainable development. For example, a misuse of funding for sustainable development projects could be enforced by the criminal law but it has not. It is unlikely that the courts would accept an action for breach of statutory duty, since these are all directory duties which do not tend to create rights per se.[45] Indeed, a common criticism against the use of vague or unenforceable terms is that they undermine the role of law in protecting individual rights (Brandl and Bungert, 1992: 92). To this end, it is helpful to distinguish between judicial enforcement, where the court is the primary implementation mechanism, and the courts' supervisory role of administrative programmes and agencies under the normal rules for judicial review (Rubin, 1989). With one exception, none of the statutes creates a statutory right of appeal for a public body's failure to meet a sustainable development obligation.

The exception is found in the Land Reform (Scotland) Act 2003 s. 61 which allows owners, community bodies and members of the community to appeal certain decisions by ministers to the sheriff court. The sheriff may require rectification of the Register and impose conditions upon the appellant, and the decision is final. The consequences of this appeal right are threefold. First, it reduces the need for judicial review by creating a statutory right of appeal. Second, it guarantees certain actors standing to challenge decisions made under the Act. Third, as the appeal is heard by a sheriff and not the Court of Session, it should be quicker and more cost-effective.[46] Beyond these observations, however, the appeal offers no additional grounds of challenge over those which are described below under judicial review.

Challenging some of the other sustainable development provisions using judicial review is possible. The provisions all involve an element of discretion, often that discretion is limited, and many contain procedural rules. The most likely grounds of challenge include: no authority to act; a failure to follow certain procedures laid down in the authorizing statute; a failure to take into account a relevant consideration or taking into account an irrelevant one; a fettering of discretion by rigidly applying a policy; a failure to have regard to legitimate expectations; and conduct or decision making that is so unreasonable no reasonable body would do it (Wade and Forsyth, 2004).[47] Furthermore, if the conduct or decision can be challenged under the Human Rights Act 1998 for a breach of a right under the European Convention on Human Rights, or as contrary to EC law, then 'the principle of proportionality' may also apply, whereby the administrative measure must not be more drastic than is necessary for attaining the desired result.[48]

As revealed above, the provisions are not alike and range from formulations which are so vague they would be very difficult to challenge, to legal rules which impose very clear procedural requirements.

Some of the provisions are framed as aspirational goals or objectives that are clearly to be treated as material considerations by the decision maker. The English courts have acknowledged 'sustainability' as a material consideration in planning decisions and that it is capable of being a main issue in planning law decisions and may deserve significant weight.[49] The Town and Country Planning Act 1990 itself is silent about sustainable development in relation to decisions on individual applications for planning permission, but it has been a key policy objective in development control for many years (UK Government, 1997). In *Horsham DC v First Secretary of State, Devine Homes plc*,[50] the Council had refused planning permission for a proposed residential development in a village, described as remote from the nearest large settlement, with inadequate services. The Council's Settlement Sustainability Analysis had determined that this site was relatively unsustainable for new residential development. The inspector allowed the appeal and granted planning permission subject to conditions. He reasoned that there was inadequate public transport but then reduced the car parking places in line with recommendations in national policy guidance (PPG 3). Sullivan J quashed the inspector's decision and found that the inspector had failed to correctly apply the advice in PPG 3 when considering the issue of sustainability and that the inspector's reasoning on sustainability was inadequate and his conclusion on the issue flawed.[51] While *Horsham* saw a positive outcome and the court willing to intervene on a sustainability matter, it remains the case that judicial review is reactive. It does not ensure compliance with the provision at an early stage and for many 'sustainable development' decisions, this is essential. The most one can hope for is that following an adverse decision, administrators alter their behaviour to prevent further challenge. Judicial review is also costly and time-consuming. Finally, regardless of the test, as many of the formulations are so vague, it would be very difficult to hold that a decision was unreasonable.

However, as suggested above, some of the sustainable objectives and duties go further and could be treated as legal rules that serve to confine and structure the decision maker's discretion and, as a result, provide a mechanism or framework for making the decision. The Parliamentary Under-Secretary for International Development set out a hypothetical example involving the provisions in the International Development Act 2002, where he clearly intends it to be used as a legal rule:

> the Secretary of State may provide development assistance only if she is satisfied that such assistance is 'likely to contribute to a reduction of poverty' through sustainable development promoting the welfare of people. Any use of aid that does not respect the primacy of the poverty requirement, when it applies, and the two development purposes would fall outside the provisions of the Bill, and any such use would therefore be challengeable in court.[52]

However, similar case law indicates that the court is unlikely to interpret these provisions as legal rules. The Waste Framework Directive Article 4 provides that 'Member States shall take the necessary measures to ensure that waste is recovered or disposed of without endangering human health and without using processes or methods which could harm the environment'. A literal approach to this provision would mean that 'no waste disposal licence would ever be granted since it is axiomatic that waste disposal causes some harm to the environment' (Bell, 2003: 77). This is formulated as a legal rule and could easily have been interpreted as such (Bell, 2003: 78). However, the Court of Appeal in *R (Thornby Farms Ltd) v Daventry DC and R (Murray) v Derbyshire CC* chose instead to treat the provision as an objective. Pill LJ held that the objective was to be treated as distinct from material considerations and 'an objective which is obligatory must always be kept in mind when making a decision even while the decision maker has regard to other material considerations'.[53]

Bell (2003) notes that while this approach appears to add emphasis to the objective, the effect of the distinction is minimal and, in practice, it will only be necessary for a decision maker to state that any relevant decision has been taken with the objectives in mind and specify which considerations have been taken into account. So long as this is done, he argues that it is unlikely that a court would intervene. Bell (2003: 81) further criticizes the 'objectives' approach noting that 'on the basis of these cases, if the aim isn't achieved, and reality suggests that in many cases it won't be, it doesn't really matter as long as the proper procedures are gone through'.

The European Court of Justice has also exercised judicial self-restraint in its interpretation of the environmental principles set out in Article 174 EC (formerly 130r). In *Safety Hi-Tech* the Court held that:

> in view of the need to strike a balance between certain of those objectives and principles mentioned in Article 130r and of the complexity of the

implementation of those criteria, review by the Court must necessarily be limited to the question whether, in adopting particular rules, the legislature committed a manifest error of appraisal regarding the conditions for the application of Article 130r of the Treaty.[54]

Havercroft and Macrory conclude that the courts appear to have taken the view that the volume of modern environmental legislation means that new principles relating to the environment should be the responsibility of the executive and legislature, and not the courts. However, the principles are still making an impact due to their increasing presence in policy documents and plans which have led the courts to feel more entitled to rely on them as policy considerations which cannot be ignored by decision makers (Havercroft and Macrory, 2004: 212).

If the courts are not the primary implementation tool and judicial review is reserved to only the most extreme decisions, what value do these provisions add? The answer in many instances is that the formulations cannot, in any formal sense, be monitored or enforced, nor was there any legislative intent that they should be. The provisions may be purely symbolic and this alone may warrant their existence – for educational, policy and reassurance reasons. However, in many instances, alternative means of enforcement, scrutiny and review do exist. The statutory provisions may give rise to a moral or societal expectation (which is probably not legally enforceable) and a failure to act in accordance with it may result in criticism from a higher level of government, the media, interest groups, neighbours or the general public.

The sustainable development provisions may also be monitored and enforced pursuant to procedural requirements set out in the statute itself. Adding some sort of procedural requirement to a duty substantially improves a provision's enforceability both inside and outside court. As noted above, several of the sustainable development provisions are much more enforceable outside the courtroom. Recall that under the Land Reform (Scotland) Act 2003 s. 34(4), if a community body does not have sustainable development as its main purpose, it cannot be entered on the Register.

The procedures can also help inside court. One of the reasons the Council in *Horsham* was successful was because it could point to something tangible – specific national planning guidance on sustainability – that was being applied irrationally. Furthermore, while not every procedural error invalidates administrative action, and the courts' jurisdiction is discretionary,[55] the failure to comply with a mandatory requirement may give rise to a separate ground of judicial review if it can be shown that the failure has resulted either from a breach of the principles of natural justice[56] or in the body acting *ultra vires*.[57]

Bell's concerns – about procedures being met and yet the broader substantive aims being lost – remain. These could possibly be resolved if some of the procedures had more of a substantive content. Hendry (2005) suggests using more precise sustainability indicators to improve the specificity of the duty whereby, for example, Scottish Water could show compliance with its sustainable development duty by demonstrating that it was on balance, making progress in some way to a set of sustainability indicators.[58] This leads back to the value of using targets for sustainable development discussed earlier. Using targets or indicators as evidence of compliance or non-compliance with a duty would not only make the duty more robust, but would also give the sustainability indicators some much-needed policy relevance. This approach is considered more thoroughly in Chapters 9 and 13 below.

Symbolic by its absence

While there has been an increase in the use of sustainable development in statutes, it is still the case that the vast majority of statutes enacted by the UK, Scottish and Northern Ireland legislatures do not contain any reference to sustainable development or sustainability in the environmental sense, yet many of these have significant economic, social and environmental implications.

There are some instances where the relevant administration does not believe that sustainable development is relevant for a particular regime or agency. Often, the sustainable development issue has been considered even if it does not show up in the final legislative product. In the Scottish Parliament, all Executive bills must be accompanied by a statement of sustainable development in the policy memorandum[59] and there are examples in both the UK and Scottish Parliaments where the issue was discussed during the legislative passing of the bill but not included in the final Act. There may be several reasons for this. The arguments put forward at the beginning of this chapter clearly hold true and there is a preference for guidance and administrative structures and for specific provisions that address issues more directly. It was decided that there was no need to include sustainable development in the Railways Bill since, as argued by the Minister, 'Sustainable development, sustainability and the environmental dimension are already in the body of the legislation affecting the [Office of Rail Regulation] and will remain so under the Bill'.[60]

During the Environment and Rural Development Committee's discussions on the Nature Conservation (Scotland) Bill the minister noted that:

> We have to take a view of sustainable development. We are all aware . . . that sustainable development has various component parts. If we try to turn every bill into a sustainable development strategy, we will have missed the point . . . We should recognize that the bill is essentially about nature conservation, notwithstanding the fact that it will play an important part in an overarching sustainable development strategy.[61]

This argument shows an improved understanding of sustainable development by a government leader than was previously evident. As discussed in Chapter 4, sustainable development policy in the past has often been considered to be an 'environmental' matter and this acknowledgment that policy on the environment and conservation should be distinct from sustainable development shows very significant advancement in the Executive's understanding of sustainable development (Jenkins, 2002: 601; Ross, 2003: 66).

Thus, the fact that sustainable development is absent from some statutes may be an oversight; in others, it may be by design. The same holds true for the strength afforded to sustainable development in those statutes where it does appear.

Analysis and conclusions

The term 'sustainable development' is being referred to in more and more UK, Scottish and, recently, Northern Ireland legislation. This reflects an acceptance of sustainable development as a policy tool and has been encouraged by devolution and the increased status of the concept at EC level. Probably due to its vague and evolutionary nature, none of the statutes studied attempts to define sustainable development. Instead, these statutes rely on government guidance to provide a consistent, yet flexible, approach. Sustainable development has not achieved the status of a *legal principle* as such in UK law. However, it does appear in a variety of legal forms, including as duties, objectives and procedural requirements.

There appears to be no hierarchy between these different forms. Some objectives are very powerful, others much less so, and the same is true for the duties. Importantly, different formulations can create very different legal impacts. Some of the provisions are almost purely symbolic, some are simply material considerations to be taken into account in the decision, some may create a legal rule dictating how a decision is to be made, and others may create a mandatory procedural requirement.

The most common provisions relating to sustainable development are duties. While the more recent provisions are much clearer than their predecessors, there is still no standard form of duty. The strength of the provisions varies enormously, but all involve some element of discretion. While there remain a few instances where the discretion conferred is very broad, in most cases, the discretion has been somehow confined or structured, either by limiting the scope of the provision, subjecting it to qualifications, or by requiring a reference to guidance or other monitoring devices. There are some statutes where sustainable development is the primary duty, but in most cases it is one of several duties or objectives. Some statutes include qualifications and mechanisms for prioritizing between duties, but in others this is left to the decision maker. There is some evidence that in some statutes the sustainable development duty could act as the mechanism for balancing other duties or objectives. In these cases, it could be interpreted as a legal rule and provide a much needed framework for decision making.

None of the substantive provisions are supported by criminal sanctions and only one includes a statutory appeal mechanism. Many provisions do not include any obvious enforcement mechanisms but may still be effective from a more symbolic perspective – acting to educate, inform and heighten awareness. Also, the provision and any breach thereof may attract the attention of the public, interest groups, parliamentary committees or a higher level of government, and result in more informal, ad hoc enforcement. Judicial review is possible but is only appropriate in those rare instances where a public body has acted irrationally, illegally or procedurally improperly. It is also generally reactive, costly and time-consuming.

The courts have demonstrated a willingness to accept sustainable development as a material consideration in decisions; however, drawing on the experience of similar-type provisions, a stronger approach may still be a way off.

Moreover, a review conducted in 2005 by the IHPC to investigate the impact of statutory sustainable development duties on bodies with existing duties in England, Scotland and Wales, concluded that duties alone were insufficient to ensure progress in mainstreaming sustainable development (Cussons, 2006). Leadership on sustainable development and mechanisms for scrutinizing the delivery of the duties were more influential. While, as discussed in Chapter 5, strong leadership on sustainable development is sporadic and, in many instances, dependent on an individual or group, scrutiny procedures can be introduced and, interestingly, these can be used to support not only sustainable development duties, but indeed leadership as well.

Increasingly, legislators are attaching procedural requirements to sustainable development provisions. These can be obligations to produce or follow guidance, regulations, directions, strategies or reports, or they may require notice, audit or publicity. These procedures bring several benefits. First, a failure to comply with a statutory procedure is much easier to enforce and monitor not only under judicial review, but also, importantly, by central government, interest groups and the public. Thus, the procedures can significantly enhance the potential impact of a given provision. The procedural provisions may also reduce the need to include substantive provisions, since by complying with the procedures, the public body may still need to direct its mind to the substance behind the procedure. The Welsh Assembly's obligation to produce a scheme of sustainable development and report on it regularly is a good example. It also may be beneficial to include more substantive content in the procedures themselves – for example, requiring a reference to progress towards certain sustainability targets or indicators in guidance. This could improve the specificity of the duty.

More procedural monitoring of the sustainable development duties would improve their impact. This is also true for the procedures themselves. It makes no sense to require the production of a report, for example, if there are no consequences for failing to do so or no obligation to act on its findings, publicize it or allow others to comment on, discuss or scrutinize it. Finally, the majority of statutes do not contain any reference to sustainable development and while in some cases this may be an oversight, in many others it is deliberate and there is some evidence of an emerging understanding by legislators and leaders that environmental protection and sustainable development objectives are distinct.

In conclusion, sustainable development provisions have a place in UK legislation. However, if a provision is to be more than simply symbolic, then, ideally, there should be some statutory (often formal) means to monitor and review compliance using administrative, political, legal or other mechanisms. At present, while some statutes do this, many do not. As will be discussed in later chapters, where the sustainable development duty is intended to create a framework to aid decision making, the legislation needs to be more explicit about this role to encourage the courts to recognize it. The current piecemeal approach to sustainable development does lead to inconsistency.

Following her review of the UK Parliament's use of sustainable development duties in 2002, Jenkins revealed a number of inconsistencies in the Government's understanding of the term 'sustainable development' and recommended replacing the various individual duties with one overriding primary statutory duty for all public bodies to contribute to the achievement of sustainable development (Jenkins, 2002: 601). Robust general duties on public bodies for each administration could provide some consistency. As is discussed in detail in Chapter 13, the procedural obligations set out in the Government of Wales Act 2006 provide an excellent starting point in this regard, despite not being accompanied by substantive duties in relation to sustainable development.

Recently, both the Scottish and Northern Ireland Executives have experimented, albeit tentatively, with general substantive duties in the Northern Ireland (Miscellaneous Provisions) Act 2006 and the Climate Change (Scotland) Act 2009. The Northern Ireland (Miscellaneous Provisions) Act 2006 s. 25, for example requires departments and district councils to exercise their functions in the manner they consider best calculated to promote the achievement of sustainable development. Unlike the Welsh obligation, which is entirely procedural and requires the production and review of a scheme of sustainable development, the duty in Northern Ireland is substantive. The potential impact of such duties is significant – they provide a mandate for public sector bodies to direct their activities to achieve positive sustainable development outcomes, and to do so without compromising their other existing statutory obligations. However, both in Northern Ireland and Scotland, the duties have not proven to be effective. First, by being hidden away in unrelated statutes, the provisions do not even manage to have any symbolic effect. Second, they are not supported by the appropriate procedures. At a very minimum these general duties, like their specific counterparts discussed above, need to be supported by strong procedures for consultation, reporting, monitoring and review, which are ideally linked to a clear vision of sustainable development set out in guidance which is consistently used. Finally, like many of the specific provisions, at the moment, these general duties provide no guidance as to priority. The Northern Ireland Executive itself reports that the impact of the duty, as of 2010, appears to have been marginal as it has proved difficult to interpret for public sector bodies (Northern Ireland Executive, 2010: 9).

As is argued in Chapters 12 and 13, a clear and consistent interpretation of sustainable development which sets defined priorities is essential for both general and specific provisions to operate effectively.

Notes

1 This chapter is an updated and revised version of an article published by the author in 2008: Ross, A. (2008) 'Why legislate for sustainable development? An examination of sustainable development provisions in UK and Scottish statutes', *Journal of Environmental Law*, 20(1): 35–68.
2 The Natural Heritage (Scotland) Act 1991 ch. 28 s. 1(1).
3 The Resource Management Act 1991 s. 5 introduced an overarching purpose of sustainable management 'to guide regulation of land and water use, pollution control and coastal marine activities'. Sustainable management is defined in s. 5(2). The sustainable management approach arguably slowed progress towards sustainable development in New Zealand, as the term was interpreted inconsistently. Subsequently the Local Government Act 2002 promotes a sustainable development approach in New Zealand.
4 Town and Country Planning (Scotland) Act 1997 ch. 5 s. 72.
5 See, for Scotland: Scottish Executive (2002) and for England: UK Government (1997) (now superseded by UK Government (2005)). Included in the Planning and Compulsory Purchase Act 2004 ch. 5; Planning *etc.* (Scotland) Act 2006 asp 17 and Planning Act (Northern Ireland) 2011, ch. 25.
6 The National Parks (Scotland) Act 2000 asp 10 and the Land Reform (Scotland) Act 2003 asp 2.
7 The Climate Change (Scotland) Act 2009 s. 44(1).
8 The Northern Ireland (Miscellaneous Provisions) Act 2006 s. 25. Planning Act (Northern Ireland) 2011; Local Government (Wales) Measure 2009 s. 4, s. 37.
9 See the Consolidated version of the Treaty establishing the European Community, *Official Journal of the European Union* (OJ) (2002), C 325/33, Article 174(2), and Winter (2004: 13).
10 The Consolidated version of the Treaty establishing the European Community OJ (2002), C 325/33, Article 2 provides that 'The Community shall have as its task . . . to promote throughout the Community a harmonious, balanced and sustainable development of economic activities'. Article 6 provides that 'Environmental protection requirements must be integrated into the definition and implementation of the Community policies and activities referred to in Article 3, in particular with a view to promoting sustainable development'.
11 The various water statutes (such as the Water Services and Water Environment (Scotland) Act 2003 asp 3) have been heavily influenced by the Water Framework Directive: Directive 2000/60/EC EU Water Framework Directive OJ (2000), L 327.
12 The International Development Act 2002 ch. 1 s. 1(3) provides that for the purposes of subs. (2)(a), 'sustainable development' includes 'any development that is, in the opinion of the Secretary of State, prudent having regard to the likelihood of its generating lasting benefits for the population of the country or countries in relation to which it is provided'.
13 House of Commons Standing Committee, G pt 5, Column 279, 21 January 2003.
14 Lord Whitty, House of Lords Debates, Local Government Bill, Column 1482, 25 January 2000. For a fuller discussion, see Jenkins (2002).
15 *Sharpe v Wakefield* (1888) 22 QBD 239 (CA) Lord Fisher MR at 241. More recently, see *Legal Aid Board v Russell* [1990] 2 QB 607 (CA) affirmed [1991] 2 AC 317 (HL).
16 [1998] AC 147.
17 [1998] AC 147, 159.
18 *Pepper v Hart* [1993] AC 593 (HL). See Kavanagh (2005: 98).

19 *Wilson v First County Trust (no 2)* [2003] UKHL 40; [2004] 1 AC 816.
20 See *Stringer v MHLG* [1970] 1 WLR 1281.
21 The Environment Act 1995 s. 31, s. 40.
22 The Planning and Compulsory Purchase Act 2004 s. 39(3).
23 The Clean Neighbourhoods and Environment Act 2005 ch 16 s. 88(9).
24 Winter (2004) uses these distinctions in the context of environmental law in national and EC law. The relationship is much more blurred in the context of international law.
25 The Consolidated version of the Treaty establishing the European Community OJ (2002), C 325/33, Article 2 explicitly sets out sustainable development as a task of the Community.
26 *Pepper v Hart* [1993] AC 593 (HL); *Wilson v First County Trust (no 2)* [2003] UKHL 40; [2004] 1 AC 816.
27 The Environment Act 1995 s. 31(2).
28 House of Commons Standing Committee, E, 5 February 1998.
29 Sections 13(3) and 58(2).
30 Subject to the courts' supervisory discretion. See *Padfield v Minister of Agriculture, Fisheries and Food* [1968] AC 997.
31 House of Commons Standing Committee, G pt 1, column 4, 21 January 2003.
32 *Simpson v Edinburgh Corporation* [1960] SC 313; 1961 SLT 17.
33 The Transport Act 2000 s. 207(2)(b); the Water Industry (Scotland) Act 2002 s. 51; the Water Environment and Water Services (Scotland) Act 2003 s. 2(4); the Northern Ireland (Miscellaneous Provisions) Act 2006 s. 25
34 To quote Richard Page (South West Hertfordshire) in the Committee stage of the Energy Bill, 'I contribute to flag days by buying a flag for various charities, but I hardly think that my contribution will be absolutely vital to achieving their aims'. House of Lords Standing Committee, B pt 5, Column 245, 8 June 2004.
35 Principal purposes are: (a) promoting economic development and wealth creation in Greater London; (b) promoting social development in Greater London; and (c) promoting the improvement of the environment in Greater London.
36 See s. 34(4).
37 House of Commons Standing Committee, D pt 13, Column 213, 14 October 2003.
38 For other examples of qualifications, see the Water Services and Water Environment (Scotland) Act 2003 s. 2(4); and the Greater London Authority Act 1999 s. 30(5).
39 For example, see the Land Reform (Scotland) Act 2003 s. 34, s. 51.
40 See the Regional Development Agencies Bill (Hansard HC Standing Committee E, 5 Feb 1998); the Greater London Authority Bill (Hansard HC Standing Committee A pt 12, 2 Feb 1999); the Local Government Bill (Hansard HC Standing Committee A pt 9, 9 May 2000); and the Further and Higher Education (Scotland) Bill (2004).
41 Section 13(3) and (6)(e)(i).
42 Section 25(2) and (3). Note the Buildings Act 1984 s. 1(1) as amended by the Sustainable and Secure Buildings Act 2004 s. 1(1) contains similar provisions for England.
43 Section 7(3).
44 Replaces the Government of Wales Act 1998 s. 121(1).
45 *Calveley v Chief Constable of Merseyside Police* [1989] AC 1228.
46 See *Holmehill Limited v the Scottish Minister* 2006 SLT (Sh Ct) 79.
47 See, generally, Wade and Forsyth (2004). See *Associated Provincial Picture Houses Ltd v Wednesbury Corporation* [1948] 1 KB 223.
48 *R v Home Secretary ex p Brind* [1991] 1 AC 696; *R (Alconbury) v Secretary of State for the Environment, Transport and the Regions* [2001] 2 WLR 1389, 1406; *R (Association of British Civilian Internees – Far East Region) v Secretary of State for Defence* [2003] 3 WLR 80.

49 *R (Ludlam) v the First Secretary of State, Derbyshire DC* [2004] EWHC 99; *Barchester Healthcare Limited v Secretary of State for Communities and Local Government; Sevenoaks District Council* [2010] EWHC 2784 (Admin).
50 [2004] EWHC 769 (Admin).
51 [2004] EWHC 769 (Admin) para. 29 .
52 House of Commons Standing Committee, D pt 5, 22 November 2001.
53 [2002] EWCA Civ 31; [2002] Env LR 28.
54 C-284/95 *Safety Hi-Tech* [1998] ECR I-4301. See also the very restrictive approach taken by the UK courts with the precautionary principle in *R v Secretary of State for Trade and Industry ex parte Duddridge and Others* (1995) 7 JEL, 224. Recent case law acknowledges the possibility of the principle having some significance at a national level: *R (Amvac Chemical Ltd) v Secretary of State for Environment, Food and Rural Affairs and Others* [2001] EWHC 1011 (Admin).
55 *London and Clydeside Estates Ltd v Aberdeen DC* [1979] 3 All ER 876.
56 *B v W. Wardship: Appeal* [1979] 3 All ER 83. A failure to comply with a procedural requirement may also be contrary to the European Convention on Human Rights Article 6(1).
57 *Bradbury v London Borough of Enfield* [1967] 3 All ER 434.
58 The Water Industry (Scotland) Act 2002 s. 51.
59 Scottish Parliament Standing Order 9.3.3 c – see Ross (2006: 20). For a fuller discussion on the role of pre-legislative scrutiny, see Oliver (2006).
60 House of Commons Standing Committee, A pt 9, Column 73, 14 December 2004.
61 Environment and Rural Development Committee, Column 529, 26 November 2003.

References

Bell, S. (2003) 'Statutory pollution prevention objectives: Are they rules or aims?', *Journal of Environmental Law*, 15(1): 59–85.
Bosselmann, K. and Grinlinton, D. (2002) *Environmental Law for a Sustainable Society*, Auckland: New Zealand Centre for Environmental Law.
Brandl, E. and Bungert, H. (1992) 'Constitutional entrenchment of environmental protection: A comparative analysis of experiences abroad', *Harvard Environmental Law Review*, 16(1): 1–100.
CAG Consultants (2003) *How Effectively has the National Assembly for Wales Promoted Sustainable Development?*, Report to the Welsh Assembly Government.
CAG Consultants (2004) *Is the Scottish Executive Structured and Positioned to Deliver Sustainable Development?*, 10th Report, vol. 2, Edinburgh: Environment and Rural Development Committee.
Collar, N. (1999) *Planning*, 2nd edition, Edinburgh: W. Green.
Curran, S. (2004) 'Sustainable development v sustainable management: The interface between the Local Government Act and the Resource Management Act', *New Zealand Journal Environmental Law*, 8: 267–94.
Cussons, S. (2006) *Review of Statutory Sustainable Development Duties*, London: In House Policy Consultancy/DEFRA.
Davis, K. (1970) *Discretionary Justice: A Preliminary Inquiry*, Baton Rouge: Louisiana State University Press.
De Sadeleer, N. (2005) *Environmental Principles: From Political Slogans to Legal Rules*, Oxford: Oxford University Press.

Department of Environment, Food and Rural Affairs (DEFRA) (1994) *Sustainable Development: The UK Strategy*, Cm 2426, London: DEFRA.

DEFRA (1999) *A Better Quality of Life: A Strategy for Sustainable Development for the United Kingdom*, London: DEFRA.

Department of Environment, Transport and the Regions (DETR) (2000) *Achieving a Better Quality of Life: Review of Progress towards Sustainable Development: Government Annual Report*, London: DETR.

Dworkin, R. (1977) *Taking Rights Seriously*, Cambridge, MA: Harvard University Press.

European Commission (2009) *Mainstreaming Sustainable Development into EU Policies: 2009 Review of the European Union Strategy for Sustainable Development*, Com 400, Brussels: EC.

Fox, A. (2007) 'Update on the right to buy land', Proceedings from the Rural Law Conference, Glasgow: CLT.

Havercroft, I. and Macrory, R. (2004) 'Environmental principles in the United Kingdom', in R. Macrory (ed.) *Principles of European Environmental Law*, Groningen: Europa Law Publishing.

Hendry, S. (2005) 'Worth the paper it's written on? An analysis of statutory duty in modern environmental law', *Journal of Planning & Environmental Law*: 1145–58.

HM Government, Scottish Executive, Welsh Assembly Government, Northern Ireland Office (2005) *One future – different paths: The UK's shared framework for sustainable development*, London: DEFRA.

Jenkins, V. (2002) 'Placing sustainable development at the heart of government in the UK: The role of law in the evolution of sustainable development as the central organising principle of government', *Legal Studies*, 22(4): 578–601.

Kavanagh, A. (2005) 'Constitutional law; Parliamentary Debates; Statutory Interpretation *Pepper v Hart* and matters of constitutional principle', *Law Quarterly Review*, 121: 98–122.

Lee, M. (2005) *EU Environmental Law: Challenges, Change and Decision-Making*, Oxford: Hart.

Lee, M. and Abbot, C. (2003) 'The Usual suspects? Public participation under the Aarhus Convention', *Modern Law Review*, 66(1): 80–108.

Macrory, R. (ed.) (2004) *Principles of European Environmental Law*, Groningen: Europa Law Publishing.

Mader, L. (2001) 'Evaluating effects: A contribution to the quality of legislation', *Statute Law Review*, 22(2): 119–31.

Northern Ireland Executive (2010) *Everyone's Involved: Sustainable Development Strategy*, Belfast. Northern Ireland Executive.

Oliver, D. (2006) 'Improving the scrutiny of bills: The case for standards and checklists', *Public Law*, Summer: 219–46.

Roberts, I. (2004) 'Statutory general nature conservation duties: More appearance than substance?', LLM thesis, University of Dundee.

Ross, A. (2003) 'Is the environment getting squeezed out of sustainable development?', *Public Law*, Summer: 249–59.

Ross, A. (2005) 'The UK approach to delivering sustainable development in government: A case study in joined-up working', *Journal of Environmental Law*, 17(1): 27–49.

Ross, A. (2006) 'Sustainable development in Scotland post devolution', *Environmental Law Review*, 8: 6–32.

Ross, A. (2008) 'Why legislate for sustainable development? An examination of sustainable development provisions in UK and Scottish statutes', *Journal of Environmental Law*, 20(1): 35–68.

Ross, A., Rowan Robinson, J. and Walton, W. (1995) 'Sustainable development in Scotland: The Role of Scottish Natural Heritage', *Land Use Policy*, 12(3): 237–52.

Rubin, E. (1989) 'Law and legislation in the administrative state', *Columbia Law Review*, 89: 369–426.

Scottish Executive (2002) *Scottish Planning Policy 1: The Planning System*, Edinburgh: Scottish Executive.

Scottish Labour Party and Scottish Liberal Democrats (2003) *A Partnership for a Better Scotland: Partnership Agreement*, Edinburgh: Scottish Government.

Scottish Natural Heritage (SNH) (1993) *Sustainable Development and the Natural Heritage: The SNH Approach*, Edinburgh: SNH.

UK Government (1997) *Planning Policy Guidance 1: General Policies and Principles*, London: UK Government.

UK Government (2005) *Planning Policy Statement 1: Delivering Sustainable Development*, London: UK Government.

Wade, W. and Forsyth, C. (2004) *Administrative Law*, Ninth edition, Oxford: Oxford University Press.

Welsh Assembly Government (WAG) (2004a) *Sustainable Development Annual Report 2004*, Cardiff: WAG.

WAG (2004b) *Sustainable Development Action Plan 2004–2007*, Cardiff: WAG.

WAG (2008) *Sustainable Development Annual Report 2007–2008*, Cardiff: WAG.

Winter, G. (2004) 'The legal nature of environmental principles in international, EC and German law', in R. Macrory (ed.) *Principles of European Environmental Law*, Groningen: Europa Law Publishing.

World Commission on Environment and Development (WCED) (1987) *Our Common Future*, Oxford: Oxford University Press.

9 Mechanisms – sustainable development indicators

> What gets measured gets done. If you don't measure results, you can't tell success from failure. If you can't see success, you can't reward it. If you can't see success, you can't learn from it. If you can't recognize failure, you can't correct it. And if you can demonstrate results, you can win public support.
>
> (WWF *et al.*, 2005: 3)

From its inception as a policy goal, advocates of sustainable development have emphasized the need to measure progress using suitable sustainability indicators. Even the early rhetoric on sustainable development recognized the importance of measuring progress and sustainable development indicators (SDIs) have long been seen as one of the essential tools for implementation. Indeed, following the 1992 Rio Summit on Environment and Development, countries were urged to 'develop indicators of sustainable development' in a way that would 'contribute to a self-regulating sustainability of integrated environment and development systems' (UNGA, 1992: para. 40.4).

This chapter examines the history and purpose of using indicators for the implementation of sustainable development and the types of indicators available. It then examines the sets of sustainable development indicators currently being used by the UK and devolved administrations. Subsequently, it considers how certain scientific and governance failings mean that SDI trends are ignored, and more generally, how they have little policy relevance and are not used to their full potential. The approaches used in the UK to select SDIs are then analyzed and compared to proven good practice to explain why indicators fail to deliver. Indeed, this chapter's analysis of the research into SDIs and their selection reveals not only an impressive depth of knowledge surrounding what is considered good practice, but also a fair bit of agreement. Yet, despite rhetoric to the contrary, this agreed good practice is often ignored by policymakers in relation to the actual SDI sets used (Bell and Morse, 2008: 3–44). Though the focus is on the UK and its devolved administrations, broader themes are nevertheless noticeable and highlighted where relevant.

History of sustainable development indicators in the UK

Indicators have a long history in science and in measuring economic progress. Essentially, the packaging of data into indicators is a way of simplifying complex and detailed information (Bell and Morse, 2008: 3–44). The late 1940s saw the start of the modern process of assessing progress using systems of national accounts and the introduction of annual calculation of gross domestic (or national) product (GDP or GNP) (Hodge and Hardi, 1997: 7). As regards sustainable development, *Agenda 21* urged countries to 'develop indicators of sustainable development' in a way that would 'contribute to a self-regulating sustainability of integrated environment and development systems' (UNGA, 1992: para. 40.4). The World Summit on Sustainable Development in 2002 encouraged further work on indicators for sustainable development by countries in line with their national conditions and priorities, and invited the international community to support efforts of developing countries in this regard (UN, 2002: para. 130). The subsequent sessions of the UN Commission on Sustainable Development (CSD) continue to confirm this mandate (Division for Sustainable Development, UNDESA, 2006: 8).

As well as urging individual countries to develop SDIs, *Agenda 21* also urged the international community to work on the development of SDI sets. The CSD completed its first indicator set in 1996 (UN, 1996), and has since revised it twice: in 2001 and 2006 (UN, 2001, 2006). The UK and the EU have been very involved in testing and developing the CSD indicator sets and many of the UK indicators have their origins in these sets (Eurostat, 2001). The initial CSD indicator set and, as a result, the UK's initial set of indicators, were criticized for containing too many indicators and being too complicated, and for not including a sufficient social dimension (DETR, 1998). The subsequent CSD sets have been shorter and emphasize the need for frameworks and the need to adapt the indicators to national conditions and priorities. The overarching purpose of the CSD indicators has been to inform policy at the national level, but they do have the benefit of also encouraging some form of homogeneity among the SDI sets of different nations which, among other things, allows international comparisons to be made (UN, 2007: 30–1).

Since Rio, there have been three UK-wide SDI sets, all of which make reference to the relevant UK sustainable development strategy. The first set was produced in 1996 and was based on the UK's first Strategy for Sustainable Development produced in 1994, which largely interpreted sustainable development as a trade-off between economic and environmental factors (DETR, 1996). Following a wide consultation (DETR, 1998) and research using focus groups (EAC, 2002, Annex 1), a second set of indicators, *Quality of Life Counts*, was produced, based on *A Better Quality of Life: A Strategy for Sustainable Development for the United Kingdom* (the 1999 strategy), which advocated a three-pronged approach to sustainable development, encompassing economic, environmental and social factors (DETR, 1999). Over and above the Government's own annual reporting on progress, the *Quality of Life Counts* indicators included 13 headline indicators which were reviewed by the House of Commons Environmental Audit Committee (EAC) and later the Sustainable Development Commission (SDC) (EAC, 2002; SDC, 2004).

Devolution posed new challenges in relation to the UK's sustainable development strategy given the division of competences with the new devolved administrations. Post-1999, responsibility for education, health and land use planning is now largely, and to varying degrees, in the hands of the administrations in Scotland, Wales and Northern Ireland.[1] Inevitably, the *Quality of Life Counts* indicators suffered from geographical inconsistencies among the regions (EAC, 2002: para. 51). Therefore, in 2005, a third set of UK-wide indicators was produced jointly by all the UK administrations (noting however, that at the time, devolution in Northern Ireland was suspended) *One future – different paths: The UK's shared framework for sustainable development* (HM Government *et al.*, 2005). This set of indicators interprets sustainable development using the five key principles: living within environmental limits, ensuring a healthy and just society, achieving a sustainable economy, promoting good governance, and using sound science responsibly (HM Government *et al.*, 2005: 8). At the same time, the UK administration produced a UK Strategy for Sustainable Development entitled *Securing our Future* which deals with reserved (or UK-wide) issues and those issues, which following devolution, only pertain to (mainly) England (DEFRA, 2005). The devolved administrations also produced their own strategies for sustainable development, and Scotland and Wales produced indicator sets (Chapter 4; WAG, 2009a). As of Summer 2011, the Northern Ireland Executive still had not produced its first indicator set. After the Scottish National Party's success in the Scottish Parliamentary election in May 2007, it replaced the previous government's sustainable development strategy with *The Government's Economic Strategy* and national performance indicators, along with one single objective of 'increasing sustainable economic growth' (Scottish Government, 2007, 2009). The Scottish Government claims this is consistent with the UK Framework, although it appears to move away from the common approach previously developed (SDCS, 2008, 2009; Scottish Government, 2010). At the municipal level, following on from Local Agenda 21, many local authorities across the UK now produce their own SDIs (Cartwright, 2000; SDC, 2009). Indicators are also produced on a sectoral basis by public and private bodies and for specific projects. The focus of this chapter is however on the UK indicators and those produced by the devolved administrations.

The purpose of sustainable development indicators

There are differing views as to the purpose and potential uses of indicators in the quest for sustainable development. The UK Government, in 2003, warned that there are limits to what SDIs can achieve, noting that 'the primary purpose of the UK indicators is to monitor and report on progress as a package. It may be expecting too much of them that they should also drive the progress they monitor in specific areas' (EAC, 2004: para. 7). Russell and Thomson argue that this narrow vision of indicators is unambitious:

SDIs do not just measure performance. Instead, they have the power to operationally define sustainable development priorities, establish thresholds that divide 'sustainable' actions from 'unsustainable' actions, help evaluate the sustainability of policy options and legitimate the use of powers by governments or regulatory agencies.

(Russell and Thomson, 2008: 367)

Moreover, in a brief for the Organisation for Economic Co-operation and Development (OECD), Stevens states that:

Indicators are needed to illustrate to policymakers and the public the linkages and trade-offs between economic, environmental and social values; to evaluate the longer-term implications of current decisions and behaviours; and to monitor progress towards sustainable development goals by establishing baseline conditions and trends.

(Stevens, 2005: 2)

The truth is that indicators come in a variety of shapes and sizes and not all of them are used for the same purpose. Some are quantitative measurements, framed to capture the current state, trends or targets. Many of these can be used not only to inform policy, but also as evidence for holding the responsible authorities (such as water authorities which have statutory duties in relation to water quality) to account. Others act simply as indicators and, in many instances, an aggregate of individual choices, action or inaction. It would be difficult to allocate responsibility to a particular public body for increasing the number of people who choose to do volunteer work, even though that is a very useful guide to issues such as social inclusion. Consequently, these indicators are useful in providing evidence of the indirect consequences of the world we live in and provide insights about society as a group of individuals behaving in a certain way. While these could not be used to hold public authorities to account, they nevertheless still should be sufficiently credible and reliable that public authorities feel confident in using them to make policy decisions. As the UN Department of Economic and Social Affairs (UNDESA) notes, 'the application of sustainable development indicators is important in several phases, from the identification of strategic priorities, through the planning and implementation of specific policy interventions, monitoring progress and learning from success and failures' (Division for Sustainable Development, UNDESA, 2006: 6). The argument put forth in this chapter is relevant to all these indicators as it relates to their credibility and policy relevance.

Types of indicators

As indicated above, several different types or frameworks of indicators are used in the context of sustainable development. Some of these are more prevalent in the UK sets than others.

The need to classify SDIs should not be underestimated, as classification ensures that the decision-making process is using indicators that cover/measure each of the dimensions of sustainable development, and is also essential for a holistic approach. As discussed below in the context of indicator selection, ideally conceptual frameworks for indicators are used to help to focus and clarify what to measure, what to expect from measurement and what kinds of indicators to use. Popular forms of categorization include versions of the driver, state, response frameworks, issue- or theme-based frameworks, capital frameworks, aggregated indicators and headline indicators. Often, a particular indicator set includes aspects of several of these, even though more generally, the indicators may be conceptually built around a particular framework. The theme-based frameworks used in the UK, for example, use headline indicators, including a range of driving force, pressures, state, impact and response (DPSIR) indicators and aggregated indicators such as the ecological footprint.

Driver (or driving force), pressure, state, impact and response frameworks

The initial set of 134 CSD indicators, published in 1996, was organized in a driving force, state and response (DSR) framework (UN, 1996). Driving force indicators describe processes or activities that have a positive or a negative impact on sustainable development (for example, pollution or school enrolment). State indicators describe the current situation (for example, nutritional status of children or land covered by forests), whereas response indicators reflect societal actions aimed at moving towards sustainable development. The first CSD indicators were additionally grouped according to the dimensions of sustainable development – social, economic, environmental and institutional, and matched to the relevant chapters of *Agenda 21* (UN, 2007: 39, 40). The benefit of DSR is that it allows indicators to be examined as a process and highlights the relationships between certain measurable indicators. Another variation further develops these inter-linkages by adding the categories of pressure and impact. The state may be caused by certain measured pressures, which in turn can be linked to a particular measured driver. Moreover, the particular measured state may be having an undesirable measured impact. The strength of the DPSIR framework is its focus on relationships between the elements that introduce dynamics into the framework. From a legal/regulatory perspective, this type of analysis is useful because regulatory responses can be introduced at various points along the production pathway (Bell and Etherington, 2009).

Whereas variations of the DSR framework continue to be used in more environmentally oriented indicator sets, the revision of the CSD indicators in 2001 discontinued this approach, mainly because it was not suited to addressing the very complex inter-linkages among sustainable development issues: the classification of indicators into driving force, state or response was often ambiguous; there were uncertainties over causal linkages; and it did not adequately highlight the relationship between the indicators and policy issues.

The difficulty is distinguishing what is the underlying cause of a subsequent problem and what is a consequence of the problems. Using DSR/DPSIR to rigidly categorize indicators is problematic as it is often possible to categorize one indicator as a state, impact and pressure indicator.

Is the crime rate a state indicator, as it then leads to other impacts such as prison overcrowding, feelings of safety and environmental degradation, or is it an impact indicator, the result of child poverty, homelessness and drug usage? These should not discredit the indicator but, instead, should add to its value. The important thing is not to get too bogged down in the categorization and, importantly, to explicitly accept the multiple attributes of the indicator. Instead of the crime rate being seen only as a consequence or a symptom, it is simultaneously viewed as both a cause and as a symptom.

This insight can improve the approach used to respond to rising crime rates. As the indicator can be used in many different ways, it is important that its purpose is clearly set out. The important point for those developing regulatory, market, education and policy solutions is to understand how each of the indicators impacts on the others, and to develop the most appropriate solution.

Thus, the indicators not only need to be linked to a policy objective, they also need to inform the policy objective so that responses do not simply address symptoms but actually address the root causes of unsustainable behaviours or outcomes. In this way, legal and policy responses should ideally become drivers of change. Consequently, the second CSD indicators, which were still organized along the four dimensions of sustainable development, were embedded in a more flexible theme/sub-theme framework (UN, 2007: 39, 40).

Theme-based or issue-based frameworks

Theme- or issue-based frameworks are the most widely used type of frameworks, especially in official national indicator sets. In these frameworks, indicators are grouped into various different issues relating to sustainable development. The issues or themes are typically determined on the basis of policy relevance (UN, 2007: 41). Thus, using the example from above, instead of the rate of crime being measured as a driver or a pressure on the natural environment, it is used as an indicator of the state of the social structure. In this way, the crime indicator can be viewed in a number of ways and used for multiple purposes.

Most countries that have developed national sustainable development indicators, including the UK and each of the devolved administrations, have based them on a thematic framework. The EU also uses this approach. A main reason for the prominence of thematic frameworks is their ability to link indicators to policy processes and targets. This provides a clear and direct message to decision makers and facilitates both communicating with, and raising the awareness of, the public. A thematic framework for indicators should be also, in theory, well suited to monitor progress in attaining the objectives and goals stipulated in national sustainable development strategies. It is flexible enough to adjust to new priorities and policy targets over time (UN, 2007: 41).

Capital frameworks

The capital approach attempts to calculate national wealth as a function of the sum of, and interaction among, different kinds of capital, and includes not only financial capital and produced capital goods, but also natural, human, social and institutional capital. This requires that all forms of capital be expressed in common (usually monetary) terms (UN, 2007: 41). While the SDI frameworks based on this approach vary, they all try to identify, first, what development is, and then how development can be made sustainable. The focus is on what resources are available today and whether these can be managed in ways to maintain and further develop the resource base over time (UN, 2007: 41).

In Canada and Norway, the capital approach puts the focus of measurement on the stocks and flows of different national assets: natural capital, financial capital, produced assets, human capital, and so on. Thus, in Norway, natural capital is measured in terms of ecosystems and renewable resources, while financial capital is captured in terms of net national income per capita and petroleum-adjusted savings. As noted by Stevens (2005: 3), 'Here, the question of sustainability is framed as whether the country is managing its resource base – as embodied in different types of national wealth – in a way that secures its maintenance over time'.

There remain many challenges to the actual use of capital frameworks (UN, 2008: 11). Among them are: disagreement about how to express all forms of capital in monetary terms; problems of data availability; questions about substitution; and the integration of intra-generational equity concerns within and across countries. Nonetheless, the concept of using capital as a way to track sustainable development could be a powerful tool for decision making (UN, 2007: 41). This is particularly true if the aim is to involve treasury and finance ministries more in the delivery of sustainable development, and if sustainable development was the central organizing principle of government (Chapter 13).

Aggregated indicators

Several aggregated indicators have been developed to capture elements of sustainable development. The value of these indicators is primarily to raise public awareness and media attention. Aggregated indicators do not offer a comprehensive view of sustainable development, as many of these indicators are specifically focused on the environmental dimension of sustainable development and resource management. Examples of such indicators include the Ecological Footprint, the Environmental Sustainability Index (ESI) and the Index of Sustainable Economic Welfare (ISEW) and these are described briefly below.

Ecological footprints represent a quantitative assessment of the biologically productive area (the amount of nature) required to produce the resources (food, energy and materials) and to absorb the wastes of an individual, city, region or country. To be sustainable, the global ecological footprint must remain within the Earth's limits. If those limits are exceeded, then resources are used faster than they can be renewed, the environment becomes degraded and the ability of the Earth to sustain life and economic activity is further reduced (Rees, 2002: 267–8; Venetoulis *et al.*, 2004: 7).

Both ESI and the Environmental Performance Index (EPI) were developed by the Center for Environmental Law and Policy at Yale University and the Center of International Earth Science Information Network at Columbia University in collaboration with the World Economic Forum and others. The ESI integrates 76 data sets – tracking natural resource endowments, past and present pollution levels, environmental management efforts and the capacity of a society to improve its environmental performance – into 21 indicators, and finally into a single number. The EPI aggregates 16 indicators related to resource depletion, pollution, environmental impact and energy efficiency into an index aimed at measuring policy impact (Center for Environmental Law and Policy, n.d.).

More comprehensive aggregated indicators on sustainable development exist and are being developed. For example, the ISEW attempts to measure the portion of economic activity that delivers genuine increases in our quality of life (Daly and Cobb, 1989). For example, it makes a subtraction for air pollution caused by economic activity and makes an addition to count unpaid household labour such as cleaning and childcare. It also covers areas such as income inequality, other environmental damage and depletion of environmental assets. To date, the ISEW is not universal and has only been computed for a handful of countries. Case studies in the UK, the USA and Australia show that the growth rate of the ISEW has been lower than that of GDP since 1945, and that since the 1980s the growth rate of the ISEW has become negative, while GDP was steadily increasing (Lawn, 2003). The ISEW has its critics who claim that it only promotes 'weak' sustainability and measures collective welfare from an individualist perspective (Ziegler, 2007).

The aggregated indicators provide little of the detail needed for effective policymaking. However, they are very useful for publicizing trends and they allow comparisons among states, regions, companies, individuals and over time. For these reasons, the ecological footprint is now used in all the UK indicator sets and is included as a headline indicator in some.

Other indicator approaches used in the UK

There are other approaches to using indicators for sustainable development outside formal frameworks. For example, there is a trend of constructing issue-specific SDI sets. At the national level, these are more likely to be used by ministries or non-governmental organizations to track policy implementation and to inform the public. For example an annual report is produced which measures the UK's progress towards the internationally agreed target of significantly reducing the loss of biodiversity by 2010 (DEFRA, 2010b). Another report measures progress on the sustainable tourism indicators (DCMS, n.d.).

There is also an increasing use of headline indicators by both countries and organizations. These tend to be small core sets of indicators closely linked to policy priorities which provide quick and visible signals to policymakers and the general public. Headline indicators usually coexist with larger sets of indicators for more comprehensive policymaking and monitoring. A potential problem with headline indicators is that they could be used for politics, rather than policy. In other words, their choice could reflect current political priorities rather than significant issues influencing future sustainability. Used correctly, however, headline indicators are excellent means of attracting media attention, raising public awareness and supplementing pedagogical materials for education and training (UN, 2007: 45–6).

Recent indicator sets used in the EU, the UK and devolved administrations

The SDI sets used across the UK administrations and over the past 20 years are remarkably similar. They are all linked around certain themes using the relevant sustainable development strategy as their conceptual framework and include both headline and aggregated indicators. The few variations and innovations are highlighted below. Assimilation is largely due to the fact that each of the administrations is subject to similar constraints. They all must contribute to the UK's entries in international indicator programmes such as those run by the CSD, which impose certain constraints in relation to what is measured, how it is measured and when it is measured, to allow for comparisons among states. The same is true for the UK Framework's headline indicators. Further constraints are imposed as to what is measurable and what is possible. The devolved administrations in Wales and Scotland, however, have demonstrated both positive and negative innovation to lead them away from the UK norm.

The UK Shared Framework introduced a new set of 20 high-level indicators – the 'UK Framework Indicators' to give an overview of sustainable development and cover key impacts and outcomes that reflect the priority areas shared across the UK. The 20 headline indicators are:

1 Greenhouse gas emissions: Kyoto target and carbon dioxide emissions
2 Resource use: Domestic Material Consumption and GDP
3 Waste: arising by (a) sector and (b) method of disposal
4 Bird populations: bird population indices (a) farmland birds (b) woodland birds and (c) birds of coasts and estuaries
5 Fish stocks: fish stocks around the UK within sustainable limits
6 Ecological impacts of air pollution: area of the UK habitat sensitive to acidification and eutrophication with critical load exceedances
7 River quality: rivers of good (a) biological and (b) chemical quality
8 Economic output: GDP
9 Active community participation: civic participation, and informal and formal volunteering at least once a month

10   Crime: crime survey and recorded crime for (a) vehicles (b) domestic burglary and (c) violence

11   Employment: people of working age in employment

12   Workless households: population living in workless households: (a) children and (b) working age

13   Childhood poverty: children in relative low-income households (a) before housing costs and (b) after housing costs

14   Pensioner poverty: pensioners in relative low-income households (a) before housing costs and (b) after housing costs

15   Education: 19 year olds with level 2 qualifications and above

16   Health inequality: (a) infant mortality (by socio-economic group) (b) life expectancy (by area) for men and women

17   Mobility: (a) number of trips per person by mode (b) distance travelled per person per year by broad trip purpose

18   Social justice: (*social measures to be developed*)

19   Environmental equality: (*environmental measures to be developed*)

20   Wellbeing: (*wellbeing measures to be developed if supported by the evidence*).

The UK Government is responsible for reporting progress on delivering the framework indicators and it does so along with its report on progress on its own more detailed set of indicators, as set out in its Strategy for Sustainable Development, *Securing our Future*. The Environmental Statistics Service in DEFRA report annually on 68 indicators. As a National Statistics Compendium publication, the report is produced pursuant to high professional standards as set out in the National Statistics Code of Practice. They undergo regular quality assurance reviews to ensure that they meet customer needs and are produced free from political interference.

The reports all link the 68 indicators to each of the four themes set out in the Framework and the Strategy: sustainable consumption and production; climate change and energy; protecting natural resources and enhancing the environment; and creating sustainable communities.

The indicators are not assessed in terms of whether targets have been reached or whether we are living sustainably, but instead, in terms of whether there has been improvement, deterioration or no change compared, with how things were a few years ago. The January 2010 report shows that compared with the position in 2003, 57 measures show improvement (representing over half of those for which it is possible to make an assessment) and 24 show little or no change. Notably, the downturn in the economy resulted in a deterioration between 2008 and 2009. A wide range of measures show improvement, including renewable electricity, emissions of air pollutants and manufacturing emissions, fossil fuels used for electricity generation, waste and land recycling, agricultural emissions and land stewardship, crime, fear of crime, mortality rates, road accidents, rough sleepers and homeless households. Fossil fuels used for electricity generation have improved since 2003. Those measures showing deterioration since 2003 are specifically (DEFRA, 2010a: 6–8):

- Aviation emissions of greenhouse gases
- Shipping emissions of greenhouse gases
- Carbon dioxide emissions from road freight
- Carbon dioxide emissions from the service sector
- Energy supply (consumption exceeding UK production)
- Farmland bird populations
- Community participation
- Range of life expectancy between local authorities
- Walking and cycling
- Households living in fuel poverty.

It is interesting that a disproportionately high number of the above relate to the state of the environment. In addition to the Government's own reporting on progress up until July 2010, the SDC also provided an analysis of progress on the indicators (SDC, 2004; Porritt, 2009; SDC, 2010).

The Scottish Government has been innovative in completely embedding its indicators in the Government's approach to governance. The Scottish vision for success for Scotland is described and measured in four parts, which support and reinforce each other:

- The Government's Purpose (sustainable economic growth) and associated targets
- Five Strategic Objectives that are the focus of actions
- 15 National Outcomes describing what the Government wants to achieve
- 45 National Indicators to track progress.

The 45 indicators are in addition to those in the Shared Framework, although there is some overlap. The 2009 report from the Scottish Government showed that of the 45 indicators, there has been improvement over the previous year in 21 indicators, but for eight the situation had worsened, 12 had stayed level and five continued to be incapable of measurement (Scottish Government, 2009).

The focus of these indicators is very much on the social and economic aspects of sustainable development. Progress on the indicators is reported annually and, up until 2011, was included in the annual review conducted by the SDC in Scotland. In the 2009 review, the SDC concluded that it did not feel that 'all indicators selected were the most appropriate in illustrating the core sustainable development challenge' (SDCS, 2009, Annex 2: 2). Moreover, the marginal positive results disguise a lack of urgency. For example, given its ambitious climate change targets, the Scottish Government is making inadequate progress, as annual emission reductions of 1.1 per cent are well below the 3 per cent per annum cuts required to meet the aims in the Climate Change (Scotland) Act 2009 (SDCS, 2009, Annex 2: 1). Furthermore, the SDC reported that:

> the Government's latest ecological footprint data . . . shows that Scotland's ecological footprint grew by 14% and its carbon footprint by 13% between

1992 and 2006. The challenge going forward will be to ensure that, despite budgetary restraints, sufficient investment is made to deliver a low carbon and sustainable economy.

(SDCS, 2009: 15)

Wales has led the way in relation to indicator selection. Wales was the first administration to formally include its ecological footprint in its indicator set and subsequently to actually report on it. The 2009 Welsh strategy contains 29 indicators over and above those in the Shared Framework. In sharp contrast to Scotland, these indicators are much more focused on environmental concerns, including limits, and 14 of the 29 are related to the environment. The *In Your Pocket* booklet on Sustainable Development Indicators for Wales 2009 provides measures of health, housing, jobs, crime, education and the environment. The statistical release presents some background to the publication and a summary table from the booklet (WAG, 2009b: 15–17).

The Welsh booklet presents comparison with the UK indicators, where available. The summary table from the publication shows that: 18 of 41 indicator assessments show a clear improvement; 14 of 41 indicator assessments show little or no change; five of 41 indicator assessments show clear deterioration; and four of 41 indicator assessments have insufficient or no comparable data. Unfortunately, this emphasis has not guaranteed progress and the situation has worsened for five of the environmental indicators: short-term changes in bird populations; the ecological impacts of pollution from nitrates; the waste arising by sector; household waste; and the number of people walking or cycling.

Both the previous strategy and implementation plan for Northern Ireland included commitments to produce an indicator set for Northern Ireland. An indicator set for Northern Ireland is promised, linked to the new strategy – *Everyone's Involved* (Northern Ireland Executive, 2010). A Plan of Implementation *Focus on the Future* was published in April 2011 (Northern Ireland Executive, 2011) which uses a hierarchical approach to implementation, with six priority areas for action and 32 strategic objectives. These strategic objectives are to provide direction and support the delivery of the outcomes in the strategy. They include vague objectives such as increase the number of jobs in the low-carbon economy and take action to halt biodiversity loss. In the Plan, the OFMDFM commits to developing a set of indicators but, as at May 2011, there was still no indicator set in place. It is simply not a priority for the Northern Ireland Executive and, as discussed in Chapter 7, it is common for administrations to 'talk' about sustainable development and make big announcements and then fail when it comes to introducing 'hard tools' like indicators which will disclose action or inaction (Jacob *et al.*, 2008: 42; and see Chapter 7).

While most extreme in Northern Ireland, the same can be said for all the administrations, since even when the indicators exist, nothing seems to be done when – year in and year out – they show insufficient progress or even clear deterioration. Moreover, even the minutest progress is celebrated, and this often masks the lack of urgency in making substantial change (See Chapter 10 for more detail). One way of dealing with this failing would be to use the target as the indicator instead of measuring any progress in the right direction. The measure would be positive when it is met or exceeded and negative if it falls short, regardless of any lesser amount of progress.

Criticisms of the UK sustainable development indicators

All the indicator sets have received criticisms over the years and indeed the summary from the progress reports above leads nicely on to the first criticism. The indicator sets are simply not leading to the improvements and progress necessary to move us towards a sustainable UK. The most recent sets all show positive trends in less than half of the indicators used. Thus, the existence of negative and concerning trends shown in the indicators does not appear to have any influence on government behaviour. It appears that bad news is not enough to compel action. This is indicative of the priority afforded sustainable development, the sustainable development strategies and the indicators within the administrations. Addressing this concern is the focus of Part III of this book.

There are, however, other problems inherent in the indicators themselves that need to be addressed and are capable of resolution. While there has been an attempt in later sets to correct problems raised earlier and some improvements have been made,[2] the indicators and their selection and use continue to receive criticism. In several instances, the same types of problems reoccur, and in other cases, the new indicators are, in some respects, more problematic than those they are replacing. In the discussion that follows, examples are taken from the criticisms raised in specific indicator sets to highlight generic issues across all the sets. The criticisms can largely be grouped as problems relating to the scientific reliability of the indicators and those levelled at the actual process of selection.

The first criticism relates to the importance of a particular indicator being actually representative of what it is supposed to represent. In 2008, the SDC found several such flaws in a number of Scotland's performance indicators. It noted, for instance, and purely for illustrative purposes, that the indicator to increase the proportion of journeys to work made by public or active transport does not tell us whether the overall usage of private cars for journeys is in decline. Similarly, there was no way of telling whether the target to reduce the proportion of driver journeys delayed due to traffic congestion had been achieved through enhancement of public transport alternatives or by increased road building (SDCS, 2008: 37). Another concern is that key information is often missing, either because of the lack of a specific indicator or because of the way a particular indicator is calculated. In 2004, the SDC noted 'Air travel growth threatens to negate any gains made on the ground, but aircraft emissions are excluded from the indicators and targets, and government policy appears to be to accommodate most of the currently predicted growth in demand' (SDC, 2004: 13).

As Bell and Morse (2008: 41) explain, the difficulty is that indicators 'attempt to encapsulate complex and diverse processes in a relatively few measures' and as a result, sometimes they tell the wrong story or are misleading. In 2004, the SDC concluded that:

> the Government sees a set of indicators most of which are showing reasonable progress towards sustainability. We see a set of indicators several of which are either inappropriate for measuring sustainability, or for which the targets and timetables that have been established are insufficiently demanding to represent significant progress towards sustainability.
>
> (SDC, 2004: 10)

That said, changing the methodology can also cause problems. For example, even though Wales was the first administration to include the ecological footprint in its indicator set, the 2009 annual report still states that the data on Wales' progress in relation to its ecological footprint is not available. The reasons are that although the same footprint methodology is used, calculation improvements mean that the 2001 and 2003 ecological footprint figures for Wales are not directly comparable (WAG, 2009b: 18).

There are other process- or governance-based problems. First, there is an ongoing difficulty in relation to the public's involvement and understanding of the indicators. As noted by Reed *et al.* (2006: 406–7), 'The majority of existing indicators are based on a top-down definition of sustainability that is fed by national-level data. This may miss critical sustainable development issues at a local level and may fail to measure what is important to the local communities'.

Moreover, there are concerns about the perceived legitimacy of the indicators and reporting of progress. In 2003, the EAC noted that:

> The unavoidably subjective nature of the assessments, compounded by the absence of any independent validation and the absence of any published criteria for judgements made, continues to give us cause for concern. The assessments should be independently validated each year, prior to publication, and a statement of validation included in the annual report.
>
> (EAC, 2003: para. 18)

In particular, given the UK approach of linking the SDIs to the sustainable development strategy, a potential risk is that each new change of government, with its corresponding new view of sustainable development, would result in a constantly changing set of SDIs, thus inhibiting comparisons and reducing comprehensibility. As described above, the UK Government's interpretation of sustainable development has undergone three significant metamorphoses (Ross, 2009), yet in fact, the reverse has turned out to be the real concern, as these changes have not led to radical changes in the SDI sets. Indeed, research has revealed that despite the stated relationship to the relevant sustainable development strategies, each of the indicator sets has been criticized for being insufficiently linked to the policy objectives set out in the relevant sustainable development strategies. Research into the indicators in Scotland by Russell and Thomson:

did not find any link between changes in the composition of the [Scottish sustainable development] strategies and changes in the SDI set, nor did we find any discussion as to the rationale for changes in the indicators used . . . In all three strategies, the Scottish government appears to have revisited its current programmes of government and re-branded them within their sustainable development strategies. Each indicator was designed with a particular purpose which often predated the sustainable development strategies and in some cases the Scottish Parliament.

(Russell and Thomson, 2008: 270)

When the problems relating to the scientific credibility of the indicators are combined with the difficulties relating to governance, the result is that indicators often lack policy relevance. They are not used by stakeholders to monitor progress or by policymakers to publicly promote the sustainable development agenda, let alone drive policy forward. The problem is not exclusive to the UK. In the USA, Innes and Booher (2000: 174) observe that 'Millions of dollars and much time . . . has been wasted on preparing national, state and local indicator reports that remain on the shelf gathering dust'. The Division for Sustainable Development recently reported that:

While sustainability indicators, indices and reporting systems have gained growing popularity in both the public and private sectors, their effectiveness in influencing actual policy and practices often remained limited. The gap between the large *potential* but small *actual* influence suggests that indicators could play a stronger role in articulating and tracking progress towards sustainability in a wide range of settings.

(Division for Sustainable Development, UNDESA, 2006: 4)

Essentially, the usefulness of the indicators is dependent on their legitimacy and this is often affected by issues of procedural fairness. As Oliver (1999: 96) notes, 'Fair procedures may affect the substantive quality of the decision'. Elsewhere, she notes that 'participation, in the sense of consultation and being listened to on the part of those affected by possible policy changes, may result in better-prepared and thought out proposals being implemented' (Oliver, 2003: 34–5). This will clearly affect legitimacy which, according to Freeman (1999), is when the public accepts decisions without having to be coerced. It follows that indicators and their selection process which make sense to the public and stakeholders will be widely accepted and legitimate, which will improve their policy relevance and usability.

Research into indicator selection

In recent years, a lot of time and effort have gone into research examining the characteristics of good indicators and indicator sets, and the best processes for developing such sets (Bell and Morse, 2008: 153–94). Chambers *et al.* (2000:

16) contend that SDIs should be resonant, understandable and relevant to users and valid, and as such, they must use comprehensive and credible data in a transparent manner. They should also be motivational and thus capable of 'provoking and inspiring' change.

Thus, two separate but linked concerns need to be addressed. First, indicator selection should be based on the best knowledge available. It should rely on the most advanced and credible science available. The approach should provide representative, measurable and comparable results. All of the UK administrations, for instance, are committed to using sound science responsibly, as set out in the UK Government and devolved administrations joint Strategic Framework, *One Future, Different Paths*, which involves ensuring policy is developed and implemented on the basis of strong scientific evidence, whilst taking into account scientific uncertainty (through the precautionary principle) as well as public attitudes and values (HM Government *et al.*, 2005: 8).

However, these often complex and detailed decisions also need to be comprehensible and relevant to other, often non-technical, users including policymakers, regulators, the regulated and the wider public. As such, indicators need to be understandable, realistic and accessible. As noted above, the indicators should be capable of provoking and inspiring change. These features are inherent within the notion of good governance. The UK Shared Framework describes good governance as 'Actively promoting effective, participative systems of governance in all levels of society – engaging people's creativity, energy, and diversity' (HM Government *et al.*, 2005: 8).

Meeting the tensions in developing and selecting indicators is not an easy process, and a strict adherence to one or the other of these two principles can generate very different approaches to indicator selection: one which is top-down and reductionist, and the other which is bottom-up or grassroots (Bell and Morse, 2008: 3–4). Historically, the development of SDIs has been dominated by experts and top-down approaches, which often, sensibly, focus on what is and can be authoritatively measured and allow for suitable comparisons. For example, the ESI uses a top-down approach, whereby a single number is derived mathematically from a list of indicators which creators at Yale and Colombia Universities feel are important for environmental sustainability. Countries are then 'ranked' (Bell and Morse, 2008: 37). Bell and Morse (2008: 38) conclude that 'for the most part the SIs [sustainability indicators], or at least the methodology for developing SIs have been set by outsiders, with perhaps a nod in the direction of those whom the SIs are ultimately meant to serve'. Reed *et al.* (2008) agree: 'the majority of indicators are still developed by academic researchers and/or policy-makers. While often accurate, these indicators are rarely accessible, meaningful, or useful to people who manage the land, who often lack time, money, and specialist training or equipment'.

The alternative is to use more bottom-up approaches, which favour local perceptions, wishes and views. Reed *et al.* note however that:

> Community control in and of itself is irrelevant to sustainability if local
> people fall prey to the same beliefs and values that have led to unsustainable

positions . . . although qualitative indicators developed through participatory research can promote community learning and action . . . it is not always possible to guarantee the accuracy, reliability or sensitivity of indicators. For this reason, monitoring results may not be as useful as they could be, or they may even be misleading.

(Reed *et al.*, 2006: 414)

As such, some commonly held beliefs by stakeholders about the sustainability of a particular project, programme or policy may not prove scientifically significant. For example, a perceived beneficial increase in the population of a particular species may actually indicate a rise in certain pollutants in a river or may be influenced by another factor. Moreover, it cannot be assumed that 'inclusion' guarantees meaningful participation (Biggs, 1995: 4–5).

A key feature of much of the recent research into the selection and use of SDIs has been to develop holistic approaches which incorporate both top-down and bottom-up assessment processes (Hodge and Hardi 1997: 7; Reed *et al.*, 2006: 406–7; Bell and Morse, 2008: 3–4). Hodge and Hardi observe that, ideally:

the assessment process [should] merge 'values expertise' with 'technical expertise' through a broadly participatory reflective process that can address and take creative advantage of the inevitable tensions. A linked, 'bottom up, top-down' assessment process is therefore essential to ensure that a range of values receive fair consideration; that participants recognize the role that they play in creation of the problem in the first place; and to facilitate early ownership of problem solutions that emerge.

(Hodge and Hardi, 1997: 18–19)

Research by Reed *et al.* (2006: 414) on project-based indicator selection found that 'by empirically testing indicators developed through participatory research, it is possible to retain community ownership of indicators whilst improving accuracy, reliability and sensitivity . . . By combining quantitative and qualitative approaches in this way, it is possible to enhance learning by both community members and researchers'.

While the concerns and challenges are slightly different on a national scale,[3] these systemic holistic approaches to indicator selection have found favour with the international bodies. As explained by the CSD, 'holistic and inclusive processes are needed to achieve headline indicators reflecting societal priorities for achieving sustainable development' (Division for Sustainable Development, UNDESA, 2006: 5). The general consensus in recent years is that the process of selecting national SDIs should be based on a framework which looks holistically at sustainability, rather than its individual parts. Stevens (2005: 2) claims that 'Frameworks are important to structure work on indicators and on underlying statistics . . . Such frameworks should be simple and understandable so as to link the indicators to policy questions and make them useful to decision makers and the public'. Hodge and Hardi (1997: 10) add that 'With a conceptual framework in place, indicators emerge more naturally, and can be adjusted to the needs of a given locale or set of decision-makers'.

Many different frameworks have been adopted and are being tested. The CSD has reported that:

> The diversity of core values, indicator processes and sustainable development theories resulted in the development and application of different conceptual frameworks . . . The main differences among frameworks are the way in which they conceptualize the key dimensions of sustainable development, the inter-linkages among these dimensions, the way they group the issues to be measured, and the concepts by which they justify the selection and aggregation of indicators.
>
> (Division for Sustainable Development, UNDESA, 2006: 5)

Approaches, such as those used in the UK, that rely on the national strategy combined with themes around economy, environment and society tend to be well regarded in the literature as 'whole systems approaches' which capture multiple aspects of a system (Hodge and Hardi, 1997: 10). Indeed, the consultation document predating the *Quality of Life* indicators, *Sustainability Counts*, clearly demonstrates holistic thinking:

> The individual indicators . . . have been selected to reflect the key issues, but it is important to recognize the interactions between them. Categorizing them as 'economic', 'social', 'environmental' or 'resource' indicators is in some ways an artificial split . . . It is therefore important that the indicators are seen together as a package; it is only by looking at them all together that we can assess whether, overall, we are on a sustainable track.
>
> (DETR, 1998)

Yet, much of the recent guidance setting out the actual criteria for indicator selection still falls short of reflecting a truly systemic approach to indicator selection (DETR, 1998: para. 5.1; HM Government *et al.*, 2005: 11–12). For example, the UK Shared Framework (HM Government *et al.*, 2005: 11–12) provides that:

> wherever possible, measures are chosen that:
>
> - are linked to the purpose and priorities within the UK Framework;
> - are agreed as high priorities by the UK Government and Devolved Administrations;
> - have UK coverage (though there are some data constraints);
> - have trends available;
> - highlight challenges;
> - are statistically robust and meaningful.

The criteria for SDI selection lack any explicit reference to it being an iterative, holistic, participatory and transparent process. Instead, the focus of the criteria remains firmly on the science. Thus, while the research has produced and tested a variety of methods which can deliver more transparent, inclusive, responsive and holistic indicators, and the various strategies place emphasis on these issues, when it comes down to actually selecting indicators, these mechanisms are not used.

One of the likely causes of this failure can be explained using institutional theories such as path dependency and disjointed incrementalism, whereby institutions tend to resist change and fall back on well-established behaviours or paths (Lindblom, 1959, 1979). In addition, one cannot ignore the political pressures facing governments. Ideally, the selection of indicators should positively reflect a political vision and, as noted by Stevens, 'through this selection, governments convey a sense of their priorities, make commitments to take action, and indicate that they are ready to respond to their electorates for failures to make progress' (Stevens, 2005: 6). Unfortunately, as explained by the UN Division for Sustainable Development, the danger is that SDIs 'simply reflect current political priorities or the influence of special interest groups rather than focus on significant issues influencing future sustainability' and to prevent this from occurring 'holistic and inclusive processes are needed to achieve headline indicators reflecting societal priorities for achieving sustainable development' (Division for Sustainable Development, UNDESA, 2006: 5). Thus, an argument can be made that mechanisms are needed to ensure that decisions about the selection of SDIs use proven methodologies and are protected from time pressures, path dependency and political whim. Mechanisms need to be introduced which provide structure and protect certain values, while at the same time encouraging and permitting contextualization and evolution.

Conclusion

Consistently, the UK, Welsh and Scottish Governments have demonstrated their commitment to the development and review of SDIs. This commitment has not been demonstrated by the Northern Ireland Executive, because, as of the spring of 2011, not a single set had been produced. It is also safe to say that outside Northern Ireland, SDIs are an established component of UK policy and, moreover, are considered to be essential means of measuring progress towards the objectives set out in the relevant sustainable development strategy.

However, the truth is that indicator sets are simply not leading to the improvements and progress necessary to move us to a sustainable UK. Each of the indicator sets for the UK, Scotland and Wales are reporting negative or unsustainable trends in a substantial number of the indicators used. Thus, the existence of negative and concerning trends shown in the indicators does not appear to have any influence on government behaviour. Addressing this concern is the focus of Part III of this book.

One possible reason for this lack of action could be the fact that neither the national SDI nor the national sustainable development strategy has any statutory footing at UK or devolved level. Thus, like many other policy initiatives that are not part of UK law, while generally accepted, indicators are lacking the legitimacy and authority that come with legal recognition. Moreover, while the processes for their selection, development, use and review are much improved under the UK's new Sustainable Development programme (HM Government *et al.*, 2005), they still lack the benefits of legal formality as they are not binding or widely publicized.

A holistic process is essential for the successful implementation of sustainable development. As noted in the quote at the beginning of this chapter, what gets measured gets done and, as a result, indicators ought to play an important role because they are the tools which measure success and failure. As discussed above, we need to be sure we measure the right things and improvements in indicator selection are necessary. However, this is not enough and, to continue from the quote, we need to reward success, and learn from failure and correct it. Indicators provide important information. It is essential that other mechanisms are put in place to use that information to generate sustainable outcomes by rewarding success and correcting failure. Chapter 10 which follows addresses the crucial issue of ensuring legitimacy and accountability through the use of various means of reporting, monitoring and review. Chapter 13 explores such options in detail including indicators.

Notes

1 The Scotland Act 1998 ch. 46; the Northern Ireland Act 1998 ch. 47; the Government of Wales Act 1998 ch. 38; the Government of Wales Act 2006 ch. 32.
2 For example, according to the EAC (2004: para. 24), 'We welcome the inclusion of the new sub-indicator on road traffic intensity which, together with the existing indicator on road traffic volumes, presents a clearer, more rounded picture of traffic levels and growth than has been the case in previous years'.
3 These include: the magnitude and wide range of government functions; the large and varied number of stakeholders who want or ought to be involved; the four-year electoral cycle and politics; and the need to comply with international obligations while also providing a framework for local indicators.

References

Bell, S. and Etherington, L. (2009) '(Re)connecting the global and local: Europe's regional seas', *Journal of Law and Society*, 36(1): 75–93.
Bell, S. and Morse, S. (2008) *Sustainability Indicators: Measuring the Immeasurable?*, 2nd edition, London: Earthscan.
Biggs, S.D. (1995) *Contending Coalitions in Participatory Technology Development: Challenges to the New Orthodoxy: The Limits of Participation*, London: Intermediate Technology.
Cartwright, L.E. (2000) 'Selecting local sustainable development indicators: Does consensus exist in their choice and purpose?', *Planning Practice & Research*, 15(1–2): 65–78.
Center for Environmental Law and Policy (n.d.) 'Environmental Performance Management Project', http://www.yale.edu/epi/, accessed 1 September 2010.

Chambers, N., Simmons, C. and Wackernagel, M. (2000) *Sharing Nature's Interest: Ecological Footprints as an Indicator of Sustainability*, London: Earthscan.

Daly, H. and Cobb, J.B. (1989) *For the Common Good: Redirecting the Economy toward the Community, the Environment and a Sustainable Future*, Boston: Beacon Press.

Department for Culture, Media and Sport (DCMS) (n.d.) *Tourism Division National Sustainable Tourism Indicators Getting it Right: Monitoring Progress towards Sustainable Tourism in England*, London: DCMS.

Department of Environment, Food and Rural Affairs (DEFRA) (1999) *A Better Quality of Life: A Strategy for Sustainable Development for the United Kingdom*, London: DEFRA.

DEFRA (2005) *The UK Strategy for Sustainable Development: Securing the Future*, London: DEFRA.

DEFRA (2010a) *National Statistics Compendium, Measuring Progress: Sustainable Development Indicators*, London: DEFRA.

DEFRA (on behalf of the UK Biodiversity Partnership) (2010b) *UK Biodiversity Indicators in Your Pocket 2010: Measuring Progress towards Halting Biodiversity Loss*, London: DEFRA.

Department of Environment, Transport and the Regions (DETR) (1996) *Indicators of Sustainable Development for the UK*, London: Government Statistical Service.

DETR (1998) *Sustainability Counts: Consultation Paper on a Set of 'Headline' Indicators of Sustainable Development*, London: DETR.

DETR (1999) *Quality of Life Counts*, London: DETR.

Division for Sustainable Development, UNDESA (2006) 'Global Trends and Status of Indicators of Sustainable Development', Background Paper No. 2, DESA/DSD/2006/2, UN.

Environmental Audit Committee (EAC) (2002) *Fourth Report Measuring the Quality of Life: The 2001 Sustainable Development Headline Indicators*, HC 824, London: EAC.

EAC (2003) *Eleventh Report Sustainable Development Headline Indicators 2002*, HC 1080, London: EAC.

EAC (2004) *Government Response to the Eleventh Report of 2002–03, the Sustainable Development Headline Indicators 2002, Second Special Report*, HC 320, London: EAC.

Eurostat (2001) *Measuring Progress towards a More Sustainable Europe: Proposed Indicators for Sustainable Development*, Brussels: EC.

Freeman, J. (1999) 'Private parties, public function and the real democracy problem in the new administrative law?', in D. Dyzenhous (ed.) *Recrafting the Rule of Law*, Oxford: Hart.

HM Government, Scottish Executive, Welsh Assembly Government, Northern Ireland Office (2005) *One future – different paths: The UK's shared framework for sustainable development*, London: DEFRA.

Hodge, R.A. and Hardi, P. (1997) 'The need for guidelines: The rationale underlying the Bellagio Principles for assessment', in P. Hardi and T. Zdan (eds) *Assessing Sustainable Development: Principles in Practice*, Winnipeg: International Institute for Sustainable Development.

Innes, J.E. and Boohcr, D.E. (2000) 'Indicators for sustainable communities: A strategy building on complexity theory and distributed intelligence', *Planning Theory and Practice*, 1(2): 173–86.

Jacob, K., Volkery, A. and Lenschow, A. (2008) 'Instruments for environmental policy integration in 30 OECD countries', in A. Jordan and A. Lenschow (eds) *Innovation in Environmental Policy: Integrating the Environment for Sustainability*, Cheltenham: Edward Elgar.

Lawn, P.A. (2003) 'A theoretical foundation to support the Index of Sustainable Economic Welfare (ISEW), Genuine Progress Indicator (GPI), and other related indexes', *Ecological Economics*, 44(1): 105–18.

Lindblom, C.E. (1959) 'The science of muddling through', *Public Administration Review*, 19(2): 79–88.

Lindblom, C.E. (1979) 'Still muddling, not yet through', *Public Administration Review*, 39(6): 517–26.

National Assembly for Wales (2006) *Starting to Live Differently: The Sustainable Development Scheme of the National Assembly for Wales*, Cardiff: National Assembly for Wales.

Northern Ireland Office (2006) *Sustainable Development Strategy for Northern Ireland: First Steps towards Sustainability*, Belfast: Northern Ireland Office.

Northern Ireland Executive (2010) *Everyone's Involved: Sustainable Development Strategy*, Belfast: Northern Ireland Executive.

Northern Ireland Executive (2011) *Focus on the Future: Sustainable Development Implementation Plan* 2011–2014, Belfast, OFMDFM.

Oliver, D. (1999) *Common Values and the Public-Private Divide*, Butterworths, London.

Oliver, D. (2003) *Constitutional Reform in the UK*, Oxford: Oxford University Press.

Porritt, J. (2009) 'The standing of sustainable development in government', http://www.jonathonporritt.com/pages/2009/11/the_standing_of_sustainable_de.html, accessed 12 April 2010.

Reed, M.S., Dougill, A.J. and Baker, T.R. (2008) 'Participatory indicator development: What can ecologists and local communities learn from each other?', *Ecological Applications*, 18(5): 1253–69.

Reed, M.S., Fraser, E.D.G. and Dougill, A.J. (2006) 'An adaptive learning process for developing and applying sustainability indicators with local communities', *Ecological Economics*, 59(4): 406–18.

Rees, W.E. (2002) 'Footprint: Our impact on the earth is getting heavier', *Nature*, 420: 267–8.

Ross, A. (2009) 'Modern interpretations of sustainable development', *Journal of Law and Society*, 36(1): 32–54.

Russell, S.L. and Thompson, I. (2008) 'Accounting for a sustainable Scotland', *Public Money and Management*, 28(6): 367–74.

Scottish Executive (2005) *Choosing our Future: Scotland's Sustainable Development Strategy*, Edinburgh: Scottish Executive.

Scottish Government (2007) *The Government's Economic Strategy*, Edinburgh: Scottish Government.

Scottish Government (2009) 'National Indicators', http://www.scotland.gov.uk/About/scotPerforms/indicators, accessed 27 August 2010.

Scottish Government (2010) *Scottish Planning Policy*, Edinburgh: Scottish Government.

Stevens, C. (2005) 'Measuring sustainable development', *OECD Statistics Brief*, 10: 1–8.

Sustainable Development Commission (SDC) (2004) *Shows Promise. But Must Try Harder: An Assessment by the Sustainable Development Commission of the Government's Reported Progress on Sustainable Development over the Past Five Years*, London: SDC.

SDC (2009) *Local Sustainable Development Lens: Final Proposal Overview Paper*, London: SDC.

SDC (2010) *Becoming the 'Greenest Government Ever': Sustainable Development in Government 2006–2009*, London: SDC.

Sustainable Development Commission Scotland (SDCS) (2008) *Sustainable Development: A Review of Progress by the Scottish Government*, Edinburgh: SDCS.

SDCS (2009) *Sustainable Development: Third Annual Assessment of Progress by the Scottish Government*, Edinburgh: SDCS.

United Nations (UN) (1996) *Indicators of Sustainable Development Framework and Methodologies*, No.E.96.II.A.16, New York: UN.

UN (2001) *Indicators of Sustainable Development: Guidelines and Methodologies*, 2nd edition, No.E.01.II.A.6, New York: UN.

UN (2002) *Plan of Implementation of the World Summit on Sustainable Development*, A/CONF.199/20/Res.2, New York: UN.

UN (2006) *Global Trends and Status of Indicators of Sustainable Development: Background Paper No.2 DESA/DSD/2006/2*, New York: UN Department of Economic and Social Affairs.

UN (2007) *Indicators of Sustainable Development: Guidelines and Methodologies*, 3rd edition, No.E.08.II.A.2, New York: UN.

UN (2008) *Measuring Sustainable Development: Report of the Joint UNECE/OECD/ Eurostat Working Group on Statistics for Sustainable Development*, New York: UN.

UN General Assembly (UNGA) (1992) *Agenda 21*, A/CONF.151/26 Vol. 1, New York: UN.

Venetoulis, J., Chazan, D. and Gaudet, C. (2004) *Ecological Footprint of Nations*, San Francisco: Redefining Progress.

Welsh Assembly Government (WAG) (2009a) *One Wales: One Planet: The Sustainable Development Scheme of the Welsh Assembly Government*, Cardiff: WAG.

WAG (2009b) *Sustainable Development Indicators for Wales*, Cardiff: National Statistics for Wales.

World Wildlife Fund, Oxfam, Poverty Alliance, Scottish Executive, Sustainable Development Commission (2005) *Scotland's Global Footprint: Are We Measuring up to Sustainable Development? Summary Report of Seminar Held 14 June 2005*, London: WWF.

Ziegler, R. (2007) 'Political perception and ensemble of macro objectives and measures: The paradox of the Index for Sustainable Economic Welfare', *Environmental Values*, 16(1): 43–60.

10 Mechanisms – reporting, review, monitoring and accountability

In 1999, UK Prime Minister Tony Blair acknowledged that:

> Talking about sustainable development is not enough. We have to know what it is, to see how our policies are working on the ground. We must hold ourselves to account – as a government but also as a country . . . All this depends on devising new ways of assessing how we are doing.
>
> (DEFRA, 1999)

Reporting on progress on sustainable development and holding the government to account for its successes and failures are crucial aspects of good governance and sound public management. Therefore, like other areas of strategic public management, sustainable development strategies and approaches need monitoring and review mechanisms whereby public bodies account for their actions or inaction and explain what they have learned and how they intend to improve. Such a process promotes more ethical, open, iterative and transparent government processes. These in turn promote reflexive governance or more self-conscious, holistic and communicative forms of reason' (Meadowcroft, 2007: 19). In the context of sustainable development, Meadowcroft argues that reflexive governance involves a specific kind of 'societal self steering' – one that demands continuous reflection about the path that has been traversed and the future we have yet to build (2007: 19).

Moreover, calling the government to account for its actions or inaction is essential to the legitimacy of government processes. As noted elsewhere, legitimacy is when the public accepts decisions without having to be coerced (Freeman, 1999). It follows that decisions that have been independently validated, tested, scrutinized and justified will be more widely accepted, and this, in turn, will improve their policy relevance and usability.

This view is consistent with the research on best practice for implementing sustainable development. The criteria produced by the Organisation for Economic Co-operation and Development (OECD) for improving policy coherence and integration for sustainable development include several aspects related to reporting, monitoring and scrutiny. Specifically, the criteria focus on the government's use of evaluation and reporting mechanisms such as indicators and environmental impact assessments, as well as its use of specific and independent auditing and reporting mechanisms (OECD, 2002: 9–10). Similarly, Principle 10 of the Bellagio Principles requires that the assessment of progress towards sustainable development be assured by clearly assigning responsibility and providing ongoing support in the decision-making process, and also providing institutional capacity for data collection, maintenance and documentation (Hodge and Hardi, 1997: 19–20).

However, as noted by Hodge and Hardi (1997: 19), it is not enough to have one-off reporting obligations. 'Trends identified in an initial assessment and the conclusions that result require testing over time to develop confidence and ensure credibility'. Continuous review has two main benefits. First, there is a strategic need for monitoring the success of actions taken over time and results-oriented management. Second, there is a substantive need to enhance our knowledge base by revealing new insights and it identifies other unknowns to be explained (Principle 9 of the Bellagio Principles).

Thus, there is no point in having the good policies and mechanisms set out in Chapters 4–9 above if their use is not reviewed, reported, monitored and enforced, and those responsible held to account. The UK has been proactive in its introduction of monitoring and review mechanisms in relation to its sustainable development agenda. This chapter examines in detail the use of various mechanisms in the EU, UK and devolved administrations for monitoring and reviewing the implementation of sustainable development. Such mechanisms include targets and indicators, internal review and reporting, independent or external review and reporting, and the various forms of scrutiny, focusing in particular on parliamentary scrutiny. Within the discussion, the role played by the UK Sustainable Development Commission (SDC) in monitoring and review across the UK administrations is a common theme. The chapter ends by considering the loss of the SDC and alternative means of accountability.

Targets, indicators and accurate measures of progress

The previous chapter examines the role of indicators in the implementation of sustainable development, and similarly, in Chapter 4, the role of clear targets with timetables is reviewed. It is important to briefly return to these measurement devices in the context of monitoring and review. As Meadowcroft explains, 'measurement is vital for defining and understanding social and environmental phenomena, establishing long term goals and intermediate targets, tracking temporal development and assessing success, and revising policy' (Meadowcroft, 2007: 16). As Dernbach (2002–2003: 106) observes, 'targets and timetables are only useful if they are effectively implemented – if the targets and timetables are actually achieved. Monitoring and public reporting of progress (or lack of progress) toward targets and timetables is one way to help ensure that they are met'. The converse is also true. There is no point in having a parliamentary committee monitoring progress towards targets that are easily met or have no timetable attached to them. Moreover, if the indicators being used are based on incomplete data, are not representative of overall strategic objectives or are incapable of being compared from year to year, then the monitoring is of limited value. While improvements have been made in establishing indicators that include clear targets as to what constitutes a sustainable level of performance in any particular area and the same means of data collection are used among all the administrations, problems still remain. In the 2005 UK-wide Framework for Sustainable Development *One future – different paths: The UK's shared framework for sustainable development,* three of the 20 indicators were yet to be developed (HM Government *et al.,* 2005: 12).[1] The UK is not alone and, 'state of the environment' reporting remains uneven and comparisons across time and jurisdictions are difficult (Meadowcroft, 2007: 16).

Finally, as is discussed in detail below, progress towards the targets and indicators needs to be reviewed and reported in a way that is perceived as legitimate. In other words, relying solely on internally produced progress reports has limited value, and independent review and validation by the National Audit Office, the Office of National Statistics, the SDC or independent consultants is essential for the reporting to be legitimate.

Internal reviews and reporting

Clear aims, targets, indicators and timetables are essential for monitoring sustainable development, but they must be accompanied by obligations on public bodies to produce regular reports on their progress towards sustainable development. Internal reporting includes a wide range of reporting activities. In each of the administrations, there are significant reporting obligations imposed on the administration as a whole (such as annual progress reports relating to the national strategies, indicators, operations, and so on), and on individual departments, directorates and agencies (such as annual reports on progress towards sustainable development action plans). Some of these obligations are set out in policy documents such as the relevant national sustainable development strategy. Others, as discussed in Chapter 8, may appear as statutory obligations, such as the reporting obligations under the Climate Change Act 2008, the Nature Conservation (Scotland) Act 2004 and the Transport Act 2000 (see Chapter 8).

Duties to operate in a certain way or to take certain things into account are very difficult to evaluate, especially for outsiders. Internal reporting obligations – requiring public bodies to keep their own records of their policy decisions, purchases, energy use, and so on, which are then set out in regular reports – provide the basis for much of the scrutiny that follows. In relation to sustainable development, administrations tend to report very well in relation to their operational side of sustainable development, yet are much more wary about reporting on policy achievements or failings.

Reporting on operations

Regular reporting on the environmental performance of the government estate or its operations, including procurement, has been used in the UK since the mid-1990s and the mechanisms are continuously improving. Reporting progress on operations is easily measured. Quantifiable data on the amount of water, energy, carbon or waste used by the estate in a given year is available and this is then used to compare one year to the next. This data is also used to compare progress in any given year against relevant targets. There are established international and European standards and tools for measuring and comparing the environmental performance of institutions. Government departments and agencies are encouraged to work towards accredited certified environmental management systems, that is, ISO 14001, EMAS or British Standard BS 8555; and adopt a whole-organization approach to carbon management, such as the Carbon Trust's Carbon Management Programme or equivalent. Thus, reporting on progress in sustainable development in the government estate or operations is relatively straightforward. These reports may also be necessary to meet obligations under certain statutes. For example, under the Climate Change (Scotland) Act 2009 s. 46, the Scottish ministers may make an order requiring all public bodies to prepare reports on compliance with climate change duties.

Over time, the UK Government's approach to sustainable development in government has become more refined, with more and more ambitious targets subject to stricter timetables (DEFRA, 2002, 2004a, 2006). The processes are continually being reported upon and reviewed. The 2006 review of the Sustainable Operations on the Government Estate (SOGE) process found it to be effective but limited because it only applied to non-departmental public bodies on a voluntary basis, set unambitious targets and appeared not to be delivering results fast enough.

The subsequent Sustainable Development in Government (SDiG) framework was agreed in 2010 and covers the UK-based estates and operations of all English central Government departments and their Executive Agencies, as well as non-ministerial departments and executive Non-Departmental Public Bodies (subject to certain minimum criteria). The Office of Government Commerce is now responsible for providing leadership, challenge and support on Government delivery against the SOGE and SDiG frameworks. It publishes the Government's Delivery Plan Update on Progress against the targets every six months and an annual report on performance (OGC, 2010).

The Scottish Executive's first *Environmental Report* for the year 2000/01, focused on the greening of the Executive's operations: procurement, energy efficiency of buildings and fleet management. Subsequently, the Scottish Executive and now, the Scottish Government, produce an Annual Report on Environmental Performance of the Scottish Government estate, for each financial year. The 2010 report for the year 2008/09 covers carbon emissions, energy, waste, transport and travel, carbon neutrality, water, biodiversity and the use of environmental management systems. The report shows positive change towards targets for four of the indicators, no change and behind year-on-year projected targets for five and, alarmingly, a worsening of performance from the previous year and behind year-on-year projected targets for four indicators, including the two targets for carbon dioxide emissions (Scottish Government, 2010: 10–13).

Progress in the Scottish Government estate has been noticeably slower than in the UK Government estate and, on the recommendations of the SDC, the Scottish Government is exploring how it can use the UK's SDiG framework in future.

In Wales, the environmental performance of the government has been measured against the Green Dragon Standard (an environmental management system equivalent to ISO 14001) since 2003. It encompasses any policy or business operation impacting on in-house environmental performance (WAG, 2009b: 1). The 5th Annual Report on environmental performance across the Welsh Assembly Government's (WAG's) in-house business operations and core administrative estate covering the period 1 April 2008 to 31 March 2009 highlights improvements and admits when the WAG is off target, but fails to indicate clearly how far off it is from the target. In fact, the reporting is misleading as worsening areas are highlighted as successes. For example, the report proudly states that 83 per cent of everyday paper consumption was from recycled sources, even though in fact this is a decrease against the previous year's 89 per cent. Moreover, while some improvements have been made, the report shows other areas worsening. Indeed, emissions from business travel increased by 1.4 per cent compared to 2007/08 to 3,570 tonnes (WAG, 2009b: 3). As of 2009, the WAG is also adapting its reporting to the broader SDiG regime used by the UK Government.

Reporting on the environmental performance of the operations of the Northern Ireland Executive is still in its infancy. The long-term ambitions of the new Northern Ireland Strategy are to be translated into SMART (specific, measurable, attainable, relevant and timely) Targets in the implementation plan, and government departments are to review progress against these targets on an annual basis, and supplement this with a succession of three-year implementation plans which integrate with, and match the timing of, future programmes for government cycles (Northern Ireland Executive, 2010: 37).

Reporting on policy

Reporting on the policy of sustainable development relates largely to reporting on the non-operational aims set out in the relevant sustainable development strategy. These often measure progress outside the direct control of government and may or may not be accurate measures of successful or unsuccessful government policy. Some of these aims may be linked to quantifiable indicators such as the number of incidents of bullying at school, expected years of healthy life or wild bird populations, and some of these may be linked to targets. Still others may need to be assessed on actions taken and the reporting of progress in relation to sustainable development action plans may be relevant here. For example, an action plan may state that new legislation will be introduced in the next year. This may or may not have happened and progress should be reported.

The UK Government did report on its sustainable development policy between 1999 and 2002, following a recommendation by the Environmental Audit Committee of the House of Commons (EAC). During that time, the Green Ministers' Committee (GMC) and its successor Cabinet sub-committee ENV(G) produced annual reports and tabled these before larger Cabinet Committee (ENV) (see Chapter 5). Three annual reports were published under the Greening Government Initiative, each improving on the previous report. For example, the first report by the GMC in 1999 was criticized as light on comparable information and exposing failings on reporting and policy appraisal (the ENDS Report, 1999). The second report remedied this and, although lacking in quantifiable data, contained several tables comparing Departments' performance in areas such as environmental management systems, policy appraisals and training. This made it possible to identify leaders and laggards. All of the reports were presented in a relatively clear fashion and presented the bad news as well as the good. The government admitted when its performance was disappointing and tried to examine where it was going wrong when targets were not achieved.

Unfortunately, in 2002 the Greening Government Initiative was repackaged as SDiG, and a decision taken to only report on the performance of the Government estate in the Annual Sustainable Development in Government reports. Therefore, the second report on Sustainable Development in Government only covers operations and, essentially, is silent on the policymaking agenda. Policy was supposed to be covered within the much more general annual reports on the UK Sustainable Development Strategy (DEFRA, 2003, 2004b). It is not surprising that the subsequent reporting on the policymaking agenda has been inadequate compared to the previous Greening Government reports. For example, in the 2004 report, environmental appraisal by departments was not even mentioned (DEFRA, 2004b). In 2005, under the *Securing our Future* strategy, the pattern continued, and overall responsibility for reporting on progress made by the UK Government was removed from the Green ministers and given to a stronger SDC. Unlike in Scotland however, the SDC did not report annually, but instead, produced reports for each strategic period (SDC, 2004, 2010). Thus, there has been no overall annual reporting of progress towards the UK's sustainable development policy targets.

Nevertheless, the 2005 strategy does require departments and executive agencies to produce annual progress reports to demonstrate the progress they have made against their sustainable development action plans (SDAP) which are a key mechanisms for converting good intentions into action (see Chapter 7). These SDAPs set out how each department or agency will contribute to the Government's overall sustainable development goals, through policymaking as well as internal operations, procurement and workforce management. According to the SDC's first review in 2007, the quality of the reports varied, as did progress towards the actions set out in the plans. The assessments conducted between 2008 and 2010 have led to improvements in both the quality of new SDAPs and real change in the way that departments operate to deliver their business more sustainably (SDC, 2010: 34).

In Scotland, progress on sustainable development policy is reported internally on the Purpose Targets and National Indicators of Scotland's National Performance Framework, using a live online resource, with information and assessments being updated as new data comes on-stream, so that the latest available overview of Scotland's progress is available to all. This resource simply records progress towards certain policy targets and indicators and does not analyze how or why changes have occurred (Scottish Government, n.d.). It provides no reporting on the numbers, quality or form of any type of policy appraisal such as strategic environmental assessment (SEA).

Given that the strategic process in Northern Ireland is still at an early stage, it is not surprising that the Northern Ireland Executive has not produced any report on its progress towards sustainable development policy. That said, there is clear evidence of progress. Its Plan of Implementation published in April 2011 provides that:

> a lead department has been identified for each of the 32 strategic objectives, each of whom will be responsible for overseeing progress against targets and communicating this to the OFMDFM. The OFMDFM will, in turn, report annually on the overall progression of Priority Areas for Action through the use of indicators.
>
> (Northern Ireland Executive, 2011: 15)

Unlike the other administrations, the WAG is under a statutory commitment under the Government of Wales Act 2006 s.79 to publish an annual report on the progress towards the objectives in its strategy. For example, the 2009/10 report reviews the WAG's progress in 2009/10 towards: embedding sustainable development as the central organizing principle of the Welsh Government; delivering key policy and programme changes towards becoming a fairer and more just society; and using only Wales's fair share of resources within the lifetime of a generation. Progress is measured for: each theme's vision; key outcomes; headline indicators of sustainable development; and specific strategic actions (WAG, 2010: 5).

Interestingly, the report contains external commentary about the report from both the SDC and Sustain Wales. Unfortunately, the actual reporting on appraisal systems again is the weak link. The SDC notes that:

> Internal mechanisms, such as the Policy Integration Toolkit and the Sustainable Procurement Action Framework, both cited in this year's Annual Report are important steps in the right direction. However, the Annual Report does not outline how successful such mechanisms have been, what change has occurred as a result, what challenges were faced and lessons learnt.
>
> (WAG, 2010: 11)

Unfortunately, then there is a worrying lack of enthusiasm about reporting on the quality or quantity of any forms of policy appraisal at both UK and devolved levels (Ross, 2005). No details are provided about the number or content of appraisals conducted in any of the administrations (see the discussion on the National Audit Office (NAO) below). Yet, as evidenced by the WAG's statutory reporting and by the reporting on SDAPs, internal reporting can lead to genuine improvements.

The EU has set up processes for internal reporting of progress towards its sustainable development policy goals which are worth examining. The Eurostat monitoring report, based on the EU's set of sustainable development indicators, provides an objective, statistical picture of progress towards the goals and objectives of the EU sustainable development strategy. It is published every two years and underpins and complements the policy analysis provided in the European Commission's progress report on the implementation of the strategy (Eurostat, 2009: 2). The reports produced by Eurostat are technically internal to the Commission and are essential for all decision making and provide transparency and openness.

Each report updates and adapts the previous edition, analysing progress in the implementation of the Strategy's objectives and targets. The indicators are evaluated against the policy objectives and targets of the EU sustainable development strategy. The approach is essentially quantitative, and focuses on the EU's set of sustainable development indicators as of a specified date (Eurostat, 2009: 32).

Every two years (starting from September 2007), the Commission submits a progress report on implementation of the sustainable development strategy in the EU and its Member States, also including future priorities, orientations and actions. The Commission's analysis draws on: a comprehensive set of sustainable development indicators, taking account of the Eurostat Monitoring Report; the latest scientific evidence; and developments in relation to key EU activities (strategies, action plans, legislation) (European Council, 2006: 26).

The benefit of internal reporting of progress towards sustainable development or any other objective is that it immediately puts the body in question on notice of its own successes and failures and allows that body to analyse the reasons behind the results. It also gives the body the chance to address problems quickly itself, perhaps without triggering 'bad press'.

Unfortunately, as shown above in relation to the WAG's 2008 figures on paper recycling, internal data can also be skewed, held out in a favourable light and, as such, external validation and review of these reports is essential for accountability of the body in question and for the legitimacy of the process as a whole (EAC, 2004b: para. 18). Indeed, in its independent review of the UK's 1999 strategic process, the SDC noted that:

> there is a significant gap between the Government's assessment of progress and our own. The Government presents a picture of widespread activity in many Government departments, and in society, designed to advance the objectives of sustainability. While recognizing that much remains to be done, it presents a picture of reasonable progress on most fronts. Our own assessment is that neither the UK Government, nor the devolved administrations nor our society as a whole have as yet fully assimilated how far the goals of sustainable development represent a radical critique of present policies and achievements, how far adrift we are from meeting our global and national responsibilities and creating a fully sustainable society, and how very much

more needs to be done in engaging society as a whole in facing up to the challenges of sustainability.

(SDC, 2004: 8, 9)

Independent or external review and reporting

Internal reporting of sustainable development has its limits. Without external validation, the progress reported on internally may not be credible. Moreover, if the report does not go anywhere or does not form part of a wider independent scrutiny process, then the danger is that it will be ignored. As discussed in Chapter 8 in relation to the statutory duties to produce strategies, plans and reports, it is vital that these obligations are accompanied by an obligation for them to be reviewed, monitored and used.

Meadowcroft, in his review of various studies for the implementation of sustainable development, observes that outside review and audit play a key role. Specifically, he claims that:

> if strategic decision making for sustainable development is to be continuously improved, the process should be subject to critical scrutiny from agencies outside governmental apparatus. This includes: parliamentary oversight (through legislative committees and/or parliamentary audit bodies); evaluation by independent public agencies (such as sustainable development commissions), and studies of social and environmental conditions, trends, pressures, and policy responses by publicly financed research institutes.
>
> (Meadowcroft, 2007: 16)

The focus in this section is on external or independent reviews of government progress towards sustainable development. The opportunities for monitoring and scrutiny are discussed separately in the next section.

The administrations in the UK are subject – and, impressively, subject themselves – to a wide variety of independent and external review by various bodies such as international institutions, non-governmental organizations (NGOs), and academic and environmental consultants. Importantly, each of the administrations has had the benefit of additional reviews being conducted by the relevant Audit Office, and up until 2011, the SDC. The role of these bodies is discussed at the end of this section.

First, however it is important to note that the UK's progress is monitored and reviewed as part of more global or EU-wide studies of progress towards sustainable development. These international external reviews are key sources of information that can be used to hold governments to account, often by comparing countries. For example, the Environmental Performance Index (EPI) is an aggregate indicator that allows direct comparisons among countries. In 2010, it ranked 163 countries on 25 performance indicators tracked across ten policy categories, covering both environmental public health and ecosystem vitality. These indicators provide a gauge at a national government scale of how close countries are to established environmental policy goals (EPI, n.d.). The OECD regularly reviews its members' progress towards sustainable development and publishes its results, highlighting areas of good practice (OECD, 2006). Similarly, the UN Commission on Sustainable Development, in conjunction with the International Institute for Sustainable Development (IISD), the World Bank and others, publishes studies of progress on a vast number of sustainable development targets, including progress towards the Millennium Development Goals, global trends in sustainable energy investment, the greening of water law, sustainable tourism and sustainable agriculture (IISD, n.d.). These comparative studies of progress can be used to embarrass governments and can be a means of compelling even the most reluctant administrations to at least appear to comply with international standards and norms, such as those on waste reduction, the use of EIA, climate change targets and aspects of good governance, such as stakeholder and public involvement.

Moreover, various NGOs such as the Green Alliance, the Royal Society for the Protection of Birds and Friends of the Earth undertake reviews of aspects of sustainable development progress (Batty, 2011). The impact of external reviews and reporting should not be underestimated. To illustrate, a 2002 WWF report found that there was no forum in Scotland for the bodies that needed to work together on sustainable development to do so, neither was there any channel of communication with those outside government. Following the criticisms, the Scottish Executive appointed external experts to the Cabinet sub-committee and established a range of stakeholder bodies such as the Scottish Coastal Forum, the Scottish Biodiversity Forum, the Organic Stakeholders Group, the Sustainable Development Forum and the Sustainable Development Network (Birley, 2001, 2002).

External reviews can also offer a different perspective on the data, and different external reviewers may take account of different sources and use alternative methods. These may differ from those used for the internal reviews and those used by past reviewers, often due to differences in expertise, discipline and priorities. For example, it may be desirable that the reports also take into account the views of stakeholders. Expert reviewers may feel a process is flawed or exemplary, while those using the system may believe otherwise. To address the need to consider alternative perceptions, the process used for the SDC Scotland's 2009 review not only used evidence from relevant strategies, policies, meeting minutes and frameworks and discussions and consultations with Scottish Government officials, but was also guided by an expert advisory group of external stakeholders which included representatives of Audit Scotland, Scottish Sustainable Development Forum, Sustainable Scotland Network, WWF Scotland, Scottish Environmental Protection Agency, Scottish Natural Heritage and Scottish Enterprise. In addition, the SDCS conducted an online survey of members of the Scottish Sustainable Development Forum, Scottish members of the Commission's Panel and other stakeholders to inform the appraisal more widely (SDCS, 2009a: 8).

In Wales, external independent review of the sustainable development scheme is statutorily required and includes the policy content of the scheme. In contrast to Scotland, while the SDC in Wales has been involved in the process, often publishing the report, the reviews have largely been managed by independent consultants and the result is that, over the years, different reviewers have used different methodologies, depending on their backgrounds. Flynn and Marsden (2006) uniquely chose to set their findings within the ongoing process of devolution within the UK, and thus not only examined the Assembly's sustainable development Action Plan, but also the UK Framework for Sustainable Development and *The UK Strategy for Sustainable Development: Securing the Future* (the 2005 strategy). Material for the report was gathered from a mixture of key person interviews and documentary review, and they developed a matrix-based analysis to assess the contribution of the Welsh Action Plan to the UK Framework for Sustainable Development (Flynn and Marsden, 2006).

Thus, variations in methodology can contribute significantly to the knowledge base and can highlight different concerns or validate issues raised elsewhere.

The Sustainable Development Commission

Until recently, the key external reviews of progress by the UK and devolved administrations towards sustainable development have been undertaken or commissioned by the SDC. Founded in October 2000, the SDC was the government's independent adviser on sustainable development, reporting to the Prime Minister, the First Ministers of Scotland and Wales and the First Minister and Deputy First Minister of Northern Ireland. Since its inception, the SDC provided informed, evidence-based advice to government on finding solutions to problems which help the government to meet its commitment to sustainable development, promoted and developed the attitudes, skills and knowledge in government to make the best decisions for today and the future, and importantly, held government to account on progress towards sustainability. In the context of an external reporting body, it produced numerous independent reports on progress under the various strategies, specific topics such as climate change and sustainable communities, and transport (SDC, n.d.).

While reporting to the leaders of each of the administrations, the remit of the SDC in each administration differed significantly and as a result, so did its impact.

In 2005, under the 2005 strategy, the SDC's role was increased to that of an independent watchdog, scrutinizing the UK Government's progress on implementing the strategy, and monitoring targets on the sustainable management of the Government estate and sustainable procurement (DEFRA, 2005). In 2009, its status was further strengthened from an advisory non-departmental public body to an executive non-departmental body registered with the Cabinet Office and registered with Companies House as a company limited by guarantee. As a separate legal entity, the SDC: reinforced its remit as the UK Government's sustainable development watchdog and adviser; had more freedom to make decisions over staffing and finances; and continued to have a close working relationship with the UK Government and the devolved administrations (SDC, n.d.).

The SDC's review of the UK administration has included annual reviews of operations across the whole estate (for example, SDC, 2009), reviews of individual departmental SDAPs (SDC, 2008), and overall periodic assessments of sustainable development in Government in the context of the relevant strategy (SDC, 2004, 2010). The SDC provided eight annual assessments of central Government performance on operations and procurement against the targets and commitments of the SOGE Framework. The benefit of the SDC reviews was that they provided annual reports on progress that could be compared from one year to the next. For example, the 2009 annual report on operations highlights the fact that while individual departmental performance remains mixed, 2008/09 was the first time that the four largest departments, which together represent 80 per cent of Government in terms of size, all achieved four out of a possible five stars for the primary SOGE targets. The 2009 report is positive about progress, yet emphasizes the need to avoid complacency. For example, the Government has made some significant progress on carbon from offices over the period and if it continues with the rate of progress achieved in 2008/09, it should be on track to meet this target. However, the Government has shown no progress since the previous reporting period on combined heat and power and needs to refocus its efforts to get on track (SDC, 2009).

Some of the best reporting came from the Scottish arm of the Sustainable Development Commission. In Scotland, the SDC was the Scottish Government's adviser and 'critical friend' on sustainability issues, reporting directly to the First Minister. Its main task was to report on the Government's delivery of sustainable development and use its recommendations to work with the Government to improve policy. Every year the SDC published an assessment of the Scottish Government's progress in aligning policies with sustainable development principles. Moreover, while internal reporting on policy in Scotland has been found lacking (see above), the external reviews conducted by the SDC in Scotland reviewed progress in relation to sustainable development policy by examining, for example, progress towards each of the Scottish Government's overall policy objectives towards sustainable Scotland and in relation to leadership (SDCS, 2007, 2008, 2009b, 2010). This is because the reports do not simply rely on the indicators for progress, they also rely on a variety of methodologies including literature, legal and policy reviews, surveys, and an expert advisory panel. Moreover, the reports are tailored to objectives, the approach taken by the Government and what has actually been going on inside and outside the Government in a given year. Where the Government changed these, the SDC reviewed the new objectives and approach. Where these stayed the same, the reviews focused more on delivery (SDCS, 2010).

The SDC in Scotland also undertook work on specific areas of policy and governance when asked by Government or on its own initiative in Scotland, and regularly provided written reports to Parliamentary committees. For example, the SDCS reviewed and reported on Scotland's second National Planning Framework (SDCS, 2009a).

SDC Wales (SDCW) was the WAG's independent advisory body on sustainable development. The Commission reported directly to the First Minister for Wales on key policy areas, including local government, regeneration and health. It tended to commission and publish the statutory reviews of the Welsh sustainable development scheme using different consultants (see discussion on methodology above). Rather than full annual reviews like those conducted in Scotland, it preferred to provide targeted commentary and responses to WAG and other reports, actions and decisions. In 2009, the Welsh Green Dragon Report that deals with sustainable operations also became subject to the external scrutiny of the SDC (SDCW, 2009). This is attributed to the clearly augmented remit for the SDC in Wales as set out in *One Wales: One Planet: The Sustainable Development Scheme of the Welsh Assembly Government*, which requires the SDC to assess and report on the WAG's operations across its administrative estate (WAG, 2009a).

The role of the SDC was more abstract in Northern Ireland, where its aim was simply to provide advocacy, advice and capability building and help to put sustainable development at the heart of government policy in Northern Ireland. In Northern Ireland, the Commission contributed to inquiries on climate change and sustainable transport, as well as providing expert advice on renewable energy projects and construction skills initiatives. The failure to give the SDC a heightened role like that in Scotland in the latest strategy is a missed opportunity and more evidence of the lack of commitment to the agenda in Northern Ireland. Indeed, there are no external reporting or monitoring mechanisms mentioned in the strategy or in the Plan of Implementation (Northern Ireland Executive, 2010, 2011).

In July 2010, the new Secretary of State for the Department of Environment, Food and Rural Affairs (DEFRA), Caroline Spelman MP, announced that the UK Coalition Government intended to withdraw its funding for the SDC from the next financial year, and later that year, the administrations in Scotland and Northern Ireland followed suit. It has only been the Welsh institutions who have seen a continued need for external review and, in March 2011, the Welsh Environment Minister, Jane Davidson, appointed a new Commissioner for Sustainable Futures, Peter Davies, who previously served as SDC Wales Commissioner, to provide leadership for sustainable development in Wales. Cynnal Cymru took on the additional remit of providing independent policy advice to ministers, and supporting the Commissioner in his work (Davidson, 2011).

The UK Government's rationale for effectively dispensing with the SDC appears to be to reduce and reallocate expenditure, and to change the leadership of sustainable development. The Secretary of State told the EAC that the funding cut for the SDC was based on a decision to remove 'arm's length' scrutiny and take more control of the sustainability agenda (EAC, 2011: 10). The Prime Minister told the House of Commons Liaison Committee that the decision was made to reserve funding for other projects 'like the green deal, like carbon capture and storage, and like a green investment bank, which will have real money to spend – rather than have quite so much monitoring and evaluation' (Liaison Committee, 2010).

The work of the SDC delivered efficiency savings many times what it cost any of the administrations and contributed towards much greater sustainability in each of the administrations. Andrew Lee, the SDC Chief Executive, told the EAC that the value of the benefits from better management of carbon, energy, travel, waste and water in 2008/09 can be estimated at between £62.3 million and £66.1 million, although these savings do not take account of the expenditure required to deliver them and it is impossible to assign the savings solely to SDC activities (EAC, 2011: 11).

Moreover, the SDC was held in very high regard internationally, and there are regularly calls for similar bodies to be set up in other countries (Abbott and Marchant, 2010: 1934–6). In particular, the reporting of progress by an external independent expert body has been consistently held up as one of the UK's great successes in the implementation of sustainable development (Dalal-Clayton and Bass, 2007: 103–4). These points are developed in the conclusion of this chapter and in Part III of this volume.

Audit offices

Before moving to the importance of external scrutiny mechanisms, it is essential to also discuss the contribution of the audit offices.

The National Audit Office (NAO), Audit Scotland, Audit Wales and the Northern Ireland Audit Office are all independent of government and report directly to the legislature. Generally, the audit offices scrutinize public spending on behalf of the relevant legislature, helping it to hold government departments to account and helping public service managers improve performance and service delivery. They conduct two types of inquiries. First, they examine and certify the financial accounts of relevant administrations and their sponsored or related public bodies, and second, they report the results to the relevant legislature. In 2009/10, the UK NAO audited expenditure and revenue amounting to some £950 billion across 475 accounts (NAO, n.d.).

Each office has a statutory power to report to the relevant legislature on the economy, efficiency and effectiveness with which the administrations have used, and may improve the use of, their resources in discharging their functions. Inquiries into progress towards sustainable development fall within these 'value for money' inquiries and can be very broad-ranging.

Indeed, value for money inquiries offer a significant opportunity for thorough investigations on a wide range of topics relevant to the implementation of sustainable development, ranging from coastal erosion and tidal flooding risks in Wales (Wales Audit Office, 2009) to the environmental impacts of government procurement (NAO, 2009). They can make important contributions to assessment of progress towards sustainability. For example, the Northern Ireland Audit Office conducted a value for money inquiry into the performance of the planning system in Northern Ireland and concluded, among other things, that:

> Targets and performance measurement are largely activity- and output-based (for example, the Agency's main measures relate to processing times and delivery of Development Plans). There are no indicators which measure the

outcomes and impacts of the Agency in terms of its ultimate aims of sustainable development, protecting the environment and promoting economic growth.

(NIAO, 2009: 30)

Each audit office submits its reports for scrutiny to the relevant parliamentary Public Accounts committee and may provide briefings and other reports to other committees. This role is vital to the scrutiny committees in both the UK and Wales. Indeed, a special relationship has evolved between the NAO and the EAC, whereby the NAO supports the work of the EAC by providing it with briefings and reports. For example, the NAO contributed to the EAC's 2004 *Greening Government* report by conducting an analysis of departmental data provided in relation to greening operations in the SDiG Report 2003 (EAC, 2004a). In 2006, at the request of the EAC, the NAO completed its first report on regulatory impact assessments and found that the coverage of sustainability issues in the assessments was limited, thus supporting claims that this more integrated form of appraisal was failing to adequately protect the environment (NAO, 2006).

A potential solution to the hole in the process of external review of sustainable development left by the demise of the SDC would be enhancing the role of the audit offices. This has been done in other countries. Canada, for example, gave explicit powers to conduct 'environmental audits' to its audit office and created a Commissioner for Sustainable Development within the office[2] (Ross, 1998). Even with the loss of the SDC, this seems unlikely in the UK, and in a letter to the EAC the Comptroller and Auditor General states:

we hope to continue to assist the Committee with its inquiries. Should the Committee take on a broader remit, we would seek to support it across the range of its activities where we can provide relevant skills and knowledge. I am not, however, in a position to enter into binding long-term commitments, or to take on functions which the Government has decided it should no longer fund.

(EAC, 2011: 25–6)

Scrutiny, accountability and legitimacy mechanisms

There is some overlap between review and scrutiny. For the purposes of this chapter, scrutiny differs from reporting or review in that it adds an element of being called to account for one's actions or inaction. In other words, scrutiny mechanisms ideally include some form of consequences for failure to meet obligations. These, in turn, add legitimacy to the decision-making and policymaking processes and to governance for sustainability generally.

The accountability measures in the UK are heavily dependent on internal public reporting (Ross, 2005). Thus, the starting point for accountability is that the variable reporting discussed above impacts on the quality of scrutiny possible. Without reliable data, it is very difficult to monitor progress and call government to account. Even the most diligent of scrutiny bodies will be left toothless if it has nothing to scrutinize. The input of the Office for National Statistics is significant here and the annual reports on sustainable development indicators are now accompanied by the following statement: 'This is a National Statistics Compendium publication which are produced to high professional standards set out in the National Statistics Code of Practice. They undergo regular quality assurance reviews to ensure that they meet customer needs and importantly are produced free from political interference' (DEFRA, 2010). These reports are then used by various sources of scrutiny, including government-funded expert bodies like the SDC, external bodies such as the WWF and, importantly, used by members of the various legislatures for scrutiny in parliamentary debates and in committees.

Indeed, scrutiny can come from a variety of places and a key question for any state or organization is who is best placed to scrutinize the decisions, reports, policies and programmes and then hold those responsible to account. A key factor here is the amount of influence the particular source of scrutiny has in that state or organization. In some countries, embarrassment in front of the international community may be very powerful, while in others it is largely irrelevant. In some countries, judicial scrutiny may play an important role, especially where there is a strong tradition of an active constitutional and administrative judiciary. In the USA, a statutory obligation is placed on all public bodies to consider the environmental or sustainable development consequences of their actions. This is enforceable in the courts.[3]

As discussed in Chapter 8, a duty has been placed on public bodies in Scotland under the Climate Change (Scotland) Act 2009 s. 44(1) to act in exercising its functions *in a way that it considers is most sustainable* and, similarly, the Northern Ireland (Miscellaneous Provisions) Act 2006 s. 25 requires all public bodies to exercise their powers *in the way best calculated to contribute* to the achievement of sustainable development. Neither these nor any of the specific obligations set out in statute are at present considered to be enforceable in court. It is unlikely that the UK courts would accept an action for breach of statutory duty based on these provisions, since these are all directory duties that do not tend to create rights per se. Indeed, a common criticism against the use of vague or unenforceable terms is that they undermine the role of law in protecting individual rights (Brandl and Bungert, 1992: 92). To this end, it is helpful to distinguish between judicial enforcement where the court is the primary implementation mechanism and the courts' supervisory role of administrative programmes and agencies under the normal rules for judicial review (Rubin, 1989). As discussed in Chapters 8 and 13, there have been cases for judicial review relating to sustainability, and the chances of success, where there has been a failure to comply with a procedural obligation, are quite high. However, this approach is not preventative, timely or cost-effective. As argued in both Chapters 8 and 13, the courts should be given an increased role, but for the reasons set out above, they should not be the main source of scrutiny.

Another possibility is to rely on public scrutiny. The most obvious way the public holds the government to account is through the electoral process every four to five years. This is a blunt instrument and other more tailored devices that use more participative techniques can be very effective. Expert political interviewers may question ministers on television, or critical blogs, editorials and commentaries may be published in newspapers, magazines and online. NGOS and academic experts may do the same. This can embarrass the government into action or, at least, require some form of response. Maintaining consistent and thorough public scrutiny is difficult, as certain prerequisites are necessary, such as a strong independent media, an active research community, powerful NGOs and a fair bit of electoral choice. Public scrutiny can be reinforced with other forms of scrutiny. For example, in Ontario, members of the public have standing in court to challenge the public sector on the environmental content of its decisions.[4] There is no similar mechanism in the UK.[5] However, following the demise of the SDC, the UK Government has emphasized how much of its watchdog role could be taken up by NGOs and academics. The WWF has told the EAC that in the past the consultation with civil society has come at too late a stage (EAC, 2011: 26–7). As part of a wider agenda of assisting scrutiny through greater transparency of its activities, the Government aims to make data on its sustainable development performance more accessible to the public. Arguably then, the public, academics, NGOs and community groups can use this data to hold the Government to account. Moreover, the EAC has asked the Government to formalize the meetings the Secretary of State is undertaking to have with NGOs every couple of months to ensure that they last. NGOs and academics can play a valuable role in bringing new ideas into the policymaking process, especially when the capacity of the public sector and the government to develop sustainable policies might be restricted (EAC, 2011: 26–7).

Parliamentary scrutiny

In practice, where the UK has been most innovative and progressive in its approach to the implementation of sustainable development is in its expansion of the legislature's supervisory role to accommodate the crosscutting nature of sustainable development. The Scottish Government, Welsh Assembly and House of Commons have all introduced innovations in their committee systems to improve government scrutiny. In relation to holding government to account for its record on sustainable development, some of these innovations have been more successful than others and the focus of the remainder of this section is on the use of parliamentary scrutiny in the implementation of sustainable development.

Question Time, parliamentary debates and the role of pre-legislative scrutiny

Sustainable development issues have been debated on the floors of all the legislatures in the UK. Debates can be very useful. Most recently, the decision to cease funding the SDC attracted a great deal of parliamentary attention in all of the UK legislatures.[6]

The situation in Scotland is particularly interesting, as in Scotland, there is a requirement for all bills to be accompanied by pre-legislative statements in relation to sustainable development (see Chapter 7). These ought to affect the subsequent parliamentary debates on bills. However, during the debate on sustainable development on 6 November 2003, Sarah Boyack, MSP observed:

> Every bill is meant to address sustainable development principles; however, I can think of only two bills that have done that properly – the National Parks (Scotland) Bill and the Water Environment and Water Services (Scotland) Bill. Sustainable development was at the core of both those bills and was debated extensively in committee, even making it to the chamber for debate. However, no member could put their hand up and say that every bill that we have debated has covered sustainable development and that we have tested all the legislative provisions that the Parliament has discussed.[7]

A study commissioned by the Scottish Parliament's Environment and Rural Development (ERD) Committee was slightly more positive. Its examination of five bills[8] introduced between September 2001 and September 2002 revealed that while the Committee and parliamentary discussions on these bills failed to address all sustainable development issues, they did touch on many relevant ones, even when these were not mentioned in the policy memorandum. However, sustainable development was rarely deliberately addressed and, instead, the discussions usually only strayed into a topic (CAG Consultants, 2004: 42–3).

Parliamentary committees

Most parliamentary committees are set up on a sectoral basis, mirroring departmental responsibilities or ministerial portfolios. Often, they are further divided up between scrutiny committees (select committees) and legislative committees (standing committees). The difficulty is that accountability relying on this type of ministerial/departmental responsibility to Parliament was never designed to cope with multi-organizational policy systems such as those required by sustainable development. Instead, they perpetuate sectoral or 'silo' thinking. The Scottish, UK and Welsh Parliaments have sought to modernize the traditional committee system to improve integration, but some of these attempts have been more effective than others.

For example, when it was introduced, the Scottish Parliament chose to adopt an integrated committee system whereby committees can initiate legislation, and scrutinize and amend Scottish Executive proposals, as well as exercise a range of investigative functions. While this means that the committee that reviews government activity can also use that information to initiate or review legislation, the process remains sector-based. For example, the committee charged with sustainable development is actually the Rural Affairs and the Environment (RAE) Committee (formerly the ERD Committee). Its remit is limited to considering and reporting on matters relating to rural development, environment and natural heritage, agriculture and fisheries, and such other matters as fall within the responsibility of the Minister for Environment and Rural Development. Under the system, the RAE committee also has legislative commitments. For example, it was the lead committee considering the Strategic Environmental Assessment Bill.

The ERD Committee published a report on sustainable development in September 2004 based on independent research it commissioned into sustainable development within Scotland (CAG Consultants, 2004). Since then, its successor, the RAE Committee, has conducted very few inquiries, but has, instead, focused almost entirely on legislative scrutiny. Nevertheless, it is not specifically charged with sustainable development and its jurisdiction does not cover the whole of the Scottish Executive or its competences (RAE, n.d.). Since 2007, there has also been a committee devoted to Transport, Infrastructure and Climate Change (TICC). The TICC has been more active on general sustainable development matters and meetings in both 2010 and 2011 have included items on finance and sustainable growth, and the future of the Sustainable Development Commission (Scottish Parliament TICC, 2010, 2011) but these are not full inquiries. The Policy Commission on a Sustainable Scotland, in its report *Working Together for a Sustainable Scotland*,[9] recommended the creation of a new parliamentary sustainable development committee similar to the EAC to scrutinize all policy and legislative proposals (Scott, 2003; Ross, 2005).

The current situation is problematic. Pursuant to the Nature Conservation (Scotland) Act 2004, every three years, a report regarding the implementation of the Scottish Biodiversity Strategy is to be laid by the Scottish ministers before the Scottish Parliament.[10] One would have thought that the RAE Committee or some cross-departmental committee would take responsibility for the proper scrutiny of this innovative, legally required report. This has not happened and instead, for instance, the 2007 Progress Report was reviewed in plenary and approved with little discussion (Scottish Parliament, 2008). Moreover, there is no scrutiny of the sustainability of the Scottish Government's finances. At present, both the RAE and TICC Committees' roles in scrutinizing the budget is limited to considering the proposals of the relevant Cabinet secretaries and ministers (thus limited to rural affairs and the environment or transport, infrastructure and climate change) and reporting to the Finance Committee in late spring. A crosscutting committee like those in the UK and Welsh legislatures could also examine, in more detail, the sustainable development statements in policy memoranda attached to all bills and provide the much-needed external scrutiny of the spending review process.

Indeed, the legislatures in both the UK and Wales have gone that step further and recognized that crosscutting policy demands new forms of accountability and scrutiny that do not inhibit inter-organizational working, reinforce boundaries or prevent sensible risk-taking. Flinders observes that:

if cross-departmental working is taken to its logical conclusion the depart-
mentally related select committee structure would have to be reformed to
reflect cross-cutting policies ... joined-up government replaces individual
ministerial responsibility with collegiate responsibility among any number
of ministers. The fear would be that, without parliamentary reform, responsibility would become opaque as ministers attempted to shift responsibility
to other ministerial stakeholders.

(Flinders, 2002: 68)

The need for some form of monitoring device to audit departments on their
environmental performance was set out by the Labour Party in its environment
policy paper of 1994 entitled *In Trust for Tomorrow*. Following the Labour
victory in May 1997, the EAC, a cross-departmental Select Committee, was
introduced. Its remit is to consider the extent to which any government activity contributes to environmental protection and sustainable development, and
to audit departments' progress against targets set by ministers. In the original
manifesto proposal, the EAC was to be supported by an expanded NAO that
would actually carry out 'environmental audits' on certain departmental projects
in addition to its usual financial audits. However, the Committee, as initially set
up, did not have the support of an extended NAO.

The EAC has been very successful at examining the policies and programmes
of government as a whole regarding the extent to which they contribute to
environmental protection and sustainable development. Since its inception, the
EAC has sought out policies and programmes which are not primarily environmental, but which do have a significant environmental dimension for its inquiries (Ross, 2000). Every inquiry the EAC has conducted involved major
policy issues such as the budget, greening government and climate change, and
this has become the main focus of its work.

A narrower reading of its remit would require the EAC to review specific
departmental policies, programmes and decisions in terms of their impacts on
sustainable development or environmental protection, as well as to audit departmental performance against operational targets set by ministers. The EAC has
largely avoided such work, since to do so, it would need additional resources
such as those available to the Public Accounts Committee via the NAO (EAC,
2001). That said, the EAC has been instrumental in pressuring the Government
to set targets and to ensure that these are audited. As targets are set, the EAC's
audit function has become more significant. However, it still cannot cope with
a very detailed departmental review, but it has benefited from data produced by
other sources such as NAO briefings, value for money reports and the SDC
annual reports (see below).

Overall, the establishment of this crosscutting select Committee has made
a valuable contribution to both the SDiG agenda and to improving environmental and sustainable development integration within government. Indeed,
preparing documentation for an inquiry, appearing before the Committee and
writing responses, may force officials to consider the environmental implications

of departmental policies and programmes, irrespective of how benign they may seem at first glance (Ross, 2000). In assessing its role without the work of SDC, the EAC has stated that it will continue to monitor the Government's SOGE data and reporting process, and changes anticipated for the indicators system, as well as assess the Government's performance against its ambition of becoming the 'greenest government ever'. Moreover, it also wants to review the appraisal of government policies across Government and the impact of these policies on sustainable development (by, for example, examining impact assessments of key policy programmes). To date, both the reporting and scrutiny on policy appraisal have been sadly lacking, especially at UK level, and this is a very welcome addition to the remit and well worth doing in the other committees.

The UK Government itself, at least in its rhetoric, claims that the EAC is an important part of the process of integrating sustainable development into government decision making and that the Committee is seen as something that cannot, and should not, be ignored (DEFRA, 1999: Introduction; HM Government, 1999: para. 6.112). However, while there are occasions when the recommendations in Committee reports have been accepted or placed under review (Ross, 2000), in its 2011 inquiry into embedding sustainable development, the EAC explicitly called for the Government to engage with its scrutiny work in a more constructive and considered way, as often, Government responses have dismissed recommendations without providing a robust account for those judgements (EAC, 2011: 26).

The Welsh Assembly, like the UK Parliament, has a crosscutting scrutiny committee dealing with sustainable development matters. Scrutiny committees are established to last for the life of the current Assembly to examine the Government's policies, actions and spending in their particular fields. One of the key roles of these committees is to conduct inquiries, collect evidence and report back to the legislature. This role gives not only stakeholders including regulators the chance to voice their views on progress, it also provides an opportunity for scrutiny (National Assembly for Wales, n.d.). The Sustainability Committee can call ministers to account and also keep an eye on government bodies and agencies within those fields. Its remit covers climate change, energy, rural affairs and agriculture, environment and planning. Arguably, this is a bit narrow and, to date, its inquiries and reports have been limited to the energy and environmental side of sustainable development. Its remit, however, crosses departmental and division boundaries so it can call any part of the WAG to account.

The impact of the loss of the SDC on the work of the legislative committees

While the UK Government expects DEFRA to take the lead in helping departments to apply sustainable development principles, DEFRA has no intention of taking on the SDC's watchdog role. Similarly, although the Centre of Expertise in Sustainable Procurement (CESP) based in the Office of Government Commerce will continue to collect SOGE performance data, it has told the EAC that it does not have the capacity to comment on the results of the data. The Government appears to wish to leave this to the EAC (EAC, 2011: 4).

The EAC was set up to scrutinize Government environmental and sustainability performance and to report on it to Parliament. The Welsh Sustainability Committee has a similar purpose. As pointed out by the EAC, a distinction needs to be drawn between scrutiny that assists Government – either to encourage better performance or to bring further transparency to its operations – and scrutiny that aids accountability to Parliament. The work of the SDC contributed mainly to assist Government, although it did also provide useful material for parliamentary scrutiny. There is also a distinction between scrutinizing Government at arm's length from the 'outside', as done by legislatures, the courts and the media, and scrutinizing Government from within, as the SDC has been able to do by embedding staff within departments. Minas Jacob from the SDC explained to EAC:

> I would say it is actually pretty much impossible to do scrutiny from the outside. Unless you are just going to be looking at people's electricity bills or statements that Government departments produce, you have to work with departments to understand their circumstances; otherwise you are producing watchdog reports, or attempting to, on information that doesn't even exist.
>
> (EAC, 2011: 25)

Thus, without the detailed reports on the progress on SDAPs (in the UK) or the detailed annual reports on SDiG, the parliamentary committees' scrutiny roles are significantly limited. Once again, effective scrutiny demands effective, reliable and independent review and reporting. In this sense, the loss of the SDC is significant to all the administrations. In many ways, it is the equivalent to asking the Public Accounts Committee to do its job without the aid of the NAO.

Accountability of the UK administrations to one another

One final point in relation to coordination and scrutiny warrants discussion. Devolution creates a fine line as to how different levels of government should report back to one another. Obviously, UK-wide targets and obligations require some monitoring and require the various parts of the UK to take responsibility for meeting those obligations within their competence. However, to what extent can and should the centre pressure the devolved administrations in relation to their progress? Flynn and Marsden (2006) note that while the Welsh devolution Acts require reporting on the Assembly Government's performance on sustainable development to the Welsh Assembly, they make no mention of reporting to, or of monitoring by, the UK Government of the Assembly's sustainability activities. Indeed, they note that any efforts to establish new reporting or monitoring arrangements might well upset the devolution settlement. They quote one interviewee who commented: 'what we do as a government here in terms of responsibility for SD we are accountable to the Assembly for . . . We wouldn't report back to anyone in the UK anyway because we are not responsible to them' (Flynn and Marsden, 2006: 10).

Legally speaking, where a devolved administration takes action or fails to take action in a manner that is incompatible with the UK's international obligations, the UK may order that such action is taken or not taken, using its powers under the relevant devolution Act (Scotland Act 1998 s. 58; Northern Ireland Act 1998 s. 26; Government of Wales Act 2006 s. 82). However, this could run counter to the purpose of devolution and is likely to be politically difficult. Resort to other measures for resolving disputes both informal and as contained in the relevant memoranda of understanding such as the Joint Ministerial Committee, is much more likely.

More recently, the converse has occurred. The UK's decision to cease funding the SDC was made unilaterally with virtually no consultation with the devolved administrations. No assessment of the impacts on the devolved administrations was made before DEFRA's initial decision to remove its funding from the SDC, even though the devolved administrations also contributed to its funding. The Secretary of State and her officials explained to the EAC that there were discussions with the administrations before a 'final' decision was taken, and that at that time, the devolved administrations did not 'raise a major objection' with the decision. When the EAC raised this with the devolved administrations, the Scottish Government said they would have preferred that DEFRA had not withdrawn funding from the SDC and the WAG announced its 'disappointment' with the Secretary of State's decision. The Northern Ireland Executive wrote (EAC, 2011: 12–13), stating: 'We are disappointed with DEFRA's decision to withdraw funding from the SDC. Progression and achievement of sustainable development does by its very nature, both in principle and in practice, require unilateral understanding and co-operation across and between Governments'. The EAC concludes that decisions like this that impinge on a shared strategy should not be undertaken lightly or unilaterally (EAC, 2011: 12–13).

This highlights a lack of coordination in the UK coalition Government's approach to sustainable development and is a serious concern. If the UK Government can in one swoop undo all the good efforts of its predecessor and the devolved administrations, what hope is there for a coordinated, consistent and effective approach for a sustainable UK? Moreover, this is significant for the constitutional settlement and likely should be addressed by the Joint Ministerial Committee in a future meeting and, if possible, consultation provisions explicitly added to the memoranda of understanding that govern relations between the administrations.

Conclusion

Simply providing opportunities for monitoring progress towards sustainable development is not enough. Quality scrutiny that genuinely calls government

to account for its actions depends very much on four factors. First, those scru
tinizing need a clear standard to measure progress. This requires clear objectives
and aims that are supported by indicators, targets and timetables. The UK and
the devolved administrations, with the exception of Northern Ireland, have
shown steady improvement in this area.

Second, effective scrutiny depends heavily on quality reporting of progress,
both internally and externally. Regular reporting on sustainable development in
government operations is now standard in most of the administrations. The
Office for National Statistics is now validating many of the quantitative reports
produced by the administrations, and the relevant audit offices are also using
their powers to conduct value for money audits in the wider context of sustainable development. Furthermore, there remains a worrying lack of enthusiasm
about reporting on sustainable development policy and, in particular, the use
of environmental, sustainability and the more general impact appraisals. The loss
of the SDC is significant here. In reviewing departments' SDAPs and progress
towards the strategies, the SDC played a primary role in the monitoring and
reporting of policy. In the context of operations, not only did the SDC report
annually on progress, it used these reports to compare progress among the
administrations and promote the extension of the UK's very successful SDiG
programme for operations to the devolved administrations. One needs to question who will produce all of this important independent data in future.

Third, there needs to be independent scrutiny of government action and
inaction by those who can genuinely hold the government to account. This
scrutiny should also be accompanied by consequences for failure to deliver. In
the UK, most of this scrutiny of government has been conducted by the relevant
legislatures, although the media, NGOs and academics have been playing an
increasing role and are expected to play an even larger role in the future.

To this end, crosscutting parliamentary committees are very effective sources
of scrutiny of the implementation of sustainable development. It would be
beneficial for both Scotland and Northern Ireland to introduce crosscutting
sustainability committees whose remit extends beyond one or two departments
to the whole of government and who can call all ministers and others to account.

Instead, Scotland relied heavily on the SDC to review and scrutinize its
policy so even if a committee was established some alternative source of data
on policy appraisal is needed for this scrutiny to be effective. The EAC's ambition
to regularly review the appraisal of government policies across Government is
exciting. This could act as a significant catalyst to achieving a much more consistent integration of environment and sustainable development in government
policy and decision making.

Finally, those involved in the scrutiny process, whether MPs, interviewers
in the media or judges in court, must be sustainably literate and understand
why sustainable development is important and what its delivery actually requires.
So much depends on their knowledge and understanding of sustainable development. As such, scrutiny will only be effective once there is a useable vision of
sustainable development which sets out clear priorities and a framework for

decision making and assessment, as well as suitable training so that these scrutinizers and others understand and can apply sustainable development.

Notes

1 These are social justice, environmental equality and wellbeing.
2 Auditor General Act 1985 R.S.C. 1985 c. A-17, ss. 21.1–23, Federal Sustainable Development Act 2008 S.C. 2008 c. 33.
3 The National Environmental Policy Act 1969 (NEPA) 42 U.S.C. s. 4332(c) s. 102 requires all federal agencies to include in every recommendation or report on proposals for legislation and other major federal actions significantly affecting the quality of the human environment, a detailed statement by the responsible official on, among other things, the environmental impact of the proposed action. Failure to observe these requirements may result in enforcement through the courts. For a critique, see the Council for Environmental Quality (1997).
4 Environmental Bill of Rights, SO 1993 ch. 28.
5 Although, if a member of the public had participated and specifically drawn a decision maker's attention to an applicable sustainable development policy document and the decision maker subsequently ignored the policy, there may be a case for judicial review or an appeal under certain regimes such as planning.
6 Scottish Parliament, Official Report, columns 2957–86, 6 November 2003.
7 House of Commons Written Answers to Questions 19 October 2010: Column 633W; Scottish Parliament Official Report Meeting of the Parliament 9 December 2010; National Assembly for Wales Record of Proceedings, 28 September 2010 (Sustainable Development annual report); Northern Ireland Assembly Official Report, 13 September 2010, AQO 1529/11.
8 Scottish Parliament, Official Report, column 2968, 6 November 2003.
9 The Criminal Justice Bill, the Freedom of Information Bill, the Local Government in Scotland Bill, the Mental Health Bill and the Water Environment and Water Services Bill.
10 The 'Policy Commission on a Sustainable Scotland' is an initiative of the Scottish Centre for Public Policy chaired by Sarah Boyack MSP and includes representatives from industry including the Scottish Council on Development and Industry and leading NGOs.
11 The Nature Conservation (Scotland) Act 2004 asp 6 s. 2(7).

References

Abbott, K.W. and Marchant, G.E. (2010) 'Institutionalizing sustainability across the Federal Government', *Sustainability*, 2(7): 1924–42.

Batty, D. (2011) 'David Cameron in danger of breaking green pledge warn green groups', *Guardian*, 14 May.

Birley, T. (2001) *Reality Check: A Review of Scottish Executive Activity on Sustainable Development*, Aberfeldy: WWF.

Birley, T. (2002) *Reality Check 2002: A Review of Scottish Executive Activity on Sustainable Development*, Aberfeldy: WWF.

Brandl, E. and Bungert, H. (1992) 'Constitutional entrenchment of environmental protection: A comparative analysis of experiences abroad', *Harvard Environmental Law Review*, 16(1): 1–100.

CAG Consultants (2004) *Is the Scottish Executive Structured and Positioned to Deliver Sustainable Development?*, 10th Report, vol. 2, Edinburgh: Environment and Rural Development Committee.

Council on Environmental Quality (1997) *The National Environmental Policy Act: A Study of its Effectiveness after Twenty-five years*, http://ceq.hss.doe.gov/nepa/nepa25fn. pdf, accessed 25 May 2011.

Dalal-Clayton, B. and Bass, S. (2007) 'Monitoring and reviewing national sustainable development strategies', in OECD, *Institutionalizing Sustainable Development*, Paris: OECD.

Davidson, J. (2011) Written Statement to the Welsh Assembly on the Commissioner for Sustainable Futures, 1 March.

Davies, P. (2010) *SDC Wales Response to DEFRA Funding Announcement*, Cardiff: Sustainable Development Commission Wales.

Department of Environment, Food and Rural Affairs (DEFRA) (1999) *A Better Quality of Life: A Strategy for Sustainable Development for the United Kingdom*, London: DEFRA.

DEFRA (2002) *Framework for Sustainable Development on the Government Estate*, London: DEFRA.

DEFRA (2003) Achieving a Better Quality of Life: Review of progress towards Sustainable Development government annual report 2002, London: DEFRA.

DEFRA (2004a) *Framework for Sustainable Development on the Government Estate*, London: DEFRA.

DEFRA (2004b) Achieving a Better Quality of Life: Review of progress towards Sustainable Development government annual report 2003, London: DEFRA.

DEFRA (2005) *The UK Strategy for Sustainable Development: Securing the Future*, London: DEFRA.

DEFRA (2006) *Sustainable Operations on the Government Estate*, DEFRA, http://www. defra.gov.uk/sustainable/government/documents/Targets.pdf, accessed 5 September 2010.

DEFRA (2010) *National Statistics Compendium, Measuring Progress: Sustainable Development Indicators*, London: DEFRA.

Dernbach, J. (2002–2003) 'Targets, timetables and effective implementing mechanisms: Necessary building blocks for sustainable development', *William & Mary Environmental Law and Policy Review*, 27: 79–136.

Environmental Audit Committee (EAC) (2001) *Departmental Responsibilities for Sustainable Development First Report 2001–02*, HC 326, London: EAC.

EAC (2004a) *Greening Government, Eighth Report 2003–04*, HC 881, London: EAC.

EAC (2004b) *The Sustainable Development Strategy: Illusion or Reality? Thirteenth Report 2003–04*, HC 624-1, London: EAC.

EAC (2011) *Embedding Sustainable Development across Government, First Report 2010–2011*, HC 504, London: EAC.

Environmental Performance Index (EPI) 2010 (n.d.) http://epi.yale.edu/Countries, accessed 24 March 2011.

European Commission (2009) *Mainstreaming Sustainable Development into EU Policies: 2009 Review of the European Union Strategy for Sustainable Development*, Com 400, Brussels: EC.

European Council (2006) *Review of the EU Sustainable Development Strategy- Renewed Strategy*, Brussels: European Council.

Eurostat (2009) *Sustainable development in the European Union: 2009 monitoring report of the EU sustainable development strategy*, Luxembourg: Office for Official Publications of the European Communities.

Flinders, M. (2002) 'Governance in Whitehall', *Public Administration*, 80(1): 51–75.

Flynn, A. and Marsden, T. (2006) *Aiming Higher: Assessing the Sustainable Development Plans and Actions of the Welsh Assembly in terms of its Commitments in the UK wide*

Strategy: A Report to the Sustainable Development Commission, Cardiff: Cardiff School of City and Regional Planning.

Freeman, J. (1999) 'Private parties, public function and the real democracy problem in the new administrative law?', in D. Dyzenhous (ed.) *Recrafting the Rule of Law*, Oxford: Hart.

HM Government (1999) *Stability and Steady Growth for Britain: Pre Budget Report*, Cm 4479, London: HMSO.

HM Government, Scottish Executive, Welsh Assembly Government, Northern Ireland Office (2005) *One future – different paths: The UK's shared framework for sustainable development*, London: DEFRA.

Hodge, R.A. and Hardi, P. (1997) 'The need for guidelines: The rationale underlying the Bellagio Principles for assessment', in P. Hardi and T. Zdan (eds) *Assessing Sustainable Development: Principles in Practice*, Winnipeg: International Institute for Sustainable Development.

International Institute for Sustainable Development (IISD) (n.d.) Linkages: Key publications and online resources on sustainable development, http://www.iisd.ca/publications-resources/sust_devt.htm, accessed 15 March 2011.

Liaison Committee (2010) Oral evidence given by Rt Hon David Cameron taken before the Liaison Committee, HC 608-i, Q 77.

Meadowcroft, J. (2007) 'National sustainable development strategies: Features, challenges and reflexivity', *European Environment*, 17(3): 152–63.

National Assembly for Wales (n.d.) Sustainability Committee website, http://www.assemblywales.org/bus-home/bus-committees/bus-committees-scrutiny-committees/bus-committees-third-sc-home.htm, accessed 16 March 2011.

National Audit Office (NAO) (2006) *Regulatory Impact Assessment and Sustainable Development: A Briefing for the Environmental Audit Committee*, London: NAO.

NAO (2009) Addressing the Environmental Impacts of Government Procurement, London: NAO.

NAO (n.d.) *What we do*, http://www.nao.org.uk/about_us/what_we_do.aspx, accessed 24 March 2011.

Northern Ireland Audit Office (NIAO) (2009) *The Performance of the Planning Service*, Belfast: NIAO.

Northern Ireland Executive (2010) *Everyone's Involved: Sustainable Development Strategy*, Belfast: Northern Ireland Executive.

Northern Ireland Executive (2011) *Focus on the Future: Sustainable Development Implementation Plan*, Belfast: Northern Ireland Executive.

Organisation for Economic Co-operation and Development (OECD) (2002) *Improving Policy Coherence and Integration for Sustainable Development: A Checklist*, Paris: OECD.

OECD (2006) *Sustainable Development Studies Good Practices in the National Sustainable Development Strategies of OECD Countries*, Paris: OECD.

Office of the First Minister and Deputy First Minister (n.d.) 'Sustainable operations on the Government estate', http://www.ofmdfmni.gov.uk/index/economic-policy/economic-policy-sustainable-development/sustainable-development-sustainable-operations.htm, accessed 5 September 2010.

Office of Government Commerce (OGC) (2010) 'Government delivery', http://www.ogc.gov.uk/sustainability_programme_progress.asp, accessed 30 August 2010.

OGC (n.d.) 'What's new', http://www.ogc.gov.uk/index.asp, accessed 5 September 2010.

Ross, A. (1998) 'Monitoring environmental performance in government: The role of the new Environmental Audit Committee of the House of Commons', *Public Law*, Summer: 190–200.

Ross, A. (2000) 'Greening government: Tales from the new sustainability watchdog', *Journal of Environmental Law*, 12(2): 175–96.

Ross, A. (2003) 'Is the environment getting squeezed out of sustainable development?', *Public Law*, Summer: 249–59.

Ross, A. (2005) 'The UK approach to delivering sustainable development in government: A case study in joined up working', *Journal of Environmental Law*, 17(1): 27–49.

Rubin, E.L. (1989) 'Law and legislation in the administrative state', *Columbia Law Review*, 89(3): 369–426.

Scott, E. (2003) *Scottish Parliamentary Debates Official Report*, column 2986, Edinburgh: Scottish Parliament.

Scottish Executive (2002) *Meeting the Needs: Priorities, Actions and Targets for Sustainable Development in Scotland*, Edinburgh: Scottish Executive Environment Group.

Scottish Executive (2003) *Sustaining Our Working Environment Annual Report 2002/2003*, Edinburgh: Scottish Executive.

Scottish Executive (2004) *Environment Group Indicators of Sustainable Development for Scotland: Progress Report 200 Paper 2004/3*, Edinburgh: Scottish Executive Environment Group.

Scottish Government (2010) *Scottish Government Estate Environmental Performance: Annual Report 2008/09*, Edinburgh: Scottish Government.

Scottish Government (n.d.) 'Performance at a glance', http://www.scotland.gov.uk/About/scotPerforms/performance, accessed 4 March 2011.

Scottish Parliament (2008) Official Report, 24 January, Debate on motion S3M-1204 on the Scottish biodiversity strategy report, Col 5510-5536, Edinburgh: SCPB.

Scottish Parliament, Rural Affairs and Environment Committee (n.d.) Meeting Papers and Official Reports, http://www.scottish.parliament.uk/s3/committees/rae/meetings.htm, accessed 24 March 2011.

Scottish Parliament Transport, Infrastructure and Climate Change Committee (TICC) (2010) Finance and Sustainable Growth Official Report 20th Meeting 2010, Session 3, Column 3269, Edinburgh: Scottish Parliament.

Scottish Parliament TICC (2011) Sustainable Development Official Report 1st Meeting 2011, Session 3, Column 3604, Edinburgh: Scottish Parliament.

Sustainable Development Commission (SDC) (2004) *Shows Promise. But Must Try Harder: An Assessment by the Sustainable Development Commission of the Government's Reported Progress on Sustainable Development over the Past Five Years*, London: SDC.

SDC (2008) *SDAP Progress Reports: The SDC's Key Findings*, London: SDC.

SDC (2009) Sustainable Operations on the Government Estate (SOGE) Assessment 2009, http://www.sd commission.org.uk/soge2009/, accessed 25 May 2011.

SDC (2010) *Becoming the 'Greenest Government Ever'? Sustainable Development in Government Reporting Period 2006–2009*, London: SDC.

SDC (n.d.) 'Who we are', http://www.sd-commission.org.uk/pages/about-us.html, accessed 24 March 2011.

Sustainable Development Commission Scotland (SDCS) (2007) *Sustainable Development: A Review of Progress by the Scottish Executive*, Edinburgh: SDCS.

SDCS (2008) *Sustainable Development: A Review of Progress by the Scottish Government*, Edinburgh: SDCS.

SDCS (2009a) *National Planning Framework 2: Paper Supporting Evidence to the Transport, Infrastructure and Climate Change (TICC) Committee*, Edinburgh: SDCS.

SDCS (2009b) *Sustainable Development: Third Annual Assessment of Progress by the Scottish Government*, Edinburgh: SDCS.

SDCS (2010) *Sustainable Development: Fourth Annual Assessment of Progress by the Scottish Government*, Edinburgh: SDCS.

Sustainable Development Commission Wales (SDCW) (2009) *Sustainable Development in Government Wales 2009*, Cardiff: SDCW.

Wales Audit Office (2009) *Coastal Erosion and Tidal Flooding Risks in Wales*, Cardiff: WAO.

Welsh Assembly Government (WAG) (2009a) *One Wales: One Planet: The Sustainable Development Scheme of the Welsh Assembly Government*, Cardiff: Welsh Assembly Government.

WAG (2009b) *Green Dragon Standard Environmental Report 2008–09*, Cardiff: Welsh Assembly Government.

WAG (2010) *One Wales – One Planet: Annual Report 2009–2010*, Cardiff: Welsh Assembly Government.

11 'Shows promise, but must try harder' – taking stock of implementation in the UK

This chapter takes its name from a report conducted by the Sustainable Development Commission in 2004 and, following the analysis in the previous chapters in Part II, it still rings true. The analysis shows that the UK and devolved administrations have made considerable efforts over the years to implement sustainable development and that this has resulted in some progress. Indeed, the UK's progress, compared to other countries', is enviable. However, these efforts have not been enough to ensure genuine sustainable development. As described in Chapter 9, the indicators for sustainable development show that the progress in each of the administrations appears to be mixed, haphazard and in no way sufficient to resolve the challenges facing the Earth. By May 2011 the Northern Ireland Executive had still not produced a set of sustainable development indicators. In Scotland, while renewable energy continues to grow and some business and education indicators also show positive trends, many public health indicators continue to be poor, some areas of economic performance are weak and there is no evidence of a narrowing of the gap between the highest and lowest earners. Greenhouse gas emissions were down by over 6 per cent in 2007 from the previous year but long-term trends on emissions are far below what the Government requires to meet the Climate Change (Scotland) Act 2009 SDCS, 2009: 41).

Jonathon Porritt (2009: 10), the former chairman of the UK Sustainable Development Commission (SDC), in his 2009 review of the standing of sustainable development in the UK, concluded that 'the reality, as I see it, is that the mainstreaming of sustainable development in the UK, from the margins to the centre of government, is indeed underway, but is still moving too slowly in most respects'.

Indeed, the consensus is that worldwide progress to date towards sustainable development has been at best slow and in many cases regressive. The European Commission's 2009 review notes that, despite considerable efforts to include action for sustainable development in major EU policy areas, unsustainable trends persist and the EU still needs to intensify its efforts (European Commission, 2009: 15). While the 2009 Eurostat report on EU progress towards its sustainable development indicators found moderately favourable changes for 'energy consumption of transport', 'healthy life years' and 'employment rate of older workers', both headline indicators of climate change and energy were moderately unfavourable, and trends in the conservation of fish stocks and the EU's official development assistance were clearly unfavourable (Eurostat, 2009: 9–10).

While a 'sustainable society' in reality remains a distant utopia, as noted in Chapter 3, research in a wide range of disciplines has developed proven pathways for implementing sustainable development. One of the main objectives of this book is to assess why the UK and many other countries have yet to successfully grasp hold of sustainability, and to explore ways of promoting, and if need be, compelling, progress towards sustainable development.

The previous chapters in Part II use four criteria (common understanding, leadership, stakeholder involvement and knowledge management, and integrative mechanisms) to analyze the UK's journey towards sustainable development over time and to analyze the various techniques, principles, mechanisms and institutions that both the central and devolved Governments in the UK have relied on to push the agenda forward. This chapter takes stock of the progress made by the UK and the devolved administrations to date in implementing sustainable development, based on these criteria. It begins by bringing together the findings from each of the earlier chapters in Part II, before moving to extract and analyze the common trends and factors that are hindering full implementation.

Vision and strategy

Since 2005, *One future – different paths: The UK's shared framework for sustainable development* has provided a unifying, UK-wide framework for sustainable development, and the individual strategies under this framework are all relatively modern and progressive in considering environmental limits and long-term effects (HM Government *et al.*, 2005). In research studies covering the strategies of several countries, the UK strategies have always tended to do quite well. For example, a review produced by Swanson *et al.* (2004) found that the thematic approach used in all the UK (and EU) strategies means that the strategies cover most aspects of sustainable development and are capable of acting as logical frameworks for decision making. The review highlighted the extent to which the UK strategy contained links to local levels through guidance or sub-national coordination. In a later review, Swanson and Pinter observe that:

> the UK SDS (2005) continues to be one of the good practice examples from a strategy co-ordination perspective. Not only is it comprehensive, it also involves multiple levels of government in the development of the strategy and therefore speaks to each level. The strategy includes a comprehensive framework intended to guide policy across the UK government. As well as nationally articulated strategy individual departments are asked to develop their own sustainable development strategies within the context of the more far-reaching UK Strategy.
>
> (Swanson and Pinter, 2007: 34)

Two key procedural factors are, however, missing from most of the processes used by the UK administrations for developing their strategies. First, it is only in Northern Ireland that responsibility for the sustainable development strategy rests at the highest level and, second, it is only Wales that currently has any legislative underpinning for its strategic process.

Ordinarily, these sustainable development strategies should be capable of delivering change. However, research shows that the UK strategies all lack influence and their use in practice is sporadic at best. Despite enviable strategic documentation, the UK approach is not delivering. Decisions continue to be made with little regard to the principles in the framework and strategies. The reasons can all be traced back to inconsistency in the application of both the UK Shared Framework and the individual strategies as well as their respective objectives and procedures. The reasons for inconsistency all relate back to varying priorities between decision makers and misunderstandings about the meaning of sustainable development, its role and its applicability. More specifically, this manifests itself in several ways.

First, some administrations appear more committed to the values, objectives, priorities and approach set out in the Shared Framework than others. While the UK published its strategy on the same day as the Framework, and Wales (due to its statutory obligation) already had a very similar scheme in place, it took the Scottish Executive seven months and the Northern Ireland Office over a year to publish their respective strategies. Moreover, the Scottish strategy was later completely replaced by *The Government's Economic Strategy* (the *Economic Strategy*) (Scottish Government, 2007) and a single objective of 'sustainable economic growth', which did little to improve the public's understanding of sustainable development, especially since it took two years for the Scottish Government to even attempt to realign itself with the rest of the UK by explaining how its unique approach fitted within the UK Framework (Scottish Government, 2010).

Problems also remain in the use of the term 'sustainable development' by governments, which leads to confusion and ignorance on how sustainable development relates to particular policy areas, sectors and partnerships. Flynn *et al.* (2008: 21) list several examples, including:

- The use of sustainable development in a standard list of crosscutting themes such as equality, social justice and bilingualism. This confusion is exacerbated by the issue of whether sustainable development should be given 'primacy' over the other issues
- Tokenistic use of sustainable development with no meaningful explanation of what this entails
- Confusing terminology related to environmental sustainability, longevity and robustness
- A limited number of defined action/process responsibilities related to sustainable development and a weak messaging on the need for change.

This concern is worsening under the UK coalition Government as inappropriate and inconsistent uses of the terms 'sustainable' and 'sustainable development' are littered throughout its 2011 Budget. For example, the Budget states that the

Government will 'introduce a powerful new presumption in favour of sustainable development, so that the default is "yes"' (HM Treasury, 2011: 3).

A further danger is explained by Blair and Evans (2004: 41) as follows: 'For sustainability to be mainstreamed, the frameworks of corporate management, the processes and specific tools (targets and indicators), audit, review and inspection procedures all need to be appropriately aligned and geared to a common sustainability set of criteria'. Currently this is not the case. Indeed, the process for the development, use and review of the strategies is best described as ad hoc and inconsistent. Even in Wales, the process set out in the strategy is vague with, for example, no details provided about forms of consultation. The acceptability and usefulness of any strategy is dependent on its legitimacy. While the content is very important, the procedures used for its development, use and review are equally important. Thus, a strategy whose development process makes sense to the public and stakeholders will be widely accepted as legitimate, and this will improve its policy relevance and usability. Chapter 4 has shown mixed results in relation to the formality and breadth of stakeholder involvement in the implementation of sustainable development in the UK. As the UK and Welsh administrations seem to be getting the balance right between consultation and delivery, it is unfortunate to see Scotland and Northern Ireland erring at the two extremes.

Indeed, given the importance of other mechanisms being linked to the strategy, most of the difficulties and criticisms surrounding the other mechanisms would be resolved if the criticisms directed at the development, use and review of the strategy itself were addressed. Ideally, as argued in the next chapter, every decision needs to use sustainable development as a template and sustainable development should be a 'whole systems' concept, providing the forum or 'table' to which important and more concrete objectives and values can be brought (Ross, 2010). This is not limited to the production of the strategy or its review. Used in this way, the role of the strategy is to provide guidance as to how sustainable development operates in any given decision-making process in order to ensure that certain objectives and values influence it (Ross, 2009, 2010).

The truth, however, is that all this depends on good leadership which prioritises sustainability, and leadership is the most essential criterion for delivering real change. As the UN Commission on Sustainable Development (CSD) concludes:

> Sound leadership and good governance is necessary for effective strategy development. This is key to guaranteeing that the policy and institutional changes that the strategy entails are affected, the necessary financial resources committed and institutions assume full responsibility for implementation of the strategy in their respective areas.
>
> (Division for Sustainable Development, UNDESA, 2002: 17)

Leadership and commitment

Chapter 5 lists numerous examples of mixed messages from leaders across the UK. Sustainable development requires a cultural change across departments and across levels of government, both in terms of integration and in terms of new priorities and goals. As aptly put by Schout and Jordan, 'all this begs the question of what comes first the chicken of political leadership or the egg of administrative instruments to translate it into practice?' (Schout and Jordan, 2008: 63). The conclusion from Chapter 5 is that we need both to happen concurrently now.

First, transformational leaders are needed, who are able to get the most out of their followers and indeed, encourage leadership amongst them. As Porritt observes:

> the rapid development of grassroots campaigns such as the Transition Towns suggests that just such a constituency is growing strongly. What's more, there is a large body of advocates for SD in business that is simply getting on with valuable work that could be accelerated and expanded with consistent political leadership.
>
> (Porritt, 2009: 21)

Unfortunately, our leaders are faced with mounting short-term pressures, yet must address long-term challenges. As such, any bud of sustainable development leadership needs to be supported and mainstreamed as soon as possible by institutional structures, as well as by training, advice and grassroots pressure. There is not enough of this type of support and protection in the UK in 2011. Indeed, progress on implementing sustainable development appears to be unravelling as the coalition Government aggressively seeks to reduce debt and increase growth with insufficient consideration of how this impacts on other aspects of sustainable development such as the health and wellbeing of the planet, its people and both intra-generational and intergenerational equity.

Thus, institutional protection is essential to provide the necessary support for transformational leadership. The value of high-level cabinet committees to provide the leadership for the agenda and reinforce this through a network of the Green ministers, with ministerial representation from every department and a further network of green civil servants working down from the permanent secretaries themselves, would support this change. This approach works because a clear line of responsibility exists between the centre and the departments.

The difficulty is that many of these excellent mechanisms which were introduced in the recent past and held up around the world as innovative and exemplary, such as the Green Ministers' Committe and the SDC, are slowly being side-stepped or discontinued. The heavy hand of the UK coalition Government in cutting funding to the SDC and the Royal Commission on Environmental Pollution, and ignoring much of the advice of the Environmental Audit Committee of the House of Commons (EAC) shows that sustainable development goals must also be protected from a lack of leadership through clear targets with timetables, legal obligations with real consequences, and direct lines of accountability (Batty, 2011). They need to be further supported by the appropriate training for leaders at all levels and across administrations using the joint committee structures.

Opportunities to communicate about sustainable development must be developed and maintained through high-level committees and intergovernmental groups, as well as partnerships. Innovations in sustainable development should be rewarded and protected from the pressures that the electoral system brings. Chapter 13 explores the reintroduction and protection of such measures in more detail.

Thus, although they are important stakeholders in the implementation process for sustainable development, our political leaders are not necessarily the most important ones. Especially given the unpredictable leadership for sustainable development of our leaders, it is imperative to involve stakeholders to push us towards sustainability and to use and manage knowledge responsibly and effectively.

Stakeholder involvement and efficient knowledge management

As noted by the Organisation for Economic Co-operation and Development (OECD):

> Scientific knowledge should be the basis for raising awareness in different constituencies and increasing the visibility of the sustainable development concept within and outside government (including in the media). However, since conclusive scientific evidence will not be available for many of the decisions to be made, it is crucial to ensure that sufficient debate occurs to confront values, perceptions and views, in order to take decisions that are more universally acceptable.
>
> (OECD, 2002: 3)

Hence, the views of stakeholders and the public need to be sought to promote better, more acceptable and more easily implemented decision making, and this knowledge, together with scientific data, needs to be efficiently managed. The complicated, complex and unpredictable nature of sustainable development information can make this difficult. Moreover, wide participation is sometimes not desirable. The Better Regulation agenda, for example, sets out other significant good governance requirements which often conflict with wide participation, including the timeliness of decision making, certainty in decision making and ensuring clear lines of responsibility and accountability. These require governments to judge their interventions in the policy debate appropriately – and choosing the appropriate approach is not easy.

Chapter 6 set out many examples of innovation and good practice, of stakeholder and public involvement and efficient knowledge management occurring in the approaches used in the UK and devolved administrations to deliver sustainable development. Unfortunately, these are often ad hoc instances, reliant on individuals and unsupported by review or monitoring mechanisms.

For example, while effective stakeholder involvement often simply requires the public to be informed or educated, at other times, it is necessary for the public to be more actively involved and their views fed into the decision-making process more directly. While the UK generally does well with the former approach, moving on to the latter has proved difficult. The participation exercise can become simply a hoop that decision makers need to go through and then makes no difference at all to the ultimate decision. This can occur due to late consultation, a failure to give any responses to consultation or ignoring the work of a partnership in favour of a unilateral decision. In these instances, the involvement is simply tokenism in that it does not really involve the views of stakeholders. It may improve the amount of information available to the decision maker but, often, if the decision is already made, it does not even achieve that objective (Arnstein, 1969: 217). The Scottish Government's consultations on its *Economic Strategy* and subsequent related policies are clear illustrations of consultation in name only.

A further danger is that so much time is spent consulting and involving stakeholders that no decisions are made and nothing gets done. To date, in Northern Ireland, there has been a lot of consultation for two different strategies, with very little action. The 2010 Northern Ireland strategy acknowledges this fact:

> We have consulted extensively in developing this document and listened to the views of stakeholders, but that is not enough. We need stakeholders (individuals, community groups, businesses and organizations) to take steps in driving delivery. We are now looking to those stakeholders, and to those working inside and outside of Government, to contribute to the attainment of the targets set within our Implementation Plan and support the priority areas for action.
>
> (Northern Ireland Executive, 2010)

Where the public or stakeholders are empowered with decision-making capabilities, it is vital that controls are in place to ensure they do not ignore sustainability altogether and choose unsustainable options. Public participation needs to be balanced against the need for sound science. The challenge for efficient knowledge management is to find or generate quality information within the needed timeframe, sift through it to find the information needed for the particular purpose, and share that information among a wide variety of stakeholders and the wider public in a meaningful way so that policymaking and decision making is informed, timely and as certain as possible.

Combined top-down and bottom-up approaches which rely on both expert knowledge and participation are possible, but this takes time and requires careful planning and support. However, where the mechanisms of decision making are altered to include experts, stakeholders, the public or even multiple government actors, this change must also be reflected in the accountability mechanisms (Performance and Innovation Unit, 2000; Ross, 2005).

Central to all of these challenges is the fact that poor leadership can easily undo much of the good work achieved by stakeholder involvement and efficient knowledge management. As such, stakeholder involvement and knowledge management need to be included in the holistic mechanisms put in place to deliver the aims in the national sustainable development strategy (NSDS) and based on the substantive principles contained in the strategy. They also need to be supported by review mechanisms and, where necessary, obligations which ensure certain procedures are followed, regardless of any changes in the whims of leadership.

Integration

Chapter 7 concludes that the integration of environmental protection and, more broadly, sustainable development into the activities of government is, in some respects, one of the easier tasks of the OECD criteria. There is a wide range of tools for achieving this integration, and often these tools can be introduced without having to expressly set out allegiance to a particular 'vision' of sustainable development, especially one which runs counter to the traditional pro-growth model. This is especially true in relation to addressing the sustainability of government operations. However, in relation to the broader cultural changes that integration requires, the findings in Chapters 7–10 show an inconsistent picture.

As noted by Schout and Jordan (2008: 53), most public sector coordination relies on bargaining and interaction between actors, yet this tends not to work in relation to environmental protection, for three main reasons. First, environmental quality is a public good and there is therefore little incentive for actors to routinely take environmental protection into account, and officials in sectoral ministries will not enter into conflict over environmental matters, as they do not see these as relevant or important enough to fight over. The result is that economic aspects continue to dominate decision making. Another difficulty is that environmental concerns tend to be allocated to weaker ministries, and as a result, negotiations are dominated by the immediate objectives of stronger sectoral ministries such as finance, agriculture and transport. Finally, asking other sectors to take the environment into account is also unlikely to have an enduring impact, as this requires ministries to act in ways which often deviate away from direct achievement of their main objectives (Schout and Jordan, 2008: 53). However, all of these three issues can be overcome using the right tools.

The OECD has advocated that having a variety of integration elements to pursue coordination at different levels is a necessary, but not sufficient, condition for greater integration (OECD, 2002). For example, the creation of crosscutting units, ministerial and other high-level committees to deal with specific issues both within and between administrations encourages working across organizations. The UK has often been proactive in introducing new mechanisms and yet, these often do not work well in combination. So for example, no strategic environmental assessment was conducted on the Scottish Government's *Economic Strategy* and, as detailed in Chapter 9, too many of the sustainable development indicators are unrelated to specific aims in the relevant strategy. The UK and devolved administrations' track records with policy and institutional tools

(Chapter 7), legal obligations (Chapter 8), indicators (Chapter 9) and reporting and scrutiny mechanisms (Chapter 10) are discussed separately below.

Policy and institutional integration tools

The traditional sectoral working of the UK public sector and those processes encapsulated in the term 'departmentalism' often run counter to environmental policy integration (EPI) or, more generally, the joined-up thinking required for sustainable development.

In the UK, some integration methods have been more successful than others. While significant progress has been made at improving the sustainability of government estate and operations, the UK administrations have had only very limited success at integrating environmental and sustainable development factors into policymaking and budgeting. For example, a report by the National Audit Office on regulatory impact assessments found that the coverage of sustainability issues in the assessments was limited, thus supporting claims that this more integrated form of appraisal was failing to adequately protect the environment (NAO, 2006).

Consistent with the findings of Jacob *et al.* (2008: 42), the UK has preferred to 'develop policy objectives and frameworks that flag the importance of EPI without developing operational structures and procedures that significantly alter the distribution of power among the various actors involved or decisively change the prevailing political and administrative routines of policy making'. Jacob *et al.* also note that 'the harder and more consequential instruments that make the environment a main concern for all sectoral policy makers are adopted less frequently and with far less enthusiasm'.

One success has been changes introduced at the institutional level. Thus, the creation of one single government department in Scotland, the introduction of a single Permanent Secretary in the devolved administrations and the creation of the Department of Energy and Climate Change in the UK administration, are all examples of how merging government functions can improve integration. Moreover, the mergers may give the traditionally weak 'environment department' or environment minister more responsibility, and hence, more power and clout in government and in cabinet.

Generally, the successful introduction of 'harder mechanisms' has been in relation to the operations of government and the workings of the government estate. The UK Government's sustainable development in government (SDiG) programme and its predecessor sustainable operations on the government estate (SOGE) in particular have set ever-increasing targets, introduced tough reporting and review processes, and in many areas, delivered real results. Indeed, by 2008/09 the SOGE framework targets had helped the UK Government improve its energy efficiency by 7.9 per cent, reduce carbon emissions from offices by 10 per cent, reduce waste by 13.7 per cent and water use by 19.9 per cent (SDC, 2011: 24). The UK success has been held up to the other administrations to encourage them to follow suit, and this demonstrates the value of imparting information across administrations.

The UK needs to apply its knowledge of integration in operations to policy. Of course, departments can improve the environmental or sustainability performance of their procurement policies, transport and resource use without having to engage with other departments or coordinate their actions with theirs. In this context, all that is needed is an internal shift which prioritizes ecological concerns in relation to day-to-day actions such as recycling and using video-conferencing for meetings instead of travelling, which often do not 'define' either the department or its staff. In contrast, policy integration has proven to be much harder, as addressing sustainable development concerns in this context requires departments to re-examine their priorities in relation to their overall purpose or objectives. Controversially, this may require that ecological considerations take precedence in certain instances over consumer demand for new airports and roads, the needs of local fishermen or a decision to use a particular weapon. Moreover, successful policy integration often requires coordination between different parts of government and even between governments.

It is unsurprising that progress in relation to 'greening' budgetary cycles in the UK has been mixed. Some progress is being made, especially in relation to the climate change mechanisms such as the climate change levy and investment in low-carbon technologies. However, experiments involving the introduction of sustainable development into the budgetary processes, such as through spending reviews, have been short-lived and quickly watered down. Policies aimed at environmental improvements or sustainable development are regularly dropped when they become politically or economically unpopular. For example, in 2011, the UK coalition Government not only suspended the fuel duty escalator, which would have meant an additional 1 per cent rise in petrol costs on top of inflation for the duration of that Parliament, but also cut fuel duty by 1p. The inflation-only increase is also being delayed (HM Treasury, 2011: 4). This duty is at least partly aimed at reducing addiction to private cars. Undoubtedly, the duty is unduly harsh on those in rural areas and on businesses and public services which must rely on road transport, such as the post. However, alternatives do not appear to be debated. For example, introducing tax differentials in the duty for different users would address the unfairness, while still tackling the problems of unnecessary car trips to the local shops, single occupier journeys, and so on.

The fact that many of the instruments are deployed in a very superficial and ad hoc manner, with little attention to diagnosing underlying problems, would certainly seem to support the theory that there is an undeniable tendency to deploy the 'easier' instruments (such as missions statements, weak teams and specification of task), than some of the more 'difficult' ones (such as rules and specification of outputs) (Schout and Jordan, 2008: 65). The UK's long-term poor record with policy-based requirements for environmental appraisal and more recently, sustainable development appraisals, is clear evidence of such mechanisms being ignored or misused.

Some harder mechanisms do exist in relation to policymaking. For example, the use of action plans to support objectives set out in the relevant strategy has been a major step in the right direction and these are now used in all the administrations. The loss of the SDC is significant here, as it was the SDC which regularly reviewed progress on these action plans and this was a key driver in improving policy integration.

Another 'harder mechanism' aimed at policy integration and operations is giving departmental officials clear responsibilities and incentives to engage with environmental integration initiatives, in order to think beyond their department's core sectoral interests. This has already been done at the UK level, and SDiG targets have been added to the performance goals for all Permanent Secretaries. This is a move in the right direction, but these could be further integrated into many more job descriptions, together with obligations to be involved in environmental coordination initiatives on a daily basis (Schout and Jordan, 2008: 265).

Unfortunately, the analysis in Chapter 7 also suggests that even when the UK administrations have introduced harder mechanisms, such as strategic environmental assessments, impact assessments and pre-legislative scrutiny, they have been seldom or restrictively used, and have failed to make headway towards putting sustainable development or the environment into the heart of government policymaking. Instead, they seem to have been more about making the right noises at times when the environment or sustainable development were high on the political agenda. Furthermore, some of the more effective harder mechanisms often do not last the test of time, as, especially in difficult times, new governments will remove the instigators of real change (such as the SDC) to protect conventional economic, and often short-term, objectives.

Responsibility for sustainable development is shared among the levels of government in the UK, and successful implementation requires intergovernmental coordination of environmental and sustainable development policy. In their review of progress towards sustainable development in Wales in 2006, Flynn and Marsden found and suggested that 'Even where relations with UK government are well developed there is little if any dialogue on the subject of sustainable development'. To address the deficit, they recommended, among other things, that a dialogue on sustainable development should be developed between the UK Government, the devolved administrations and England. They also suggested existing forums should be revised or new ones developed, within the constraints of devolution, to enable different tiers of government in the UK to explore and further develop the UK and devolved administrations' sustainable development agenda. This would allow all parties to contribute fully to the UK-wide dialogue on sustainability (Flynn and Marsden, 2006: 73–4).

The process of replacing the 2005 UK Shared Framework for Sustainable Development, which was jointly produced by all four UK administrations, will be a true test of how the current administrations can work together to produce something meaningful. Once again, the issue of leadership arises. Effective integration must be based on a system of mutual interdependence between the bottom and the top. Leadership from the top is needed to override departmental sectoral interests and yet the leadership needs to be compelled into action through pressure and scrutiny from environmental groups, public bodies, the wider public and, possibly, the courts.

Legal obligations

Law, as a social construct with the capacity to compel action, may offer solutions to some of the challenges to policy integration described above. As noted in Chapter 8, sustainable development is being referred to in more and more UK and Scottish legislation and even in some Northern Ireland legislation. Indeed, recently, both the Scottish and Northern Ireland Executives have experimented, albeit tentatively, with general substantive duties in the Northern Ireland (Miscellaneous Provisions) Act 2006 and the Climate Change (Scotland) Act 2009. The Northern Ireland (Miscellaneous Provisions) Act 2006 s. 25, for example, requires departments and district councils to exercise their functions in the manner they consider best calculated to promote the achievement of sustainable development. It also appears in measures of the Welsh Assembly.

This reflects an acceptance of sustainable development as a policy tool and has been encouraged by devolution and the increased status of the concept at European Community level. Probably due to its vague and evolutionary nature, none of the statutes make any serious attempts to define sustainable development. Instead, the provisions rely on tailored Government guidance which by permitting some flexibility provides little consistency between public bodies or regulatory regimes. Sustainable development has not achieved the status of a legal principle as such in UK law; however, it does appear in a variety of legal forms, including duties, objectives and procedural requirements.

Different statutes refer to sustainable development in different ways, and the obligation placed on public bodies in relation to sustainable development also varies. There appears to be no hierarchy between these different forms. Some aims are very powerful, others much less so, and the same is true for the duties. Importantly, different formulations seem to create very different legal impacts. Some of the provisions are almost purely symbolic, some are simply material considerations to be taken into account in the decision, some may create a legal rule dictating how a decision is to be made and others create a mandatory procedural requirement (see Chapter 8).

The most common provisions relating to sustainable development are duties. While the more recent provisions are much clearer than their predecessors, there is still no standard form of duty although the most common form of words is 'to contribute to the achievement of sustainable development'. The strength of the provisions varies enormously, but all involve some element of discretion. There are some statutes in which sustainable development is the primary duty, but in most cases, it is one of several duties or objectives. Some statutes include qualifications and mechanisms for prioritizing between duties, but in others, it is left to the decision maker. There is some evidence that, in some statutes, the sustainable development duty could act as the mechanism for balancing other duties or objectives. In these cases, it could be interpreted as a legal rule and provide a much-needed framework for decision making. The courts have demonstrated a willingness to accept sustainable development as a material consideration in decisions; however, drawing on the experience of similar types of provisions, a stronger interpretation may still be a way off (see Chapter 8).

Many provisions do not include any obvious enforcement mechanisms but may still be effective from a more symbolic perspective – acting to educate, inform and heighten awareness. Also, the provision and any breach thereof may attract the attention of the public, interest groups, parliamentary committees, or a higher level of government and result in more informal, ad hoc enforcement. Judicial review is possible, but is only appropriate in those rare instances where a public body has acted irrationally, illegally or procedurally improperly. It is also generally reactive, costly and time-consuming.

Increasingly, legislators are attaching procedural requirements to sustainable development provisions. These can be obligations to produce or follow guidance, regulations or directions, strategies or reports, or they may require notice, audit or publicity. A failure to comply with a statutory procedure is much easier to enforce and monitor, not only under judicial review, but also, importantly, by central government, interest groups and the public. Thus, the procedures can significantly enhance the potential impact of a given provision. More procedural monitoring of the sustainable development duties would improve their impact. This is also true for the procedures themselves. It makes no sense to require the production of a report, for example, if there are no consequences for failing to do so or no obligation to act on its findings, publicize it or allow others to comment on, discuss or scrutinize it.

Chapter 8 concludes that the statutes add little to the overall understanding or coherent thought about what exactly sustainable development means or its role in governance. Confusion remains as to whether sustainable development is simply a matter for environmental policymakers, whether it is the same as climate change, and to what extent it is compatible with the pursuit of economic growth. Moreover, uncertainty exists as to the role of sustainable development in all forms of decision making. Although flexibility may be appropriate for individual agencies in their specific contexts, there needs to be much more clarity as to the overall role of sustainable development in government.

For statutory sustainable development provisions to be more than simply symbolic, ideally, there should be some statutory (often formal) means to monitor and review compliance, using administrative, political, legal or other mechanisms. For example where a statute requires a report to be produced, this obligation should be accompanied by an obligation for it to be published, reviewed by an independent body and/or placed before the legislature where it can be debated in plenary or in committee. At present, while some statutes do this, many do not (see Chapter 8). The role of procedural obligations in this context should not be underestimated. Robust procedural general duties on public bodies for each administration could provide some consistency. As discussed in detail in Chapters 8 and 13, the procedural obligations set out in the Government of Wales Act 2006 to regularly produce and review a scheme for sustainable development provide an excellent starting point in this regard, despite not being accompanied by substantive duties in relation to sustainable development.

The potential impact of general substantive duties could also be significant in providing a mandate for public sector bodies to direct their activities to achieve positive sustainable development outcomes and to do so without compromising their other existing statutory obligations. However, both in Northern Ireland and Scotland (see above), the duties have not proven to be effective. First, by being hidden away in unrelated statutes, the provisions do not even manage to have any symbolic effect. Second, they are not supported by the appropriate procedures. At a very minimum, these general duties, like their specific counterparts discussed above, need to be supported by strong procedures for consultation, reporting, monitoring and review which are ideally linked to a clear vision of sustainable development set out in guidance which is consistently used. Finally, like many of the specific provisions, at the moment, these general duties provide no guidance as to priority.

As is discussed in later chapters, where the sustainable development duty is intended to create a framework to aid decision making, the legislation needs to be more explicit about this role to encourage the courts to recognize it. The current piecemeal approach to sustainable development does lead to inconsistency. Moreover, if these provisions are to have any meaning, a clear and consistent vision and interpretation of sustainable development is needed. Even then, research shows that duties alone are insufficient to ensure progress in mainstreaming sustainable development. Leadership on sustainable development and mechanisms for scrutinizing the delivery of the duties are essential (Cussons, 2006).

Indicators

From the analysis in Chapter 9, it is clear that consistently, the UK, Welsh and Scottish Governments have demonstrated their commitment to the development and review of sustainable development indicators. This commitment to date has not been demonstrated by the Northern Ireland Executive, as not a single set had been produced by the spring of 2011. It is also safe to say that outside Northern Ireland, sustainable development indicators are an established component of UK policy and that they are considered to be essential means of measuring progress towards the objectives set out in the relevant sustainable development strategy.

Chapter 9 concludes that the indicator sets are not leading to the improvements and progress necessary to move us to a sustainable UK. It notes that the existence of negative and concerning trends year after year in the indicators for UK, Scottish and Welsh does not appear to have had any influence on government behaviour. The UK is not alone in this regard and based on their study of indicators in the USA, Innes and Booher (2000: 174) observe that 'Millions of dollars and much time . . . has been wasted on preparing national, state and local indicator reports that remain on the shelf gathering dust'. It appears that bad news is not enough to compel action. This is indicative of the low priority afforded sustainable development, the sustainable development strategies and the indicators within the administrations.

Another possible reason is that despite the stated relationship with the relevant sustainable development strategies, research into indicator sets has regularly criticized the sets as being insufficiently linked to the policy objectives set out in the relevant sustainable development strategies.

When the problems relating to the scientific credibility of the indicators are combined with the difficulties relating to governance, the result is that indicators often lack policy relevance. They are not used by stakeholders to monitor progress or by policymakers to publicly promote the sustainable development agenda, let alone drive policy forward. At the UN, the Division for Sustainable Development recently reported that:

> While sustainability indicators, indices and reporting systems have gained growing popularity in both the public and private sectors, their effectiveness in influencing actual policy and practices often remained limited. The gap between the large *potential* but small *actual* influence suggests that indicators could play a stronger role in articulating and tracking progress towards sustainability in a wide range of settings.
>
> (UN, 2006: 4)

In addition, this lack of influence could be attributed to the fact that neither the national sustainable development indicators nor the NSDS has any statutory footing at UK or devolved level. Thus, like many of the other policy initiatives discussed in Part II of this volume that are not part of UK law, while generally accepted, indicators lack the legitimacy and authority that come with legal recognition. Moreover, while the processes for their selection, development, use and review are much improved under the UK's new Sustainable Development programme (HM Government *et al.*, 2005) these lack the benefits of legal formality, as they are neither binding nor widely publicized.

A holistic process is essential for the successful implementation of sustainable development. What gets measured gets done and, as a result, indicators ought to play an important role as they are the tools which measure success and failure. As discussed above, we need to be sure we measure the right things and improvements in indicator selection are necessary. However, this is not enough and we need to reward success, learn from failure and correct it. Indicators can provide important information needed to generate sustainable outcomes by measuring progress and then rewarding success and correcting failure. However, they are only one part of what must be a holistic, iterative and, arguably, compulsory process.

Reporting and monitoring

Chapter 10 concludes that effective scrutiny depends heavily on quality reporting of progress, both internally and externally. Regular reporting on sustainable development in government operations is now standard in most of the administrations. For instance, the Office for National Statistics now validates many of the quantitative reports produced by the administrations and the relevant audit offices also use their powers to conduct value-for-money audits.

Worryingly, there remains an apathy about reporting on sustainable development policy and, in particular, the use of environmental, sustainability and the more general impact appraisals. The loss of the SDC is significant here. In reviewing departments' sustainable development action plans (SDAPs) and their progress towards achieving the strategies, the SDC played a primary role in monitoring and reporting of policy. In the context of operations, not only did the SDC report annually on progress, it used these reports to compare progress among the administrations and promote the extension of the UK's very successful SDiG programme for operations to the devolved administrations. One needs to question who will produce all of this important independent data in future.

Crosscutting objectives like sustainable development, for which numerous departments, agencies and organizations share responsibility, require changes in the accountability structures to reflect integrated responsibilities and roles. If the component parts are jointly accountable to the same body, then this may force them to cooperate with one another and with the centre. In fact, this pressure from the outside may be the most effective incentive to work together. This outside pressure comes from reports, reviews and league tables produced by international organizations such as the OECD, the CSD or the UN Educational, Scientific and Cultural Organization (UNESCO), non-governmental organizations such as the World Wildlife Fund (WWF). The media and, occasionally, court action can also apply significant pressure. In the UK, while the scrutiny role of the media, academia and interest groups is on the rise, formal scrutiny is provided by the legislatures and their committees. The scrutiny body must have a clear remit and set objectives. The EAC and the Welsh Assembly's Sustainability Committee both provide excellent examples of effective cross-departmental scrutiny on a crosscutting issue – sustainable development in government. However, parliamentary committees are not resourced to produce their own data and reports and must rely on others such as the administrations themselves, the relevant audit and statistics offices and, in the UK, the SDC, to provide them with the necessary information. International and media reviews are often similarly limited. The loss of the SDC reports will have a significant impact on the work of all of the parliamentary committees operating in the UK as well the scrutiny of sustainable development by others such as the media.

Analysis

The earlier chapters in Part II use four criteria (common understanding, leadership, stakeholder involvement and knowledge management, and integrative mechanisms) to analyze the UK's implementation of sustainable development over time, and there is evidence in the UK of good practice and innovation for each of the criteria. Indeed, in many respects 'the UK has the architecture in place to actually start delivering sustainable development' (Porritt, 2009: 56). However, good architecture does not guarantee consistent implementation, nor has it necessarily at present, stood the test of time. Over time, while some good tools, such as the SDiG framework, have been reviewed and improved to become excellent tools, other excellent mechanisms, such as the UK and Scottish Cabinet sub-committees on sustainable development, have fallen victim to political whim or disfavour. The result is a frustratingly slow progression to which, at present, there is little sign of improvement.

This lack of progress cannot be ignored, and the UK – like every other country – needs to face up to some hard truths. The harsh reality, bluntly stated by French (2005: 25–6), is that much of the environmental change that will occur over the next 30 years has already been set in motion by past and current action, and similarly, many of the effects of environmentally relevant policies will not be apparent for 30 or more years. Also, a disproportionate amount of damage will be caused to the world's poorest communities due to the nature of environmental risk (such as desertification and flooding) and the poor's inability to resource appropriate remedial and/or adaptive strategies.

Thus, ignoring the UK's lack of progress is not an option. The Sustainable Development Commission Scotland (SDCS) has reduced the challenges to implementation of sustainable development to three key factors: scale, urgency and interconnectedness, which go to the heart of why progress in achieving sustainable development is so slow. First, the scale of the problem continues to overwhelm any efforts, and positive changes are miniscule compared to the problem. So while some continue to live well beyond their fair share of the Earth's resources, others are suffering. Second, many of these challenges are urgent. Bold and radical decisions will need to be taken to deliver the targets set. Finally, efforts to integrate and connect planning, the built environment and policies pertaining to transport, agriculture, food and waste, remain limited, and without these, delivering sustainable development is impossible (SDCS, 2009: 41).

Some argue that a new ethic is needed. Yet contrary to claims that sustainable development is an ineffectual and meaningless goal incapable of tackling the challenges now facing the Earth, most of the research into its utility has concluded that it could serve a valuable role but only if redefined (Bosselmann, 2008; Ross, 2009).

Indeed, all three of the SDC's challenges can be traced back to three failings in the UK's interpretation of, and status given to, sustainable development. First, the UK's approach to sustainable development has varied over time and between jurisdictions and sectors so that no consistent understanding of sustainable development with clear priorities and a framework for decision making exists in the UK. Second, there are misunderstandings as to the role and importance of sustainable development in decision making, especially in relation to related objectives such as economic growth and tackling climate change, and no mechanisms to support and protect initiatives against political whim and short-termism. Indeed, the final failing is that there is a lack of leadership for sustainable development in the UK to drive sustainability forward. Part III is devoted to addressing each of these failings.

Chapter 12 addresses the first failing which stems from the inappropriateness of weak sustainability as a policy tool. While sustainable development is clearly popular and has proven its resilience as a policy objective in the UK, and its strategies are good strategies, there remains no common understanding of what sustainable development means and how it applies to government action. It is also clear that sustainable development with weak sustainability as its normative core is not a worthy policy objective, and the definition has become so broad that it is in real danger of becoming meaningless and impossible to monitor. More specifically, while the UK's track record of introducing robust reporting and monitoring mechanisms is exemplary, its progress overall has been hampered by the muddled vision of sustainable development which is regularly sidestepped by the leadership, due to changes in political priorities and for short-term gain.

Chapter 12 specifically explores a more modern interpretation of sustainable development. It advocates that sustainable development needs to be redefined in a meaningful way, with clear limits and priorities that focus on ecological sustainability and wellbeing instead of economic growth. Moreover, it makes the case for raising the legal status of ecological sustainability to a fundamental legal principle and for sustainable development to be the central organizing principle of government.

Chapter 13 then considers how to ensure more consistency in the application of sustainable development and provide some alternative suggestions for addressing the second failing. As noted in Chapter 7, even when there is a clear message in the strategy and the links are present and explicit in a strategy, quite often, there are discrepancies within an administration regarding the actual delivery of sustainable development objectives or compliance with procedures. Varying levels of priority for the sustainable development objectives have a knock-on effect on mechanisms such as sustainable development action plans, SDAPs, indicators, public service agreement targets and various appraisal tools. Indeed, while there is plenty of evidence of holistic thinking and good practice across the UK, there has not been the necessary groundswell of public and institutional support needed to apply sustainable development consistently and make it the cultural norm both inside and outside government. The reasons for the inconsistency include varying priorities between decision makers and misunderstandings about the meaning of sustainable development, its role and its applicability. These are then magnified by other influential factors such as path dependency and resource constraints (Porritt, 2009).

Chapter 13 highlights the value of legislation as a tool for social engineering and makes the case that the time has come for sustainable development to receive legal backing to improve consistency. It explores how legislation could make a significant and beneficial difference in the way in which sustainable development strategies are developed, implemented and reviewed. Legislation could crystallize the policy framework already in place, and thus turn what is now, at best, good practice into meaningful legal obligations, supported by monitoring and review mechanisms that impose significant consequences for failure. Finally, legislation could set out how tools such as spending reviews, environmental assessment, procurement practice, research funding and public consultation relate to sustainable development and their role in the overall framework for implementation. This would not only improve consistency but would also support good practice and sustainable leadership.

Poor leadership for sustainable development is the third crucial failing influencing the UK's lack of success in implementing sustainable development. The means to improve sustainability leadership is the subject of some excellent books by experts from other disciplines (Parkin, 2010; Rayment and Smith, 2010). However, our leaders also need legal support. In 2011, the UK coalition Government announced its plans to discontinue SDAPs with no obvious replacement. Together with its decision to cease funding the SDC, these decisions demonstrate how even the most effective mechanisms need protection from political short-termism and how our leaders need support to avoid opting for easy short-term solutions to address mounting short-term pressures, and consider long-term challenges.

Addressing the previous two failings may also improve leadership in sustainable development. A clear definition of sustainable development will increase understanding of sustainable development among the wider community and, as such, increase the number of sustainably literate leaders. Moreover, while a lack of sustainable development leadership is often the underlying cause of inconsistency and regressive decision making, the converse is also true. Legislation could be used to compel leaders to produce strategies, use certain means of stakeholder involvement and explicitly consider environmental limits and inequities. It could also be used to support sustainable development leadership by compelling regular cross-administration working on sustainable development and even go so as far as to impose a substantive duty on all government public bodies to make sustainable development the organizing principle of government.

References

Arnstein, S. (1969) 'A ladder of citizen participation', *Journal of the American Institute of Planners*, 35(4): 216–24.

Batty, D. (2011) 'David Cameron in danger of breaking green pledge warn green groups' *Guardian* 14 May.

Blair, F. and Evans, B. (2004) *Seeing the Bigger Picture*, London: Sustainable Development Commission.

Bosselmann, K. (2008) *The Principle of Sustainability: Transforming Law and Governance*, Aldershot: Ashgate.

Cussons, S. (2006) *Review of Statutory Sustainable Development Duties*, London: In House Policy Consultancy/DEFRA.

Department of Environment, Transport and the Regions (DETR) (1998) *Sustainability Counts: Consultation Paper on a Set of 'Headline' Indicators of Sustainable Development*, London: DETR.

Division for Sustainable Development, UNDESA (2002) 'Guidance in preparing national sustainable development strategy: Managing sustainable development in the new millennium', Background Paper No. 13, DESA/DSD/PC2/BP13, Rome: Department of Economic and Social Affairs.

European Commission (2009) *Mainstreaming Sustainable Development into EU policies: 2009 Review of the European Union Strategy for Sustainable Development*, Com 400, Brussels: European Commission.

Eurostat (2009) *Sustainable development in the European Union: 2009 monitoring report of the EU sustainable development strategy*, Luxembourg: Office for Official Publications of the European Communities.

Flynn, A. and Marsden, T. (2006) *Aiming Higher: Assessing the Sustainable Development Plans and Actions of the Welsh Assembly in Terms of its Commitments in the UK-wide Strategy. A Report to the Sustainable Development Commission*, Cardiff: Cardiff School of City and Regional Planning.

Flynn, A., Marsden, T., Netherwood, A. and Pitts, R. (2008) *Final Report: The Sustainable Development Effectiveness Report for the Welsh Assembly*, Cardiff: Welsh Assembly Government.

Freeman, J. (1999) 'Private parties, public function and the real democracy problem in the new administrative law?', in D. Dyzenhous (ed.) *Recrafting the Rule of Law*, Oxford: Hart.

French, D. (2005) *International Law and Policy of Sustainable Development*, Manchester: Manchester University Press.

HM Government, Scottish Executive, Welsh Assembly Government, Northern Ireland Office (2005) *One future – different paths: The UK's shared framework for sustainable development*, London: DEFRA.

HM Treasury (2011) *Budget 2011*, HC 836, London: Treasury.

Innes, J.E. and Booher, D.E. (2000) 'Indicators for sustainable communities: A strategy building on complexity theory and distributed intelligence', *Planning Theory and Practice*, 1(2): 173–86.

Jacob, K., Volkery, A. and Lenschow, A. (2008) 'Instruments for environmental policy integration in 30 OECD countries', in A. Jordan and A. Lenschow (eds) *Innovation in Environmental Policy: Integrating the Environment for Sustainability*, Cheltenham: Edward Elgar.

MacNeill, J. (2007) 'Leadership for sustainable development', in OECD, *Institutionalizing Sustainable Development*, Paris: OECD.

Meadowcroft, J. (2007) 'National sustainable development strategies: Features, challenges and reflexivity', *European Environment*, 17(3): 152–63.

National Audit Office (NAO) (2006) *Regulatory Impact Assessment and Sustainable Development: A Briefing for the Environmental Audit Committee*, London: NAO.

Northern Ireland Executive (2010) *Everyone's Involved: Sustainable Development Strategy*, Belfast: Northern Ireland Executive.

Organisation for Economic Co-operation and Development (OECD) (2002) *Improving Policy Coherence and Integration for Sustainable Development: A Checklist*, Paris: OECD.

Oliver, D. (2003) *Constitutional Reform in the UK*, Oxford: Oxford University Press.

Parkin, S. (2010) *The Positive Deviant: Sustainability Leadership in a Perverse World*, London: Earthscan.

Performance and Innovation Unit (2000) *Wiring it up: Whitehall's Management of Cross-Cutting Policies and Services*, London: Cabinet Office.

Porritt, J. (2009) 'The standing of sustainable development in government', http://www.jonathonporritt.com/pages/2009/11/the_standing_of_sustainable_de.html, accessed 12 April 2010.

Rayment, J.J. and Smith, J.A. (2010) *MisLeadership: Prevalence, Causes and Consequences*, Aldershot: Gower.

Ross, A. (2003) 'Is the environment getting squeezed out of sustainable development?', *Public Law*, Summer: 249–59.

Ross, A. (2005) 'The UK approach to delivering sustainable development in government: A case study in joined-up working', *Journal of Environmental Law*, 17(1): 27–49.

Ross, A. (2008) 'Why legislate for sustainable development? An examination of sustainable development provisions in UK and Scottish statutes', *Journal of Environmental Law*, 20(1): 35–68.

Ross, A. (2009) 'Modern interpretations of sustainable development', *Journal of Law and Society*, 36(1): 32–54.

Ross, A. (2010) 'Sustainable development indicators and a putative argument for law: A case study of the UK', in D. French (ed.) *Global Justice and Sustainable Development*, Leiden: Martinus Nijhoff.

Russell, S.L. and Thompson, I. (2008) 'Accounting for a sustainable Scotland', *Public Money and Management*, 28(6): 367–437.

Schout, A. and Jordan, A. (2008) 'Administrative instruments', in A. Jordan and A. Lenschow (eds) *Innovation in Environmental Policy: Integrating the Environment for Sustainability*, Cheltenham: Edward Elgar.

Scottish Government (2007) *The Government's Economic Strategy*, Edinburgh: Scottish Government.

Scottish Government (2010) *Scottish Planning Policy*, Edinburgh: Scottish Government.

Stevens, C. (2005) 'Measuring sustainable development', *OECD Statistics Brief*, 10: 1–8.

Sustainable Development Commission (SDC) (2004) *Shows Promise. But Must Try Harder: An Assessment by the Sustainable Development Commission of the Government's Reported Progress on Sustainable Development over the Past Five Years*, London: SDC.

SDC (2008) *Sustainable Development Action Plans (SDA) Progress Reports: The Sustainable Development Commission's Key Findings*, London: SDC.

SDC (2011) *Governing for the Future – the opportunities for mainstreaming sustainable development*, SDC, London.

Sustainable Development Commission Scotland (SDCS) (2008) *Sustainable Development: A Review of Progress by the Scottish Government*, Edinburgh: SDCS.

SDCS (2009) *Sustainable Development: Third Annual Assessment of Progress by the Scottish Government*, Edinburgh: SDCS.

Swanson, D. and Pinter, L. (2007) 'Governance strategies for national sustainable development strategies', in OECD, *Institutionalizing Sustainable Development*, Paris: OECD.

Swanson, D., Pinter, L., Bregha, F., Volkery, A. and Jacob, K. (2004) *National Strategies for Sustainable Development: Challenges, Approaches and Innovations in Strategic and Coordinated Action*, Winnipeg. IISD.

United Nations (UN) (2006) *Global Trends and Status of Indicators of Sustainable Development: Background Paper No.2 DESA/DSD/2006/2*, New York: UN Department of Economic and Social Affairs.

Welsh Assembly Government (WAG) (2009) *One Wales: One Planet: The Sustainable Development Scheme of the Welsh Assembly Government*, Cardiff: WAG.

Part III

A new reality – the way forward

12 Time to get serious – ecological sustainability[1]

> Civilization exists by geological consent, subject to change without notice.
> (Durant, 1927)

The purpose of this chapter is to return to the value of sustainable development as a policy tool in the 21st century and question its relevance and importance. Given the challenges facing the Earth today, especially the climate change challenge, the early interpretations of sustainable development as a vague, malleable policy tool based on weak sustainability fail to address the fact that there are limits to the Earth's resilience; nor do they address our cultural and moral failure to curb our consumption. Instead, the demands of the 21st century require a much more meaningful instrument for framing decisions. This chapter explores more recent interpretations of sustainable development in the UK and elsewhere and the influences behind these interpretations to assess whether sustainable development can provide a useful mechanism for delivering truly 'sustainable' development.

Throughout this volume, it has been maintained that sustainable development is best viewed as a framework or forum for decision making. It resembles a table to which different concerns are brought. Sustainable development is a poor champion for any one concern, such as the environment, justice, human rights and economic development. Instead, it has the potential to set out an appropriate decision-making process. To do this, it needs to be based on clear, theoretically robust norms and values. The trouble is that in many respects, discussions about the meaning of sustainable development have been muddled with discussions about the priority society should attribute to living within the Earth's limits and the present generation's stewardship role. This chapter aims to address the prioritization issue, and lends its support to redefining sustainable development with ecological sustainability as its normative core. It sets out the case for treating ecological sustainability as a fundamental legal principle that ought to be given the same priority as other fundamental legal principles, such as justice, equality and freedom. It then also explains how this impacts on the interpretation of sustainable development and priorities for decision making. It also describes sustainable development as a framework for decision making which could be reinforced as a legal rule in appropriately drafted legislation. This approach paves the way forward for sustainable development to become the 'central organizing principle of government'.

The chapter begins with an examination of the impact to date of early interpretations of sustainable development based on 'weak sustainability' and then explores the more recent emergence and importance of 'ecological sustainability' as the moral and (potentially fundamental) legal principle underpinning the concept of sustainable development. This shift towards ecological sustainability has undoubtedly been influenced by the climate change agenda, considering that climate change is one of the key challenges facing the Earth today. Consequently, the chapter next explores the influence of the climate change agenda on this shift.

Having traced the development of ecological sustainability, the chapter next examines the mechanisms available to make the ethic of ecological sustainability operational. It emphasizes the importance of certain tools for establishing the Earth's limits, the ecological impact of development and the need to keep these distinct from broader sustainable development processes. It argues that with ecological sustainability at its normative core, sustainable development has the capacity to set meaningful objectives, duties and rules, and provide boundaries for decision making. Moreover, it already shows up in these roles in UK and devolved law, policy and practice. The chapter ends with the observation that even with a much more ecologically based role for sustainable development, decisions relating to improving supply and reducing impacts are much easier for governments, businesses and individuals, than moves to reduce consumption and risk in economic growth. The continued reliance on economic growth as the primary objective of governance is not leading to improvements in health, equality or the maintenance of our planet. This is true even when such economic growth is restricted to 'sustainable' growth, or where growth is decoupled from resource use. Instead, true sustainability, whereby the lives of everyone, now and in the future, are improved, is only possible through strong leadership that places sustainable development with ecological sustainability at its core as the central organizing principle (overall objective) of government.

The impact of weak interpretations of sustainability and sustainable development

> Just as reckless spending is causing recession, so reckless consumption is depleting the world's natural capital to a point where we are endangering our future prosperity.
>
> (WWF *et al.*, 2008: 1)

As explained in Chapter 4, in the UK, as in most countries, early national and business interpretations and strategies for sustainable development were underpinned by what is commonly referred to as 'weak sustainability' (Blowers, 1992: 132). Weak interpretations of sustainable development focus on development and are largely indifferent to the form in which capital stock is passed on (Pearce, 1993: 15). Pearce notes that 'on the weak sustainability interpretation of sustainable development there is no special place for the environment. The environment is simply another form of capital' (Pearce, 1993: 15–16).[2] This is reflected in the description of sustainable development as a trade-off between the environment and economic development prominent in the early 1990s (UK Government, 1994, Principle 4; UNGA, 1992). Later interpretations consider the three components of economy, environment and society as interdependent and mutually reinforcing pillars, but still favour high economic growth (DEFRA, 1999; UNGA, 2002).

Weak sustainability approaches are based on the premise that technology and international trade will ensure there are always enough resources to meet cultural or human carrying capacity. People will always find another way of meeting their needs. 'Necessity is the mother of invention'. Many of the solutions promoted, sought and developed have focused on improving the environmental credentials of the products supplied, with little attention being paid to the demand side of the equation and changing consumption patterns. The result is that while fewer resources are required per unit of energy, transport, food, etc., more units are being consumed. For instance, although modern cars are much less polluting than in the 1950s, the number of cars on British roads has increased from just under 2 million in 1950 to 26.5 million in 2006 (Department for Transport *et al.*, 2009, chs 3, 9). Technology is used to justify our erosion of the Earth's capital instead of simply living off the interest. As more and more pressure is placed on the ecosystem due to increased consumption of resources by an ever-growing population, there will come a stage where the ecosystem cannot meet all the demand.

Humanity's demand on the planet's living resources, its ecological footprint, exceeded the Earth's ecological limits by the 1980s, and has continued to rise, such that its ecological footprint now exceeds the planet's regenerative capacity by about 30 per cent (WWF *et al.*, 2008: 1).[3] The effects of this failure to protect and maintain the Earth's resources are numerous. The climate is changing: the annual mean Central England Temperature (CET) increased by about 1°C in the 20th century (DECC, 2010). Since 2000, the CET has continued to rise steadily and in 2006, had risen to 1.09°C above the average for 1961–1990 (DECC, 2010). *The Economics of Climate Change: The Stern Review* (the Stern Review) (Stern, 2007) states that even if the annual flow of emissions does not increase beyond today's rate, the stock of greenhouse gases in the atmosphere would reach double the pre-industrial levels by 2050 – that is, 550 parts per million (ppm) of carbon dioxide equivalents, and this could happen as early as 2035 (Stern, 2007: Executive Summary, iii). At this level, there is at least a 77 per cent chance of a global average temperature rise exceeding 2°C (Stern, 2007: Executive Summary, iii). The five principal pressures directly driving biodiversity loss (habitat change, over-exploitation, pollution, invasive alien species and climate change) are either constant or increasing in intensity (SCBD, 2010: 9). The number of species present in rivers, lakes and marshlands has declined, by 50 per cent (SCBD, 2006: 9). Nearly a quarter of plant species are estimated to be threatened with extinction. Habitats such as forests and river systems are the subject of 'extensive fragmentation', leading to the loss of biodiversity and ecosystems (SCBD, 2010: 9).

The dangers of the weak sustainability approach were explained by renowned economist Robert U. Ayres in 1996:

> To those who follow us we are bequeathing a more and more potent technology and significant investment in productive machinery and equipment and infrastructure. But these benefits may not compensate for a depleted natural resource base, a gravely damaged environment and a broken social contract.
>
> (Ayres, 1996: 117)

Chambers warns that:

> Our dominant culture continues to celebrate expansion in spite of its heavy toll on people and nature. In fact, we desperately try to ignore that much of today's income stems from liquidating our social and natural assets. We fool ourselves into believing that we can disregard ecological limits indefinitely.
>
> (Chambers *et al.*, 2000: 47)

Just as every flood, hurricane, drought and extinction increases our awareness of the fragility of the Earth's ecological capital, so in the autumn of 2008, the effects of high-risk borrowing started to tremble through the global economy. The same moral and cultural failure to show restraint in consumption to which the overnight destruction of many of the world's oldest and largest banks was attributed, is also true in the context of global ecological systems. The UK Government's financial support of British banks has reached £850 billion (Grice, 2009). The US borrowed $700 billion to bail out its investment banks, and other governments had to follow suit (*The Times*, 2008). The general consensus is that the privatization of profits and the nationalization of losses are not sustainable, but the issue is how we can stop borrowing from our children. Clearly, economies need to develop a social and ecological consciousness, and a sense of responsibility needs to be returned to the global market. There is some evidence of attempts to make this happen. For example, in his 2010 Budget speech the Chancellor of the UK Exchequer, George Osborne, promised:

> plans for fairer pay across the public sector, without increasing the overall pay bill, so that those at the top of organisations are paid no more than 20 times the salaries of those at the bottom. The culture of excessive pay at the very top of the public sector simply has to end.
>
> (HM Treasury, 2010a)

Moreover, despite extensive culling in the public sector, the Chancellor promised to honour commitments to provide the National Health Service with real increases throughout the Parliament, as well as the UK's international aid obligations to the poorest in the world (HM Treasury, 2010b). These initial decisions showed responsibility and a strong ethical concern for the less fortunate. Unfortunately, subsequent decisions by the coalition show that the Government's concerns about borrowing are restricted to the economy. Little attention has been paid to the cost of using the Earth's capital to finance the lifestyles of today. Furthermore, in cutting public finance, where the UK Government has wanted to relieve financial and regulatory burdens of the electorate, it has chosen to do so by reducing environmental protections such as the fuel duty and opening up the land-use planning system (see Chapter 11). These decisions reflect the UK (and Scottish and Northern Ireland) administrations' view of economic growth as the panacea to all societal problems. In his study examining the relationship between prosperity and economic growth, Jackson (2009) concluded that the financial crisis can at least in part be attributed to our current growth model. He states that the reliance on debt to finance the cycle of growth has created a deeply unstable system that makes individuals, families and communities inherently vulnerable to cycles of boom and bust. Economic growth has delivered its benefits unequally at best, with a fifth of the world's population earning just 2 per cent of global income, huge gaps between rich and poor in developing countries, and disastrous environmental consequences (Jackson, 2009: 6–19). Yet successive UK and devolved administrations continue to focus their efforts in relation to sustainable development on economic growth. Indeed, many aspects of economic policy are still centred on economic growth, as opposed to well-being and wider sustainable outcomes (SDCS, 2009: 3). For example, 'Too many development plans and local planning decisions are still, in their cumulative impact, inconsistent with the creation of low-carbon, inclusive and sustainable communities' (SDCS, 2009: 34).

Ecological sustainability as the legal principle underpinning sustainable development

'Sustainability'[4] is generally understood to mean doing things that can be continued over long periods without unacceptable consequences. The ecological changes we are experiencing are, or will soon be, creating unacceptable consequences, and this is evidence that the weak version of sustainability popular among governments and business is not working. The Stern Review concludes that:

> The evidence shows that ignoring climate change will eventually damage economic growth. Our actions over the coming few decades could create risks of major disruption to economic and social activity, later in this century and in the next, on a scale similar to those associated with the great wars and the economic depression of the first half of the 20th century.
>
> (Stern, 2007: Summary of conclusions)

A decision-making process which legitimates and promulgates 'business as usual' patterns of economic growth is unsustainable. The attempt to roll three types of sustainability (ecological, economic and social) into one overarching concept of sustainability has left it pointing in multiple directions, without any central meaning. Definitions which use such a weak sustainability approach invariably end up in a balancing act, trading off one against the other (Bosselmann, 2008: 52).

Everything we do is constrained by the Earth's ecosystem and there is a need to revisit the basic principles that govern our decision making, to ensure that environmental concerns have a greater influence. 'Strong sustainability' is often described as limiting the extent to which environmental capital may be substituted by man-made capital and defining certain environmental assets that are critical to our wellbeing and survival as critical natural capital (Blowers, 1992: 132). The difficulty with this particular conceptualization is that it fails to give guidance as to how we should determine what does or does not qualify as critical natural capital (Bowers, 1997: 194).[5] In this respect, expressing the concept as 'ecological sustainability' is more helpful. 'Ecological sustainability' imposes a duty on everyone to protect and restore the integrity of the Earth's ecological systems. It advocates the need to operate within the ecological carrying capacity of the Earth.[6] Decision making based on ecological sustainability places the discussion of trade-offs within the ecological limits of the Earth.

This is hardly a new idea, and respect for nature and the 'need for human activity to respect the requisites for its maintenance and continuance' have been present in the ideologies of many ancient civilisations.[7] While recently ignored by the industrialized world, it should be a fairly obvious observation that development must occur within the confines of the Earth's capabilities. As the Prince of Wales puts it: 'If Nature's own capital base loses its innate resilience then how long will it take for our economic systems to lose their resilience too?' (Prince of Wales, 2011).

Sound environmental management practices already advocate an ecosystem approach which 'recognises the relationships between healthy and resilient ecosystems, biodiversity conservation and human wellbeing. Various principles have evolved for decision making and action spanning the environmental, economic and social dimensions of sustainability' (WWF *et al.*, 2008: 30; Convention on Biological Diversity, 2007).

That said, to make a significant impact on the way we live, ecological sustainability needs to be more than a policy objective. Clearly, the law has a crucial role to play. 'Ecosystems don't obey the rules of private property. What one farmer does – in fencing his land, blocking animal migrations, spraying crops, introducing new crop varieties, hunting and fishing, logging, pumping groundwater or managing livestock diseases – has ramifications far beyond the farm' (Sachs as quoted in WWF *et al.*, 2008: 30). Bosselmann (2008: 43) notes that 'while a legal system cannot on its own initiate and monitor social change, it can formulate some parameters for the direction and extent of social change'. Current legal systems, preoccupied with private property and individual rights are failing to respond to our modern needs. To really make a difference, the ecological systems approach needs to be supported by a strong moral and legal normative framework. A new ethic is needed which advocates the need to operate within the ecological carrying capacity of the Earth. One way of obtaining the necessary status would be to treat ecological sustainability as a legal principle (Bosselmann, 2008: 5).

Bosselmann (2008: 48) explains that the difference between 'a policy and a legal principle is that a principle is derived from a more fundamental moral principle or ethic upon which the law is ultimately grounded'. Dworkin (1977: 22) observes that while principles set out standards which state a reason for arguing a certain way, they do not dictate the actual decision. Conflicting principles need to be balanced against one another in the decision-making process (Winter, 2004: 13–14). It is not the intention to canvas here the debates on what exactly is required to qualify as a legal principle and the role and value in law of such principles. It is, however, safe to say that certain environmental principles – such as the polluter pays, prevention and, to a lesser extent, the precautionary principles – are all at least acknowledged in UK, EU and international courts (Macrory, 2004; French, 2005). While sustainable development itself is not recognized as a legal principle in UK, EU or international law, the EU and several other states have elevated certain environmental approaches, such as the polluter pays approach, to the status of principle (Macrory, 2004; Ross, 2008: 44).[8] Moreover, the English courts have accepted 'sustainability' as a material consideration in planning decisions, and accepted that it is capable of being a main issue in planning law decisions and may deserve significant weight.[9] It is possible to see the leap to accepting ecological sustainability as a legal principle, given the ever-growing pressure on the Earth's environment, as a natural progression.

As such, the contention that ecological sustainability meets the criteria of a legal principle is legitimate. Ecological sustainability is reflective of a fundamental morality (respect for ecological integrity). It also requires action (to protect and restore). Therefore, it is capable of causing legal effect (Bosselmann, 2008: 53). Furthermore, unlike other environmental principles, such as the polluter pays and the precautionary principles, which are directive, ecological sustainability is an approach not unlike justice and equality (Bosselmann, 2008: 57). Thus, it is capable of being treated as a fundamental legal principle to be used in the same way as the principles of fairness, freedom and justice.

More importantly, and regardless of the intricacies of any theoretical debate, the main justification supporting ecological sustainability as a fundamental legal principle, is that our ability to deliver the other fundamental legal principles (freedom, equality and justice) reduces as the Earth's resources and resilience reduce. The best way to protect these other fundamental legal principles is to operate within a system based on ecological sustainability.

Significantly, this is not just some ideological whim. There is evidence of a trend towards ecological sustainability in various public and private spheres. The remainder of this chapter explores this trend and how this ethic can be made operational in the UK and devolved administrations.

Ecological sustainability and strategic vision

There is evidence at various levels of governance that 'ecological sustainability' already has some credence as a guiding ethic. One of the strongest formulations is present in the Earth Charter, which is a declaration of fundamental principles for building a just, sustainable and peaceful global society for the 21st century (Earth Charter Initiative, 2000). The idea of a new charter that would set forth fundamental principles for sustainable development was discussed in *Our Common Future* (the Brundtland Report) (WCED, 1987) and later at the UN 1992 Earth Summit held in Rio de Janeiro (Earth Charter Initiative, 2000). In 1994, Maurice Strong, the Secretary General of the Earth Summit and chairman of the Earth Council, and Mikhail Gorbachev, president of Green Cross International, launched the Earth Charter Initiative with support from the Dutch Government. The Charter is the result of a long period of wide civic engagement and consultation. Its final text was approved by consensus at a meeting at the UN Educational. Scientific and Cultural Organization (UNESCO) Headquarters in Paris in March 2000. Subsequently, the Charter has been formally endorsed by thousands of organizations representing millions of people, including the UNESCO Conference of Member States, national government ministries, national and international associations of universities, and hundreds of cities and towns in dozens of countries. It has also been endorsed by tens of thousands of individuals and publicly supported by numerous heads of state.[10]

In the Earth Charter, the environment is presented as the basis of all life. This shift from a narrow human-centred, to a broader life-centred, perspective is expressed in its overarching principles of governance: (1) Respect Earth and life in all its diversity; (2) Care for the community of life with understanding, compassion and love; (3) Build democratic societies that are just, participatory, sustainable and peaceful; (4) Secure Earth's bounty and beauty for present and future generations. It then sets out certain actions required to fulfil these four broad commitments (Earth Charter Initiative, 2000).

Change is also evident at the UK level. *One future – different paths: The UK's shared framework for sustainable development* published jointly by all the administrations in the UK sets out an approach to sustainable development based on five principles (HM Government *et al.*, 2005a: 8). The first principle is living within environmental limits: 'Respecting the limits of the planet's environment, resources and biodiversity – to improve our environment and ensure that the natural resources needed for life are unimpaired and remain so for future generations' (HM Government *et al.*, 2005a: 8). The third principle is achieving a sustainable economy: 'Building a strong, stable and sustainable economy which provides prosperity and opportunities for all, and in which environmental and social costs fall on those who impose them (Polluter Pays) and efficient resource use is incentivised' (HM Government *et al.*, 2005a: 8).[11] The reference to high economic growth is gone and this demonstrates a deeper commitment to ecological sustainability. As discussed in Chapters 4 and 11, the 2005 Framework is due to be replaced and, as discussed in Chapter 14, this will be a valuable opportunity to drive the delivery of sustainable development forward and will be a true test of the four administrations' commitment to genuine sustainable development, as well as of their willingness to work together.

The most progressive of the administrations is Wales. In *One Wales: One Planet: The Sustainable Development Scheme of the Welsh Assembly Government*, produced in 2009, the Welsh Assembly Government (WAG) sets a vision which uses sustainable development as the overarching strategic aim of all WAG policies and programmes across all ministerial portfolios and confirms that sustainable development will be the central organizing principle of the WAG. The scheme also sets out the steps to be taken to embed this approach (WAG, 2009: 4). Uniquely, it sets an explicit long-term aim for Wales to use only its fair share of the Earth's resources (WAG, 2009: 13).

There are also examples of multinational companies promoting an ecological sustainability ethic. Retailer Marks & Spencer plc, for example, is promoting Plan A: 'an eight-year, 180-point "eco" plan to . . . work with our customers and our suppliers to combat climate change, reduce waste, safeguard natural resources, trade ethically and build a healthier nation' (Marks & Spencer plc, 2010a). Plan A has ambitious targets, such as becoming carbon neutral and sending no waste to landfill by 2015 (Marks & Spencer plc, 2010b: 11).

Ecological sustainability and the influence of climate change

It would be naive to ignore the influence of the climate change agenda on any modern approach to sustainable development. Environmental law has always been disaster-driven. For instance, changes in responses to nuclear accidents only came about after the Chernobyl disaster.[12] Air quality measures were only seriously introduced following the London smog crisis in 1952, which killed almost 4,000 people.[13] Climate change is pushing environmental matters back to the forefront of political, economic and legislative discussions.

One reason climate change is grabbing headlines is that it is actually the largest threat to our continued existence. Indeed, the *Living Planet Report 2008* states that 'Potentially the greatest threat to biodiversity over the coming decades is climate change. Early impacts have been felt in polar and montane as well as coastal and marine ecosystems, such as coral reefs' (WWF *et al.*, 2008: 4). Thus, if one is genuinely concerned about wildlife and biodiversity, tackling the emissions of greenhouse gases should be a priority.

There is, however, another reason. Unlike many other environmental concepts or concerns, such as sustainable development or biodiversity, climate change can be explained in layman's terms. There is strong evidence that greenhouse gas emissions from human activities are now raising the Earth's temperature and causing other changes in the climate. Emissions are projected to rise significantly over the next few decades, and quite likely beyond, leading to significant increases in global temperatures, with profound risks for the natural environment and human society worldwide. Without action to reduce greenhouse gas emissions, global temperatures are expected to rise by between 1.4°C and 5.8°C by 2100, and sea level could also rise by between 0.09 metres and 0.88 metres compared to 1990 levels. The consequences include increased storms, floods, drought, desertification, habitat loss and melting ice caps (HM Government, 2006: 8).

Thus, the problem is clear in relation to changes to the Earth's climate. Its impact on the inhabitants of various parts of the Earth at various periods in the future is also clear. The cause of the harm is known, and what is needed to be done to reduce its impact, both in relation to limiting the change and adapting to the change, is also known. Action is much more possible, since there is a tangible concern and clear areas that can be targeted.

Securing the Future: Delivering UK Sustainable Development Strategy provides that:

> Sustainable development and climate change are two vitally important and interrelated challenges facing us in the 21st century. Our ability to develop more sustainably will determine the speed and degree of climate change we experience. And as the climate changes the choices available to us to develop sustainably will change.
>
> (HM Government, 2005: 73)

While the Strategy clearly acknowledges that sustainable development and climate change address different challenges and have different objectives, it also treats the agendas as being equal in scope. This perspective arguably increases the importance of mitigating climate change and controlling greenhouse gas emissions within the remit of sustainable development, which in turn focuses on limits and thus, promotes ecological sustainability.

There are significant benefits with this approach. First, as climate change is arguably the most significant of the environmental harms facing the Earth, this higher status may be warranted. After all, as noted above, climate change itself is the biggest threat to biodiversity (WWF *et al.*, 2008: 4). Furthermore, its more comprehensible agenda elevates the ecological sustainability platform, at least in relation to keeping our emissions within the limits that the Earth can absorb. It may also reflect the other more development-oriented aspects of sustainable development. It is arguable then that it would be better to replace the emphasis put on sustainable development with a regime entirely focused on mitigating and adapting to climate change.

The difficulty with this approach is that while the climate change agenda takes a limits-based approach, this is only in respect to one aspect of the Earth's ecosystem – the effect of increased greenhouse gas emissions on the climate – and this may not reflect ecological sustainability in relation to other aspects of the Earth's ecosystem. Despite the huge threat climate change poses to most parts of the Earth's ecosystem, it is still true that actions which simply reduce greenhouse gas emissions may actually harm other parts of the environment or may have serious negative effects on certain communities or economies. For example, a solution such as carbon capture and storage, whereby carbon dioxide is 'captured' from production sources such as fossil fuel power stations and then injected into receptacles on land, in sand or under the sea in former oil and gas reserves, while potentially very effective at tackling greenhouse gas emissions, may have its own environmental consequences caused by the transportation of the carbon dioxide and leakages that could occur during the transportation (Intergovernmental Panel on Climate Change, 2005: 11). Similarly, a decision to support nuclear energy projects would clearly reduce our reliance on fossil fuels and, as a result, reduce greenhouse gas emissions, but could seriously increase, among other things, risks of radiation and the amount of heavy metals needing disposal.

The danger of the approach in the Strategy is that it narrows the scope of sustainable development by increasing the weight afforded to the climate change agenda in any decision-making process, creating the risk of ecological sustainability being subsumed in another different agenda.

The development of renewable energy sources contributes to a reduction of greenhouse gas emissions and provides increased energy security by offering local alternatives to oil and gas. However, renewables, in the wider context of environmental sustainability and sustainable development are not necessarily a panacea without their own environmental consequences. As Li (2005: 2240) explains, too many cars powered with fuel cells add to the water vapour in the air (humidity) which will affect the climate and both the natural and built environment. The production of biofuels takes away land used for food production and this affects the price of certain foods. The intensification of agriculture can also result in increased runoff of nutrients, thus leading to increased eutrophication of lakes, rivers and seas. Tidal projects can have biodiversity consequences. Wind power can require a great deal of land and needs to be carefully planned around existing uses to minimize the effects on biodiversity and amenity (Li, 2005: 2242). There are other examples of the climate change agenda subsuming sustainable development. The UK Cabinet sub-committee on Sustainable Development in Government was quietly abolished and replaced by the Committee for Energy and Climate Change which was then further downgraded to a sub-committee during the Brown administration (Woolf, 2007). More worryingly, the Cameron Cabinet contains no committee or sub-committee dedicated to either agenda although he has maintained the sub-committee for the London Olympics in 2012 (Cabinet Office, 2010).

The SDC expressed some concern about this asymmetric vein of the climate change agenda. In its response to the consultation on the Scottish Climate Change Bill, the Commission emphasized that 'Government will need to ensure that action to tackle climate change will not impact upon wider sustainable development' (SDCS, 2008). While this quote can be used to support an argument based on ecological sustainability, it could also be supporting a business-as-usual weak sustainability approach.

At this stage, it is also comforting to remember that tackling climate change does not only concern mitigating greenhouse gas emissions. It also concerns adaptation measures to address the effects of climate change (which many scientists now believe are inevitable) on the various regions and communities of the Earth. The climate change agenda also seeks to address the economic, social, environmental and other impacts of rising sea levels, increasing temperatures, desertification, melting ice caps, etc. The UK Strategy reflects this reality: 'Adaptation must be brought in to all aspects of sustainable development and climate change has been considered in relation to each aspect of this strategy' (HM Government, 2005: 92). As is discussed below, despite the danger of ecological sustainability and, in turn, sustainable development becoming subsumed into the climate change agenda, both the Climate Change Act 2008 and the Climate Change (Scotland) Act 2009 appear to be based around a much more holistic vision of ecological sustainability which uses sustainable development as the framework for climate change decision making.[14] For example, the UK Act requires the policies and objectives within adaptation programmes to contribute to sustainable development.[15]

Establishing limits for ecological sustainability

From the discussion above, ecological sustainability is highly dependent on science to establish what the carrying capacity of a certain ecosystem is in relation to certain impacts and being able to compare and prioritize between local, neighbouring and global limits. These are not easy tasks and the development of tools capable of generating robust data on limits and impacts is currently a major area of research. It is becoming possible to identify and quantify planetary boundaries that must not be transgressed, to help prevent human activities from causing unacceptable environmental change. In a paper for *Nature*, an impressive team of scientists (Rockström *et al.*, 2009) proposed a new approach for defining preconditions for human development, identifying nine processes which can define planetary boundaries: climate change; rate of biodiversity loss; interference with the nitrogen and phosphorus cycles; stratospheric ozone depletion; ocean acidification; global freshwater use; change in land use; chemical pollution; and atmospheric aerosol loading. Crossing certain biophysical thresholds for each of these processes could have disastrous consequences for humanity. Already, three of the nine interlinked planetary boundaries have already been overstepped. The researchers emphasize that, 'we do not have the luxury of concentrating our efforts on any one of them in isolation from the others. If one boundary is transgressed, then other boundaries are also under serious risk' (Rockström *et al.*, 2009: 474). Ecological footprinting[16] and environmental assessment, including strategic environmental assessment,[17] are useful tools for this purpose and others are continually being developed. For example, sustainability wedges are used to break down the various contributing factors of ecological overshoot across different sectors and drivers. Each of the proposed solutions can be represented as a wedge. So for example, one wedge may represent how much of the required annual reductions in carbon emissions of 7 billion tonnes can be achieved by home insulation, reforestation or carbon capture and storage (Pacala and Socolow, 2004: 968–72; WWF *et al.*, 2008: 1, 23, 25).

The argument put forward here is that to promote ecological sustainability, it is essential that these tools continue to focus on the integrity of the environment and remain separate from any broader sustainability measures that include social and economic impacts. These tools are the starting point for decision making, by providing the necessary information about the ecological limits or carrying capacity of systems at local, regional and global levels. Local limits may need to be exceeded for the global good and vice versa. Developing and improving the tools capable of comparing local and global impacts must be a priority. Once a determination has been made about the baseline critical natural capital, further decisions will need to balance local needs and cumulative effects in relation to the social and economic concerns in addition to other less critical aspects of the environment. As French (2005: 25–6) argues simply taking action on environmental issues is regressive if it exacerbates the economic, social and power disparities between countries and without a pro-poor approach, many of the world's fundamental causes of environmental degradation will not be resolved.

This is the role of sustainable development.

Delivering ecological sustainability – the role of sustainable development

Humans have a need to improve, ask questions and seek answers. We seek fulfilment and this yearning is encapsulated by the term 'development'. The key measures of development in industrialized countries, such as gross domestic product, have largely focused on economic development, consumption and wealth (Grainger, 2004: 10). More recently, there has been recognition that wealth does not necessarily equate to wellbeing or happiness and newer measures of development include mortality rates, employment and wellbeing (UNDP, 2007: 229). To quote the Earth Charter 'We must realise that when basic needs have been met, human development is primarily about being more, not having more' (Earth Charter Initiative, 2000).

The original purpose of the sustainable development agenda was to bring the economic development and environmental protection agendas together (WCED, 1987; Sands, 2003: 9). In so doing, sustainable development can usefully be viewed as either a product or a process. As a product, it is an aim to which every project and action should aspire. For example, a given wind farm or strategic policy can be considered to be 'sustainable development' in and of itself, or it can be viewed as part of a larger project on regional, national or global 'sustainable development'. For most purposes, it is more useful to focus on the role of sustainable development as a process. In this context, as Stallworthy (2008: 174) observes, 'sustainable development provides a foundation for integration of environmental and other considerations within the process of decision making and a means whereby environmental impacts of our activities, previously uncosted, can be internalised'.

However, the term needs to do more than simply bundle together the economic, environmental and social policy strands. The conflicts internal to the term 'sustainable development' and its imprecise nature have meant that it has been manipulated to support or refute different policy outcomes based on different objectives and the amount of weight attached to them. One decision may be sustainable because it attaches more weight to economic considerations over social or environmental ones; another decision may favour environmental factors, and so on. 'The lack of a norm at the heart of the three pillar approach leads to "mock compromises", "sacrifices of nature . . . commanded by short term economic and social interests"' (Winter, 2008: 28). To be effective, sustainable development needs to provide more guidance as to the way these strands relate to one another.

Elkins (1992: 280) claims that 'sustainable development requires the adoption of ecological sustainability as the principle economic objective in place of economic growth'. With ecological sustainability at the core of sustainable development, it is then possible to relate the social and economic components of sustainable development to a central point of reference within defined boundaries (Bosselmann, 2008: 52). Sustainable development becomes a more meaningful organizational framework for balancing the Earth's sustainability with our human need to develop. Thus, 'a development is sustainable if it tends to preserve the integrity and continued existence of ecological systems; it is unsustainable if it tends to do otherwise' (Bosselmann, 2008: 52). The emphasis is on determining the ecological limits first and then establishing what development is feasible within those limits.[18] This is also consistent with calls for sustainable development to be the central organizing principle of government. As Jackson notes, 'The idea of an economy whose task is to provide capabilities for flourishing within ecological limits offers the most credible vision to put in its place. But this can only happen through changes that support social behaviours and reduce the structural incentives to unproductive status competition' (2009: 91).

Indeed, once the limits are agreed, then the balancing and trade-offs must still occur, but not in relation to the Earth's natural capital. As discussed elsewhere, the approach taken in the UK Framework (HM Government *et al.*, 2005a) is capable of such an interpretation, whereby the principles are separated into two groups so that two of the principles cover the overarching ambitions of the Strategy:

- Living within environmental limits
- Ensuring a strong, healthy, just and equal society.

And then the four further principles describe the necessary conditions for the achievement of sustainable development:

- Achieving a sustainable economy
- Promoting good governance
- Using sound science responsibility
- Promoting opportunity and innovation.

Apparent changes of emphasis, however, may not be all they seem. For example, moves to simply decouple economic growth from resource use do not go far enough. The European Commission has stated that 'the great challenge faced by economies today is to integrate environmental sustainability with economic growth and welfare by decoupling environmental degradation from economic growth and doing more with less'. Indeed decoupling is signalled as being 'one of the key objectives of the European Union'.[19] In contrast to the model proposed here, whereby growth is remodelled to reflect an acceptance of the limits imposed by 'the ability of the biosphere to absorb the effects of human activities', the decoupling approach reflects ecological modernization's emphasis on reducing the negative environmental impact of economic growth – relative improvements rather than absolute ones.

Real change requires sustainable development with ecological sustainability at its core to be the central organizing principle, or, put another way, to be the overall objective of government. The current approach of tinkering with growth is not enough.

Delivering sustainable development based on ecological sustainability – new ways of using existing mechanisms

Given sustainable development's opaque historical meaning, it is not surprising that translating it into meaningful legal formulations has proven problematic and most instruments have tended to be highly generalized (Stallworthy, 2008: 174). As discussed in Chapter 8, early legislative formulations were so vague and diluted that they could only be interpreted as symbolic or, at best, aspirational objectives.[20]

However, especially since 1999, references to sustainable development in UK, Scottish, and slowly, Northern Irish statutes have been on the increase and in much clearer and more powerful legal forms. Sustainable development appears as duties, objectives and procedural requirements. While the vast majority of the provisions do not attempt to define sustainable development, some consistency is provided by a reliance on Government guidance (Ross, 2008: 44),[21] which, in turn, allows flexibility for the normative core of sustainable development to evolve and shift to become more ecologically based without requiring amendment of the statutory provisions.

Chapter 8 shows how sustainable development most often appears as an objective or duty for a regulatory regime or authority. The Planning and Compulsory Purchase Act 2004 ch. 5 s. 39(2) provides that those bodies involved in development planning in England and Wales must exercise their function with the objective of contributing to sustainable development. In this example, sustainable development is the primary duty; however, in most cases it is one of several duties or objectives. Some statutes include qualifications and mechanisms for prioritizing between duties, but in others it is left to the decision maker. In some instances, it is simply one of several competing objectives to balance against one another.[22]

There are instances where the sustainable development duty or objective appears to be the mechanism for balancing other duties or objectives. In these cases, it acts as a legal rule. A common phrase is 'shall exercise its powers *in the way best calculated to contribute* to the achievement of sustainable development'.[23] This formulation sets out the mechanism for decision making as a legal rule, but is couched with discretionary language, which means other factors will influence the decision. This does not prohibit these from being considered legal rules (Dworkin, 1977: 28). As a result, rules may be formulated to allow the balancing of opposing concerns within the scope of the rule (De Sadeleer, 2005: 311).[24] In these cases, only the policies and concepts referred to in the rule may be used to influence an agency's decision making generally or a particular type of decision.[25]

The approach taken in the UK Climate Change Act 2008 clearly permits the sustainable development provision to be treated as a legal rule. The Act amends the Energy Act 2004 to include s. 125A(2) which provides that:

> It is the duty of the Administrator to promote the supply of renewable transport fuel whose production, supply or use –
>
> (a) causes or contributes to the reduction of carbon emissions, and
> (b) contributes to sustainable development or the protection or enhancement of the environment generally.[26]

If the supply does not contribute to sustainable development then, arguably, the administrator has not complied with its legal duty.

Thus, while sustainable development as a material consideration can, at best, only suggest ecological sustainability as a worthwhile objective, sustainable development as a legal rule providing either some procedural requirement or as a framework for making the ultimate decision, can actually impose and deliver ecological sustainability. As a result, these provisions have the capacity to deliver the real change needed to ensure development is kept within the Earth's ecological limits, but whether they actually will do so largely depends on leadership.

Leadership, ecological sustainability and curbing consumption

Technology makes resource use more efficient; yet, technological changes that enhance productivity, instead of reducing consumption, often result in increased exploitation of natural resources.[27] Analogous to a weak sustainability approach, as technology has improved, very little attempt has been made to alter human behaviour so that we consume less resources. As evidenced from the discussion above, the solutions presented for dealing with climate change remain focused on technology.

Clearly, the most effective way of dealing with climate change and contributing to sustainable development is to reduce our consumption of energy. If we use less energy, then fewer harmful emissions are emitted into the atmosphere, and if we use less energy, then there will be less demand for energy, so new, safe and secure sources of energy become less pressured. The SDC has noted that 'climate change can be most effectively halted if Government tackles unsustainable policies that encourage unsustainable actions within society. End of pipe interventions alone will not deliver the long term emissions reductions required' (SDCS, 2008). Indeed, the pressure to meet the USA's unyielding demand for secure supplies of oil was one of the key contributors to the 2010 deep sea oil exploration disaster in the Gulf of Mexico. In his address to the nation, President Barak Obama showed real leadership and a clear understanding of the American contribution to the situation and its solution:

> The tragedy unfolding on our coast is the most painful and powerful reminder yet that the time to embrace a clean energy future is now . . . there are some who believe that we can't afford those costs right now. I say we can't afford not to change how we produce and use energy – because the long-term costs to our economy, our national security, and our environment are far greater.
>
> (White House, 2010)

Many environmental, social and economic concerns can be addressed by tackling consumption. The mechanisms used to reduce energy consumption include a culture of making things last and then reusing them, reducing what we use and recycling wherever possible. Some actions, such as improvements in home insulation, are one-off changes. Other actions require a concerted cultural and perhaps, moral, change that will often need to be motivated by the government, using market and other regulatory incentives and penalties. While improvements in the public transport network are necessary to provide the opportunity for people to alter their behaviour, it may not be sufficient, especially if road transport (that is, private, as opposed to public, road transport) and air transport continue to be more attractive in relation to comfort, cost and timing. In these instances, taxes that address the true cost of these transport options do work. Indeed, more generally, mechanisms aimed at reducing consumption, while often unpopular, have proven effective. Experience with the congestion charge for London shows a substantial decrease in the number of individuals taking their cars into central London (Transport for London, 2008).[28] In the Republic of Ireland, charging consumers for plastic bags resulted in an immediate 90 per cent drop in their use (Department of Environment, Heritage and Local Government, n.d.).[29]

So why are environmental taxes and charges not used more often? Leadership has repeatedly been cited as the most important aspect for sustainable development governance (Chapter 11; Cussons, 2006: 16; Ross, 2006: 14). Yet, the immediate response to concerns about rising energy costs and energy security focused on the development and provision of alternative sources of energy, including fossil fuels.[30] Furthermore, the previous UK Government seemed to take the view that for every decision made to tackle climate change or promote sustainable development, two should be made to counteract any benefit, often in the name of economic growth. The day after the Secretary of State for Climate Change Ed Miliband announced a legally binding pledge to cut Britain's greenhouse gas emissions by 80 per cent by 2050 covering all sectors of the economy, including shipping and aviation (*Independent*, 2008a), the Prime Minister Gordon Brown was threatening petrol companies with an inquiry under competition laws if they refused to pass on lower oil prices to motorists (Grice, 2008). The previous week, the Government had backed plans to allow the expansion of Stansted Airport to handle an extra 10 million passengers a year and increase the number of flights from 241,000 to 264,000 (*Independent*, 2008b). By continuing to provide secure supplies of cheap oil and gas, there is little incentive for anyone to consume less fuel or switch to alternative fuels or alternative transport.

The difficulties continue. A sustainable economy is a key tool for delivering sustainable development, but it should not be its primary objective. Ecological sustainability, or making sure our planet meets our needs and the wellbeing of present and future generations, surely are the real objectives behind sustainable development and ought to take priority. As set out in the 2005 Framework, a sustainable economy ought to be one of the means of achieving ecological sustainability and wellbeing. In October 2010, the UK Government was paying, at a rate of £120 million a day, £43 billion a year in debt interest (HM Treasury, 2010b). This is hardly sustainable and the Government's commitment to reducing the debt is admirable. The spending cuts announced by the Chancellor, George Osborne, in October 2010, include changes to incapacity benefit, housing benefit, council tax benefit and working tax credit, a rise in state pension age and reductions in public sector pensions and tuition fees (HM Treasury, 2010b). The Government admits these welfare cuts are regressive but that the whole review is progressive. The Institute for Fiscal Studies disagrees and claims that the cuts hit the most vulnerable the hardest. Its analysis shows that families with children will suffer the most but so will the disabled, the elderly, the poor and women (Institute for Fiscal Studies, 2010). Any interpretation of sustainable development which puts the health of the economy ahead of the wellbeing of society's most vulnerable has to be questioned.

Conclusion

Weak sustainability, whereby environmental factors are traded-off against social and economic ones, have meant that today's income comes from liquidating our social and natural assets capital. Moreover, the UK's affinity for economic growth has led to further environmental degradation and increased disparity between the rich and poor. Decoupling growth from resource use is not enough to make a real difference. 'Ecological sustainability' imposes a duty on everyone to protect and restore the integrity of the Earth's ecological systems. Decision making based around ecological sustainability places the discussion of trade-offs within the ecological limits of the Earth. Like justice and equality, ecological sustainability is an approach and should be considered a fundamental legal principle. This legal status is deserved, since our ability to deliver the other fundamental legal principles (freedom, equality and justice) reduces as the Earth's resources and resilience reduce, and the best way to protect these other fundamental legal principles is to operate within a system based on ecological sustainability. With ecological sustainability at its core, sustainable development has the capacity to set meaningful objectives, duties and rules, and provide boundaries for decision making, as these roles are already present in recent UK and devolved legislation.

However, this is not enough. We know the way forward and we know what is required. The difficulty is that without a consistent message and powerful support for best practice, short-term gains will continue to trump long-term objectives. This is simply not sustainable and requires good leadership supported by binding obligations. The next chapter makes the case for legislating more generally for sustainable development, by imposing on all public bodies, a general, overarching duty related to sustainable development. Over and above its symbolic and educational value, specific legislation in relation to sustainable development generally, and in relation to the production, use and review of the national or sub-national sustainable development strategy more specifically, would impose mandatory obligations on policymakers and decision makers, often with meaningful consequences both inside and outside the courtroom. However, legislation cannot bring about the change discussed in this chapter. It cannot explain to leaders the importance of operating within the Earth's limits. Ideally, ecological sustainability would underpin any general legislative action. However, there are ways of imposing legislative obligations that would make a significant difference, even if the government in power is not at the stage politically to explicitly prioritize ecological sustainability. As such, the next chapter explores three legislative models that would be suitable in the UK and its devolved administrations to support the implementation of sustainable development building on experience in Wales and Canada. All three models have the capacity to deliver increased consistency in decision making by turning what may currently be established good practice or policy into legally binding obligations that can deliver real change.

Notes

1 This chapter reworks and updates material previously published in Ross, A. (2009) 'Modern interpretations of sustainable development', *Journal of Law and Society*, 36(1): 32–54.

2 Capital comprises the stock of man-made capital – machines and infrastructure, together with the stock of knowledge and skills, or human capital, as well as the stock of natural capital including natural resources (renewable and non-renewable), biological diversity, habitat, clean air, water, and so on (Pearce, 1993: 14). 'Weak sustainability is indifferent to the form in which we pass on capital stock. We can pass on less of the environment so long as we offset this loss by increasing the stock of roads and machinery or other man-made capital' (Pearce, 1993: 15). The weak

sustainability interpretation of sustainable development still requires that the depletion of natural resources that are in fixed supply – non-renewable resources – should be accompanied by investment in substitute sources (Pearce, 1993: 15–16). For a slightly stronger view, see Bowers, 1997: 194.

3 The ecological footprint measures the amount of biologically productive land and water area required to produce the resources an individual, population or activity consumes and to absorb the waste it generates, given prevailing technology and resource management.

4 The term 'sustainability' is problematic since it is used to describe many different attributes, including the success of a particular business or its succession plans and the state of an economy more generally.

5 Bowers argues that while the concept of natural capital is problematic, sustainability requirements can be more simply expressed as a set of constraints on decision making.

6 How such capacity is determined is discussed below in the text (see Rees, 2002; Venetoulis *et al.*, 2004).

7 See Judge Weeramantry's separate opinion in the *Gabçikovo-Nagymaros Project Case* (*Hungary/Slovakia*), Judgment, ICJ Reports: 7.

8 Consolidated version of the Treaty on European Union *Official Journal of the European Union* (OJ) (2008), C 115/13 Article 3(3)(5), Article 178. For a fuller examination, see Judge Weeramantry's separate opinion in the *Gabçikovo-Nagymaros Project Case* (*Hungary/Slovakia*), Judgment, ICJ Reports: 7.

9 *Horsham DC v First Secretary of State, Devine Homes plc* [2004] EWHC 769 (Admin).

10 For example, see the Government of Mexico (Earth Charter Initiative, 2007).

11 The other three principles are: ensuring a strong, healthy and just society; promoting good governance; and using sound science responsibly (HM Government *et al.*, 2005: 8).

12 Convention on Early Notification of a Nuclear Accident, 25 *International Legal Materials* (ILM) 1370 (1986). See Cameron *et al.*, 1988.

13 The Clean Air Act 1956 ch. 52.

14 The Climate Change Act 2008 ch. 27; the Climate Change (Scotland) Act 2009 asp 12.

15 The Climate Change Act 2008 s. 58(2).

16 See Chapter 9; Rees, 2002: 267–8; Venetoulis *et al.*, 2004: 7.

17 See Chapter 7.

18 This is no easy feat, as the impacts of any decision need to be considered in the context of the local ecosystems, foreign ecosystems and that of the Earth as a whole. See Directive 2001/42/EC on the assessment of certain plans and programmes on the environment (OJ) (2001), L 197/30; Rees, 2002; Venetoulis *et al.*, 2004; Pacala and Socolow, 2004; WWF *et al.*, 2008.

19 Sustainable Consumption and Production and Sustainable Industrial Policy Action Plan COM (2008) 397 final.

20 See the Environment Act 1995 ch. 25 ss. 4(1), 31(2). Arguably, given the importance of these agencies, they should have more modern duties.

21 An exception may be the International Development Act 2002 ch. 1 s. 1(3).

22 See, for example, the Further and Higher Education (Scotland) Act 2005 asp 6 s. 20.

23 See the Transport Act 2000 ch. 38 s. 207(2)(b); the Water Industry (Scotland) Act 2002 asp 3 s. 51; the Water Environment and Water Services (Scotland) Act 2003 asp 3 s. 2(4).

24 De Sadeleer (2005: 311) describes these as rules of indeterminate content and argues that such rules may be created so long as they appear in normative text and are formulated in a sufficiently prescriptive manner.

25 See, for example, the Land Reform (Scotland) Act 2003 asp 2 ss. 34, 51.

26 The Climate Change Act 2008 s. 78, Schedule 7.

27 For a fuller discussion about this observation, see Beder, 2006: ch. 1.

28 Since the Congestion Charge scheme started, traffic entering the original charging zone remains 21 per cent lower than pre-charge levels (70,000 fewer cars a day) and there has been a 6 per cent increase in bus passengers during charging hours (Transport for London, 2008).

29 The plastic bag levy introduced on 4 March 2002 had an immediate effect on consumer behaviour – with plastic bag per capita usage decreasing overnight from an estimated 328 bags to 21 (roughly 90 per cent) (Department of Environment, Heritage and Local Government, n.d.).

30 For example, previously unviable sources of oil and gas are becoming attractive due to the higher price of energy and the fact they are in secure locations. Many of these sources, such as the tar sands in Alberta, Canada are becoming more viable economically to exploit, but remain environmentally costly. For instance, oil production in the tar sands requires substantial amounts of natural gas and water, and there are also biodiversity issues related to these sources, as well as social considerations relating to health and safety impacts on the local community (Climate Action Network Canada, 2008: 4).

References

Ayres, R.U. (1996) 'Limits to the growth paradigm', *Ecological Economics*, 19(2): 117–34.

Beder, S. (2006) *Environmental Principles and Policies: An Interdisciplinary Introduction*, Sydney: University of New South Wales Press.

Blowers, A. (1992) 'Planning a sustainable future: Problems, principles and prospects', *Town and Country Planning*, 61(5): 132–35.

Bosselmann, K. (2008) *The Principle of Sustainability: Transforming Law and Governance*, Aldershot: Ashgate.

Bowers, J. (1997) *Sustainability and Environmental Economics: An Alternative Text*, Harlow: Longman.

Cabinet Office (2010) The Cabinet Committees System and list of Cabinet Committees, http://www.cabinetoffice.gov.uk/resource-library/cabinet-committees-system-and-list-cabinet-committees, accessed 25 May 2011.

Cameron, D., Hancher, L. and Kuhn, W. (eds) (1988) *Nuclear Energy Law after Chernobyl*, London: Graham & Trotman/International Bar Association.

Chambers, N., Simmons, C. and Wackernagel, M. (2000) *Sharing Nature's Interest: Ecological Footprints as an Indicator of Sustainability*, London: Earthscan.

Climate Action Network Canada (2008) *Stuck in the Tar Sands: How the Federal Government's Proposed Climate Change Strategy Lets Oil Companies off the Hook*, Ottawa: CANC.

Convention on Biological Diversity (2007) 'Principles', http://www.cbd.int/ecosystem/principles.shtml, accessed 12 August 2010.

Cussons, S. (2006) *Review of Statutory Sustainable Development Duties*, London: In House Policy Consultancy/DEFRA.

Department for Transport, Scottish Executive, Welsh Assembly Government (2009) *Transport Statistics for Great Britain 2009*, 35th edition, London: Department for Transport.

Department of Energy and Climate Change (DECC) (2010) *Average Surface Temperature: 1772–2009*, DECC, http://www.decc.gov.uk/assets/decc/statistics/climate_change/1_20100319151831_e_@@_surfacetemperaturesummary.pdf. accessed 27 May 2011.

Department of Environment, Food and Rural Affairs (DEFRA) (1999) *A Better Quality of Life: A Strategy for Sustainable Development for the United Kingdom*, London: DEFRA.

Department of Environment, Heritage and Local Government (n.d.) 'Plastic Bags', http://www.environ.ie/en/Environment/Waste/PlasticBags/, accessed 15 August 2010.

De Sadeleer, N. (2005) *Environmental Principles: From Political Slogans to Legal Rules*, Oxford: Oxford University Press.

Durant, W.J. (1927) *The Story of Philosophy: The Lives and Opinions of the Greater Philosophers*, New York: Garden City Publishing.

Dworkin, R. (1977) *Taking Rights Seriously*, London: Duckworth.

Earth Charter Initiative (2000) *The Earth Charter*, http://www.earthinaction.org/invent/images/uploads/echarter_english.pdf, accessed 12 August 2010.

Earth Charter Initiative (2007) 'A wonderful week for the Earth Charter – Mexico reaffirms its support and commitment', http://www.earthcharterinaction.org/content/articles/122/1/A-Wonderful-week-for-the-Earth-Charter.html, accessed 12 August 2010.

Elkins, P. (1992) '"Limits to growth" and "sustainable development": grappling with ecological realities', *Ecological Economics*, 8(3): 269–88.

French, D. (2005) *International Law and Policy of Sustainable Development*, Manchester: Manchester University Press.

Grainger, A. (2004) 'Introduction', in M. Purvis and A. Grainger (eds) *Exploring Sustainable Development: Geographical Perspectives*, London: Earthscan.

Grice, A. (2008) 'Brown: Petrol firms must lower fuel prices or face OFT inquiry', *Independent*, 17 October.

Grice, A. (2009) '£850bn: Official cost of the bank bailout', *Independent*, 4 December.

HM Government (2005) *Securing the Future: Delivering UK Sustainable Development Strategy*, London: DEFRA.

HM Government (2006) *Climate Change: The UK Programme 2006*, London: DEFRA.

HM Government, Scottish Executive, Welsh Assembly Government, Northern Ireland Office (2005a) *One future – different paths: The UK's shared framework for sustainable development*, London: DEFRA.

HM Treasury (2010a) 'Budget statement by the Chancellor of the Exchequer, the Rt Hon George Osborne MP' 22 June 2010, http://www.hm-treasury.gov.uk/junebudget_speech.htm, accessed 12 October 2010.

HM Treasury (2010b) 'Spending Review statement by the Chancellor of the Exchequer, the Rt Hon George Osborne MP' 20 October 2010, http://www.hm-treasury.gov.uk/spend_sr2010_speech.htm, accessed 22 October 2010.

HM Treasury (2011) *Budget 2011*, HC 836, London: HM Treasury.

Independent (2008a) 'Britain to pledge legally binding emissions cut', *Independent*, 16 October.

Independent (2008b) 'Government green light for Stansted expansion', *Independent*, 9 October.

Institute for Fiscal Studies (2010) *Spending Review Analysis 2010*, http://www.ifs.org.uk/publications/5314, accessed 22 October 2010.

Intergovernmental Panel on Climate Change (2005) *Special Report on Carbon Dioxide Capture and Storage*, Cambridge: Cambridge University Press.

Jackson, T. (2009) *Prosperity Without Growth: Transition to a Sustainable Economy*, London: SDC.

Li, X. (2005) 'Diversification and localization of energy systems for sustainable development and energy security', *Energy Policy*, 33(17): 2237–43.

Macrory, R. (ed.) (2004) *Principles of European Environmental Law*, Groningen: Europa Law Publishing.

Marks & Spencer plc (2010a) 'About Plan A', http://plana.marksandspencers.com/about, accessed 12 August 2010.

Marks & Spencer plc (2010b) *Our Plan A Commitments: 2010–2015*, London: Marks & Spencer Group plc.

Pacala, S. and Socolow, R. (2004) 'Stabilization wedges: Solving the climate problem for the next 50 years with current technologies', *Science*, 305(5686): 968–72.

Pearce, D. (1993) *Blueprint 3: Measuring Sustainable Development*, London: Earthscan.

Prince of Wales (2011) 'An article by HRH The Prince of Wales for *The Times* on economic growth and the environment', 9 February 2011, http://www.princeofwales. gov.uk/speechesandarticles/an_article_by_hrh_the_prince_of_wales_for_the_times_on_ econo_1719068971.html, accessed 28 May 2011.

Rees, W.E. (2002) 'Footprint: Our impact on the earth is getting heavier', *Nature*, 420: 267–8.

Rockström, J. *et al.* (2009) 'A safe operating space for humanity', *Nature*, 461: 472–5.

Ross, A. (2006) 'Sustainable development in Scotland post devolution', *Environmental Law Review*, 8: 6–32.

Ross, A. (2008) 'Why legislate for sustainable development? An examination of sustainable development provisions in UK and Scottish statutes', *Journal of Environmental Law*, 20(1): 35–68.

Sachs, J.D. (2008) quoted in WWF/Zoological Society of London/Global Footprint Network (2008) *Living Planet Report 2008*, Gland: WWF Switzerland.

Sands, P. (2003) *Principles of International Environmental Law*, 2nd edition, Cambridge: Cambridge University Press.

Scottish Government (2010) *Scottish Planning Policy*, Edinburgh: Scottish Government.

Secretariat of the Convention on Biological Diversity (SCBD) (2006) *Global Biodiversity Outlook (GBO-2)*, Montreal: Convention on Biological Diversity.

SCBD (2010) *Global Biodiversity Outlook (GBO-3)*, Montreal: Convention on Biological Diversity.

Stallworthy, M. (2008) *Understanding Environmental Law*, London: Sweet & Maxwell.

Stern, N. (2007) *The Economics of Climate Change: The Stern Review*, Cambridge: Cambridge University Press.

Sustainable Development Commission Scotland (SDCS) (2008) *Sustainable Development Commission Scotland's response to the Scottish Government Consultation on a Scottish Climate Change Bill*, Edinburgh: SDCS.

SDCS (2009) *Sustainable Development: Third Annual Assessment of Progress by the Scottish Government*, Edinburgh· SDCS.

The Times (2008) 'Q&A: $700 billion US bailout plan', *The Times*, 25 September.

Transport for London (2008) *Central London Congestion Charging Impacts Monitoring, Sixth Annual Report*, London: Transport for London.

UK Government (1994) *Sustainable Development: The UK Strategy*, London: HMSO, Cm 2426.

UN Development Programme (UNDP) (2007) *Human Development Report 2007/2008: Fighting Climate Change*, New York: UNDP.

UN General Assembly (UNGA) (1992) *The Rio Declaration on Environment and Development*, A/CONF.151/26 Vol. 1, New York: UN.

UNGA (2002) *Programme of Implementation of the World Summit on Sustainable Development, Johannesburg*, A/CONF.199/20, New York: UN.

Venetoulis, J., Chazan, D. and Gaudet, C. (2004) *Ecological Footprint of Nations*, San Francisco: Redefining Progress.

Welsh Assembly Government (WAG) (2009) *One Wales: One Planet: The Sustainable Development Scheme of the Welsh Assembly Government*, Cardiff: WAG.

White House (2010) 'Remarks by the President to the Nation on the BP Oil Spill', 15 June 2010, http://www.whitehouse.gov/the-press-office/remarks-president-nation-bp-oil-spill, accessed 12 October 2010.

Winter, G. (2004) 'The legal nature of environmental principles in international, EC and German law', in R. Macrory (ed.) *Principles of European Environmental Law*, Groningen: Europa Law Publishing.

Winter, G. (2008) 'A fundament and two pillars: The concept of sustainable development 20 years after the Brundtland Report', in H. Bugge and C. Voigt (eds) *Sustainable Development in International and National Law*, Groningen: Europa Law Publishing.

Woolf, M. (2007) 'Brown downgrades cabinet committee on climate change', *Independent*, 5 August.

World Commission on Environment and Development (WCED) (1987) *Our Common Future*, Oxford: Oxford University Press.

World Wildlife Fund (WWF), Zoological Society of London and Global Footprint Network (2008) *Living Planet Report 2008*, Gland: WWF.

13 Compelling action – the case for legislation[1]

The UK has been successful in developing effective tools for delivering sustainable development. Its strategies for sustainable development are some of the best in the world. The remit and work of the Sustainable Development Commission (SDC) is renowned and copied elsewhere and in the Environmental Audit Committee of the House of Commons (EAC), an effective and high level of parliamentary scrutiny exists. Yet, the UK is still a long way off from being sustainable. In November 2009, the former SDC Chairman, Jonathon Porritt, concluded that 'the reality, as I see it, is that the mainstreaming of sustainable development in the UK, from the margins to the centre of government, is indeed underway, but is still moving too slowly in most respects' (Porritt, 2009a: 10).

The UK is not alone in being at an impasse in its implementation of sustainable development. Other countries and regions are also struggling to make the big changes necessary to actually move from rhetoric to full sustainability, and although the mechanisms so far developed have potential, this potential is not being fully exploited. This chapter offers a way over the hurdles that countries face. It explores the value of using legislation to educate and promote change, and it contends that the time has come to use law to force the hand of decision makers and compel them to take the actions required to implement sustainable development.

As observed by Dernbach (2008: 94), 'While it is difficult to envision how sustainable development can occur without a legal foundation, the issue of an appropriate legal foundation for sustainable development at the national level has received less attention than it deserves'. Very few countries have actually provided the foundation referred to above by using legislation to drive their sustainable development programmes forward. As discussed in Chapter 8, in the UK, sustainable development regularly appears in statutes as a legal objective, a procedural obligation, and, arguably, a legal rule providing a framework for decision making. However, these provisions are specific to particular regimes and to individual public authorities or groups of public authorities, such as the Environment Agency or planning authorities. Despite calls for a general sustainable development duty which extends to all government actors or activities, there remains no such obligation at UK level (Jenkins, 2002: 578). The Northern

Ireland Assembly has imposed a duty to promote sustainable development, as provided for in the Northern Ireland (Miscellaneous Provisions) Act 2006 s. 25, which requires departments and district councils to exercise their functions in the manner they consider best calculated to promote the achievement of sustainable development. Unfortunately, this substantive duty is not supported by procedural requirements and, to date, has had very limited impact. Indeed, in the UK, Scotland and Northern Ireland, there is no statutory obligation to produce a national sustainable development strategy nor are there substantive or procedural obligations in place to regulate how it is produced, to secure its use and to ensure it is regularly reviewed. As discussed below, while there is a procedural obligation imposed on the Welsh institutions to produce a scheme of sustainable development,[2] progress towards sustainable development in Wales has been hindered by a lack of supporting detail in the procedures and, arguably, a lack of substantive content. Thus, while they are generally accepted, sustainable development strategies in the UK – along with their indicators and other implementation mechanisms – lack the legitimacy and authority that come with legal recognition.

The main argument presented here is that the UK is now at a stage where specific legislation is required to further drive the implementation of sustainable development forward. Legislation directed at the implementation of sustainable development could potentially address many of the current shortcomings by, among other things, increasing the priority, support and protection afforded to sustainable development as a long-term policy objective across governments. Legislation could have a significant symbolic and educational impact in making stakeholders and the general public understand what is at stake. Moreover, it could crystallize the policy framework already in place and thus, turn what is now, at best, good practice into meaningful legal obligations, supported by monitoring and review mechanisms that impose significant consequences for failure. Finally, legislation could set out how tools such as spending reviews, environmental assessment, procurement practice, research funding and public consultation relate to sustainable development and their role in the overall framework for implementation.

This chapter begins by setting out the basic premise that any programme for sustainable development must include a clear understanding or vision, a framework for decision making and a strong operational toolkit (or armoury of mechanisms). As discussed in the previous two chapters, the UK has been only partially successful in meeting these requirements and the criticisms of the UK approach to sustainable development can all be attributed to inconsistencies in the application of the relevant strategy, and its objectives and procedures. Over and above its symbolic and educational value, legislation in relation to sustainable development, and specifically, in relation to the production, use and review of the national or sub-national sustainable development strategy, would have meaningful consequences both inside and outside the courtroom. Three alternative legislative models that would be suitable for the UK and its devolved administrations to support the implementation of sustainable development are explored here using examples from Wales and Canada. The first possible model would be purely procedural. The second possible model would aim to make the strategy the central reference point or framework for all policy and decision making (this approach could be weakened by limiting its application to policy and decision making relating to sustainable development). The final possible model used for this analysis is the most ambitious – making sustainable development the central organizing principle of government.

The practical benefits of procedural obligations, both operating alone and as back up for more substantive obligations, are emphasized, as is the possibility of certain well-worded substantive duties capable of being treated as actual legal rules which govern decision making. The benefits and drawbacks of including a definition of 'sustainable development', and of referring to specific underlying principles such as the precautionary principle also are reviewed. While perhaps very useful in other jurisdictions, these definitions and references may not be necessary or suitable in the UK.

Throughout this volume, it is contended that sustainable development ought to be the central organizing principle of government in the UK. However, the chapter argues that even if a weaker and less ambitious formulation is preferred, providing some legislative backing for the production, use and review of the strategies would still be valuable and consistent with calls for reflexive governance for sustainable development. If this is the case, legislation for sustainable development could be enacted in a staged fashion, focusing initially on the most important procedural obligations and then later supplementing them with the more substantive obligations, as awareness and acceptance of sustainable development develop.

The evaluation in this chapter is restricted to those legislative provisions relating to the production, use and review of a sustainable development strategy, and to the need for other mechanisms, such as environmental assessments and procurement practices, to reflect its aims and priorities. This is done for good reason. The strategy initiates a process and, as Dernbach explains, this involves:

> the development of an overall sustainability vision and objectives based on an iterative and open process; Identification of the institutions and policies that will be used to achieve those objectives; adoption and implementation of the needed laws and policies; and a monitoring, learning and adaptation process that informs and perhaps changes objectives policies, and implementation.
>
> (Dernbach, 2008: 103)

Moreover, many of the difficulties and criticisms levelled at the other mechanisms would be resolved if the criticisms directed at the development, use and review of the strategy itself are addressed.

The various recommendations made for the UK, Wales, Scotland and Northern Ireland are, in many cases, adapted from those developed elsewhere and they can readily be transposed to other jurisdictions. Each jurisdiction, however, needs to tailor its legislation to its own circumstances, keeping in mind its own constitutional and administrative arrangements and political and legal culture (Turner, 2006a: 55–87; 2006b: 245–75; 2007: 422–58).[3]

Implementing sustainable development

As discussed in Chapter 3, a great deal of research and experience into the optimal requirements for delivering sustainable development now exist, and the essentials are now pretty much settled. The Organisation for Economic Co-operation and Development (OECD) has stated that 'Good governance and sound public management are preconditions for the implementation of sustainable development policies' (OECD, 2002: 2). The SDC fleshes out this vision by explaining that to be meaningful, sustainable development needs to operate at three different levels. First, people must be helped to understand the 'big picture' or what is actually at stake (SDC, 2004: 10; Porrit, 2009a: 11–15). As described by the OECD, what is needed is a common understanding of sustainable development. Obviously, strong leadership is a key factor for actually achieving this (OECD, 2002: 2). As noted in Chapter 5, leadership, however, is a double-edged sword. When it is present, policies flourish, when it disappears, policies like sustainable development flounder (Kavanagh and Richards, 2001: 1, 17). While law can have little influence on ensuring leadership, it can provide symbolic evidence of the importance of sustainable development, as well as suitable and lasting protection against a lack of leadership in the short term by protecting certain values and imposing certain substantive and procedural obligations. If the SDC's role had been set out in statute, it would have been much more difficult for the UK Coalition Government to cut its funding.

The SDC's second requirement is that sustainable development must provide a comprehensive framework within which to integrate potentially conflicting priorities (Porritt, 2009a: 15–22). As in many other countries, the various UK administrations have opted to use their national sustainable development strategies as the framework for the implementation of sustainable development. Approaches which use the national strategy combined with themes around economy, environment and society tend to be well regarded in the literature as 'whole-systems approaches' which capture multiple aspects of a system (Hodge and Hardi, 1997: 7–21; UN, 2006: 9). As discussed in Chapters 4 and 12, as a whole-systems concept, sustainable development must not be too closely linked to one particular concern including environmental protection, human rights or climate change. Consequently, sustainable development cannot be an effective champion for any of its component parts on their own. These concerns need their own champions (Ross, 2009: 45). Instead, sustainable development is most appropriately viewed as providing the forum or 'table' to which important and more concrete objectives and values can be brought (Ross, 2009: 45). Used in this way, sustainable development can offer a framework for decision making which ensures these objectives and values influence the decision-making process

(Ross, 2009: 45). Legislation can be used to support this role by requiring certain procedures, such as the production of reports and wide consultation, or by imposing substantive duties requiring decisions to be made in a particular way by taking into account certain factors, and importantly, introducing certain priorities.

Finally, the SDC maintains that sustainable development must also provide an operational tool kit – in terms of policymaking, performance appraisal, management systems, procurement, and so on (Porritt, 2009a: 23–8). The OECD similarly expects countries to develop specific institutional mechanisms to steer integration (including enforcement and monitoring) along with effective stakeholder involvement and efficient knowledge management (OECD, 2002). Chapters 7, 8, 9 and 10 of this volume explore numerous tools in the armoury for implementing sustainable development, including: government procurement practices, dealing with the government estate; allocation of resources through public service agreements and spending reviews; legal duties; and the use of various assessment, reporting and monitoring tools. Many effective tools are not fully utilized, or they have been ignored or revoked. Again, legislation could support these tools and provide consequences for a failure to comply.

Criticisms of the current UK Framework and strategies

One future – different paths: The UK's shared framework for sustainable development (HM Government *et al.*, 2005) is a unifying, UK-wide framework for sustainable development, and the individual strategies are all relatively modern and progressive in considering environmental limits and long-term effects. These should be capable of delivering change. However, as summarized in Chapter 11, research shows that the Framework and each of the strategies lack influence and legal and political clout, and their use in practice is sporadic at best. Hence, at the moment, despite enviable strategic documentation, decisions continue to be made with little regard to the principles in the Framework and strategies. Moreover, the Framework and the strategies are not delivering in the three areas the SDC notes as vital for the proper implementation of sustainable development: improving understanding; providing a comprehensive framework to integrate potentially conflicting priorities; and providing an operational toolkit.

As set out in the previous chapters, the criticisms can all be reduced to a lack of leadership and a failure to set out and commit to a clear vision of sustainable development which, in turn, establishes a clear hierarchy of priority. This manifests itself through inconsistencies in the application of the strategy, and its objectives and procedures. The reasons for the inconsistencies include varying priorities between decision makers and misunderstandings about the meaning of sustainable development, its role and its applicability. These are magnified by other influential factors such as path dependency and resource constraints (Porritt, 2009a: 8–30). The contention here is that legislation can make a significant and beneficial difference in the way in which sustainable development strategies are developed, implemented and reviewed. Over and above its symbolic and educational value, legislation can turn good practice and policy into binding obligations, with meaningful consequences both inside and outside the court-room, and it can make a significant difference to delivering on all three levels set out by the SDC.

Possible legislative options for sustainable development

Any legislative solution to the difficulties described in Chapter 11 needs to take into account the legislative options actually available to a given country or administration, and its institutional framework and legal culture. For the UK, devolution, a preference towards legislating sparingly, avoiding unenforceable substantive provisions and, where possible, leaving decision makers ample discretion to ensure flexibility, all figure prominently in this regard. Keeping this in mind, and building on experiences in Wales and Canada, three possible legislative models and the provisions needed by each are explored below. The models start from different political and cultural perspectives, yet they are not mutually exclusive. Indeed, it may be preferable to introduce the legislation in a staged fashion, initially setting out more detailed procedural obligations and then, over time, supporting these with more powerful substantive duties as public and political opinion becomes more accustomed to using sustainable development as the central organizing principle of government.

As Rubin (1989: 374) explains, in a modern state, contemporary legislation serves a range of purposes. These include: creating direct prohibitions, regulatory controls and administrative agencies; conferring benefits on groups or individuals; issuing guidance; conferring grants of jurisdiction and statutory duties; imposing enforcement and implementation procedures; and facilitating private arrangements. Some legislation is simply symbolic expressing the political authorities' awareness of an issue and that something needs to be done about it (Mader, 2001: 119, 122).

Different countries will use legislation for big policy issues (like sustainable development) in different ways and for different purposes. Different countries will also have different legislative options available to them and any suggested legislative approach must take account of the constitutional and administrative arrangements in a particular state. In many countries, if one wanted to truly embed sustainable development into government, the answer would be to seek a constitutional amendment and, in fact, sustainable development appears in the Constitutions of South Africa, Poland and the EU.[4] While the UK can pass legislation which impacts on its Constitution, such as the devolution Acts and the European Communities Act 1972,[5] there is no individual or identifiable collection of documents which are 'the UK Constitution', so a constitutional approach is not available for the UK.

Before discussing any legislative option, it is essential to review the legal culture and institutions of the UK. The UK's initial approach to the sustainable development agenda was largely non-legislative (Ross, 2005: 27–49). Indeed, in 2000, the Government dismissed the need for legislation, stating that sustainable development could be placed at the heart of an organization by policy directions from the executive or by the inclusion of non-statutory aims and objectives (DETR, 2000: paras 5.2 and 5.4). There is also a view that the needs of sustainable development are better served by specific provisions, such as targets to improve water quality or reduce hospital waiting lists, than by any general overarching duty or objective (CAG Consultants, 2004: 43). However, references to sustainable development have become much more commonplace in statutes of both the UK and Scottish Parliaments (Ross, 2008: 66, Chapter 8) and occasionally now in Northern Ireland. One possible reason is that over the last decade, sustainable development has proven its acceptability and resilience as a policy tool, and crystallizing it in statute has become more palatable. For example, sustainable development has been a key policy objective of the planning systems both north and south of the border for many years (UK Government, 1997; Scottish Executive, 2002), but it was only included in a relevant English statute in 2004 and in the Scottish equivalent in late 2006.[6] Also, while it is not one of the EU's core environmental principles (Winter, 2004: 13),[7] sustainable development has been elevated in status to one of its general aims. This is reflected in the EU's legislation, such as the Treaty on the European Union Article 3(3)(5),[8] which has influenced the content of legislation at both UK and devolved levels.[9]

In light of the above, as well as the Welsh experience discussed below, legislation specifically directed at an administration's approach to sustainable development would seem not to be out of step with modern UK legal culture. However, any legislation would also need to take account of the institutional structures that exist in the UK. The key challenge in this regard is devolution and the fact that legislative and administrative competence often does not lie with the UK Government, but instead, with the devolved institutions. Enacting legislation that binds the UK and devolved governments to certain policy goals would not be easy, since it largely counteracts the purpose of devolution (Reid, 2009a).[10] Therefore, any legal formalization in relation to the production, review and use of the UK Shared Framework for Sustainable Development and its indicators is not a realistic possibility. Instead, such formalization needs to remain as a joint policy initiative among the administrations. The current informal approach works well at this level because successful cooperation is often underpinned by its non-binding nature. Indeed, much of the actual workings of the devolution settlement are set down in a memorandum of understanding and various other concordats, rather than in the devolution legislation itself (Bulmer *et al.*, 2006: 75–85; Ross and Nash, 2009: 564–95). The SDC used to play an important role here, keeping the governments of Scotland, Wales, Northern Ireland and the UK in touch with one another over sustainable development strategies and policy experience, and helping them to maintain a sense of common cause in the spirit of *One Future, Different Paths* (Porritt, 2009a: 39). As discussed in Chapter 14, coordinating the replacement framework without the SDC's assistance will be a challenge.

Legislation directed at a single administration is possible, as shown in Canada, where the Federal Sustainable Development Act 2008 covers the areas of competence of the federal government.[11] Additionally, three of the ten Canadian provinces have opted to pass their own sustainable development Acts.[12] A similar approach would be suitable in the UK. Ideally, the individual statutes would include a reference to a shared framework or some other coordinated UK-wide effort.

At this stage, it is important to emphasize the value of legislating at the sub-national level. Porritt hypothesizes that sustainable development may be an easier concept to operationalize at the sub-national level. In his review of the standing of sustainable development in government in the UK, he notes that the new devolved system has opened up political space for innovation in Scotland and Wales, and that there has been a potentially helpful break with 'path dependence' (Porritt, 2009a: 45, 46). This is supported by the new Welsh strategy and by Ross's finding that the Scottish Parliament has shown a greater willingness to legislate on sustainable development than its UK counterpart (Ross, 2008: 37). Moreover, from the review below, the Canadian provinces also appear more proactive in their legislation than the federal government. Porritt (2009a: 46) suggests that particular regions or states can be laboratories for policy changes, and Scotland and Wales could enlarge policymakers' sense of what is politically possible in relation to sustainable development.

Three legislative models

So what is the best approach for the UK? The answer is that it depends on what the particular UK administration wants the legislation to do. Since a framework approach to sustainable development is supposed to be iterative and capable of review and change, crystallizing the content of any existing strategy itself into law is not desirable. Instead, law reform is needed to support the selection, development, use and review of national sustainable development strategies and, arguably, the overall approach to implementing sustainable development. It is imperative for any legislation on sustainable development to be very clear as to its overall purpose. This section explores three possible models and the legislative approaches that each model requires, drawing on examples from Wales, Canada and the Canadian provinces of Manitoba and Quebec.

Procedural model

The first model is purely procedural. Its objective is to ensure that certain events happen at certain times in a certain way. This approach introduces procedural obligations in relation to the production, use and review of the sustainable development strategy, and employs tools such as indicators and action plans. These procedural obligations could also implicitly embody the substance of certain principles (Ross, 2008: 56–60). For example, procedural obligations could require the production of the strategy, provide consultation opportunities or require regular reports on progress.

These procedures are characteristic of reflexive law which aims to provide information to government agencies and institutions on the effectiveness and impacts of particular laws and policies, which can then be used to modify those laws and policies (Kemp *et al.*, 2005: 23–6). These reflexive procedures can also be used to encourage or prod non-governmental entities, including businesses, to make their activities more sustainable, without being overly prescriptive (Orts, 1995: 1311–13). Ideally, in the context of sustainable development, effective reflexive law encourages self-reflection in institutions by requiring the generation and public disclosure of knowledge that would help institutions make their activities responsive and adaptable to future events – by anticipating and avoiding unwanted side effects in current decision making, by the iterative development of sustainability goals, and by the development and implementation of appropriate strategies in conjunction with stakeholders (Voss and Kemp, 2006: 17–20). These approaches or strategies, in turn, must be capable of informing and learning from all relevant levels of governance and all relevant governance institutions (Voss *et al.*, 2006: 427–9, 435).

There is already an effective UK example of this approach in Wales. When the UK Parliament established the National Assembly for Wales (the Assembly) under the Government of Wales Act 1998, it included, in s. 121, a requirement to produce a scheme of sustainable development.[13] Similar duties were not included in the Scottish and Northern Ireland settlements, as these settlements created parliaments with legislative power and it was thought that imposing such a duty would be contrary to the spirit of devolution. Importantly, the Welsh provisions need to be distinguished, as they were, at least formally, imposed on the Assembly and later the Welsh Assembly Government (WAG) rather than being introduced by the institutions themselves. That said, the WAG is proud that sustainable development is a core principle within its founding statute (WAG, 2009: 4).

The Government of Wales Act 2006 s. 79 requires the Welsh Ministers to produce a scheme setting out how they propose, in the exercise of their functions, to promote sustainable development, and to report annually on how all functions were carried out. Every four years, the Assembly is to report on the effectiveness of the proposals (WAG, 2008: 5). The provisions are confined to these procedural obligations. Although there is a very weak substantive obligation imposed on the Assembly Commission, the contracting arm of the legislature, by Schedule 2, clause 8(2) that 'in the exercise of the functions of the Assembly Commission due regard must be had to the principle of promoting sustainable development', there is no definition of sustainable development, nor does the Act impose a substantive duty on the key Welsh institutions. Moreover, the procedures are very vague. For example, under s. 79(3), the Welsh Ministers must consult such persons as 'they consider appropriate'. Even these minimal procedural requirements have made an impact. The Welsh institutions have been much faster than their counterparts in Scotland and Northern Ireland to incorporate sustainable development into their policies and the exercise of their functions, to review their progress regularly and to respond accordingly. The Assembly, and subsequently, the Welsh Ministers have produced the required effectiveness reports on their first two sustainable development schemes. Both reports, produced by independent consultants, strongly commended the commitments to sustainable development made by the Assembly, but pointed to difficulties in driving those commitments through to delivery (CAG Consultants, 2003; Flynn *et al.*, 2008). Nevertheless, the SDC in 2005 criticized the Welsh institutions for starting well but having unambitious commitments, failing to join up the delivery of commitments and failing to embed sustainable development across the Welsh public sector (SDC, 2006). Munday and Roberts add that:

> Although the commitment to sustainable development has become a legal duty, there has been very little elucidation of precisely what sustainable development means, in economic, environmental, social and cultural terms, and, as importantly, how to identify whether or not the region is becoming more sustainable.
>
> (Munday and Roberts, 2006)

One of the unique challenges for Wales is that often it does not have the legislative competence to introduce the necessary changes. Nonetheless, in 2009, it addressed concerns over the imprecise meaning of sustainable development by making the most of its policymaking powers. The most recent scheme, entitled *One Wales: One Planet: The Sustainable Development Scheme of the Welsh Assembly Government*, is arguably the most ambitious of the UK strategies to date (WAG, 2009). Specifically, it sets a clear vision which uses sustainable development as the overarching strategic aim of all WAG policies and programmes across all ministerial portfolios, and confirms that sustainable development will be the central organizing principle of the WAG, as well as the steps to be taken to embed this approach. Uniquely, it sets an explicit long-term aim for Wales to use only its fair share of the Earth's resources (WAG, 2009: 13).

Thus, for Wales, the UK government opted for a purely procedural legislative approach relying on a minimum number of procedural duties. From the experience in Wales, it is safe to argue that introducing these types of legal procedures elsewhere in the UK would make a significant difference to the embedding of sustainable development into government activities. The evidence also suggests, however, that the Welsh provisions could benefit from some additional detail – for example, on the consultation process and the role of the Commissioner for Sustainable Futures.

One argument against the use of a sustainable development statute that sets out procedural obligations is that the obligations may already exist in specific legislation. Unfortunately, as shown in Chapters 7 and 8, specific legislation, for example, on the strategic environmental assessment of plans and programmes, has been of limited success. One reason may be that the procedures exist without a broader context and their role in the overall sustainable development process may not be evident. In contrast, primary legislation on sustainable development that specifically refers to certain procedures as tools to be used to implement sustainable development goals will set those tools in context.

The statutes of Canada and the Canadian provinces of Quebec and Manitoba offer examples of more detailed procedural regimes. As a federal state, Canada divides legislative competences between the federal and provincial governments. The sustainability Acts noted below all focus on the activities of a single administration. All three Acts also impose obligations on the government to produce a sustainable development strategy, as well as component strategies for individual departments.[14] All three allocate specific responsibilities to the relevant environment department in relation to the strategies.[15] In addition, these three Acts have increased the powers of the relevant Auditor General's office to include review of the implementation of sustainable development across departments and public bodies.[16] Both provincial governments have established special funds to encourage sustainable development research and innovation and include procedures for the development of sustainable development indicators.[17] The Canadian and Manitoba Acts also create advisory bodies or roundtables.[18]

Thus, in the UK, legislatively adopted procedures could explicitly require the production of departmental sustainable development action plans and clarify the roles of the National Audit Office, the SDC and, for the UK administration, the role of the EAC in reviewing and monitoring the various strategies. It would be simple enough to put their policy remits into statute. The process for the selection, development, use and review of national or sub-national indicators could also be set out, and require compliance with, the principles and objectives set forth in the relevant sustainable development strategy.

Such procedures would bring several benefits to the UK. First, a failure to comply with a statutory procedure is much easier to enforce and monitor than non-compliance with some vague substantive duty, not only using judicial review but also, importantly, by the central government, interest groups and the public (Ross, 2008: 60). Moreover, the procedures can be introduced without having to address politically sensitive issues, such as clarifying the substantive meaning of sustainable development and any principles underpinning it, or delineating its specific status within UK governance. Arguably, the appropriate procedural provisions may reduce the need to include substantive provisions. A key benefit of such reflexive law is that by complying with the procedures, the public body will still need to direct its mind to the substance behind the procedure. The Welsh Assembly's obligation to produce a scheme of sustainable development and report on it regularly is a good example.

Unfortunately, less successful examples also exist. The Scottish Parliament requires most bills to be accompanied by a pre-legislative memorandum that includes a statement of the bill's impact on sustainable development. Studies show that the quality of these statements has always varied and continues to be variable, often reflecting a significant lack of understanding among policymakers and draftsmen and their conflicting priorities (Ross, 2006; Reid, 2010b). These failings point to the need for a substantive provision to clarify the role and meaning of the term 'sustainable development'.

Thus, while providing support for a strong operational toolkit for sustainable development, an exclusively procedural approach fails to address the SDC's remaining objectives: promoting a common understanding and creating a framework for decision making. Exclusive reliance on procedural mechanisms creates a danger that any symbolic statement on sustainable development will be lost and the required procedures will be reduced to mere box-ticking exercises.

Establishing the strategy as the framework for sustainable development

The second model explicitly establishes the relevant sustainable development strategy as the framework for the implementation of sustainable development. Ideally, this approach explicitly sets out the sustainable development strategy as the primary reference point for all decision making across an administration. At present, the duties imposed on various public bodies to 'exercise [their] powers in the way best calculated to contribute to the achievement of sustainable development' do not refer specifically to the relevant sustainable development strategy.[19] Instead, as noted in Chapter 8, the different statutes refer to all sorts of different guidance to assist in the interpretation of sustainable development. While allowing contextualization and flexibility arguably this also creates confusion and inconsistency (Ross, 2008: 67). Reference to the strategy ensures a more consistent interpretation of sustainable development across an administration. This appears to be the approach taken in the Canadian Federal Sustainable Development Act s. 3, which provides that 'the purpose of this Act is to provide the legal framework for developing and implementing a Federal Sustainable Development Strategy that will make environmental decision-making more transparent and accountable to Parliament'. Regrettably, the purpose is limited to environmental decision making rather than being extended to all government decision making.

This model also has the advantage of creating additional substantive obligations in relation to the indicative content and structure of the strategy and its use. For example, in Canada, the federal statute requires the strategy to be based on a specific definition of the precautionary principle. The federal and Quebec Acts require the inclusion of certain substantive content: goals, targets, an implementation strategy for each target, and an allocation of responsibility to individual ministers.[20] In contrast, the Manitoba statute creates no explicit substantive requirements for the strategy's content. Instead, it sets out that the strategy is intended for the purpose of, but not limited to, establishing provincial sustainable development goals, establishing a framework for sustainable development policy development, and guiding the preparation of specific economic, environmental, resource, human health and social policy component strategies.[21] Arguably, this description implicitly sets out certain substantive content.

In the UK, this type of approach would increase the status of the sustainable development strategy in decision making, both generally and in relation to those existing obligations that require particular agencies to 'contribute to sustainable development'. It would add value by making the strategy the mandatory point of reference for these bodies, rather than leaving it to the various sources of guidance referred to in present legislation (see Chapter 8). To be truly effective, this type of provision needs to be accompanied by the procedural obligations set out above. This approach still falls short of delivering any significant cultural change, however, since it says nothing about the role of sustainable development itself in the workings of government.

Establishing sustainable development as the central organizing principle of governance

Finally, an Act could establish sustainable development as the central organizing principle of governance in the UK and/or its devolved administrations. In Jonathon Porritt's final blog as Chairman of the SDC, he notes:

> The 'mainstreaming' imperative that drives all our work ('to make sustainable development the central organising principle of everything Government does') may not as yet have got as far as we would have liked, but it has got a lot further than many may once have thought possible.
>
> (Porritt, 2009b)

Jackson maintains that:

> The idea of an economy whose task is to provide capabilities for flourishing within ecological limits offers the most credible vision to put in its place. But this can only happen through changes that support social behaviours and reduce the structural incentives to unproductive status competition.
>
> (Jackson, 2009: 91)

Such legislation would cause a massive cultural shift for governance in the UK, encouraging and driving sustainable development forward, rewarding compliance and penalizing non-compliance. For this third model to be operational, two additional legislative provisions are needed. First, there must be a clear declaration of purpose by government about the role of sustainable development in all its activities. Second, the legislation must impose meaningful substantive duties on all government bodies.

Thus, the legislation needs to include an explicit statement of purpose. The most forceful example is that used in the Quebec statute: 'the object of this Act is to establish a new management framework within the Administration to ensure that powers and responsibilities are exercised in the pursuit of sustainable development'.[22] The aim in Manitoba is less forceful: to 'create a framework through which sustainable development will be implemented in the provincial public sector and promoted in private industry and in society generally'.[23] The declaration in the Canadian Federal Act states: 'The Government of Canada accepts the basic principle that sustainable development is based on an ecologically efficient use of natural, social and economic resources and acknowledges the need to integrate environmental, economic and social factors in the making of all decisions by government'.[24] While usefully referencing the ecological priority, the use of the words 'accepts' and 'acknowledges' makes this statement particularly weak – and insufficient to make any impact. In contrast, a provision based on the commitment in the Welsh strategy would work very well as a statement of purpose:

> sustainable development (the process that leads to Wales becoming a sustainable nation) will be the central organising principle of Government, and we will encourage and enable others to embrace sustainable development as their central organising principle and a general duty imposed on all public bodies.
>
> (WAG, 2009: 13)

If a statute is going make such a commitment to sustainable development, then some argue that it should be accompanied by a definition of sustainable development. All three of the Canadian administrations, in their sustainable development acts have chosen to define sustainable development using the Brundtland definition: 'development that meets the needs of the present without compromising the ability of future generations to meet their own needs' and, where considered necessary, adding to it.[25] This is the 'safe' option and common in other countries. However, as discussed in Chapter 4, this definition provides little guidance on prioritization and can be used to justify 'business as usual' pro-growth decision making. In contrast, Regulation (EC) No 2493/2000 of the European Parliament and of the Council of 7 November 2000 on measures to promote the full integration of the environmental dimension in the development process of developing countries provides that:

> For the purposes of this Regulation: 'sustainable development' means the improvement of the standard of living and welfare of the relevant populations within the limits of the capacity of the ecosystems by maintaining natural assets and their biological diversity for the benefit of present and future generations.[26]

This definition makes no mention of economic growth and would be useful in adding clarity and priorities to the interpretation of sustainable development. Unfortunately, it was ahead of its time politically, and on 1 January 2007, it was repealed and replaced with a new financing instrument for development cooperation which does not contain an equivalent definition. Instead it merely acknowledges that the concept comprises political, economic, social and environmental elements.[27]

There are strong arguments in favour of providing some definition of sustainable development. First, without a clear definition, the imprecise nature of sustainable development introduces a lack of consistency, both internally within a regime or public body and externally between regimes or public bodies.

Second, there may be a lack of continuity in the meaning of the term over time. This may result in confusion as to meaning and expectations, both for those implementing the legislation and those subject to it. Finally, imprecision may give the executive (a public body) too much discretion, while needlessly taking power away from the judiciary and the legislature (Ross, 2008: 41).

These arguments have all been raised in the UK in relation to the specific provisions for public bodies in various Acts (Ross, 2008: 41). While the number of UK statutes that refer to sustainable development is on the increase, to date, the UK has resisted defining sustainable development in its legislation. Experience with such terms as 'planning' has shown that it is better that the legislation allow the precise meaning and interpretation to evolve over time and be contextualized to suit a wide range of circumstances (Collar, 1990: 10). The non-binding nature of guidance is attractive to policymakers, as it allows them to take greater risks and introduce more ambitious approaches than they would attempt with legislation. This approach has proven very effective in the UK. So, for instance, any definition or interpretation set out in legislation produced in 1994 on sustainable development would be out of step with the more ecologically focused interpretation of sustainable development in the UK shared Framework.

However, as noted in Chapter 8 the experience with land-use planning is not directly transferable to sustainable development. The term 'planning' is largely only used in one sense and one context. Moreover, its meaning at any given time is largely accepted and comes from one source, that being the government guidance on planning. In contrast, the term 'sustainable development' is used in a wide range of contexts, the guidance provisions are not in any standard form and in many instances, the legislature has tailored them to the needs of the particular regime. The type and extent of the power that Parliament has delegated to the executive differ depending on the formulation of the provision. However, this differentiated approach to guidance may run counter to the actual implementation of sustainable development and a more consistent reference to specific guidance (for example, the relevant sustainable development strategy) which sets out a clear vision may be more desirable.

The approach set out in the second model described above which adds a statutory obligation to produce a strategy and sets out a clear vision of sustainable development would provide additional continuity and consistency for the interpretation of sustainable development without the need for a statutory definition. It would also establish the strategy as the single point of reference for interpreting the term.

A related question is whether certain component principles of sustainable development, such as acting within the Earth's ecological limits and seeking a fair and just society, should be defined in statute or receive other statutory protection. Such provisions could set out certain principles, objectives or rules that must be taken into account, and thus explicitly incorporate certain established values or principles into decision-making processes. Both Quebec and Manitoba have adopted this arrangement. The list of substantive principles in

Quebec's Sustainable Development Act must be taken into account by the Administration when framing its actions. The principles also influence the production of the sustainable development strategy.[28] However, once again the danger is that this prescriptive approach may restrict opportunities for the principles to evolve over time and to be contextualized for certain circumstances. It could also potentially limit the discretion of future administrations and increase the chances that the provisions will be watered down to the lowest acceptable level. The Manitoba statute contains both substantive principles and guidelines for sustainable development. However, the Manitoba Government only needs to 'have regard' to sustainable development and the listed principles and guidelines.[29] Once again, provision which refers to the relevant sustainable development strategy may resolve this issue if the principles are listed in it.

The second additional provision required to make sustainable development become the central organizing principle of government is a substantive duty imposed on all public bodies. This is not an easy task. The UK tends not to legislate on substantive principles, and even dominant policy changes have tended not to be explicitly legislated. Thus, for example, until recently, very few statutes expressly mention equality, democracy and freedom of speech.

However, the modern UK legal tradition does use this type of provision. As noted above, the Northern Ireland Assembly has already imposed such a general substantive duty on all public bodies in Northern Ireland. The Northern Ireland (Miscellaneous Provisions) Act 2006 s. 25 requires departments and district councils to exercise their functions in the manner they consider best calculated to promote the achievement of sustainable development. The obligation is, however, far from perfect. It is weakly worded and hidden away in a miscellaneous provisions Act instead of being a showpiece for sustainability in Northern Ireland and, unsurprisingly, it has had little impact on sustainability in Northern Ireland (Porritt, 2009a: 44; Northern Ireland Executive, 2010: 9).

Moreover, some of the duties that already exist in relation to sustainable development for specific public bodies are next to meaningless (Roberts and Reid, 2005: 162–8). For example, the duty imposed on Scottish Natural Heritage (SNH) in the Natural Heritage Scotland Act 1991 – 'to have regard to the desirability of securing that anything done whether by SNH or any other person, in relation to the natural heritage of Scotland is undertaken in a manner which is sustainable' – is so diluted that it can only be interpreted as a rather vague objective. On the other hand, the strongest possible phrasing would impose a duty to achieve sustainable development. Given the definitional issues surrounding the term, this would be a tall order and none of the UK statutes go that far.[30] Instead, they are couched in phrases which add layers of discretion. The more recent formulations use 'contribute to the achievement of' or 'contribute to' sustainable development. So long as these are not further watered down with qualifications such as 'reasonableness' or 'as costs allow', they could form the basis of a strong general obligation to be imposed on all public bodies. Arguably, this formulation is sufficient to create a legal rule and to allow sustainable development to provide the framework for decision making (Ross, 2008: 66). At present, case law indicates that the courts are likely to interpret these provisions as objectives rather than as legal rules (Bell, 2003: 78–81). Nevertheless, any change needs to start in the legislature.

As discussed in Chapter 8, one way of giving greater legitimacy to substantive duties is to phrase them as 'targets'. Targets set clear goals that are capable of being acted upon. Recently, there has been an increase in the use of targets in UK statutes, especially in areas such as fuel poverty, climate change and biodiversity.[31] The enforceability of these targets in court is questionable however, and one has to question what might be achieved by bringing an action against the government for failing to meet established targets. Moreover, it is hard to see how a target for sustainable development can be set that would attract the same sort of public attention as those for climate change or biodiversity. Sustainable development reflects a holistic view that is difficult to express as a single indicator or target. However, as discussed in Chapter 8, targets have a role in any legislative approach to sustainable development, both as precise deadlines for producing documentation and as benchmarks for specific sustainable development indicators that are essential to drive forward progress. More indirectly, specific climate change, biodiversity, fuel, poverty and other targets could be used as evidence to assess progress towards sustainable development.

Consequences of breach and the case for a staged approach

The consequences of a failure to comply must be explored fully to ensure any legislation is effective. In the UK, a failure to meet a procedural obligation is much easier to challenge and enforce than a breach of substantive duty, as a required procedure would either have been performed correctly and on time or not. In contrast, substantive duties are often more subjective and give the person responsible significant discretion. While procedural obligations on their own can make a difference, the same cannot be said about substantive obligations. Thus, the ideal model uses both. Regardless of the model chosen, it is imperative that both substantive and procedural obligations are supported by requirements for reporting, review, publication and audit that have real consequences if breached

A key question is whether the legislation should be focused on keeping generally willing people in line or aimed at forcing a change in behaviour among unwilling parties? In the context of the UK, it is likely that any legislation would have to be directed at dealing with both challenges. There will be inadvertent errors of judgement in pursing sustainable development. However, there will also be people who are determined to flout the system by putting their own personal short-term gain ahead of wider long-term public benefit. At present, none of the existing substantive provisions in UK or Scottish statutes are supported by criminal sanctions and only one provision includes a statutory appeal mechanism (Chapter 8). It is difficult to see how criminal sanctions could be introduced into a sustainable development act. However, given the well-documented likelihood that certain public bodies will resist change for reasons such as path dependency, resource constraints and poor leadership (Cussons, 2006: 16), some deterrence mechanisms, such as naming and shaming and budgetary penalties, are probably necessary.

On their own, many substantive provisions, such as statements of purpose or declarations, could not realistically be accompanied by any obvious enforcement mechanisms. However, they may still be effective from a more symbolic perspective – acting to educate, inform and heighten awareness. Moreover, any breach of these provisions is still likely to attract the attention of the public, interest groups, parliamentary committees or a higher level of government and result in more informal, ad hoc enforcement.

Judicial review is only appropriate in instances where a body has acted procedurally improperly, or, more rarely, where a public body has acted irrationally or illegally. It is also generally reactive, costly and time-consuming. Courts are very reluctant to intervene in any case where the argument is essentially about the merits of government policy and the allocation of resources. That said, the UK courts have demonstrated a willingness to accept sustainable development as a material consideration in decisions, even without any statutory obligation.[32] They would probably treat a generally applicable substantive provision in the same way. Ideally, the provision would be so worded to allow the court the possibility of interpreting it as a legal rule. As noted above, however, previous research on similar provisions in other areas has revealed unwillingness on the part of the judiciary to treat such vague provisions as legal rules (Bell, 2003: 78–81).[33]

To be most effective then, Reid suggests that:

> any legal duty should be phrased in such a way as to be enforceable, and policy targets should be strengthened not by unenforceable statutory duties but through the establishment of specific monitoring, reporting and scrutiny mechanisms that will allow effective political accountability to be achieved.
>
> (Reid, 2009b: 44; 2010b: 15)

As a result, where possible, the substantive objectives must be accompanied by a meaningful toolkit of procedural duties. These include obligations to produce an annual report or require notice, audit or publicity. Failure to comply with these statutory procedures is much easier to enforce and monitor than non-compliance with broad principles, both under judicial review and by central government, interest groups and the public. There is precedent in the UK for supporting a general duty with an obligation to produce a strategy. The Nature Conservation (Scotland) Act 2004 s. 1, for example, imposes a general duty on all public bodies and office holders to exercise their functions to further the conservation of biodiversity.[34] This duty is supported by an accompanying duty to produce a Scottish Biodiversity Strategy. Procedures such as these can significantly enhance the potential impact of a given provision.

The needed cultural change may have to come in stages – initially in the legislature and then later in the courts. Given the continued public and political indifference to the challenges facing the Earth, it may be that the best immediate approach is to simply introduce the necessary procedures under the first model described above. Even on their own, reflexive procedures can secure significant progress. By compelling action, informing decision makers and encouraging them to learn about the effects of their actions, decision makers are given the opportunity to make adjustments, correct errors and improve their overall understanding (Dernbach, 2008: 104). With public, media and political support, these ideally ought to be used to support explicit, rather than implicit, substantive obligations in relation to the sustainable development strategy, its development, use and review, as well as to link to other governance tools. Ultimately, a further substantive obligation that pronounces sustainable development as the central organizing principle of governance should also be enacted. Depending on the level of public and political support, it may be necessary to use a staged legislative approach, whereby these substantive duties are introduced later as political and public understanding improves itself as a consequence of the procedural obligations taking effect.

Moreover, due to the asymmetrical nature of devolution, the means of making these changes differ across the UK. The administrations of the UK, Scotland and Northern Ireland could simply enact their own sustainable development statutes. The Government of Wales Act 2006 provides an excellent starting place for Wales, but does not go far enough, even if a minimalist procedural objective is used. More specific procedures are needed about consultation and the role of the Commissioner for Sustainable Futures in particular. As Wales has only limited legislative power, it would be up to the UK Government to either devolve to Wales the power to do this under the 2006 Act or to legislate for Wales itself.

Finally, as noted above, the UK courts have been hesitant to interpret substantive obligations as anything more than general objectives or material considerations to be taken into account, and it may take longer to get the courts to fully enforce these obligations, especially those that could be treated as legal rules. Without legislation actually in place, however, there is nothing for the courts to interpret. Experience indicates that it may take time to reach the stage where strong substantive obligations are interpreted by the courts as legal rules that actually secure sustainable development as the central organizing principle of government. Indeed, it was only in 1991 that the House of Lords finally struck down UK legislation as incompatible with European law despite the supremacy of European Community law being set out in the European Communities Act 1972.[35]

Conclusion

Unfortunately, the UK's continued preference for a policy approach based on weak sustainability and supported by only minimal legislation is not delivering the cultural change required to make the UK sustainable. Legislation is now needed to compel compliance and adherence to best practice, and to promote consistency in interpretation and use.

This chapter explores three legislative models that would be suitable in the UK and its devolved administrations to support the implementation of sustainable development and the legislative provisions necessary for their delivery, using examples from Wales and Canada. All three models have the capacity to deliver increased consistency in decision making by turning what may currently be established good practice or policy into legally binding obligations that can compel compliance.

The first possible model is purely procedural to, among other things, produce and review a strategy. The imposition of obligations to produce a strategy and pursue other measures such as action plans, spending reviews, indicators and targets, and set out key monitoring and enforcement tools for bodies such as the Audit Offices or Parliamentary committees would be a major step forward in making the 'sustainable development toolkit' operational.

The second possible model would explicitly establish the sustainable development strategy as the framework or central point of reference for all decision making. A weaker version would do so, but only for all decisions and policies relating to the environment. This approach gives the strategy legal status, provides a clear point of reference for those bodies with substantive obligations relating to sustainable development and generally improves the understanding of the term. It does not explicitly set out the role of sustainable development in the workings of government, however. This omission misses out on important symbolic benefits and fails to address directly any inconsistencies in the interpretation and application of sustainable development.

The final possible model used for this analysis is the most ambitious – to make sustainable development the central organizing principle of government. Arguably, this is the only way to truly secure the cultural change required for genuine sustainability. As set out in Chapter 12, for this model to be effective, sustainable development would need to be redefined – with ecological sustainability, as opposed to economic growth or sustainable growth, at its core. Furthermore, in legislation based on this model, sustainable development would need to be more than just a material consideration or one objective to be balanced against others, and there is precedent for a better approach in previous statutes. The Planning and Compulsory Purchase Act 2004 in relation to development planning provides in s. 39(2) that 'The person or body must exercise the function with the objective of contributing to the achievement of sustainable development'. This phrasing is strong enough to potentially give such legislation the role of a legal rule and hence, truly provide a framework for all decision making across government.

Thus, there are significant practical benefits to using procedural obligations alone and to backup more substantive obligations. There is also merit in introducing certain well-worded substantive duties which are treated as not simply objectives, but as legal rules which govern decision making.

There are both benefits and drawbacks of including a definition of 'sustainable development' or referring to specific underlying principles such as the precautionary principle. While perhaps very useful in other jurisdictions, it is debatable as to whether these are necessary or suitable for the UK. This chapter contends that sustainable development as defined in Chapter 12, with ecological sustainability at its normative core, ought to be the central organizing principle of government in the UK. It argues, however, that even if a weaker and less ambitious formulation is preferred, providing some legislative backing for the production, use and review of sustainable development strategies would still improve understanding, provide a framework for decision making and could clarify the use and importance of other implementation devices such as appraisal tools, action plans and indicators. Moreover, the legislation could be staged, starting with the necessary provisions for the first procedural model and, over time, move towards the substantive provisions necessary for the third model.

Arguably, the real challenge for legal drafters in the UK is to design a system that contains legal tools to create a meaningful framework for decision making based on sustainable development, while ensuring that this framework is iterative and flexible.

Notes

1 This chapter reworks and updates some of the material and ideas set out in Ross, A. (2010) 'It's time to get serious: Why legislation is needed to make sustainable development a reality in the UK', *Sustainability*, 2(4): 1101–27; doi:10.3390/su2041101, http://www.mdpi.com/2071-1050/2/4/1101/.
2 The Government of Wales Act 2006 ch. 32 s. 79.
3 Many of the points raised for Scotland apply equally to Northern Ireland. However, progress in Northern Ireland on sustainable development lags well behind the rest of the UK due to, among other things, the suspension of devolution from 2002 to 2007 and the power-sharing arrangements for government which often lead to deadlock.
4 See the Constitution for the Republic of South Africa 1996 Article 24; the Constitution of the Republic of Poland 1997 Article 5; the Consolidated version of The Treaty on European Union *Official Journal of the European Union* (OJ) (2008), C 115/13 Article 3(3)(5). Article 3(3) provides that '[the Union] shall work for the sustainable development of Europe'. Article 3(5) similarly requires the Union to 'contribute to the sustainable development of the Earth'.
5 See the European Communities Act 1972 ch. 68; the Scotland Act 1998 ch. 46; the Northern Ireland Act 1998 ch. 47; the Government of Wales Act 2006 ch. 32.
6 See the Planning and Compulsory Purchase Act 2004 ch. 5; the Scottish Parliament (2006) Planning *etc.* (Scotland) Act 2006 asp 17.
7 See the Treaty on the Functioning of the European Union OJ (2008), C 115/47. Articles 11 and 191–3 set out the integration, polluter pays, preventative and precautionary principles.
8 OJ (2008), C 115/13.
9 See Directive 2000/60/EC EU Water Framework Directive OJ (2004), L 327.
10 The Joint Nature Conservancy Council in the Natural Environment and Rural Communities Act 2006 ch. 16 Schedule 4 is an example of all the UK administrations working together.
11 The Federal Sustainable Development Act 2008 c. 33.

12 The Sustainable Development Act 1997 S.M c.61 as amended; the Sustainable Development Act 2006 RSQ cD-8.1.1; the Sustainable Development Act 2007 SNL cS-34. Note that the statute for Newfoundland and Labrador is limited to the sustainable development of natural resources in the province and, as such, is of only limited use in a UK context.

13 The Government of Wales Act 1998 ch. 38 s. 121.

14 The Sustainable Development Act 1997 S.M s. 7; the Sustainable Development Act 2006 RSQ ss. 5–12, 15; the Federal Sustainable Development Act 2008 ss. 9–11.

15 The Sustainable Development Act 1997 S.M s. 5; the Sustainable Development Act 2006 RSQ ss. 8, 12, 13; the Federal Sustainable Development Act 2008 s. 7.

16 See the Auditor General Act 1985 RSC 1985 A-17 as amended s. 7, ss. 21.1–23; the Sustainable Development Act 1997 S.M s. 16(1)(b); the Sustainable Development Act 2006 RSQ s. 31.

17 The Sustainable Development Act 1997 S.M s. 9, 17; the Sustainable Development Act 2006 RSQ ss. 7, 13, 26.

18 The Sustainable Development Act 1997 S.M s. 4; the Federal Sustainable Development Act 2008 ss. 6, 8.

19 The Transport Act 2000 ch. 38 s. 207(2)(b); the Water Environment and Water Services (Scotland) Act 2003 asp 3 s. 2(4).

20 The Sustainable Development Act 2006 RSQ s. 11; the Federal Sustainable Development Act 2008 ss. 9, 10.

21 The Sustainable Development Act 1997 S.M s. 7(2).

22 The Sustainable Development Act 2006 RSQ s. 1.

23 The Sustainable Development Act 1997 S.M s. 2.

24 The Federal Sustainable Development Act 2008 s. 5.

25 The Sustainable Development Act 1997 S.M s. 1; the Sustainable Development Act 2006 RSQ s. 2; the Federal Sustainable Development Act 2008 s. 2.

26 (2000) OJ L 288, art 2.

27 Regulation (EC) No 1905/2006 of the European Parliament and of the Council of 18 December 2006 establishing a financing instrument for development cooperation (2006) OJ L 348.

28 The Sustainable Development Act 2006 RSQ ss. 6, 7.

29 The Sustainable Development Act 1997 S.M s. 3.

30 In contrast, see Abu Dhabi Law No. (16) of 2005 Reorganization of the Abu Dhabi Environment Agency, Article 3 which states that 'To fulfil the above objectives, the Agency has the following responsibilities: 22 – Achieve sustainable development through environmental activities'.

31 See the Climate Change Act 2008 ch. 27 s. 1(1): 'It is the duty of the Secretary of State to ensure that the net UK carbon account for the year 2050 is at least 80% lower than the 1990 baseline'.

32 See, for instance, *Horsham DC v First Secretary of State, Devine Homes plc* [2004] EWHC 769 (Admin); *R (Ludham) v the First Secretary of State, Derbyshire DC* [2004] EWHC 99.

33 *Friends of the Earth v Secretary of State for Energy and Climate Change* [2009] EWCA Civ 810.

34 The Nature Conservation (Scotland) Act 2004 asp 6.

35 *Factortame v Sec of State for Transport (No. 1)* [1989] 2 WLR 997 (HL); *(No. 2)* [1990] 3 WLR 818 (HL); [1991] 3 All ER 769.

References

Bell, S. (2003) 'Statutory pollution prevention objectives: Are they rules or aims?', *Journal of Environmental Law*, 15(1): 59–85.

Bulmer, S., Burch, M., Hogwood, P. and Scott, A. (2006) 'UK devolution and the European Union: A tale of cooperative asymmetry', *Publius*, 36(1): 75–85.

CAG Consultants (2003) *How Effectively has the National Assembly for Wales Promoted Sustainable Development?*, Report to the Welsh Assembly Government.

CAG Consultants (2004) *Is the Scottish Executive Structured and Positioned to Deliver Sustainable Development?*, 10th Report, vol. 2, Edinburgh: Environment and Rural Development Committee 2nd.

Collar, N. (1990) *Planning*, 2nd edition, Edinburgh: W. Green.

Cussons, S. (2006) *Review of Statutory Sustainable Development Duties*, London: In House Policy Consultancy/DEFRA.

Department of Environment, Transport and the Regions (DETR) (2000) *Achieving a Better Quality of Life: Review of Progress towards Sustainable Development: Government Annual Report*, London: DETR.

Dernbach, J. (2008) 'Navigating the U.S. transition to sustainability: Matching national governance challenges with appropriate legal tools', *Tulsa Law Review*, 44: 93–120.

Flynn, A., Marsden, T., Netherwood, A. and Pitts, R. (2008) *Final Report: The Sustainable Development Effectiveness Report for the Welsh Assembly*, Cardiff: Welsh Assembly Government.

HM Government, Scottish Executive, Welsh Assembly Government, Northern Ireland Office (2005) *One Future, Different Paths: The UK's Shared Framework for Sustainable Development*, London: DEFRA.

Hodge, R.A. and Hardi, P. (1997) 'The need for guidelines: The rationale underlying the Bellagio Principles for Assessment', in P. Hardi and T. Zdan (eds) *Assessing Sustainable Development: Principles in Practice*, Winnipeg: International Institute for Sustainable Development.

Jackson, T. (2009) *Prosperity without Growth: Transition to a Sustainable Economy*, London: Sustainable Development Commission.

Jenkins, V. (2002) 'Placing sustainable development at the heart of government in the UK: The role of law in the evolution of sustainable development as the central organising principle of government', *Legal Studies*, 22(4): 578–601.

Kavanagh, D. and Richards, D. (2001) 'Departmentalism and joined-up government: Back to the future?', *Parliamentary Affairs*, 54(1): 1–18.

Kemp, R., Parto, S. and Gibson, R.B. (2005) 'Governance for sustainable development: Moving from theory to practice,' *International Journal of Sustainable Development*, 8(1–2): 12–30.

Mader, L. (2001) 'Evaluating effects: A contribution to the quality of legislation', *Statute Law Review*, 22(2): 119–31.

Munday, M. and Roberts, A. (2006) 'Developing approaches to measuring and monitoring sustainable development in Wales', *Regional Studies*, 40(5): 535–54.

Northern Ireland Executive (2010) *Everyone's Involved: Sustainable Development Strategy*, Belfast: Northern Ireland Executive.

Organisation for Economic Co-operation and Development (OECD) (2002) *Improving Policy Coherence and Integration for Sustainable Development: A Checklist*, Paris: OECD.

Orts, E.W. (1995) 'Reflexive Environmental Law', *Northwestern University Law Journal*, 89(4): 1227–340.

Porritt, J. (2009a) 'The Standing of sustainable development in government', http://www.jonathonporritt.com/pages/2009/11/the_standing_of_sustainable_de.html, accessed 12 April 2010.

Porritt, J. (2009b) 'Looking back on nine years at the Sustainable Development Commission', http://www.forumforthefuture.org/blog/looking-back-on-nine-years-at-the-SDC, accessed on 12 April 2010.

Reid, C.T. (2009a) *Nature Conservation Law*, 3rd edition, Edinburgh: W. Green.

Reid, C.T. (2009b) 'Enforcement of policy duties', *Scottish Planning & Environmental Law*, 132: 44–5.

Reid, C.T. (2010a) 'Environment and sustainable development', in E.E. Sutherland, K.E. Goodall, G.F.M. Little and F. Davidson (eds) *Law Making and the Scottish Parliament: The Early Years*, Edinburgh: Edinburgh University Press.

Reid, C.T. (2010b) 'Enforcement of policy duties Part II', *Scottish Planning & Environmental Law*, 137: 15.

Roberts, I.R. and Reid, C.T. (2005) 'Nature conservation duties: more appearance than substance', *Environmental Law & Management*, 17(4): 162–8.

Ross, A. (2005) 'The UK approach to delivering sustainable development in government: A case study in joined-up working', *Journal of Environmental Law*, 17(1): 27–49.

Ross, A. (2006) 'Sustainable development in Scotland post devolution', *Environmental Law* Review, 8: 6–32.

Ross, A. (2008) 'Why legislate for sustainable development? An examination of sustainable development provisions in UK and Scottish statutes', *Journal of Environmental Law*, 20(1): 35–68.

Ross, A. (2009) 'Modern Interpretations of Sustainable Development', *Journal of Law and Society*, 36(1): 32–54.

Ross, A. (2010) 'Sustainable development indicators and a putative argument for law: A case study of the UK', in D. French (ed.) *Global Justice and Sustainable Development*, Leiden: Martinus Nijhoff.

Ross, A. and Nash, H. (2009) 'European Union environmental law: Who legislates for whom in a devolved Great Britain?', *Public Law*, July: 564–94.

Rubin, E.L. (1989) 'Law and legislation in the administrative state', *Columbia Law Review*, 89(3): 369–426.

Scottish Executive (2002) *Scottish Planning Policy (SPP) 1: The Planning System*, Edinburgh: Scottish Executive.

Sustainable Development Commission (SDC) (2004) *Shows Promise. But Must Try Harder: An Assessment by the Sustainable Development Commission of the Government's Reported Progress on Sustainable Development over the Past Five Years*, London: SDC.

SDC (2006) *Sustainable Development in Wales: From Pioneer to Delivery*, London: SDC.

Turner, S. (2006a) 'Transforming environmental governance in Northern Ireland. Part One: The process of policy renewal', *Journal of Environmental Law*, 18(1): 55–87.

Turner, S. (2006b) 'Transforming environmental governance in Northern Ireland. Part Two: The case of environmental regulation', *Journal of Environmental Law*, 18(2): 245–75.

Turner, S. (2007) 'Laying the foundations for a sustainable Northern Ireland: The review of environmental governance', *Northern Ireland Legal Quarterly*, 58(4): 422–58.

UK Government (1997) *Planning Policy Guidance (PPG) 1: General Policies and Principles*, London: UK Government.

United Nations (UN) (2006) *Global Trends and Status of Indicators of Sustainable Development: Background Paper No.2 DESA/DSD/2006/2*, New York: UN Department of Economic and Social Affairs.

Voss, J.P. and Kemp, R. (2006) 'Sustainability and reflexive governance: Introduction', in J.P. Voss, D. Bauknecht and R. Kemp (eds) *Reflexive Governance for Sustainable Development,* Cheltenham: Edward Elgar.

Voss, J.P., Kemp, R. and Bauknecht, D. (2006) 'Reflexive governance: A view on an emerging path', in J.P. Voss, D. Bauknecht and R. Kemp (eds) *Reflexive Governance for Sustainable Development,* Cheltenham: Edward Elgar.

Welsh Assembly Government (WAG) (2008) *Sustainable Development Annual Report 2007–2008,* Cardiff: WAG.

WAG (2009) *One Wales: One Planet: The Sustainable Development Scheme of the Welsh Assembly Government,* Cardiff: WAG.

Winter, G. (2004) 'The legal nature of environmental principles in international, EC and German Law', in R. Macrory (ed.) *Principles of European Environmental Law,* Groningen: Europa Law Publishing.

14 Moving from rhetoric to reality

This chapter brings together the analysis of the UK's progress towards delivering sustainable development set out in Chapter 11 with the arguments made in Chapters 12 and 13 regarding a way forward.

Four criteria (common understanding; leadership; stakeholder involvement and knowledge management; and integrative mechanisms) are used in Part II to analyse the UK's journey towards sustainable development over time and the various techniques, principles, mechanisms and institutions that both the central and devolved governments in the UK have relied upon to push the sustainable development agenda forward. However, as the analysis in Chapter 11 shows, although much of the architecture is in place for moving towards a sustainable UK, this architecture lacks vision, leaders are easily swayed by misguided short-termism and, crucially, good practice and institutional innovations are not supported or protected.

As described in Chapter 3, the research into sustainable development in this volume and elsewhere broadly agrees that two significant changes are required for effective implementation. The first change needed is a cultural acceptance and understanding that prioritizes operating within the Earth's limits and thinking about the long-term effects of policies and decisions. The success of this first change depends on the second significant change, which is the full integration of environmental protection concerns, and more broadly, sustainable development, into all forms of policy and decision making. As discussed throughout this volume, both changes need to be supported by effective leadership for sustainable development and a strong institutional and legislative framework.

The Welsh experience described in Chapters 12 and 13 shows that sustainable development is capable of being the central organizing principle or overall objective of government. For this to happen, however, the meaning of sustainable development itself needs to be properly understood and those advocating it need to share common priorities and fully understand the consequences of decisions based on sustainable development. At present, in the UK, this is not the case. Moreover, and more importantly, the general substantive understanding of sustainable development needs to be turned on its head. Weak sustainable development approaches in which economic growth remains the main objective and environmental factors are traded off against social and economic ones, have led to a liquidation of social and natural assets. Essentially, we have been living off the Earth's capital instead of off the interest and, as such, we are essentially borrowing from our children, with little chance of paying them back. The vision proposed in Chapter 12, which is based on ecological sustainability, imposes on everyone a duty to protect and restore the integrity of the Earth's ecological systems. With ecological sustainability at its core, sustainable development has the capacity to become useful again.

The possible legal significance of this approach should not be ignored. Decision making based on ecological sustainability places the discussion of trade-offs within the ecological limits of the Earth. Like justice, liberty and equality, ecological sustainability could be considered a fundamental legal principle. This status is deserved because the ability to deliver the other fundamental legal principles (freedom, equality and justice) reduces as the Earth's resources and resilience reduce, and the best way to protect these other fundamental legal principles is to operate within a system based on ecological sustainability.

The starting point in the UK is to replace *One future – different paths: The UK's shared framework for sustainable development* (HM Government *et al.*, 2005) with a new framework that reflects the new challenges facing the whole and parts of the UK, the EU and the world in 2011 and beyond. The 2005 Framework did not foresee the economic crisis that descended on the UK and other countries in 2008. Neither does it reflect the changed political, demographic, environmental and social issues including Japan's triple disasters (earthquake, tsunami and nuclear threat), social and political unrest in North Africa, new scientific evidence on climate change, biodiversity, and human health and happiness, and the new technological and other responses to these developments. A new UK-wide framework is needed, that sets out a coordinated and agreed vision of sustainable development among the four UK administrations, and that includes clear priorities which are easily understood. Modern strategies such as the Earth Charter and *One Wales: One Planet: The Sustainable Development Scheme of the Welsh Assembly Government* (*One Wales: One Planet*) (WAG, 2009) show that there is a growing shift in favour of more ecologically based interpretations of sustainable development. These interpretations recognize that our ability to justly meet the needs of both present and future generations decreases the more we use up the Earth's capital. Past UK administrations have been leaders in their strategic innovations, and the opportunity to continue this role by introducing a strong vision of sustainable development based on ecological sustainability should be not be missed. The individual administrations would then need to build on this framework to produce more detailed strategies for their own jurisdictions and competences. Ideally, the production of these new strategies would be the responsibility of ministers at the highest level, in order to ensure that the process and results are widely accepted and promoted across government.

It is important that addressing the challenges presented by climate change does not dominate this shift towards ecological sustainability. As it is relatively easy to understand, climate change has the potential to be a champion for all aspects of the Earth's ecosystems, not just the Earth's ability to absorb greenhouse gases. If this is the case, however, it is essential that strategies and actions which address the climate change agenda are based on the principle of ecological sustainability and contribute to sustainable development more generally.

With ecological sustainability at its core, sustainable development has the capacity to set meaningful objectives, duties and policy rules. It can also provide boundaries for decision making, as these roles are already present in recent UK and devolved legislation. What this requires, as Wackneragel and Rees observe, is that we need to 'shift our emphasis from "managing resources" to managing ourselves so that we learn to live as part of nature' (1996: 4).

As a consequence of this approach, certain specific mechanisms are necessary to actually establish the carrying capacity of the Earth's ecosystems. Such mechanisms include targets, indicators, stabilization wedges, environmental assessment and ecological footprints. These need to be continuously refined and improved, especially in relation to knowledge management. They must remain firmly focused on ecological limits and be kept separate from broader sustainable development tools such as the strategies themselves, sustainability appraisals and the wider impact assessment and sustainable development duties, as it is essential that these mechanisms also address social and economic concerns.

Once these limits (that is, the carrying capacity of the Earth's ecosystems) are understood, it is then the role of sustainable development to promote and encourage social and economic development within them. As explained by Andrew Lee, Chief Executive Officer of the Sustainable Development Commission (SDC):

> Sustainable development [itself] is a hugely powerful toolkit for finding new solutions to old problems, an operating system which has the potential to sit behind everything that our government departments, companies, schools, hospitals, local authorities and grassroots organizations do, delivering better economic, social and environmental outcomes.
>
> (SDC, 2011: 5)

Part II of this volume lists numerous examples of innovative and exciting developments in relation to promoting leadership, stakeholder involvement and knowledge management, which are three of the Organisation for Economic Co-operation and Development's criteria for delivering sustainable development. It also gave many excellent examples of robust innovations aimed at policy integration (such as action plans), sustainable development in government operations, institutional developments such as the creation of the Department of Energy and Climate Change, legal duties such as those imposed by the Government of Wales Act 2006, and reporting and review processes, such as those provided by the SDC and the Environmental Audit Committee of the House of Commons. At the moment however, these sustainable development tools are inconsistently used. For instance, indicators are often of little policy relevance, as they are not explicitly linked to clear objectives in the national strategy. Budget decisions, such as those capping environmental taxes, continue to be made for short-term electoral gains.

Moreover, there are also examples of useful sustainable development mechanisms falling into disuse or being discontinued. Some of these losses are significant and several are retrograde steps. These include the failure of the Scottish Government to consult widely on *The Government's Economic Strategy* (Scottish Government, 2007), the loss of both the Scottish and UK Cabinet committees on sustainable development and the decision to cease the funding of the SDC.

Hence, even if a new vision based on ecological sustainability is widely accepted, there are no guarantees that it would be consistently applied, as there will always be those pushing alternative short-term agendas. Thus, success also depends on leadership and a long-term view which addresses both consumption and supply. The policy approach supported by only minimal legislation is not delivering the cultural change required to meet these aspirations for sustainable development. It does not protect these innovative and crucial procedures, institutions and goals from electoral short-termism and, importantly, it does not support and promote real leaders in sustainable development. These leaders need support and, arguably, legal backing. The more we erode the Earth's carrying capacity, the more the capacity of leaders to provide answers to economic and social crises diminishes.

As argued in Chapter 13, sustainable development has proven itself to be a resilient and valuable policy tool in the UK, and it is time for the UK administrations to give it legislative backing. Legislation could compel compliance and adherence to best practice and promote consistency in interpretation and use. It could also create a meaningful framework for decision making based on sustainable development, while ensuring that this framework is iterative and flexible.

A UK-wide statute on sustainable development that binds both central and devolved administrations alike is unfeasible following devolution. However, it would not be out of step with modern UK legal culture for the UK, Scotland and Northern Ireland legislatures to enact their own legislation on sustainable development. Under the current devolution arrangements the UK would need to do this on behalf of Wales or devolve this power to the Welsh Assembly.

A key issue for legislators to decide is which legislative model for sustainable development should be adopted. Chapter 13 sets out three possible models that reflect different levels of political commitment to sustainable development. The first model focuses on creating binding legal procedures considered vital to implement sustainable development fully, such as the production of a strategy, reports on progress and wide consultation in the process. The typical examples have a general obligation in the statute and follow this up with either detailed guidelines or regulations. More protection and more certainty will inevitably require more detail and more binding rules at the expense of flexibility. Ensuring an appropriate balance between the general and the specific, as well as between the binding and the persuasive, is essential to success and must reflect the realities and practice of the existing legal culture and political environment. For example, where the system relies on trust and professionalism, and it works, it should continue to do so.

Procedures alone will not necessarily deliver a cultural change within governments. The second model aims to enhance the status of the sustainable development strategy by introducing a substantive duty across government to ensure that its activities, policies and decisions are consistent with the objectives and principles set out in the sustainable development strategy. This approach gives the strategy legal status, provides a clear point of reference for those bodies with substantive obligations relating to sustainable development and, generally, improves the understanding of the term. It also would ensure more consistency in its use and application. However, this approach does not explicitly set out the role of sustainable development in the workings of government. This omission misses out on important symbolic benefits and fails to directly address any inconsistencies in the interpretation and application of sustainable development.

If the real cultural change described earlier is actually going to happen, then it may be that the various UK legislatures need to legislate to make sustainable development the central organizing principle of governance in each of their respective parts of the UK. This is the third model described in Chapter 13. Here, two additional legislative provisions are needed. First, there must be a clear declaration of purpose by government about the role of sustainable development in all its activities. The statement in *One Wales: One Planet* works well as a declaration of purpose: 'sustainable development (the process that leads to Wales becoming a sustainable nation) will be the central organizing principle of Government, and we will encourage and enable others to embrace sustainable development as their central organizing principle and a general duty imposed on all public bodies' (WAG, 2009: 13).

Second, the legislation must impose meaningful substantive duties on all government bodies. These duties should do more than simply require these bodies to 'have regard to' or 'take account of' sustainable development. Sustainable development needs to be more than a material consideration, or one objective to be balanced against others and there is precedent in previous statutes of a better approach. For example, the Local Government in Scotland Act 2003 s. 1(5) provides that 'the local authority shall discharge its duties under this section in a way which contributes to the achievement of sustainable development'. This phrasing is strong enough to potentially give the provisions the status of legal rule and hence, truly provide a framework for all decision making across government.

In the past, this author has been unconvinced of the value of legislating to define sustainable development or of referring to certain underlying principles, such as good governance or sound science (Ross, 2008). More recently, however, some more specific definitions/interpretations have been set out which provide more detailed limits than the Brundtland definition, while still retaining some flexibility. Moreover, certain clear priorities set out in the legislation would be very helpful for promoting a consistent approach. A useful sample definition was provided in Regulation (EC) No 2493/2000 of the European Parliament and of the Council of 7 November 2000, on measures to promote the full integration of the environmental dimension in the development process of developing countries, which provides that:

> For the purposes of this Regulation 'sustainable development' means the improvement of the standard of living and welfare of the relevant populations within the limits of the capacity of the ecosystems by maintaining natural assets and their biological diversity for the benefit of present and future generations.[1]

This definition makes no mention of economic growth and would be useful in adding clarity and priorities to the interpretation of sustainable development. More research is needed into how best to deliver these more substantive goals while still retaining the flexibility needed to allow sustainable development to be contextualized and to evolve over time.

Legal formalization would raise the status of the sustainable development strategy and of sustainable development itself. It would also upgrade the framework approach from a nice idea to a legal obligation. Failure to produce a strategy or to observe the legislated procedural requirements would not only be subject to judicial review, but would also attract considerable public attention and thus, significantly improve scrutiny and accounting on sustainable development. This would also provide vital support to sustainable leadership. Most importantly, legal recognition will improve the educational value of the strategy and heighten its status in the public eye.

Finally, the implementation of sustainable development to date has been a staged process in the UK and elsewhere. There is no reason to believe it will not continue to be so. While legislation which adopts the SDC's vision of sustainable development as the central organizing principle of governance in the UK is arguably needed now and, is the likely way forward, it may take the UK administrations a while to be willing to give this legislative backing. It will likely take the UK courts longer still to recognize such a change in priorities. Chapter 13 explains how such legislation can be staged, and how even the most basic procedures can significantly improve the implementation of sustainable development.

This book revealed an abundance of good and evolving practice based on the expertise of a wide range of scientists, social scientists, professionals, public servants, voluntary and community groups, businesses and individuals. Unfortunately, the hurdles these initiatives face are often significant and result in good practice being frustratingly ignored, abandoned or repealed. By examining sustainable development from a legal perspective and exploring the options that the law offers in relation to its understanding and implementation, the hope is that the analysis and arguments set out in this book will generate discussion both inside and outside the legal community and inspire calls to protect and support good practice for sustainable development.

Note

1 Regulation (EC) No 2493/2000 of the European Parliament and of the Council of 7 November 2000 on measures to promote the full integration of the environmental dimension in the development process of developing countries [2000] OJ L288, Article 2. Note that this regulation was repealed by Regulation (EC) No 1905/2006 of the European Parliament and of the Council of 18 December 2006 establishing a financing instrument for development co-operation (2006) OJ L 348, which contains no such definition of sustainable development.

References

HM Government, Scottish Executive, Welsh Assembly Government, Northern Ireland Office (2005) *One future – different paths: The UK's shared framework for sustainable development*, London: DEFRA.

Ross, A. (2008) 'Why legislate for sustainable development? An examination of sustainable development provisions in UK and Scottish statutes', *Journal of Environmental Law*, 20(1): 35–68.

Scottish Government (2007) *The Government's Economic Strategy*, Edinburgh: Scottish Government.

Sustainable Development Commission (SDC) (2011) *Governing for the Future: The Opportunities for Mainstreaming Sustainable Development*, London: SDC.

Wackneragel, M. and Rees, W.E. (1996) *Our Ecological Footprint: Reducing the Human Impact on the Earth*, Gabriola Island, Canada: New Society Publishers.

Welsh Assembly Government (WAG) (2009) *One Wales: One Planet: The Sustainable Development Scheme of the Welsh Assembly Government*, Cardiff: WAG.

Index